STIRRING *the* SOUL *of* CATHOLIC EDUCATION

Formation for Mission

By
Jill Gowdie

**BBI – THE AUSTRALIAN INSTITUTE OF
THEOLOGICAL EDUCATION
MISSION AND EDUCATION SERIES**

Published in Australia by
Vaughan Publishing
32 Glenvale Crescent
Mulgrave VIC 3170

Vaughan Publishing
A joint imprint of BBI – The Australian Institute of Theological Education and
Garratt Publishing

Typesetting: Mike Kuszla, J&M Typesetting
Cover image – istock.com

Printed by Lightning Source

Nihil Obstat: Reverend Monsignor Gerard Diamond MA (Oxon), LSS, D. Theol
             Diocesan Censor

Imprimatur: Monsignor Greg Bennet MS STL VG EV
             Vicar General

Date: 27 March 2017

The Nihil Obstat and Imprimatur are official declarations that a book or pamphlet is free of
doctrinal or moral error. No implication is contained therein that those who have granted the
Nihil Obstat and Imprimatur agree with the contents, opinions or statements expressed. They do
not necessarily signify that the work is approved as a basic text for catechetical instruction.

Cataloguing-in-Publication information is available from the National Library of Australia
www.nla.gov.au

DEDICATION

This book is dedicated to the great host of women and men who sense the world of the Divine imagination and keep the rumour of angels alive. They are teachers, companions, leaders and soul friends who, age after age, lean into the world and reflect the heart of God.

Jill Gowdie February 2017.

ACKNOWLEDGEMENTS

Financial Support

Since the inception of the program, the Mission and Education series has received financial support from a number of Catholic Education authorities. Their assistance with research and publication costs is gratefully acknowledged:

- *Queensland* – the Catholic Education Offices of Brisbane, Cairns, Rockhampton, Toowoomba and Townsville.
- *New South Wales* – the Catholic Education Offices of Armidale, Bathurst, Broken Bay, Maitland-Newcastle, Parramatta, Sydney and Wagga.
- *Australian Capital Territory* – the Catholic Education Office of Canberra-Goulburn.
- *Victoria* – the Catholic Education Offices of Ballarat, Sale and Sandhurst.
- *South Australia* – Catholic Education South Australia (Archdiocese of Adelaide and Diocese of Port Pirie).
- *Tasmania* – the Catholic Education Office of Hobart.
- *Northern Territory* – the Catholic Education Office of Darwin.
- *Religious Congregations* – the Good Samaritan Sisters, Marist Brothers (Sydney Province), Marist Brothers National, Edmund Rice Education Australia and De La Salle Brothers.

BBI – THE AUSTRALIAN INSTITUTE OF THEOLOGICAL EDUCATION MISSION AND EDUCATION SERIES

The Mission and Education publishing project is divided into two series. The *Exploratory Series* seeks to serve leaders in Catholic education. It explores aspects of contemporary Catholic education in the light of the Church's official teaching on mission, and the experience of those who attempt to embrace this mission in their personal and professional lives. The *Educator's Guide Series* is being prepared specifically for teachers in Catholic schools.

The richness of the resources now at the disposal of those who seek to explore education theologically can come as a surprise. Because the faith held by the Catholic community is a living faith, Catholic Church teaching on mission has developed, and continues to develop, in the light of contemporary societal and cultural changes. Similarly, Scripture continues to yield its treasures. Only now, for example, is the Bible being widely recognised as a witness to God's purpose or mission in the created universe, and as an account of human response to the unfolding of that mission.

We live in a period of rapid cultural change driven by global dynamics. This has its impact on how we understand what knowledge is, how it is acquired, and how schools are best led and organised so as to maximise student learning, and the economic and social benefits that are presumed to flow from sound educational policies. Very often the emphasis in such policies shifts from 'the learning student' to the more abstract concept of 'student learning'. This sits uneasily with the concept of a Catholic education.

The consequence of rapid societal change is that, in our time, new areas of mission present themselves with real urgency. It is now clearly necessary to include within the mission agenda both the processes of knowledge construction and meaning-making, and the modes of Christian participation in the new public space created by both globalisation and the communications media. These new areas of mission take their place alongside those fields already familiar to the faith community.

The Mission and Education Series seeks to bring together, in the one conversation, the light that human experience, culture and faith throw on particular topics now central to the future development of Catholic education. It also seeks to honour the significant efforts that Catholic educators make, on behalf of young people, to address the contemporary mission agendas within the total process of education. It provides a forum designed to stimulate further conversation about the 'what' and the 'how' of Catholic education as a work of the Gospel in our complex society and culture.

It is the hope of the Mission and Education Editorial Board that Catholic educators, both in Australia and beyond, will view the series as an invitation to contribute their own creativity to this vital conversation.

Therese D'Orsa
Commissioning Editor
BBI – The Australian Institute of Theological Education

Also in this series

CONTENTS

PART C
MINING THE WISDOM: ADULT SPIRITUALITY, EDUCATIONAL CULTURE AND THE FAITH TRADITION

Introduction to Part C   57

PART D
FRAMING A NEW APPROACH
Introduction to Part D   170

PART E
PRACTICE WISDOM: CASE STUDIES IN THE AUSTRALIAN CATHOLIC EDUCATIONAL LANDSCAPE
Introduction to Part E   224

PART F
CONCLUDING REFLECTIONS
Introduction to Part F   282

PROLOGUE

'Traditions, traditions!' says Tevye ... 'Without our traditions, our lives would be as shaky as ... as ... as a fiddler on the roof!'[1] Yet, as Tevye finds out in the great unfolding story of the *Fiddler on the Roof*, neither tradition nor identity are static things, passed down fixed and unchanging from generation to generation. A living tradition – an authentic identity – is an adaptive thing that can continue to speak meaning to culture.

The Christian tradition has always been shaped by a dialogue between faith and culture. Christianity has only ever continued to be relevant in as much as it has offered meaning within the context in which it lives. When either faith or culture becomes deaf to the other, both lose relevance. Something dies in each, something of rich meaning-making is lost unless a new dynamic emerges, one that is less like a fiddler trying to keep balance on a roof and more like a dancer inviting partners onto the floor.

The challenge of teacher and leader formation in Catholic education in Australia stands at the nexus of just such an emergent time – a liminal time – a time in which the provision of formation that opens the individual to the rich horizon of the Christian worldview is only as relevant as it makes profound meaning in the cultural context in which people live.

In this book we grapple with the question of how to frame a re-imagined understanding of formation for the Catholic educator and leader. In doing so, we mine the learnings of the great thinking and engagement in this area, and explore a new model of formation for Catholic educators, a model responsive to our time and place.

As you are introduced to the many writers and thinkers included within the pages of this book, I invite you to see them as colleagues and friends who, with you, grapple with the questions of purpose and faith, of role and soul, of teaching and leading, of being and calling.

Always remember, you are in very good company!

---

1   N. Jewison et al. 2006, *Fiddler on the Roof*, (movie).

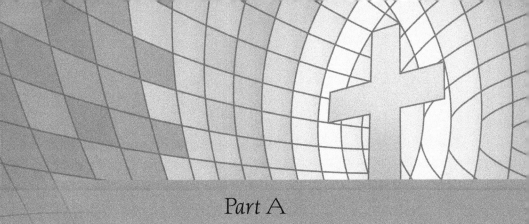

Part A
THE CHALLENGE OF FORMATION IN CONTEXT

My mission of being in the heart of the people is not just a part of my life or a badge I can take off; it is not an 'extra' or just another moment in life. Instead, it is something I cannot uproot from my being without destroying my very self. I am a mission on this earth; that is the reason why I am here in this world. We have to regard ourselves as sealed, even branded, by this mission of bringing light, blessing, enlivening, raising up, healing and freeing. All around us we begin to see nurses with soul, teachers with soul, politicians with soul, people who have chosen deep down to be with others and for others.

Pope Francis, 2013,
Evangelli Gaudium Notes,
133-134 and 273.

INTRODUCTION TO PART A: 'WE ARE!'

The year is 2016.

The place: The Convention and Exhibition Centre, Perth, Australia.

The event: A national broadcast hosted by Australian media presenter Tony Jones for the quinquennial National Catholic Education Conference.

The moment: Tony Jones poses the question to the esteemed panel following a short discussion about the diminishing numbers in religious orders: 'And so who is going to carry the torch in the place of these religious brothers and sisters [while] only 19 per cent of teachers in Catholic schools are practicing Catholics?'

The proclamation: 1600 voices in the darkness erupt spontaneously as one in response: '*We are!*'

This was a powerful moment for all those present. The media host was taken aback as the unseen audience suddenly 'stole the oxygen'. The panel too, though less surprised, were drawn from their own pool of light on stage to the vocal sea of darkness before them. The audience itself, 1600 teachers and leaders of Catholic schools and systems from across the country, surprised itself with its own united and strong voice. What followed in the moment was clapping and laughing from that audience, surprised at their own audacity and impassioned eruption.

So now, what does this mean – *We are!*

This book opens up the vibrancy and opportunity reflected in that remarkable moment and the challenge inherent in that multi-dimensional question.

1

SETTING THE SCENE

The growth of Catholic education in Australia and the role of Catholic educators has been an extraordinary tale. Catholic schools today cater for 1 in 5 Australian students and span the country.[2] Catholic education is currently Australia's largest non-government employer. Even amidst the continuing devastation of the child abuse crisis that has ruptured the church globally and locally,[3] Australian catholic schools remain well supported by parents and enjoy strong credibility in the wider community. The provision of Catholic education in Australia today is characterised by a sophisticated national and diocesan organisational structure, significant government funding, as well as strong academic patronage through the Australian Catholic University and other Catholic higher education providers. Added to this, Catholic education in Australia has had a unique history amid the unfolding of the years since Vatican II. This history offers a distinctive lived reality that has much to celebrate and build upon for future Catholic education in this country. The proclamation, 'We are!' gives expression to the goodwill, the energy and the enormous commitment of Catholic education staff to the ministry of Catholic education.

At the same time, Australian Catholic education shares the significant international challenges of secularisation, de-institutionalisation, pluralisation and ecclesial fracture. There is no doubt we are in a liminal time[4] where a continuing anxiety and sense of uncertainty is appreciable among all stakeholders around the nature, purpose and future of Catholic schools. Of particular concern, among many factors, is the erosion of

---

2   NCEC, 2015.
3   The Royal Commission into Institutional Responses to Child Sexual Abuse has uncovered widespread criminal behaviour and a tragic past in the administration and practices within the Australian Church. This is causing unimaginable harm to thousands of Catholics and their families and friends. The result has been enormous hostility by both Catholics and the broader community towards the Church and its hierarchy, with the reputation of the Church and its institutions seriously diminished.
4   See D'Orsa & D'Orsa, 2013, pp. 2-4 for a description of phases and the convergent factors in the current liminal time.

confidence in Church authority, the 'unbundling'[5] among the parent body and the emerging generation of school staff and leaders about what it means to be Catholic, and changing aspirations of parents and teachers with respect to outcomes of Catholic schooling. These shifts are exacerbated by mega-trends in education including escalation of accountability provisions for educational outcomes, an increased corporatisation of system processes including staff development, and the emergence of neo-liberal ideology in publicly funded education.[6] And so, the proclamation 'We are!' also begs the questions: what does it mean now to 'carry the torch,' and what is needed for our educators and leaders to sustain the fire into the future?

Theologically, I write this book from my own inner perspective as a Catholic Christian, who from my own tradition reflects upon the Christian faith in dialogue within the current context. I write from the perspective that the need for meaning-making in the midst of this liminal landscape is both an enormous challenge and a critical opportunity. In particular, the need to make meaning of 'mission' in the context of Catholic education demands not only radical re-thinking in terms of what mission is as it applies to Catholic educators, but also a concomitant re-imagining of formation for educators and leaders.

Our exploration unfolds within a complex and layered setting. It is a setting to which both you and I bring our own particular experience, and our own eyes and mind and heart. To engage in this journey together I offer that we do so within the master-narrative of Luke 24 – *The Road to Emmaus*. This story, at once familiar and foreign, provides for us both a window and a mirror to the mysterious dynamic of dialogue, encounter and new meaning-making in which any company of strangers comes to understand Jesus in their midst. At some time in our lives, we all flee our Jerusalems, die with our own spent dreams. And yet there remains something in us that has the capacity to turn heart to home; to be called into a deeper reality. It requires its own courage. But the simple shift is transformative. And cannot be undone. This is the essence of what the formative process is about – a turning to the deep down, an understanding of being in the world that is compelling, sustaining, enlivening. And in our tradition, it happens only in and through each other 'on the way'.

We might also frame this in missiological terms. Noel Connolly in reference to Pope Francis's missiology summarises three challenges for the broader church:

---

5   This is a term coined by Charles Taylor to describe the unravelling of forms of belonging, and of spiritual and other activities previously gathered under the Church.
6   For a useful account of the impact of the neo-liberal agenda in Catholic education, see Gleeson, 2015.

The first challenge is for the church and we as individuals to return to the Gospels, to encounter Jesus. The second challenge is a reform of the church, not just the individual. The third challenge is to surpass the one-directional perspective and enter into reciprocity and dialogue.[7]

Let us bear both the invitations and challenges of our own hearts, our own minds and our own experience, to the journey here together. And see what happens – on the way!

THE CONNECTIONS: MISSION, FORMATION AND CATHOLIC EDUCATION

In recent decades, an understanding of mission that reflects the broadening consensus of engaged leaders across the globe has been developed within the magisterial documents of the Catholic Church.[8] That understanding is grounded in a missional theology which befriends culture and human experience and the living religious tradition. In Catholic education, this requires an orientation of the heart that can hold the tensions of those three dimensions, and where each of us and the community as a whole follow the tracks of the Divine in a very fluid world context.

The lens of 'mission thinking'[9] in Catholic education today is very much focused on those Who and Why questions: *Who are we? Why are we? Who are we with? Why are we doing what we're doing?* These questions involve the intersection of the lives of Catholic educators and leaders, the culture in which they live, and the faith tradition in which stands Catholic education. Crucially, it is a lens that recognises that God is already working, and has been working within all cultures, revealing Godself.[10] This in turn implies that spirituality is not 'an additional dimension of mission to be considered when all the doctrinal and practical apparatus is already in place. Rather, the spiritual dimension is the first thing around which everything else ought to revolve'.[11] God is the primary agent of mission and works through the power of the Holy Spirit. Openness to the Spirit – *joining in with the Spirit* – is therefore what mission is about. Hence, it is more authentic to say

---

7   Connolly, 2016, p. 7. Taken originally from a reference by Enzo Biemmi in a paper, 'For a truly "new" evangelisation: A re-reading of the Synod' given at the 2013 Conference of SEDOS in Rome.

8   For an interpretive summary of the development of official church teaching on mission and evangelisation, see Jim and Therese D'Orsa, 'Securing Mission at the Heart of the Australian Church', in Neil Ormerod, Ormond Rush, David Pascoe, Clare Johnson, and Joel Hodge (eds), *Vatican II Reception and Implementation in the Australian Church* (Mulgrave: Garratt Publishing, 2012), 240-57.

9   D'Orsa & D'Orsa, 1997, p. 269.

10   Balia and Kim, *Witnessing to Christ Today*, (Edinburgh, 2010), p. 241.

11   Ma and Ross, *Mission Spirituality and Authentic Discipleship*, p. 9.

'the mission has a church', rather than 'the church has a mission'.[12] The missiologist is concerned that the message of the Gospel permeates human cultures by engaging with and enriching what is already there. The spiritual formation specialist is concerned that the heart of God and the wisdom of the tradition enkindle a transformative dynamic within the individual and the community that changes both. For both the missiologist and the formation specialist, mission and formation must be context specific by definition.

Spiritual formation in the Catholic Christian tradition is a dynamic process of growth in following the way of Jesus in becoming one with God. 'Formation' generally refers to a set of experiences designed to prepare a person or group for a particular purpose. In preference to a word like 'training', 'formation' is most often used in the context of spiritual development and conjures images of a deep learning that involves attitudes, values, commitment to particular life directions, as well as knowledge and skills. It is the 'who' and the 'why' that informs the 'what' and the 'how' questions of our particular work in the great enterprise that is Catholic education.

The word 'formation' itself comes from the Latin *formare*, meaning 'to shape' or 'to mould'. We are all constantly being shaped and moulded by our circumstances and our surroundings, whether we are aware of it or not. When we talk of spiritual formation, we are talking about choosing what will shape and mould us, and to what we give our deepest energies!

Yet formation is also a contested term. For some, it carries negative connotations as a control word in an overly parental church busy in conforming leaders and teachers to a particular mould. For others, it carries a sense of re-creating tight community boundaries and routine practices as the way to develop mature followers of Christ. Gerald Arbuckle offers a helpful image for our time, an image of spread-out communities which live in the world, rather than in the cloister, and which inculturate the Gospel creatively and imaginatively beyond the edges of Church. This kind of formation requires flexibility and adaptability.[13]

To engage in spiritual formation then is to practice seeing the reality beneath the reality of things! In this process, grounded in that reality, occurs the integration of learning how to integrate this meaning-making of one's values and beliefs with one's behaviour in daily life – both personally and professionally. Catholic spiritual formation is about all these things in response to Jesus Christ who is seen as the Way, the Truth and the Life, and the Holy Spirit acting through the community of Christ's disciples

---

12 This phrase has been identified with Stephen Bevans who has written extensively on missiology as contextual theology. His work is explored in a later section of the book.
13 Gerald Arbuckle, 1996, p. 245.

(the Church) in the context of the mission of Catholic education, and the Catholic school in particular.

Engagement in formation means to be concerned with the ongoing transformation of individuals and their communities. Christian spiritual formation is deeply personal and radically communal in its vision and praxis. While the shape of a spiritual life is, in the end, a matter of unique mystery between God and the individual person, spirituality in the Christian tradition is developed in the company of others.

There is no such thing as a private Christian. Formation in the context of Catholic education is personal and communal. Every individual working in any capacity in Catholic school communities presents with their own personal story, their own personal spirituality and their own community (school/office). This presenting context is the starting point for all formation. Thus we approach the individual's reality with two key assumptions:

- Every person is a lifelong learner.
- God is real, present and at work at the heart of each person and in their lives.

There is also a strong relationship between vision and formation. Vision proclaims what we believe ourselves to be about. In both Greek and Latin, the root meaning of 'to believe' is 'to give one's heart to'. So, a vision expresses what a community 'gives its heart to.' It calls us and reminds us of our centre and brings us back to our centre. The sacred work of the Church as the people of God, including the ministry of Catholic education within it, is to nurture the deep water horizon of mystery in our own lives and in our shared lives. To look toward this horizon is to believe as Daniel O'Leary says, that 'as rivers flow and the winds blow, so too the human heart with its imagination, affections, and creativity, will never be – cannot ever be – other than God-bound'.[14]

Over the last ten years, the *assumptions* about formation provision for mission at a school and system level have turned into an *awareness* of the need for appropriate and effective formation, and this has translated into considerable energy being given to ways of *meeting* that need. More than ever now, the distinct questions emerging about mission and formation impel us to be attentive to those 'who' and 'why' questions of Catholic education. That, I believe, is a very good thing!

---

14   O'Leary, 2004, p. 13.

THE ROLE OF THE EDUCATOR IN THE CATHOLIC SCHOOL

The Catholic school educator encounters a range of expectations for their role, both personally and professionally. Teaching as a vocation is well described as a deep and personal calling: 'Teaching is a vocation. It is as sacred as priesthood, as innate as desire, as inseparable as the genius which compels the artist.'[15] Within the Catholic school context however, it is a role that carries specific aspirations in which the construction of teaching as a vocation or calling includes an additional lens that situates vocation in mission.

The foundational Post-Vatican II document on the identity of Catholic schools, *The Catholic School* (1977), is clear that the Catholic educator is concerned to help students integrate life, culture and faith in developing the worldview which they bring to the challenges and problems that shape their lives (*The Catholic School*, 1977, n. 37).[16] The 1988 document *Lay Catholics in Schools: Witnesses to Faith* further elaborates:

> The Catholic educator must be a source of spiritual inspiration ... The Lay Catholic educator is a person who exercises a specific mission within the Church by living in faith, a secular vocation in the communitarian structure of the school: with the best possible professional qualifications, with an apostolic intention inspired by faith, for the integral formation of the human person, in a communication of culture, in an exercise of that pedagogy which will give emphasis to direct and personal contact with students, giving spiritual inspiration to the educational community of which he or she is a member, as well as to all the different persons related to the educational community.[17]

This understanding is reiterated in more recent Vatican documents, (*Educating Together in Catholic Schools*, 2007 and *Educating Today and Tomorrow, A Renewing Passion,* 2014) where the Catholic school itself is described as '... a place of integral education of the human person through a clear educational project of which Christ is the foundation, directed at creating a synthesis between faith, culture and life'. [18]

The perceived magnitude of this responsibility for the Catholic school educator was explicitly articulated at the Second Vatican Council (1961-1965).

---

15   Pearl S Buck, cited in Gleeson, 2003, p. 80.
16   Congregation for Catholic Education, *The Catholic School,* 1977.
17   Congregation for Catholic Education, 1982, n. 24.
18   Congregation for Catholic Education, 2007, p. 3.

> Teachers must remember that it depends chiefly on them whether the Catholic school achieves its purpose (*Gravissimum Educationis*, 1965, n. 8).

> Teachers must bear testimony by their lives and by their teaching to the one Teacher, who is Christ (*Gravissimum Educationis*, 1965, n. 8).

That personal responsibility has lost none of its gravitas in the intervening sixty years:

> If modern women and men listen to teachers at all, they listen to them because they are witnesses (*Evangelii Nuntiandi*, 1975, n. 41).

The work of the Catholic educator is in fact the work of helping to form human beings:

> The teacher under discussion here is not simply a professional person who systematically transmits a body of knowledge in the context of a school; 'teacher' is to be understood as 'educator' – one who helps to form human persons. The task of a teacher goes well beyond the transmission of knowledge (CCE, 1982, n. 16).

And further to this, the role has individual and communal dimensions:

> A significant responsibility for creating the unique climate of a Christian school rests with the staff as both individual and in community, for the teacher does not write on inanimate material but on the very spirit of human beings (CCE, 1982, n. 19).

Finally, the Catholic educator has their eye on a larger horizon: not only should the teachers be personally and professionally committed, but they should also be '... sensitive to finding opportunities for allowing their students to see beyond the limited horizon of human reality'. [19]

Distinct recurring themes emerge that contribute to a 'model' of the *ideal* Catholic school educator as one who is committed to:

- community building
- lifelong spiritual growth
- lifelong professional development
- students' spiritual formation
- students' human development. [20]

---

19 Congregation for Catholic Education, 1988, n. 51.
20 Shimabukuro, 1998.

This ideal model of the Catholic educator, formulated in the language of vocation and mission, reflects a role that incorporates significant ecclesial responsibility and enormous expectation. Concomitantly, the need for 'formation' in bearing this vocational responsibility of teaching and leading in a Catholic school has been increasingly acknowledged: 'Formation, therefore, must be a part of and complement the professional formation of the Catholic school teacher.'[21]

It is apparent that both the distinctiveness of the role of the Catholic educator and the need for support in this role has developed as a priority identified in the Post-Vatican II ecclesial literature. The influence of Catholic educators is recognised and the expectations placed on them have become prominent. However, while the reality of a predominantly lay teaching staff has been noted demographically, and acknowledged by ecclesial and governance authorities, the research regarding the experience of what it means to be a teacher in an Australian Catholic school is not extensive. Yet, it is here, in the experience of the role, that the complex external world of Catholic school education intersects with the internal and deeply personal world of Catholic school educators.

THE PROFILE OF CATHOLIC SCHOOL EDUCATORS

Research about staff in Catholic schools has provided insight into the complexity of the area by drawing attention to both the striking changes in the religious/lay staffing of Catholic schools and the perspectives of the various categories of Catholic teachers. The staff demographic has changed over the last 50 years from predominantly vowed religious with a culturally homogeneous profile, to a predominantly lay staff with a culturally heterogeneous profile. Given this, and the expectations outlined above, the research exploring the values and experience of lay teachers is particularly relevant for our discussion.[22] Between the responsibility of vocation and the provision of formation lies the current reality of a staff demographic where evidence identifies increasing distance from the ecclesial Church.[23]

There are two areas which highlight particular characteristics in the profile of contemporary Catholic school educators:

---

21 Congregation for Catholic Education, 1982, n. 65.
22 Key Australian research in this area includes D'Arbon, Duignan & Duncan, 2002; Downey, 2006; Fisher, 2001; McLaughlin, 1997, 2002, 2005.
23 'The vast majority of them [Catholic educators] have reservations about the contemporary Catholic Church and, like the general Catholic population, are not practising.' McLaughlin, 2002, p. 12. Note that this 2002 research was undertaken before the abuse crisis. No extensive research is yet available on shifts in attitude and practice, but one would not expect it has reversed its trajectory.

- the generational meaning-making of staff
- the system-world and life-world of staff.

Each of these will be considered in turn.

GENERATIONAL MEANING-MAKING

Across Australian Catholic schools, Generation X includes young teachers and educational leaders, and Generation Y incorporates those in teacher education preparation or those beginning teaching. Baby boomers carry the major leadership responsibilities in Catholic education. Many of these are former religious brothers and sisters or those who have had extensive early Church enculturation.[24] We will not see the like of this Catholic educator profile again, and we have not yet fully realised nor acknowledged their unique role in the unfolding story of Catholic education. Within the broader generational change, their particular personal, professional and spiritual journey and witness in the transition of staff from religious to lay, and their legacy in maintaining such strong and deep traction in the ethos of Catholic schools, is a contribution for which we owe more than can be measured. This also reflects the general situation in Europe, America, Canada and England.[25]

One of the fundamental shifts within the global Church has been the willingness of the Catholic laity baby boomers to challenge and/or reject elements of Church teaching whilst at the same time continuing to remain active members of the Church.[26] In contrast, Gen X and Y teachers are less likely to offer such loyalty. These generations trust their own experience, distrust received 'truth', know the plurality of experience and accept the validity in the individual's perspective.[27] For them, there is a longing for a personal discovery of trustworthy certainties.[28] They are a generation of seekers, and while institutions may not have their loyalty, they value authentic behaviour and conduct.

> *If they agree with the Church on an issue, it is because the Church position makes sense to them and they actively decide to agree. If a Church teaching does not make sense to them, they will refuse to agree, no matter how often or how clearly or how authoritatively the Church has spoken on it.*[29]

---

24 It was the changing reality experienced by religious which attracted early interest as their presence in schools diminished: see Burley, 1997, 2001. The experience of ex-religious in our schools invites further work.

25 Grace & O'Keefe, 2007.

26 Dixon, 2005; Mulligan, 1994.

27 BRC, 2003.

28 Mason, Singleton & Webber, 2007.

29 McLaughlin, 2002, p. 12.

Research undertaken with Australian Catholic University undergraduate students[30] has been substantiated by more extensive Australian research[31] confirming the identified slippage of Gen X and Y from any sense of ecclesial loyalty.[32] In addition, the figures from this broader sample group and longer study indicate a strong drift away from Christianity among Gen Y; before they reach the age of 25, 'about 18% of those who used to belong to a Christian Church are already ex-members'.[33] The implications of these findings for Catholic education staff suggest that graduates coming into the Catholic education system, and graduate teachers entering Catholic schools, appear to have little sense of a Church connection or parish culture and even less sense of allegiance to Church teaching or the ecclesial dimension of their role.

The reasons for the diminishing decline in Church affiliation are endemic and deep-seated, suggesting issues of fundamental meaning-making. For some time now, researchers have identified this as the source of crisis in the institutional Church. This ...

> is far more profound than simply falling attendance at Mass, increased practice of artificial birth control, an aging clergy and a decreasing number of vocations, and the unfortunate longevity of some anachronistic customs of clerical control that simply refuse to die. These are but symptoms of the more fundamental nature of the crisis. There is today a different way of understanding reality.[34]

While each major era or stage in the human lifespan is marked by its own way of meaning-making, the recalibration demanded in building community with a 'different way of understanding reality' is compounded by a cultural insularity in contemporary society. Charles Taylor calls this 'buffering.' In other words, the insularity or buffering caused by the fragmented and individualistic culture that currently prevails obstructs the development of almost any broader community or organisational commitment.[35] Yet capturing the commitment of older staff and the engagement of younger teachers appears to require an operative community dynamic.

In trying to identify what is needed to nurture young adults (Gen Y/Millennials and iGens) to develop 'a mature commitment in a tentative world',[36] American research has identified critical factors in the

---

30 McLaughlin, 1997; 2002.
31 Hughes, 2007.
32 This was defined through weekly attendance at Mass, and belief in key teachings including divorce, contraception and pre-marital sex.
33 Mason, Singleton & Webber, 2007, pp. 301–2.
34 Mulligan, 1994, p. 99.
35 Senge, Scharmer, Jaworsk & Flowers, 2005.
36 Daloz-Parks, 2000, p. 171.

first three decades of life that predispose young adults to living a life of commitment to a larger whole. The elements that seem to operate favourably towards such a commitment, and in a variety of combinations, include contact with: 'community adults who model commitment; service opportunities; mentors and critical experiences in college or graduate school.'[37] In addition, the research identified 'habits of mind' nurtured in a healthy community dynamic that characterise this development. They are:

- dialogue
- interpersonal perspective taking
- critical systemic thought
- holistic thought.[38]

Within this dynamic, older mentors and the wider community have a unique role. The findings demonstrated that for the 17–30 year olds (those preparing for teaching or in their early teaching years), strategic mentorship is influential. Moreover, young adults are influenced not only by individual mentors but also by mentoring environments, with older adults having a powerful responsibility in this. Furthermore, the findings confirmed that the broader culture as a whole plays a mentoring influence in the formation of each new generation of young adults, shaping the future of the culture itself. This has important micro implications in the community structure of the Catholic school and its young staff for cultural renewal and meaning-making. In such a scenario, the pressure on school leaders for spiritual and faith leadership is a real and immediate challenge in creating authentic communities of witness.

Reflecting on the challenge of creating an authentic shared reality for the mission of Catholic education, practitioners in the field of teacher formation advocate for a new language that speaks to the hearts and souls of people today, 'a re-inflaming of the romantic imagination'.[39] In this endeavour, these practitioners appear to draw on the language of the mystic rather than ecclesial tradition. Indeed, the search for characteristics of a new vocabulary to engage people was one of the outcomes of an international series of symposia between 2002 and 2004 that investigated the nature of mission in contemporary secular culture.[40]

---

37   Daloz-Parks, 2000, p. 6.
38   Daloz, Keen, Keen & Daloz-Parks, 2000, p. 173.
39   Rolheiser, 2006, p. 21.
40   Oblate Communications, 2004.

THE SYSTEM-WORLD AND
LIFE-WORLD INTERFACE

The second area which highlights particular characteristics in the profile of contemporary Catholic school educators concerns life-world. The terms *life-world* and *systems-world* were coined by Jürgen Habermas to describe 'two mutually exclusive yet ideally interdependent domains.'[41] Research in Australia, Canada and the United States identifies the changing patterns and pressures in the life-world of teachers and principals in particular. Findings indicate the complexity and responsibility of contemporary family life, in addition to identified work intensification issues, heightening stress, fatigue, and professional and personal upheaval.[42] A brief overview of the key factors here is helpful in framing our later discussion.

The rise of economic rationalism on a global scale has influenced educational systems worldwide in a sweeping process of restructure and reforms.[43] In Australia, this is reflected in a thrust for greater accountability to and influence from the community; the justification and national monitoring of curriculum; individual public rating of schools; and institutionalised scrutiny of teacher performance. The impact of market-driven values on the policy of schools is an attendant concern for Catholic schools striving to maintain a values base that is countercultural to elitist and materially aspirational drivers.[44]

Adding to these wider changes exacting pressure on the 'system-world' of the Catholic educator are the 'life-world' issues and personal pressures of postmodern society. The juggling of family, community and work commitments in an individualist, materialist culture contributes to a level of busyness that has become endemic. Constant 'over busyness' is linked to burn out, with sleep deprivation a common lifestyle concern.[45]

Thus, in the midst of technological, gender, cultural and economic revolutions,[46] the current generation of Catholic school educators face the difficulty of increasing pressures in their life-world and the juggling of conflicting ideology in their system-world. There are 'few other occupations where lifestyle and work are so closely linked and where lifestyle options can so strongly affect career possibilities.'[47] As these worlds collide, there is increasing difficulty in attracting staff to engage in Catholic school leadership.[48]

---

41   Sergiovanni, 2001, p. 5.
42   This has been documented in a range of studies: Branson, 2004; Carlin, d'Arbon, Dorman, Duignan & Neidhart, 2003; Downey, 2006; Hargreaves, 1994; McMahon, 2003.
43   Hughes, 2000; O'Donoghue & Dimmock, 1998.
44   Grace, 1996, 2002; McLaughlin, 2002.
45   Downey, 2006; McMahon, 2003.
46   Mackay, 2008.
47   Tinsey, 1998, p. 36.
48   Belmonte, Cranston & Limerick, 2006; Flintham, 2007.

As this complex dynamic continues, it has become more and more apparent that much of the Church's outreach into the community is through Catholic schools.[49] For the majority of Australian Catholics – parents and students – the Catholic school is the only experience of Catholicism they choose to have.[50] Indeed, research conducted for the Queensland dioceses as far back as 2001 indicated that one third of the families associated with Catholic schools were involved with a parish or diocesan Church community; for the remaining two thirds, the Catholic school was 'the face and place of the Church'.[51]

In consequence, the pressure of responsibility on the Catholic school educator has increased. Catholic school staff have become the face of the Church, asked to be its best advocates, integrating professional, spiritual and communal qualities and commitment in their ministry. Increasingly, principals are expected to engage in more Church leadership initiatives. This expectation is heavily reinforced by ecclesial authorities. Compounding this pressured situation is the perception that ecclesial authorities, while requesting a high level of commitment and authentic witness from teachers, have viewed the role of the laity as 'an apostolate of the second string'.[52] Overlaying this system-world is a life-world for contemporary Catholic school educators which carries its own increasing pressure. In this complex dynamic, traditional approaches in the delivery of spiritual formation for Catholic educators appear inappropriate.

THE BROADER CULTURAL CONTEXT IN AUSTRALIA

The 'Life-world' issues have further nuance in the Australian cultural landscape.

The Australian Constitution precludes the Commonwealth from declaring an official religion or establishing a state church. As a result, Australian society is characterised by practical pluralism rather than strict secularism.[53]

The decision of the Australian Bureau of Statistics to list 'no religion' in the first place among options on the 2016 census implied the Bureau, for the very first time, expected that option to attract the majority of respondents that year. In his latest book, *Beyond Belief*, Hugh Mackay describes an Australia

---

49   McLaughlin, 2000b.
50   This was first noted 20 years ago in Australia (Quillinan, 1997, and McLaughlin, 2000c) and has become more and more accepted as the prevailing and continuing reality.
51   Queensland Catholic Education Commission, 2001, p. 3.
52   Lakeland, 2003, p. 98.
53   See the work of Tom Frame, 2007, for further discussion on this: https://www.cis.org.au/commentary/articles/do-secular-societies-provoke-religious-extremism

that 'has lost its appetite for conventional religion'.[54] He and other observers however do not equate the loss of support for conventional religion with an absence of value for the spiritual life in general nor a dismissal of the value carried for the cultural heritage of Christianity in particular.

> What is clear is that few Australians with little religion or spirituality have totally and explicitly rejected it. The major problem is not necessarily a philosophical one ... (rather) the day to day world does not require that they engage with religion or spirituality. They are 'practical' secularists, rather than ideological secularists.[55]

Rather, the onus is on the churches to respond to new expectations:

> Christian faith communities of all persuasions will do well to hear and respond to the cry for honesty, dialogue, relevance and an authentic participatory approach. Whether that cry comes from a middle-aged journalist, a year 10 student or a 20-something arts graduate. [56]

Australian Bishop Greg O'Kelly referring to Fr Michael Paul Gallagher's reflections, underlines the new reality by suggesting that those whose starting point (in mission) is to arrest the decline of Church practice and find ways of inviting people back to Church, will adopt a different starting point from those who wish rather to approach the process in reawakening the question of God as a personal hunger.[57] Gallagher coins the term 'longing without belonging' to describe many of the seekers of today who are not touched by present Church life and language. Consequently, the impetus for seeking after God or the numinous, comes more often through cultural and spiritual wounds from which people might suffer: the wounds in memory, belonging and imagination.[58] The collective impact of these wounds is an absence of roots with any meaning, a lack of affective belonging in community and

---

54 Mackay, 2016, p. 2. Previous to this, 61% of Australia have ticked Christian, 15% attend church once a month, 8% weekly. 22% ticked no religion (p. 7), 2.5% Buddhist, 2.2% Muslim, 1.3% Hinduism (pp. 7-8).

55 Kaldor, Hughes & Black, 2010, p. 57. Six years later, Mackay, 2016, p. 49, affirms this: 'Even in a determinedly secular society like Australia, all those non-churchgoing people who still choose to identify themselves as "Christian" are presumably saying something about the values they still aspire to, the kind of cultural heritage they still respect, and possibly the kind of intuitions they still want to preserve.'

56 Daughtry, 2002, p. 5.

57 Gallagher quotes Grace Davie who has described the phenomenon of 'believing without belonging' as a description of many of this age. Others, says Gallagher, have turned that around, pointing to the frequency of inactive, passive Church membership as 'belonging without believing.'

58 Bishop Greg O'Kelly, quoting Gallagher, 2015. French sociologist Danièle Hervieu-Léger has written a major study of religion as memory, where she argues that the decline of faith today is due to a collapse of collective memory much more than to any critiques from Enlightenment rationality.

a wounded imagination that locks us into a new kind of social imaginary centred on the self and self-gratification.[59]

This is the mission field and a new way of being is needed to be authentic within it.

THE BROADER ECCLESIAL CONTEXT IN AUSTRALIA

The general trends for Australian Catholic school communities include the following:

- a lay administration
- a lay staff
- the enrolment of children of other faiths
- an increased percentage of non-Catholic, or non-practising Catholic, teachers and pupils
- an ageing population of practising Catholics
- an identifiable secular influence in the community culture and lifestyle
- a priest who is not from the local Archdiocesan area.[60]

While these trends have had a prolonged influence on Catholic education, the last trend is a new phenomenon. As priestly numbers sharply decline in Australia, Australian Bishops are negotiating with Bishops in third-world countries to supply priests to minister in Australian parishes. This initiative reflects a noticeable shift in the global composition of the Catholic Church. [61]This intersection between post-Christian West and non-western Christianity will be a 'defining ecumenical characteristic' of the 21st century.[62]

The importance of other changes over the last 35 years has not escaped the attention of those ultimately responsible for Australian Catholic education, namely the Catholic Bishops. They have continued to advocate

---

59 Gallagher, 2004, quoting Canadian philosopher Charles Taylor, states: we live in a 'soft relativism', where a 'new expressivist self-awareness brings to the fore a different kind of social imaginary.'

60 Belmonte, Cranston & Limerick, 2006; McLaughlin, 2000b.

61 A hundred years ago, only two percent of all Christians lived in Africa. Today, nearly one in four Christians in the world is African and the 'statistical centre' of Christianity is to be found in Mali.
    Christianity has also seeing dramatic growth in Asia in the past century where it has increased at twice the rate of overall population growth. Further, much of the growth of Christianity has been in Charismatic, Pentecostal, Evangelical and non-denominational forms of expression, while mainstream denominations that were the bedrock of the 20th-century ecumenical movement are being eclipsed.

62 *Global Christianity: A Report on the Size and Distribution of the World's Christian Population* (New York: Pew Research Center, 2012), 67-69.

enthusiastically for the mission of Catholic education and the role of the educator and leader in the Catholic school through key documents and research.[63] Causal factors are acknowledged whereby 'changes in enrolment patterns and in our educational and cultural context have radically affected the composition and roles of the Catholic school in recent years'.[64] In response, the Bishops offer some prescription with regard to staffing in Catholic schools: 'People whose lives give witness to Christian values and who are committed to engage in the Church's mission of evangelisation will staff Catholic schools.'[65] Thus, a key element in the ecclesial response to the impact of changing cultural and ecclesial contexts on the school environment has been to emphasise more strongly the expectations that teachers and leaders cultivate and embody Gospel-based beliefs, values and witness.

In turning attention to implied formation needs, policy and research at the national Catholic education level of governance have progressively positioned a positive anthropology of humanity and a connection to a loving God as central to both student formation and teacher formation. This has been an important element of the National Catholic Education Commission's (NCEC) documentation as it has responded to challenges in Catholic education first identified twenty years ago. The NCEC policy also highlighted a specific need 'to provide better quality programs for the professional development of religious educators, and for the faith development of all teachers'. In particular:

> The co-ordinated development of adult education around a coherent and systematic curriculum, its resourcing and the training of its teachers and leaders, are large issues confronting us immediately.[66]

Almost ten years later, in a major report following a national forum for Directors and Heads of Religious Education in Catholic School Systems (NCEC, 2005), a number of key issues were named as challenging matters demanding a response. These included 'parish–school relationships and expectations', 'parent expectations and engagement', and 'Catholic school identity and mission'. However, echoing the urgency of a much earlier paper (*Top Ten Challenges*, 1996) the leading issue for all stakeholders was now 'teacher spirituality and formation': 'The readiness of teachers to take

---

63 Three key documents emanate from: 1. The Bishops of Queensland (QCEC: The Queensland Bishops Project – *Catholic Schools for the 21ˢᵗ Century*, 2001). 2. The Bishops of New South Wales and the ACT (*Catholic Schools at the Crossroads*, 2007) and 3. The Australian Catholic Bishops Conference *(Bishop Holohan: Re-visioning Catholic Schools in an Education Revolution*, 2009).

64 Bishops of NSW & the ACT, 2007, p. 2. In addition, one third of the students in Catholic schools are not Catholic. Half of all Catholic students are in government schools.

65 Bishops of NSW & the ACT, 2007, p. 3.

66 National Catholic Education Commission, 1996, p. 5.

up the challenge of being leaders in the religious domain and the need to design and support high quality formation programs.'[67] Three other research projects are of note: *What Strategies and Models Best Support the Faith Development of Teachers?* (1995); *Spiritual and Faith Formation for Leadership* (2005); and the *Who's Coming to School Today?* survey (2010). All of these highlighted serious challenges.[68]

Cumulatively, these three research projects signalled the need for a different kind of staff preparation for mission, additional to qualifications and professional in-service. Consequently, in the last ten years, in seeking to strengthen the missional dimension of Catholic school staff, Catholic Education policy across Australian dioceses has increasingly identified the importance of formation for both employing authorities and employees,[69] and a strengthening of expectations for employees to engage in formation experiences.[70]

While the policy and research journey of Australian Bishops and Diocesan employing authorities has continued to develop at one level, grounded action has developed apace at another. Established in 2007, a

---

67 National Catholic Education Commission, 2005, p. 11.

68 *What Strategies and Models Best Support the Faith Development of Teachers?* (1995) identified the following as formative experiences for teachers: the influence on their lives of significant other people who modelled a relationship with God; the foundational importance of experience over acquiring knowledge; the lifelong and individual nature of the spiritual journey; the role of significant times of pain in being catalysts for seeking spirituality; and the positive experience and influence of being part of a faith community (QCEC, 1995). *Spiritual and Faith Formation for Leadership* (2005) explored the landscape of theory, practice and opportunities in spiritual formation for leadership across the Queensland dioceses. The research identified serious challenges for leadership succession in Catholic education. The report included an overview of formation opportunities for those in leadership positions; a detailed report on current policy, and practice in spiritual and faith formation for leadership in diocesan and Religious Institute schools in Queensland; a preliminary review of the literature in the area; an outline of key learnings; and design principles and strategies for further development. *Who's Coming to School Today?* survey (ACER, 2010) identified the following: 1. Strong endorsement by staff for the importance of religious faith and practice in the life of the schools, with little variance in sub-groups. 2. While parents and students want more emphasis on vocational outcomes and academic success, few staff thought the best thing their school did was to generate good academic results. 3. When stakeholders are asked for the dominant thing that Catholic schools do best, they choose a 'caring community' over academic qualities. However, this co-exists with the finding that most stakeholders 'agreed'/'strongly agreed' that their school provided good academic results.

69 The most recent QCEC policy statement, *Formation for Staff in Catholic Schools in Queensland* (2010), makes explicit the responsibility of the employer: All Catholic school authorities will ensure that all staff members participate in formation experiences to assist them to grow in understanding of their ministry as part of the mission of the Catholic Church (QCEC, 2010, 1, p. 1)

70 The 2010 QCEC policy signaled an increased focus on formation rather than RE qualifications and accreditation activities. Policy for senior leadership positions reflects a similar change. The 2000 QCEC policy statement for senior leaders identified the religious dimension of Catholic leadership as a central principle and introduced some essential criteria. This policy has since been enhanced with more prescriptive religious qualifications and formation expectations required for senior leadership.

national network emerged (FACE: Formation for Australian Catholic Educators), comprising leaders in formation across Australian Catholic education, and it has continued to grow in a vibrant way. The network has provided collaboration among its members (which include religious congregations and independent operators as well as diocesan education leaders) modelling strategic, practical and collegial support. In this way, both the approach and praxis of formation for Australian Catholic educators has advanced significantly. The shared understanding has resulted in the development of a set of Principles of Approach for staff formation.[71] You will have the opportunity to engage with the depth of wisdom and experience of a number of these leaders in Part E of this book (Practice Wisdom). The NCEC is currently developing a productive formal association with this network, providing an NCEC website for resources and additional opportunities to gather and collaborate in formal and informal ways.

A QUESTION INTO THE FUTURE

Gerald Grace suggests the crucial question for the future is: Are the reserves of spiritual capital in the Catholic school system being renewed or is the system in contemporary contexts living on a declining asset?[72] If we understand culture as Pope Francis does, to be 'a dynamic reality which a people constantly recreates'[73], then dialogue between faith and culture must be two-way. In 'befriending' both the wisdom of the faith tradition and the wisdom of the cultural tradition – that is, to engage with them critically, but loyally – there must be a living into and from both the faith tradition and the cultural tradition. Authentic formation for mission has to embrace this.

CONCLUSION TO PART A

Both the context and the challenges invite an opportunity to engage, as never before, in the exploration of formation that makes personal meaning, has system-strategic application and remains ecclesially faithful. The multi-faceted nature of the challenge and the diversity of needs among Catholic educators and leaders does not diminish the responsibility to provide formation that satisfies the meaning-making needed for the contemporary mission space of Catholic education. At the same time, the possibilities for genuine transformative work that changes lives and influences the world has never been as verdant!

---

71 These principles were originally presented at the 2010 ACU Leadership Conference and more recently re-published in *Compass*.
72 Grace, *Digital Journal of Lasallian Research* (4), 2012: 07-19, p. 11.
73 Pope Francis, 2013, *Evangelii Gaudium*, n. 122.

Spiritual formation is a 'sleeping giant' for Catholic education. While it is perceived by many in system leadership as the soft edge of professional development, the reality is that authentic spiritual formation is probably the most confronting and challenging journey leaders and educators can undertake. It calls for courage to own the belief that formation is much more than informational learning, pious spiritual practice or system compliant action – it is professional and personal, individual and communal. The creation of a contemporary approach to spiritual formation that is both faithful to the evangelising mission of the Church and responsive to the personal worlds of individuals calls us to be creative and practical, to re-imagine traditional approaches, and to recover core realities. The challenge here is not only whether such a re-imagination is possible, but how it finds its place in the current ecclesial, cultural and educational landscape.

Pope Francis pulls this challenge back into the Emmaus story in describing his dream for the Church in the world ...

> *We need a Church unafraid of going forth into their night. We need a Church capable of meeting them on their way. We need a Church capable of entering into their conversation. We need a Church able to dialogue with those disciples who, having left Jerusalem behind, are wandering aimlessly, alone, with their own disappointment, disillusioned by a Christianity now considered barren, fruitless soil, incapable of generating meaning.'*[74]

While we will explore some very complex areas in this book, the under-pinning questions are the same stark and simple questions Pope Francis raises in this dream for the Church.

How do we – you and I – embrace the night-time journey in ourselves and each other? How do we make sense of living and dying and rising to give voice to a bigger, deeper, richer reality? What are we bringing to every encounter with students, with parents, with staff? Into whom and with whom are we growing? From what well of wisdom do you and I dialogue, reflect, live? And how do we honour and nurture the proclamation of those 1600 Australian Catholic educators and leaders: 'We are!'?

This is the heart of the mission formation task: the sacred work of stirring the soul of Catholic educators.

---

74 Pope Francis, Meeting with the Bishops of Brazil, Archbishop's House, Rio de Janeiro Saturday, 28/7/ 2013 http://w2.vatican.va/content/francesco/en/speeches/2013/july/documents/papafrancesco_20130727_gmg-episcopato-brasile.html

STRUCTURE OF THE BOOK

The book unfolds into 6 sections.

In Part A we have opened up the challenge of formation for mission in the multi-dimensional context of Catholic education.

In Part B we explore the models of formation available across broad disciplines and seek to mine the learnings from these for the current challenge.

In Part C we explore the three major intersecting areas of thinking and praxis that inform our conversation around formation in the context of the Catholic educator and leader.

Part D brings together the strands of our exploration, extracting rich learnings in order to frame a new model of formation for Catholic school educators, a model which is responsive to the challenge of the mission field in a contemporary Australian Catholic educational context.

Part E gives voice to Practice Wisdom across the Catholic education landscape in Australia.

Part F concludes our journey, suggesting touchstones for policy and practice into the future.

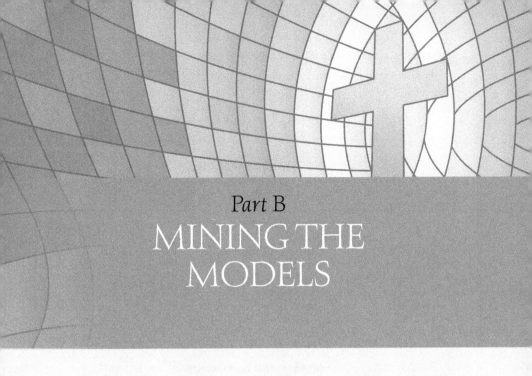

Part B
MINING THE MODELS

Spiritual formation in a Christian tradition answers a specific human question: 'What kind of person am I going to be?' … The most important thing in your life is not what you do; it's who you become. That's what you will take into eternity. You are an unceasing spiritual being with an eternal destiny in God's great universe.

Dallas Willard[1]

INTRODUCTION TO PART B

Because Australian Catholic schools were staffed almost entirely by members of religious orders until the 1960s, the predominant model of teacher formation in Catholic education has been the 'religious life' model. While we will begin Part B by considering the religious life model, we then explore a range of formation models from the broad field of research in human development and spiritual growth that offer insightful perspectives for the creation of effective and meaningful formation for the contemporary Catholic educator. In doing so, the aim is to open you to rich experiential exploration in this field, and to invite you to be attentive to those elements of each model that resonate with your own understanding. That resonance may be intuitive or it may be based on your professional experience. Both are relevant and point to the building blocks for a new and contemporary approach that grows out of the wisdom of those who've laboured before us.

---

1   Willard, quoted in Ortberg, 2014, p. 23.

Figure 1 below identifies the various models of spiritual formation that feature in Part B.

FIGURE 1: OVERVIEW OF FORMATION MODELS

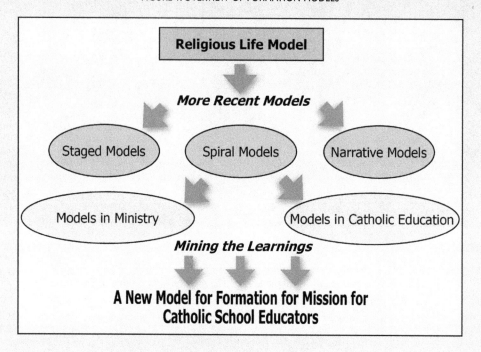

Outline of Part B

Chapter 2 outlines dominant and emerging models of Spiritual Formation in the broader landscape.

Chapter 3 explores current models and approaches in the Catholic educational context.

Chapter 4 mines the learnings for us across these available models and approaches.

As you traverse this broad landscape, be mindful of what resonates with your own experience, and hold on to those insights.

2

MODELS OF SPIRITUAL
FORMATION

THE RELIGIOUS LIFE MODEL

We begin by exploring what has come to us as the 'Religious Life' model.

The religious life model 'is the Catholic historical realisation of the monastic archetype'.[2] While monasticism is a religious phenomenon identifiable across various religious traditions, cultures and throughout history, the Catholic religious life model is distinctive in three ways:

1. It has a Christ-centric focus – a focus on the person of Jesus who is not merely an historical person whose memory gives a model to live by, but who is living and interactively present in the life of the believer.
2. It embraces a conception of salvation – based on a conviction that the one who believes in Jesus has eternal life in the here and now, and that whatever follows human death is not substantially different from the life of grace.
3. It has an ecclesial setting – where religious life is a 'form of Catholicism', not an alternative to it, and where mission and ministry in the world (even for contemplative orders) flows out of a commitment to the reign of God in the world.[3]

The traditional formation framework, which provided the foundation for the religious who once staffed Australian Catholic schools, was a staged and sustainable immersion model. For most religious orders, the journey to perpetual profession took some years and progressed through identifiable phases: juvenate; postulancy; novitiate; profession of annual vows; scholasticate and profession of lifelong vows.[4] There was a clear sense of journey, of living and learning toward a shared reality.

Formation in the religious life model is predicated on a three-step movement in spiritual development: the purgative way (moving away from

---

2   Schneiders, 2000, p. 9.
3   Schneiders, 2000, pp. 13-17.
4   Finke, 1997.

sin); the illuminative way (progression of virtue); and the unitive way (where one reconciles with God).[5] This traditional understanding has a generally static or fixed view of the formative dimension. Bernard Lonergan's theory of knowledge and process of religious conversion[6] opened up a more dynamic and transformative understanding of formation, and Kerrie Hide[7] adds a fourth and initial step – the affirmative way – to the traditional three-step movement.

A matrix framework allows for the application of Lonergan's conversion dimensions to the four-step process, situating the whole process within the journey towards Oneing – a term coined by the mystic Julian of Norwich to describe the growth toward and in union with God. Table 2.1 below illustrates this application.[8]

TABLE 2.1: CONVERSION DIMENSIONS AND THE FOUR WAYS

	Affirmative Way *Original Oneing*	Purgative Way *Oneing Through the Cross*	Illuminative Way *Becoming One in Love*	Unitive Way *Being in Love*
Intellectual Conversion	Our minds were created to reflect the wisdom of Christ in God.	Letting go of the limits of our intellectual certitude involves being prepared to embrace the cross.	Our search for knowledge opens us to new and deeper insights about the nature of wisdom and truth (mind of Christ).	Truth is more and more deeply intuitively grasped by the mind.
Affective Conversion	All things flow from God and return to God. Feelings can direct us to God.	We begin to earnestly seek to face our deepest fears that set up resistance to God.	Our physical and spiritual senses become more sensitised.	Our feelings are grounded in God enabling us to find consolation in the midst of suffering.
Moral Conversion	Our journey to God is to enable Christ to act in and through us.	There is a painful turning away from old false messages about loving.	We begin to experience oneness with all humanity. We go out to meet Christ in others.	In the way of Christ we take personal responsibility for our life and mission.
Socio-political Conversion	The whole of the human person, body and soul, is sacred, as is everyday life.	The violence in our own hearts makes us desperate to find peace and to work for peace.	There is a maturing ability to act from a place of inner freedom and to work for peace.	We can live in the midst of things but not in things.

5   Groeschel, 1984.
6   Lonergan, 1972.
7   Kerrie Hide, 2004.
8   This table was developed by Dr Kerrie Hide, 2004.

Bodily Conversion	Human beings are spiritually embodied.	Addictions begin to cause real discomfort and motivate us to address them	The wisdom of bodily knowing develops.	We live out of a holistic body-spirit unity.
Religious Conversion	God invites us to love with all our heart, all our mind and all our strength.	There is a deep unsettling desire to taste and see the goodness of God.	We have a maturing awareness that we must see all things through the eyes of God.	We know true joy and live in the eternal now.

In exploring the transformative process in a spiritual formation context, Robert Wuthrow[9] identified an ongoing journey of 'seeking' and 'dwelling'. Building on the research of James Loder and Robert Wuthrow,[10] Leron Shults and Steven Sandage[11] developed a model (Figure 2.2) that expresses the relationship between 'seeking' time and 'dwelling' time. Based on the original three-phase movement in spiritual development (purgative; illuminative; unitive), the model illustrates the progress between the inner and outer paths of dwelling and seeking.

FIGURE 2.2: BALANCING SPIRITUAL DWELLING AND SEEKING[12]

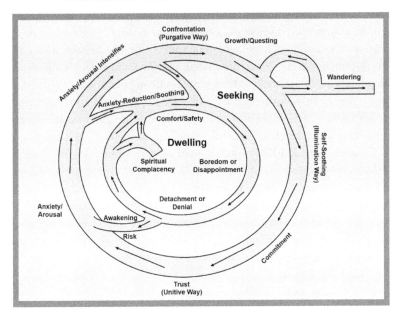

---

9   Wuthrow, 1998.
10   Loder, 1998 & Wuthnow, 1998.
11   Shults & Sandage, 2006.
12   Shults & Sandage, 2006, p. 33.

Dwelling includes 'connection to a spiritual community and tradition that legitimises certain rituals and spiritual practices and provides a sense of continuity of spiritual experience'.[13] For spiritual growth to continue, the individual is propelled at intervals to enter the path of seeking. While the model does not profile the variety of catalysing events or moments that cause the shift, it indicates the moment of transformative resolution propelling the individual into a renewed place of dwelling.

The Religious Life Model in Practice

In practice, the traditional religious life model translated into a distinctive lifestyle that had a marked influence on Catholic school identity and culture. The elements of this formative lifestyle might be summarised as:

- a commitment to the calling
- a commitment to the community
- a commitment to service.[14]

The commitment to a deep sense of calling, symbolised by dress, by title and by a direct daily vocational living, gave a clear sense of unity to purpose and mission. The commitment to living in community with its daily rhythms around communal prayer, and its expectation on the individual to serve, developed a commitment to community identity above individual identity. The commitment to service demanded that time and energy be given to long hours in the school, covering a multitude of tasks outside teaching, as well as service to the wider community needs of parish and parish families.[15]

The context of community living in religious life provided sustainable modelling which extended into the school environment. One learned how to be a religious, and how to teach, partly through observing how others did it, and by the companioning of influential individual religious and the religious community. The daily formation framework included compulsory morning prayers, communal Mass, communal rosary and night prayers. In a seamless extension into the classroom and the school community 'many other spiritual exercises filled the day.'[16] Students absorbed a religious culture communicated through aural, visual and olfactory dimensions entwined in their Catholic schooling experiences.[17]

At the same time, the day to day living out of this model exposed shortcomings that had a detrimental impact on the individual religious, as well as the school environment. As current expectations for the provision of

13   Shults & Sandage, 2006, p. 32.
14   O'Donoghue & Potts, 2004.
15   O'Donoghue & Potts, 2004, pp. 469-72.
16   Burley, 2001, p. 33.
17   O'Donoghue & Burley, 2008.

formation intensify for systemic authorities, the limitations of the religious life formation model for the contemporary context of Catholic school staff highlight issues at the core of the current challenge.

The program of 'spiritual formation' for religious sisters, brothers and priests included elements of renouncing self, family and any relational ties. Related quandaries also presented themselves for the individual religious:

> It was not long before I began to feel the contradictions inherent in the life of a nun – we were to live a life of love, of God first and above all else, and then of love for all those we worked with. Love to me implied warmth, spontaneity and generosity, but these qualities were often suppressed. For our training involved 'death to self' – a disciplined self-control of all such feelings. For me, love and death to self presented a dichotomy that could never be reconciled.[18]

This often resulted in a variety of discipline practices being adopted by teaching religious within the school environment, which were not in accordance with any official pedagogical position of the religious orders to which the members belonged.[19]

While elements of a shared community vision and integrated praxis in everyday routine are a rich and valuable source in formation, the focus in the religious life model on the purgative way of transformation often devalued individual experience. Rather than confirming a positive anthropology, the development of a deficit view of the human condition presents a major inadequacy for contemporary times.

STAGED DEVELOPMENTAL MODELS

A second group of approaches adapted for formation emanate from the staged developmental models. Models by James Fowler[20] and Lawrence Kohlberg[21], and the multiple pathway models offered by experiential practitioners Peter Jarvis[22] and William Huitt and Jennifer Robbins[23], give priority to individual experience and development in the adult learner. In contemporary culture, this emphasis has become prominent in the educative contexts.

---

18 Graham, as cited in O'Donoghue & Burley, 2008, p. 187.
19 O'Donoghue & Burley, 2008.
20 Fowler, 1981.
21 Kohlberg, 1987.
22 Jarvis, 2004.
23 Huitt & Robbins, 2003.

The Sequentially Staged Model

The most influential stage thinker in the faith development field is James Fowler.[24] Fowler defined faith development as a sequence of stages by which persons shape their relatedness to a transcendent centre.

Fowler's theoretical research identified seven stages of spiritual development across a person's lifespan. Following a linear set of stages, he claims most people attain Stage 3, shaping some kind of personal definition of faith. Fowler also believes few people ever attain Stage 7 – the development of a consciousness dealing with complex issues such as social justice, and the giving up of an egocentric focus that creates 'a universalising faith'. Importantly, Stage 5 suggests a second naïveté where an increased appreciation for the power of myth and a deeper connection to symbol emerges. It is a movement that is indicative of 'a return to the inner-child that values direct experience, while learning to affirm others' beliefs'.[25]

There are four fundamental assumptions in Fowler's work:

1. Human beings are hardwired for communion with the Divine, with connection to something greater than self.
2. Faith evolves through a complex development of sequential stages.
3. An individual's freedom of choice to deepen that communion, or move away from it, operates within the strong influences of secularity.[26]
4. This formative development happens within and is shaped by community, and its symbolic and ritual life.[27]

For the purposes of our exploration, Table 2.2 outlines the four Fowler stages which are most relevant to the participant demographic which constitutes educators in Australian Catholic schools.

While Fowler's work remains foundational, the framework is critiqued as being too cognitive and linear. The juxtaposition of Carl Jung's studies on mid-life against Fowler's stage theory has provided a thoughtful lens for researchers to expand Fowler's work. Drawing on Carl Jung's theory that the first half of life is influenced more by biology and the second half of life more by culture,[28] researchers support an approach that gives emphasis to awareness and emotion. The 'cultural' aims of mid-life 'come to fruition

---

24   Fowler, 1981; 2000.
25   Huitt & Robbins, 2003, p. 11.
26   See also Wilber, 2000.
27   See the work of English, Fenwick & Parsons, 2005.
28   See Joseph Campbell (ed), 1971, for a very useful introduction to Jung's thought on the stages of life.

by the maturation of the spirit.'[29] This proposition confirms Erikson's contention that 'generativity is the central issue in midlife'. [30]

Working with staged modelling, experiential learning scholars have contributed what they understand to be the working principle of individual differentiation. Peter Jarvis[31], building on David Kolb's work in experiential learning[32], offers a model which allows different routes and non-linear pathways in the adult learning journey. While acknowledging the reality of different learning pathways, this model foregrounds reflection and experiential praxis in progression through stages and in the creation of transformative change in the adult learner. However, insufficient reference to, and integration of, adult developmental markers remains a key limitation in this model.

TABLE 2.2: FOWLER'S STAGES OF FAITH (STAGES 4-7)

Stage	Typical Age	Defining Qualities	Influences	Major Antecedents to Transition
4. Synthetic– Conventional	15–21, plus some adults	Formation of personal identity and shaping of personal definition of faith	External sources such as school, work, friends, media and personal reflection	Internal conflict between personal beliefs and social expectations
5. Individuative – Reflective	Young adult	Unique, individualistic worldview	Independent critical thinking; beginning to balance self, others and higher power	Desire to integrate worldviews of self and others
6. Conjunctive	Mid-life and beyond	Value direct experience while affirming others' beliefs	Increasing appreciation of symbols and myths; meaningful learning experiences	Desire to reconcile the untransformed world and the personally-developed transformed vision and loyalties
7. Universalising Faith	Few ever reach	Disciplined activist seeking to impact and transform the social order	Consciousness of complex universal issues; loss of egocentric focus	

---

29 McFadden & Gerl, 1990, p. 35.
30 Erikson, 1950, cited in Huitt and Robbins, 2003, p. 12.
31 Jarvis, 1987, 2004.
32 Kolb, 1984.

A different kind of experiential approach that incorporates both staged models and spiral models is John Westerhoff's 'Rings of Faith' model.[33] Identifying 'rings' or stages, Westerhoff proposes that faith life grows and builds on these concentric rings of experience. The revised stages are identified as affiliative faith, searching faith and mature faith (Figure 2.3). This model recognises lifelong growth, where the core of mature faith rests in a childlike faith.

FIGURE 2.3: THE RINGS OF FAITH MODEL (WESTERHOFF, 1980)

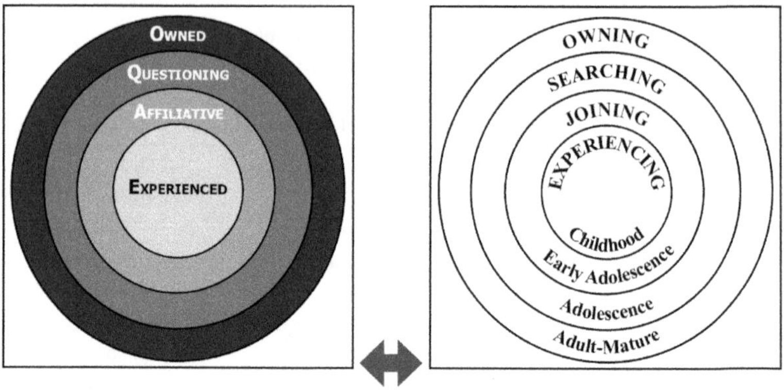

Experientially, and paradoxically, the stages of maturing spiritual growth reflect a developing interiority to a point where the individual is subsumed in God. The contribution of the mystics in the Catholic tradition to the experiential dimension of formation is well documented.

> The first theologies of the soul were also the first attempts at depth psychology. Mystical awareness of the person's inner world or soul is distinct from ordinary awareness. For St. Teresa it was an inner castle; for Catherine of Siena the soul was an interior home; for Meister Eckhart it was a little castle; for St. John of the Cross the soul was the dark and hidden part of his house.[34]

This process of deepening interiority is elaborated in three steps in the 14th century work of Christian Mysticism 'The Cloud of Unknowing'[35]:

1. A way of life where the believer is caught up more with things outside of self as opposed to within. It is a life in the world filled with good deeds and works of mercy, but not yet deepened with interior things.

---

33   Westerhoff, 1976, 1980.
34   Beck, 2003, p. 30.
35   Walker, 1998.

2. The second stage is characterised by a movement towards interiority. Within self, interior meditation on the things of the spirit is the key.

3. The believer is above and beneath self and under God – this happens through grace. Here the believer is united with God in spirit and one with God in love and desire in the Cloud of Unknowing.[36] The same paradoxical process of interiority and detachment has been re-presented as a four stage journey of spiritual growth moving from the 'chaotic/anti-social' stage into the 'formal/institutional' stage through a 'scepticism/questioning' stage and finally into the 'mystic/communal' stage.[37]

In all expressions of experiential staged learning, there is an acknowledgement of the uniqueness of the individual journey. This remains such an important contribution to contemporary understanding of the formative process.

SPIRAL MODELS

The application of spiral dynamics in spirituality has been associated with Ken Wilber in his development of 'integral spirituality'.[38] His work marks an innovative response to the challenge of re-conceptualising spirituality in the modern and post-modern context. Within a broader framework that assumes multiple pathways of development, Wilber identifies four factors that facilitate a personal transformative process that spirals into deeper awareness and being. Different in each individual depending on background, capability and life experience, the four factors are fulfilment, dissonance, insight and opening.[39] Fulfilment means that the individual has reached the completion of a particular stage or 'wave'. Some experience of dissonance then opens the individual to transformation. This experience is one of pain and disorientation in letting go and embracing the new. Eventually, out of the dissonance comes insight into a new reality. Finally, if all three factors fall into place, there is an opening up to the next wave of consciousness, a deeper and richer reality than previously experienced or imagined. For each individual, the profiling of dissonance as a catalyst for transformation resonates with what the mystics call the 'dark night of the soul' as a necessary breakthrough phase in spiritual growth.

From this meta-world of theology to the real-world setting of Catholic education, the conceptual perspective of the spiral model has had application

---

36   Walker, 1998.
37   Peck, 1993, p. 238.
38   Wilber, 2006.
39   Wilber, 2000.

in curriculum planning development since the nineteen-eighties. Maria Harris, in her work, proposed educationalists adopt curriculum planning 'from a religious and artistic angle of vision, in contrast to one that is technical and mechanical'.[40] Her pedagogy is aesthetic and formative.

> Curriculum planners should think of themselves as artists, as the potter who works with clay, so that we can 'fashion a people.' We re-order and re-create experience to give it meaning. What we do will be intuitive rather than technical ... more like a dance than something linear.[41]

In this way, Harris pioneered a new paradigm for modelling that directly reflects a way of understanding development that is cyclical rather than linear. This perspective is particularly appropriate for a formation program because of the experientially responsive nature of the work and the acknowledgement of the complex and iterative nature of individual spiritual growth.

A Spiral 'Pathways of Learning' Model

One of the most educationally engaging approaches developed through this perspective is the spiral model created by Rachael Kessler. This model highlights an understanding of learning that identifies diverse pathways. Identifying seven different innate drivers for individuals derived from the developmental research of Fowler (1981), Kohlberg (1984), Maslow (1983), Gardner (2000), Erikson (1950) and Campbell (1972), Kessler (2000) affirms distinct practices needed to nurture these different pathways in the spiritual journey.

The premise in this model is that the starting point for individuals is different yet falls into seven general pathways. Kessler calls these 'pathways to the soul.'[42] For each pathway, the experiences and activities provided progress the individual's yearning deeper and deeper into their connective soul space. Figure 2.4 illustrates the model.[43]

---

40   Harris, 1989, p. 169.
41   Harris, 1989, p. 170.
42   Kessler, 2000, p. 160.
43   Huitt &Robbins, 2003, p. 11.

FIGURE 2.4: KESSLER'S SPIRAL MODEL OF SPIRITUAL DEVELOPMENT (2000)

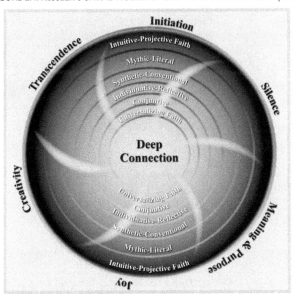

Table 2.3, following, elaborates on the descriptors for each pathway, cross-matching Kessler's identified pathways with other theories (Fowler, Gardner, Erikson, Maslow, Sternberg, Csikszentmihalyi and Campbell).

TABLE 2.3: 'PATHWAYS TO THE SOUL'[44]

Pathway	Description	Found in Other Theories
Yearning for deep connection	Describes a quality of relationship that is profoundly caring, resonant with meaning, and involves feelings of belonging	Fowler (1981) Erikson (1950) – need for belonging (to something larger than oneself); Gardner (2000) – Interpersonal intelligence (connection/others)
Longing for silence and solitude	As a respite from the tyranny of busyness and noise, silence may be a realm of reflection, of calm and rest, of prayer or contemplation.	Gardner (2000) – Intrapersonal intelligence
Search for meaning and purpose	Exploration of big questions, such as 'Why am I here?' 'Does my life have a purpose?' 'What is life for?' 'What is my destiny?' and 'Is there a God?'	Gardner (2000) – Existential intelligence; Fowler (1981) – Unique, individualistic worldview

----

44   Kessler, 2000.

Pathway	Description	Found in Other Theories
Hunger for joy and delight	Can be satisfied through experiences of great simplicity, such as play, celebration or gratitude	Csikszentmihalyi (1998) – Flow in consciousness
Creative drive	Is part of all the gateways; the awe and mystery of creating, whether developing a new idea, a work of art, a new discovery or a new lens on life	Sternberg (1988) – Creative intelligence
Urge for transcendence	The desire to go beyond perceived personal limits; not only the mystical realm, but experiences of the extraordinary in the arts, athletics, academics or human relations	Maslow (1983) – Transcendence Fowler (1981) – loss of egocentric focus
Need for initiation	Deals with rites of passage	Campbell (1972); Schlegel and Barry (1980) – Initiation

While Kessler's work is focussed on school students, the model is applicable to adults. The key to implementing this model is to provide appropriate scaffolding and opportunity to address each of the pathways in a manner that is meaningful to the developmental level of the individual. A strength in Kessler's spiral model is the cross-match analysis and integration of developmental theories with her individual pathway recognition. This contribution underlies the holistic approach to formation strongly supported in the literature. Her understanding of the critical role of environment and context also has endorsement in the wider literature.

The limitation of this framework is the reliance on the initial environmental engagement and the ability of the teacher/facilitator to propel individuals into the quest about their 'most intimate questions and longings'[45] and to continue the companioning. This is because the capacity to 'invite soul into the classroom'[46] ultimately depends on 'the identity and integrity of the teacher'[47] and attention to their own spiritual development.

---

45   Kessler, 2000, p. 18.
46   Kessler, 2000, p. 16.
47   Palmer, 2007, p. 2.

NARRATIVE MODELS

Another model for assisting adult formative learning to emerge in contemporary times is the narrative model. The construction of narrative as a mode of thought has been methodically explored in the literature, informed by the groundwork scholarship of Paul Ricour[48] and Jerome Bruner.[49] In educational research, the use of narrative is both central and influential, for 'at the heart of meaningful educational reform and change, lie the narratives'.[50]

Two pre-eminent characteristics of narrative thinking are relevant to our discussion:

1. Narrative thought contrasts with logical inductive thought, allowing for a different way of world-making.
2. Narrative reflection gives entry to a different reality that orders experience outside of chronological time and other temporal forms.[51]

In this dynamic, connection to an articulation of experience is crucial, and the outcome of that connection gives shape to one's spirituality.

The drive for self-understanding in the post-modern context has seen a stronger use of narrative across a number of disciplines. By telling and retelling their life stories, adult learners describe times of continuity and change in their lives, and give an account of their self-formation. The process of (re)reading one's narrative offers new and alternative learning[52] where 'both the narrative itself and reflections upon the narrative appear to facilitate understanding and to generate new knowledge'. [53] The use of narrative is thus a way in which teachers 'find voices to tell their own stories' [54] and gain new understandings of their lives and the communities within which they live.

Reflection is an integral part of narrative inquiry and is linked to the gaining of new understandings.[55] Transformative learning occurs when reflection on disjunctive experience leads to interpretations which change the learners' meaning perspectives and their social practice.[56] These changes are incorporated into a new version of the life narrative. In this dynamic,

---

48 Ricour, 1984.
49 1986; 2004.
50 Beattie, 2001, p. 66.
51 Bruner, 2004.
52 Johnson, 2002.
53 Chambers, 2003, pp. 404–5.
54 Beattie, 2001, p. 59.
55 Day & Harris, 2000.
56 Moxley, 2000.

imagination partners with critical reflection in the individual to re-frame life in a new and evolved way. The narrative facilitation of this transformative or hermeneutic conversation is the pivotal element in adult formative learning.

One of the contemporary narrative models pertinent to the discussion is Fred Korthagen's 'onion' model, which explores the possibilities of multifaceted reflection.[57] The general thrust for more reflectivity in educators is not accompanied in the literature by much practical guidance in developing a self-reflective practice. Cognisant of this, Korthagen's approach presents an 'umbrella model of levels of change that could serve as a framework for reflection and development'.[58] It is also responsive to the post-modern emphasis in narrative work around the beliefs people hold about themselves.

Thus, this is a model that interprets the relationship between a person's inner self and his or her behaviour in the outer world, linking core beliefs about self to professional identity.[59] The six layers of this model are:

1. the environment
2. one's behaviour in relation to this environment
3. the competencies determining one's behaviour
4. the beliefs guiding one's functioning in the outside world
5. sense of identity
6. mission.

The sixth level is also referred to as the level of *spirituality*. Reflection at this level is concerned with what inspires, with what gives meaning and significance to work or life (Faller-Mitchell, 2010). 'Mission' is 'what is deep inside us that moves us to do what we do'[60] and is about what gives meaning to one's existence. Korthagen directly links this core level to the teacher's professional development. Although Korthagen's 'onion model' was designed to help researchers frame thinking around 'what makes a good teacher', it provides a model for framing and understanding the very depths of identity formation in teachers. Figure 2.5 illustrates Korthagen's onion model and the relevant questions for each layer.

---

57   Korthagen, 2004.
58   Korthagen, 2004, p. 77.
59   Korthagen & Vasalos, 2005.
60   Korthagen, 2004, p. 85.

FIGURE 2.5: KORTHAGEN'S ONION MODEL [61]

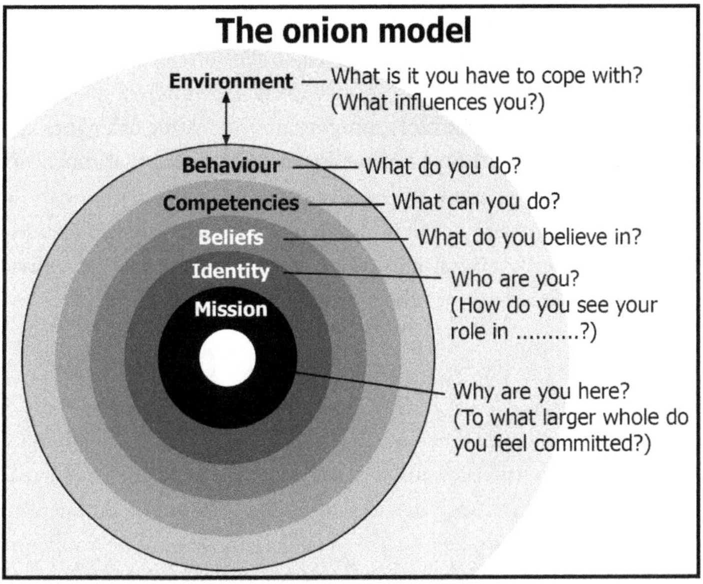

The onion model

Environment — What is it you have to cope with? (What influences you?)

Behaviour — What do you do?

Competencies — What can you do?

Beliefs — What do you believe in?

Identity — Who are you? (How do you see your role in ....?)

Mission — Why are you here? (To what larger whole do you feel committed?)

In Korthagen's model, transformative learning occurs in the learner through the ongoing interpretation of events in their inner and outer experience, during which learners compose their lives and their life stories. An important aspect of this model is the principle that the levels influence each other, with the inner and outer levels determining, at different times, how the individual operates. When there is alignment between the levels, one experiences what Mihaly Csikszentmihalyi[62] calls *flow*, that is, a state of optimal functioning in which one feels that one's expression in the real world reflects 'the real me'. In other words, there is a sense of identity and integrity.

To summarise, the alignment of teachers' inner spiritual cores with their professional context and mission is an important principle of formation in the Catholic tradition and in the adult learning literature. Korthagen's model suggests the animation of that core carries the capacity for transformative change in behaviour and outlook. Opportunities for deep professional learning arise: as soon as people are more in touch with their own identity and mission, this not only creates a change of perspective towards the daily hassles of the profession, but it also opens up doors to more transformational changes. It may also lead to new kinds of behaviour that are more in line with people's missions and inner potentials.[63]

The limitation of Korthagen's model is the inadequate recognition

---

61 Korthagen, 2004, p. 80.
62 Csikszentmihalyi, 1998.
63 Lyons, 2010.

of the role of community (others) in the individual's learning journey. Philosopher Charles Taylor affirms a positive effect of secularism in the individual seeking of self-identity, and which illuminates the 'ex-carnation' that sits in our culture, but he also points to the downside of an 'expressive' individualism that marks the contemporary period.[64] One of Taylor's central points is that human identity is primarily dialogical, and that much of our understanding of the world is necessarily shared.[65] In Taylor's view, the 'dark side of individualism' is a withdrawal into our own narcissistic pleasures and pains, involving an overly atomistic and instrumental view of individual identity, with little regard for others or society.[66]

FORMATION MODELS IN MINISTRY

The United States Conference of Catholic Bishops[67] offers an approach to formation based on the recognition of a lay ecclesial ministry. The formation framework, already in place for deacons and priests (based on *Pastores Dabo Vobis*, 1992), is applied to lay ecclesial ministers. The foundational background statement affirms a holistic approach to formation:

> *Effective formation methods address the whole person: emotions, imagination, will, heart, and mind. It is the whole person who ministers, so the whole person is the proper subject of formation.*[68]

Four inter-related areas are proposed, each considered critical in formation for any pastoral ministry: human, spiritual, intellectual and pastoral. The approach also recognises the importance of the cultural context of participants, insisting that formation should 'take the greatest account of local human culture, which contributes to formation itself.'[69]

While some have enthusiastically adopted this structure as the way forward in lay formation generally, the basic framework raises significant questions. Researchers in the psycho-spiritual field[70] understand spiritual formation to necessarily include human, intellectual and active/pastoral dimensions within the formation journey, and that to place spiritual formation separate from these other areas is unhelpful for both the process

---

64   Ex-carnation: Taylor used this term in A Secular Age (as the opposite of in-carnation) to describe what happens when we conceptualise and abstract our lives. What ends up happening is that concepts and thoughts become more important than the lived experience. See Taylor, 2015.
65   Taylor, 2015.
66   Taylor, 2007.
67   USCCB, 2005.
68   USCCB, 2005, p. 33.
69   USCCB, 2005.
70   Huitt & Robbins, 2003; Leffel, 2007; Theissen, 2005.

and integrity of spiritual formation. In her schema for spiritual formation for leaders, theologian Gesa Thiessen re-shapes the human, intellectual and pastoral elements named in the USCCB framework as *connection* (to self, community and creation), *compassion* (growing from knowledge and experience) and *contribution* (service).[71] In this way, the human context is the starting point for engagement, rather than one of the dimensions for focus.

Formation work in youth ministry and leadership ministry offers further insights relevant to our current discussion. Thomas Zanzig's prominent approach in contemporary youth ministry offers a four-step model described as a formation of discipleship: inspiration (through the witness of others); imitation (conscious daily practice); integration (into personal identity); and identification (in a way that sees the transformation of self).[72] It is a process that is sequential and ongoing, with potential application to ongoing spiritual formation.

Another approach, developed by Wendy Rosov and based on rabbinic education, offers a pedagogy framework. In this model, four key components are identified for facilitating spiritual formation: reflective deliberation; teaching text for meaning; discipling; and creating community.[73] Further research that builds on specific strategies for nurturing spiritual leadership has subsequently distinguished four conceptual dimensions as the focus for formation programs: worship, warmth, word and work.[74]

There are a number of other models used in contemporary Christian ministry preparation which rely more on non-institutionally based formation methodologies such as mentoring, retreating, and small group spiritual formation within the context of a local church or other Christian community.[75] These models signpost the integration of personal and group development research with customised elements of formation. An implication of this philosophy of ministry preparation is a focus on action orientation rather than a didactic (lecture-centred) orientation.[76] The discussion, discovery and problem-solving orientation reflects a shared wisdom approach to spiritual formation.

In practice, most ministry formation models are more commonly used outside the Catholic Church context than inside. However, they have much to offer in a time of rapidly changing contexts for both lay and ecclesial ministry formation. In particular, the profound influence of the experience of community immersion and service orientation on participants' spiritual growth is instructive.

---

71   Thiessen, 2005.
72   Zanzig, 2004.
73   Rosov, 2001.
74   Cheung, 2002.
75   Harrison, 2007; Lount & Hargie, 1998; Robinson, 2007.
76   Miedema, 1995; Dowson & McInerney, 2005.

3

CURRENT MODELS AND APPROACHES IN A CATHOLIC EDUCATION CONTEXT

Within the Catholic education context, approaches to formation contrast in both process and content. The formation for evangelisation model developed by James Mulligan (2004), the spirituality/virtues seminars model developed by Patricia Earl (2003) and the reflective retreat model developed by Parker Palmer (1997) exemplify three distinct approaches for consideration.

TEACHER FORMATION FOR EVANGELISATION SMALL GROUP MODEL

The small group model of formation created and explored in the research of Canadian, James Mulligan, CSC, provides an insightful perspective on contemporary evangelisation.[77] Teacher formation, in his view, is understood as a preparation for the ministry of Catholic education, with its goal being evangelisation. However, Mulligan maintains that formation for contemporary times must be invitational, not coercive. It needs to be designed to touch the spirit of the Catholic educator, not propagandise, and it must tend to the life experience of the educator. Mulligan's approach is dialogical, given context in the life and work of educators, and involves a community process-oriented development of knowledge.

Supported by selected readings, the themed content of the series of small group discussions that form the process in Mulligan's model focus on both cultural and ecclesial contexts for the Catholic schoolteacher. While these contexts for Catholic schooling are significantly different from the Australian environment, the underlying principles in approach are relevant and applicable. The strength in Mulligan's approach is four-fold: it allows for quality reflection and engagement; the structure of discussion allows the challenge of the present personal and ecclesial reality for the Catholic school educator to be addressed; the extended time period of the

---

77   Mulligan, 1994, 2005.

program (eight months) allows for a genuine formative experience; and the choice of participants addresses the issue of the mentoring need identified for beginning teachers. In addition, Mulligan demonstrates a sharp understanding of the needs of Catholic school educators and respectfulness for the challenge and interpretive wisdom of the experienced teacher and leader in Catholic schools. This is reflected in the shape of the program and in Mulligan's personal learning from his research journey:

> Our experience together as a group of pilgrim believers concerned about Catholic education confirms for me again the fundamental intuition that ministry in the Church today is most effective when it is done in the context of a caring, critiquing, enabling community.[78]

Mulligan's subsequent works in 2005 and 2015 reiterate his belief in the critical role of a dialogical communal dimension in formation for mission.

SPIRITUALITY/VIRTUES SEMINARS FORMATION MODEL

The contrasting approach in American research by Patricia Earl IHM is informative. It uses values as a conduit in formation for Catholic school educators. Constructed as a four-week seminar series on basic elements of spirituality, and a two-day seminar on virtues for the classroom, Earl's approach combines formation background for teachers with strategies for the classroom. The spirituality seminars provide 'a background for spirituality based on the Bible, Catholic Church documents, and the *Catechism of the Catholic Church*.'[79] The virtues seminar provides a basic theological background and understanding of virtue and how to develop it in the classroom with students. The aim of the seminars, targeted to both pre-service and practising teachers, is 'helping teachers to help students love God and love neighbour and use talents'. [80] The findings indicate that the seminars did provide theological knowledge related to virtue or character education.

> Participants identified, as a sign of God's love, such things as modelling virtue and prayer, integration of religion and concepts of moral development, and nurturing and caring for students The seminars provided teachers with not only information, but also personal formation to guide students to love God and neighbour, to develop and use their gifts and talents, and to become caring and responsible individuals.[81]

---

78   Mulligan, 1994, p. 14.
79   Earl, 2007, p. 40.
80   Earl, 2003, p. 13.
81   Earl, 2003, p. 14.

The strength of Earl's approach is in the twin targeting of personal formation and professional pedagogy, with her study indicating the seminars 'had influence on four areas: the individual, teaching pedagogy, character education, and understanding the mission of Catholic education'.[82] This is underpinned by literacy theory and theological background. It is an approach that coincides with a resurgence of interest in values education as an entry point to formation in Catholic belief and teaching in England and Scotland (e.g. *Values for Life*, Scotland CEC, 2007). In Australia, values education is being given greater emphasis. In referring to the potential of values education in all Australian schools, Terence Lovat & Neville Clement comment, 'We live in a time when our understanding of the role of the teacher and the power of values education is coalescing.'[83] Seeking to capitalise on this development, a number of dioceses are exploring values as the lever between the national educational agenda and Catholic philosophy (e.g. *Values that Matter*, Parramatta CEO, 2008; *Our Values, Our Mission*, Broken Bay CEO, 2008).

The concern in adopting this approach is two-fold. The focus on values or virtues runs the risk of losing the richness of the Catholic tradition in the search for an acceptable compromise that connects with a contemporary audience. Secondly, the seminar approach is based more on an in-service or informational model than a formation model, with limited time provided for depthing a personal journey, either theologically or spiritually. As such, the structure and process can accommodate large numbers of participants, but there is doubt about the sustainable influence of this model.

COURAGE TO TEACH REFLECTIVE RETREAT FORMATION MODEL

A retreat-centred model, developed by American educationalist Parker Palmer in conjunction with the Fetzer Institute, provides a third approach. Initially created as a renewal experience for public school teachers, it draws on Quaker practices and principles as well as scholarship in education and psychology. The approach is based on the premise that 'good teaching cannot be reduced to technique; good teaching comes from the identity and integrity of the teacher'.[84]

Focusing on the inner life of the participant, this program is structured as a series of eight retreats over two years, with six key elements in the formation approach: 'Evocative questions; Silence; Paradox; Birthright Gifts;

---

82 Earl, 2007, p. 43.
83 Lovat & Clement, 2008, p. 3.
84 Palmer, 2007, p. 10.

'Third things'; and 'Clearness Committees.'[85] In large-group, small-group and solitary settings, each three-day retreat experience explores concepts of vocation, and 'the teacher's heart'[86] through the use of personal stories; reflections on classroom practice; and insights from storytellers, poets and a variety of religious and wisdom traditions. This overall process is carefully bounded in the creation of established principles for 'the formation space'[87] which develops a dynamic of deep sharing and trust among participants.

Palmer's most influential work has been around the role of community and reflective praxis. Palmer is a strong proponent of the 'wisdom within' both the individual and the community, and the individual's own ability to find and nurture that wisdom. Independent evaluations of Palmer's *Courage to Teach* retreat program (CTT) empirically validate the approach of exploring teacher spirituality in the context of their lives and everyday work.[88] The strength of the approach lies in the carefully constructed retreat process, the personal focus, and the creative use of a variety of resources. While this approach has been readily adopted in a number of Australian dioceses, its greatest limitation is a lack of an appropriate cultural and strong theological context for the Catholic school educator.

---

85   Intrator, 2002, p. 282.
86   Palmer, 2007, p. 4.
87   Palmer, 2007, p. 76.
88   Intrator & Scribner, 2000; McMahon, 2003; Simone, 2004.

4

MINING THE LEARNINGS – FIVE LEVERS

The strengths of each model of spiritual formation so far presented offer valuable insights into the development of a new framework, and it is this framework that might meet the multiple challenges in the formation of Catholic educators today. The religious life model of formation, while no longer an appropriate, sustainable framework in its traditional form, offers foundational design elements that have the potential to be contemporised for a new context. Similarly, elements of approach and structure from the other models make useful contributions to the creation of something new.

In addition to the strengths in each model already outlined, there are five general levers we can see (following) which are instructional in further development, and which invite some further explication.

CALLING (VOCATION)

The grounding of spiritual formation processes in the context of vocation has a rich tradition for Catholic educators. In a contemporary approach, there is a connecting of one's personal story and heart to one's professional story. Vocation comes to be known in a new way 'not as a goal to be achieved but as a gift to be received.'[89] The voice of vocation is not 'out there' but within us calling us to be the person we were born to be, to fulfil the original selfhood given at birth by God.[90] Therefore, the authentic call to teach 'comes from the voice of the *teacher within* [author's italics], the voice that calls me to honour the nature of my true self'.[91]

For Catholic educators, a personal, holistic approach to vocation is organically situated within the school community, and in the contexts of the pedagogy of the reflective practitioner and a seamless Catholic curriculum:

---

89 Palmer, 1983, p. 10.
90 Palmer, 1983.
91 Palmer, 2007, p. 29.

The essence and beauty of Catholic education since the paradigmatic shift brought about by Vatican II is to promote the growth of the individual and the development of the whole person. This call to formation of the whole person in students ... insists upon the continuous formation of the teacher and subject matter that is organised relevantly to the holistic development of the student.[92]

In Figure 2.6 Gini Shimabukuro illustrates and explores this learning community dynamic in her extensive work in Catholic education.[93]

FIGURE 2.6: THE LEARNING COMMUNITY DYNAMIC

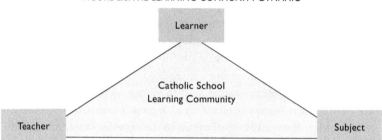

Such a paradigm implies an interior synthesis within the teacher, which permeates the Catholic school culture through the student-teacher dynamic and the staff dynamic. For this to be effective, the continuous spiritual process becomes visible through interaction with others, and there is an apparent nurturing of skill in behavioural areas, such as self-esteem, authentic caring, humility and communication. Aligning with Groome's belief that the educator's mission is 'to inform, form, and transform with the meaning and ethic of Christian faith'[94], this paradigm is an alternative call for an 'inspirational pedagogy'[95] that encourages critical thought and dialogue to develop a personally meaningful spirituality through knowledge and experience of the Reign of God. This is at the heart of the mission of the Catholic school, and it is the heart of the vocation of the Catholic school educator.[96]

---

92 Shimabukuro, 2001, p. 113.
93 Shimabukuro, 1998, 2008, 2010; and 2001, p. 114, for the diagram.
94 Groome, 1996, p. 118.
95 Grace, 2002.
96 Mulligan, 2004.

COMMUNITY

All of the models, to differing degrees, recognise the role of community. In fact, the community context is described as one of three spiritual practices of central importance to formation in the educational context. These practices are: 'the study of sacred texts, the practice of prayer and contemplation, and the gathered life of the community itself.'[97] The hallmark of Palmer's 'community of truth' is in its claim that 'reality is a web of communal relationships, and we can know reality only by being in community with it.'[98] Peck's four developmental stages of spiritual growth seek to bridge both individual and community journeys in faith.[99] An emphasis on the relational and communal aspect of spirituality demands a focus on 'living relationships' which requires personal commitment and investment of time and energy.[100] This also requires the nurturing of mutuality. The practice of mutuality requires the acquisition of certain formative habits – things that are done often and eventually with some kind of ease – to sustain a lifestyle of mutual relationships. Seven habits of mutuality are identified for regular practice:

- self-love
- taking ourselves and one another seriously
- being present to others and ourselves
- seeing the sacred in ourselves and others
- acknowledging and respecting differences
- facing conflict
- participating in supportive communities.[101]

Australian research confirms that a lack of connectivity between the reflective practice involved in spiritual formation processes and the day-to-day school environment dissipates the impact of the formation experience.[102] Furthermore, where the approach to formation remains focused on the individual, the influence appears to remain restricted to the individual.[103] Mulligan situates the formation process at the centre of his study within the wider staff and school milieu, understanding acutely the dynamic that characterises contemporary Catholic school communities and the growing of leaders:

---

97 Palmer, 1993, p. 17.
98 Palmer, 2007, p. 95 .
99 Peck, 1993. His summary of community as integrative – diverse and yet holistic – echoes the sentiment of successive Catholic church documents on the role of community in Catholic education.
100 Whelan, 1998.
101 Zappone, 1991, p. 84.
102 Bracken, 2004.
103 Downey, 2006.

The leader, the single authority figure, no longer has the same impact as the collaborative, consistent and conscientious witnessing of the group or community. In education, the commitment and the dedication of the school community will make a deeper, more relevant statement to the public than the single leader no matter how great her charisma or his public relation skills. Real authority is diffused throughout the Catholic school community. The contemporary challenge for authority in the Catholic school then is to release the potential of the core community, the Catholic educators in the school. It is to facilitate the liberation of others who will be leaders in their different spheres of influence.[104]

This collaborative development of leaders within community finds resonance elsewhere. Across the literature, there is a growing sense of the need for co-leadership to drive mission in Catholic education: '... this is best done when the partners in Catholic education, personally and collectively, live out their own vision of Catholic education in its wholeness'.[105]

SERVICE

Service as a result of spiritual formation is a particular feature associated with the Catholic Christian tradition. It is a dimension closely linked to mission and ethos in the Catholic educational context.[106] Experiential practice includes elements of social action with emphasis on a harmony of both contemplation and action in formation. 'With discipleship or apprenticeship, Christian life is a continual learning from, and empowerment by, the person of Jesus of Nazareth'.[107] Hellwig proposes the following four core characteristics for this apprenticeship:

- to learn to be thoughtful and discerning
- to learn to be countercultural and community building
- to learn to be open to uncertainty and attuned to an unending process of learning
- to learn to be practical in the public and private spheres, and ecumenical in seeking allies and inspiration wherever they may be found.[108]

Thus, personal and social transformation is developmentally and conceptually linked in Christian formation.

104   Mulligan, 2004, p. 114.
105   Grace & O'Keefe, 2007, p. 127.
106   Harris & Moran, 1998; Meyers, 1999.
107   Hellwig, 1998, p. 7.
108   Hellwig, 1998, p. 8.

In the Catholic school context, Church documents since Vatican II (consolidated by the social encyclicals of the last 150 years) have stressed the creation of an environment where the school would be 'the leaven for the community, and teach the message of hope, build community and serve all mankind so that above all, schools should be instruments of social justice'. [109] Thus, the challenge for Catholic educators is profoundly social: 'We cannot be called truly 'Catholic' unless we hear and heed the Church's call to serve those in need and work for justice and peace.' [110]

The challenge to service, particularly through social justice, remains a non-negotiable principle for Catholic Christians. In this Catholic framework of making a better world through witness and action, there is alignment with the concept of the contemporary learning organisation (discussed in Chapter 3) which involves transformational change or *metanoia* in the leaders and people of the community 'so that they can become who they are meant to be'.[111] Given the confluence of these elements in the Catholic school context, it seems that 'the idea of a mission-ed and empower-ed people is most applicable to the Catholic education reality'.[112]

INDIVIDUAL ENTRY POINTS

The contemporary models of formation acknowledge the diversity of individual context, and seek to affirm and accommodate this reality. Although the direction for everyone in Christian spiritual formation is towards God, each person is unique, and therefore 'our response to God's call will be as unique as each person, each child of God, who has ever lived.' [113] The diversity inherent in adult learners underlines the need for a holistic approach. While Maria Harris' framework for spirituality recognises cognitive dimensions, spirituality in fact 'takes us beyond cognition'[114] and allows for the creation of spaces where the future possibilities can take shape in people's imagination. Harris confirms this in her holistic view of the developmental qualities for growing an authentic spirituality: it must be appropriate, communal, expressed in service and justice, and be intelligent, requiring an openness to learning and being challenged.[115]

This approach brings together the processes of reason, memory and imagination to provide a lens of understanding that seeks 'the deep heart's

---

109   Bryk, Lee & Holland, 1993, p. 53.
110   USCCB, Communities of Salt and Light, 1993.
111   Senge, 1990, p. 13.
112   Mulligan, 1994, p. 76.
113   Guinan, 1998, p. 4.
114   Ochs, 1983, p. 9.
115   See Maria Harris (discussed in earlier chapter) and her books: 1989, 1991, 1996,1998.

core'[116] whatever one's pathway. In this way, a sacramental perspective is nurtured, 'an incarnational and holistic faith, a faith that engages the whole person, body and soul, mind and senses.'[117] This 'sacramental consciousness' is called 'a depth characteristic in Catholicism, that looks at the world and then through it to see the transcendent in the ordinary, the Creator in the created.'[118] This transformative impact of the praxis approach as used by Groome has been insightfully described:

> Contemporary life stories interact with inherited stories; and the hearing of inherited stories uncovers the depth of present experience of the gracious mystery we call our God. Most of all it is about the story of Jesus and the many ways the ancient tradition of our faith has found of telling it.[119]

Specific models offer a more sophisticated understanding of individual human pathways. Predicated on a diversity of human ability, development and growth, Wilber's complex developmental theory, referred to in the discussion on spiral models, brings together thinking across theology, philosophy, human development and metaphysics. According to Wilber, multiple lines of development or intelligences exist (e.g. cognitive, aesthetic, musical etc.) and individuals have varied patterns of development in each of these lines. Within each broad stage, there are sub-levels, and it is spiral dynamics that fully explicates this movement between stages and highlights the reality that individuals are on their own unique developmental journeys.

REFLECTIVE PRAXIS

All models discussed include a focus on the dimension of reflective praxis. Both Parker Palmer and Robert Kinast[120] are leading figures in this area. While Palmer's focus is on developing trust in the individual's ability to read their own lives and plumb the wisdom of their own lived experience to develop their spirituality, Kinast's contribution is the development of a contemporary method of theological reflection that engages the traditional three-fold movement (lived experience, Christian tradition, and practical implications for Christian living).[121]

---

116 Groome, 1998, p. 14.
117 Groome, 1998, p. 135.
118 Groome, 1998, p. 129.
119 See Doherty, 2008, p. 8. Tony Doherty is an Australian priest, writer and educator. One of his most recent contributions to Australian Catholic education has been the authoring of a series of books for new parents, new graduates and new employees in a way that engages the contemporary reader with the culture of the church. These books are used for induction and parent engagement.
120 Kinast, 1996, 2000.
121 Refer also to previous texts in this Mission series (see especially, Leading for Mission, pp. 232-237, and Catholic Curriculum, pp. 230-234).

Across all models, specific experiential practices that nurture a reflective perspective are encouraged. These experiential practices, such as prayer, meditation, reading of sacred texts, embracing song, silence and engaging in rituals, enhance the central formation focus identified in the theoretical literature: knowledge of the relationship between a person and the Creator, and the development of a relational consciousness.[122] In seeking to bring together both vocational and spiritual aspects, Stephen Brookfield offers four lenses[123] through which a reflective (theological) practice might occur for educators in the Catholic school context. They are:

1. reflecting on one's personal teaching history
2. engaging in dialogical communication with the community of learners
3. reading literature supporting the ministry of teaching
4. engaging in collegial conversation and critique.

Theological reflection as a specific kind of reflective praxis for Catholic educators is a process at the heart of mission formation. It is always contextual and its aim is practical action. All contemporary approaches to theological reflection or 'doing theology' are informed by a range of contextual theologies (including liberation, feminist, catechetical, pastoral and ecumenical) and draw on wisdom across the disciplines of scriptural exegesis, psycho-spirituality, educational and leadership theory, missiology and ecclesiology – all to make personal and shared meaning at the juncture of life, culture and faith. The nurturing of the capacity for this in the individual teacher and leader as well as in the Catholic education community has emerged as a central lever in formation for mission.

CONCLUSION TO PART B

Part B has traversed a range of formation models from broad fields of research and praxis. Different elements will have had resonance for you in your own professional and personal experience, and other elements perhaps have stirred your wondering. In addition to the rich experiential exploration that these models provide, they nurture growth in the social and psycho-spiritual understanding of the adult learner and the nature of transformative change. All of this is fertile ground for integrating insights that can support the emergence of something new for our time and context. On the way to developing a new approach, we now turn our attention to three major intersecting areas that must be engaged if we are to be authentic in our endeavour.

---

122   Stonehouse, 1998; Kessler, 2000.
123   See Brookfield, 1995; 2008; 2015.

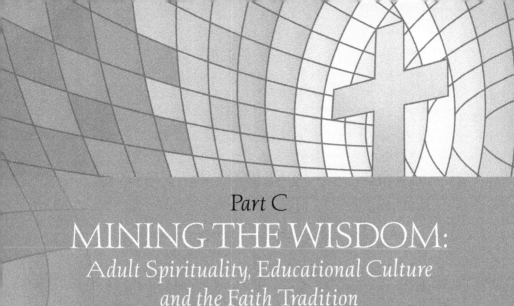

MINING THE WISDOM:
Adult Spirituality, Educational Culture and the Faith Tradition

'Teaching is a beautiful job; as it allows you to see the growth day by day of people entrusted to your care ... It is a great responsibility ... that only a mature and balanced person can undertake ... remember that no teacher is ever alone, his or her work is shared with other colleagues and with all the education community to which they belong.' (Pope Francis)[1]

INTRODUCTION TO PART C

In Part C we explore more deeply the three major intersecting areas of thinking and praxis in the context of the Catholic educator and leader. You will see how these underpin aspects of the models already discussed and at the same time stretch our thinking into the future.

The thinking and practitioner experience that informs our conversation has a wide reach – and so it should. We know that any formation approach must be context specific for it to be meaningful. For Catholic educators and leaders, this context is shaped not only by scholarly thought and practitioner experience concerning the nature of the adult spiritual journey, but also by current educative approaches and praxis in adult learning and change education, as well as a theological understanding of mission and vocation. These three broad areas themselves draw on several disciplines including theology, psychology, spirituality, educational theory, leadership theory,

---

1   Pope Francis, July 24, 2015, https://www.ncronline.org/blogs/francis.../pope-s-quotes-teaching

missiology and ecclesiology. In reality, of course, specific areas of focus and their parts intersect and interlink in a complex way. So, it is important to remember that whenever we put the spotlight on specific elements, the meta-themes have a dynamic orientation rather than a static content orientation.

Outline of Part C

We begin with an exploration of adult spirituality, how this has been understood, and what cultural factors are at play in the Australian context. The research in developmental theory and the process of spiritual formation and practice in Australia and internationally are critiqued. The historical development and understanding of Catholic faith formation and practice as it impacts on individual experience is analysed and, finally, the interface between Christian spirituality and contemporary theology is examined.

Secondly, because we are undertaking formation within an educational environment, theory and current methodologies in adult learning are essential for our understanding. The relationship of formation to learning is considered as we explore key elements of educational practice. We also consider the dynamics of change facilitation and critical mass theory for the development of whole community change, given our Catholic educational systemic context.

The third area for our attention concerns the relationship between the faith tradition and Catholic schooling. Here we examine the challenges and tensions in ecclesial expectations, school leadership, identity and purpose. The key interconnecting domains of evangelisation, Catholic school leadership, vocation and mission formation are explored.

These three areas (explored subsequently in Chapters 5, 6 and 7) engage the complex reality underpinning the challenge of appropriate spiritual formation for Catholic educators. As we progress through the following chapters, notice what connections you make between the specific area under focus and your own experience as teacher and leader. Especially look for new connections and insights I know you will make between the contexts described and the future directions for formation for Catholic educators.

These connections and insights are essentially part of a new conversation for us between life, culture and faith.

5

ADULT SPIRITUALITY

'Spirituality' and 'religion' are complex, multi-dimensional constructs that interact with each other, but the primary concern in authentic adult formation lies within the field of spirituality as distinct from religion. The term 'religion' implies a sense of belonging to an organised faith tradition and the term 'spirituality' denotes a more personal connection with something greater than oneself, including the sacred. This latter area of exploration – the connection to and articulation of the Sacred – must be our starting point within the broader frame of spiritual formation in the Catholic faith tradition. When a spiritual knowing is activated for learners of any age, religion may then offer the spirit 'a complex language, a sense of tradition and a cultural memory'.[2] So it is the development of the initial and continuing personal spiritual connection that is the central focus here, even though it is nested in and may draw toward the religious faith tradition. And in the Australian context, our culture offers a distinctive life lens to appreciate the concept of spirituality!

There are four areas of focus in this chapter:

Spirituality in Contemporary Australia
Adult Formation Theory and Praxis
Catholic Culture and the Adult Spiritual Journey
The Interface with Theology.

SPIRITUALITY IN CONTEMPORARY AUSTRALIA

Our setting is the interplay between spirituality in the Christian context and the Australian cultural milieu in a post-modern context. The characteristics of Catholic Christian spirituality in Australia are coloured by its unique history in the establishment of religious institutions. That history has unfolded within a distinctive culture, strongly characterised by an independent and laconic spirit that has an uneasy existence in authoritarian constructs.[3]

---

2 Tacey, 2003, p. 77.
3 See Mackay, 2008 & 2016, for a further sociological examination of Australian culture and

Spirituality and the Christian Context

Contemporary Catholic Christian spirituality is influenced by a growth of interest in the broader culture as well as developments in understanding within the tradition. No longer contained within institutional religion[4], spirituality is identified in current culture as 'an unusual outpouring of deep human longing'[5] alternatively identified as a 'wild explosion of spirituality'[6]. The contemporary, post-modern society which has emerged in the last 20 years perceives spirituality as a personal quest, and understands this quest to be heavily influenced by the circumstances and historical context in which people find themselves.

A Catholic understanding of spirituality is rooted in the Christian tradition of discipleship. This means it is about self-transcendence, but just as importantly it is also concerned with an orientation towards others. The 'deep human longing' is 'the radical desire of the human spirit for meaning, truth, value and love – a radical desire that is, at bottom, always a desire for God'.[7] That human longing is understood as finding authentic expression within the mystery of God in a sense of real presence – being real and fully present not just to self, but also to others, the cosmos, the Divine. It is 'a way' that is communal, incarnational and sacramental.[8]

Until recent times, the word 'spirituality' was in fact an almost exclusively Catholic term referring to the experiential and ascetical aspects of Christian life or discipleship, especially in their representation in various movements and Catholic religious orders. These have developed so that the way in which spirituality is expressed today within Eastern Orthodoxy appears very different from how it is expressed within Roman Catholicism. Further, the sacramental emphases of all Catholic traditions contrast with the evangelical traditions of Protestantism.[9] In recapturing the essence of a Christ-centred spirituality and a renewed vision of Christian life signalled by the Second Vatican Council (1961-1965), Post-Vatican II scholars turned to earlier Judeo-Christian foundations.[10]

Both Hebrew and Christian Scriptures have a concrete meaning for the word 'spirit': in both the Hebrew *ruach* and the Greek *pneuma*, the basic meaning is 'wind/breath', describing the breath of life permeating and animating all of life. The Christian theological origin of the word is Pauline.

---

beliefs.

4 For an historical outline of this shift, See Tacey, 2015.

5 Fenwick, 2001, p. 10.

6 Taylor, 1996, p. 10. Also, see Taylor's essays in Dilemmas and Connections, Selected Essays (2014).

7 Conn, 1998, pp. 72-73. Also see: Ryan, T. (2014).

8 Streeter, 2012, pp. xiv-xv

9 See Rossiter, 2005, and Drazenovich, 2004, for further details on these movements and traditions.

10 See Dreyer & Burrows, 2005; Rohr, 2010; Schneiders, 2003; Wolski Conn, 1999.

Pneumatikos (spiritual) was a new word created and applied to any person or reality seen to be filled with the Spirit. The original meaning thus had a distinctly inclusive sense that referred to the *whole* person being influenced by the Spirit or breath of God (*ruach*).

The early development of Christianity was influenced by the dualism inherent in Greek philosophical thought which emphasised a split between the body and the soul. By the twelfth century, the holistic understanding around spirituality had been recast into a dualist mind-set between the things of the Spirit and the things of the flesh. The body subsequently became identified with the lesser things of the material or temporal world and the mind identified with 'higher order' things of the spiritual or eternal world. Further, this dualism became genderised in theology. Women were associated with the lesser worlds of the body and men with the higher worlds of the mind. Already established in the normative male culture of the patristic literature, a dualist worldview became entrenched by the Middle Ages and its influence has survived into the present time.[11]

In the latter part of the twentieth century, the move in religious orders to use the language of *charism* rather than *spirituality* to describe their distinguishing characteristics, paralleled the appropriation in the secular world of the word 'spirituality' to describe the depth dimensions of human experience. At the same time, the emergence of the reference to 'lay ministry' as a result of Vatican II (further addressed later in this chapter) attracted theological and spiritual debate on the varieties of Christian experience in the world. Dialogue concerning a 'lay spirituality' emerged. This initiated a focus on 'appropriate 'psychological' expression in cultivation of habits of prayer, examination of conscience, and a humble respect for mystical gifts should they occur'.[12] Spiritual direction as a support to lay people also began to gain acceptance. Having originally grown out of the tradition of companioning, particularly common in the early Celtic Christian tradition, spiritual direction had developed as a distinctive feature in religious orders in the Middle Ages. And since 1980, the psycho-spiritual perspectives pioneered by Wicks, Parsons and Capps[13] have developed as an influential element in the contemporary understanding and approach to spiritual direction, lay ministry, and Christian formation.

As the understanding of the spiritual journey within a contemporary Catholic Christian milieu has been broadened and deepened by ecclesial and psychological scholarship, so too has it been challenged in its cultural context. Indeed, spirituality has become associated with a broad mix of religious traditions as well as non-religious practice. As this occurred, the

---

11   See Schussler Fiorenza, 1984, and Treston, 1997, for a detailed exploration.
12   Kelly, 2004.
13   Wicks, Parsons & Capps, 1993, 2003; Wicks, 2006.

dynamic nature of spirituality began to draw attention from researchers.[14] All forms of spirituality seem to have a common thread, 'the quest of the human spirit for something that is above us, that is bigger, deeper, "more than" the ordinary surface reality of life'.[15] Key characteristics of spirituality can be identified in the variety of its contexts. These characteristics are also central to the evolving understandings of Christian spirituality:

- spirituality is holistic [16]
- it is an intrinsic human capacity[17]
- it is transcendent[18]
- it is connective[19]
- it is about meaning-making.[20]

In harnessing these global characteristics to a specifically Christian focus, the following definition of spirituality, while developed many years ago by Maria Harris, serves a contemporary demand for both an expansive reach and a particular tethering:

Spirituality is our way of being in the world
in the light of the Mystery
at the core of the universe.[21]

In this definition, the dynamic mystery is God; this mystery pervades all of creation; and the 'way of being in the world', along with the individual's response to it, is uniquely influenced by a faith tradition, the wider culture, and the individual's embodied and personal reality. In Catholic Christian terms, spirituality may be further defined as 'the whole of human life viewed in terms of a conscious relationship with God, in Jesus Christ and the saints, through the indwelling of the Spirit and lived within the Church as the community of believers.'[22] Thus spiritual formation is the growth of the whole person through an intentional focus on particular perspectives, practices and relationships that reflect and nurture this way of being.

The Australian Cultural Milieu

In this dynamic, the influence of the wider culture within the Australian milieu takes specific expression. Australia displays the range of characteristics

---

14 See especially King & Boyatzis, 2004.
15 Guinan, 1998, p. 1.
16 Zohar & Marshall, 2000.
17 Benson, Roehlkepartain & Rude 2003; Hill, 2004; Tacey, 2003, 2015.
18 Zinnbauer, Pargament & Scott, 1999.
19 Rossiter, 2004; Berk, 2001; Castelli, 2000.
20 Tisdell & Tolliver, 2001.
21 Harris, 1996, p. 75.
22 Grace, 2012, p. 10, quoting Philip Sheldrake, 1998.

of a secular consciousness in the post-modern world of which it is part[23], as well as distinctive characteristics that have grown out of its own story. Key features relevant to this discussion are fragmentation, individuated meaning-making and a determined egalitarianism. Fragmentation has become part of the lexicon to describe the repercussions of compartmentalisation and standardisation in the human world since the industrial revolution. It has permeated all facets of post-modern culture for the last 20 years:

> *The first kind of fragmentation involves the separation of economic life from the environment. A second kind of fragmentation is social fragmentation. Another kind of fragmentation is within ourselves. We find ourselves disconnected from our bodies and our hearts.*[24]

A further kind of fragmentation to be identified in post-modern culture is a lack of a shared sense of meaning or mythology. Belief in any meta-narrative is questioned and there is a strong individualism in the way people construct their own meaning.[25] The staunchly defended egalitarian theme in Australian culture, where one person's position and meaning-making has no more importance than another's, provides robust scaffolding for post-modern individualism. The important thing is that it is authentic to the individual.

Given this cultural context, while statistically Australia is categorised as a 'predominantly Christian country'[26], it is not surprising that social researchers[27] claim the lived reality reflects a more complex dynamic. This derives from a social history indicating Australians as a whole have never been overtly religious, and that organised religion has not been an integral part of Australian political and cultural society other than at certain key moments. Thus, even though most Australians express a belief in God, there is a continual and marked decline in weekly Church attendance.[28] At the same time, the interest in spirituality continues to thrive. Research concludes that spirituality as expressive of individual meaning-making enjoys acceptance and a degree of popularity among Australians as it does elsewhere[29]. In Australia, David Tacey suggests that people are no longer embarrassed to speak of things of the spirit; an indicator that the divide between the social and the spiritual world is closing. As this has happened, the move has been away from traditional religious frames of reference toward an individualistic,

---

23   See Taylor, 2015; Tacey, 2015; Paranjape, 2009.

24   Senge, Scharmer, Jaworski & Flowers, 2008, p. 190.

25   See Flowers, 1988; Drane, 2000. Taylor, 2015, refers to this 'expressive individualism' as a self-orientation that has now become a common trait of our society.

26   Smith, 2006, p. 8.

27   See Holmes, 2005; Mackay, 2000, 2016.

28   National Church Life Surveys, 2001, 2006, 2011, 2016; ACBC, 2017.

29   Mitroff & Denton, 1999; Holmes, 2005; Tacey, 2016.

personal emphasis on spiritual experience and making sense of the here and now.[30] (The addition of the identification SBNR (spiritual but not religious) as part of personal profiles on social media indicates the mainstream nature of this shift). Accompanying this has been the emergence of a 'collector's mentality' critiqued as an underlying malfunction: 'Australia is "acting out" a neurosis; an increasing number of people have rejected the religious life of their own traditions and found solace in new age therapies.'[31]

Within the category of those Australians identifying as Catholic or Christian, research into their spiritual beliefs and practices has been neglected. It was not until 1978 that Australian theological literature (specifically the *Australasian Catholic Record*) began to consider elements of a distinctive Australian spirituality. Acknowledging the dearth of research about Catholic laity, Katherine Massam[32] nevertheless identifies two distinct approaches to spirituality and argues that their interaction encapsulates a central dynamic of faith in twentieth century Australia. These two strands, devotion and activism, characterised lay Catholic spirituality in the forty years before the Second Vatican Council (1961-65):

> *Australian Catholics were drawn on the one hand by a passive and highly emotive piety centred on personal holiness for the next world, and on the other by an active apostolic spirit which called for an analytical understanding of this world in order that it might be transformed.*[33]

Research in cultural history has brought spirituality to the attention of Australian cultural historians. Understanding that 'spirituality is cut from the cloth of culture, and the context in which beliefs are held shapes their expression'[34], these researchers began to 'acknowledge the spiritual dimensions of Australian life, adding depth to the understanding of the lives of ordinary people'.[35] Historians have characterised Australia as a God-forsaken land, where there is little sense of meaning and where 'the real narcotic today is that [which has] driven consumerism.'[36] However, a perspective attracting growing interest holds that this is itself a search for meaning in the midst of an uneasy identity. And such a search is a spiritual one. 'Recognising the potential sacredness of the modern experience of emptiness, is perhaps the first step toward the genuine religious revival of our civilisation.'[37]

---

30   Hughes, 2007.
31   Tacey, 2000, p. 236.
32   Massam, 1996.
33   Massam, 1996, p. 4.
34   Massam, 1996, p. 15.
35   Massam, 1996, p. 2.
36   See Clark, 1995, and Kelly, 2009.
37   Tacey, 2006, p. 2.

There is a tension between those who are responding to this search by exploring new boundaries in non-traditional ways[38], and those arguing for attention towards a more ecclesial spirituality[39]. Noting that the starting point for many people in spiritual searching is their own lived reality and experience, Rufus Black suggests that 'the resources of Christian spirituality have been too narrowly focused on the quest for God rather than on the quest for a fulfilled human life, of which the quest of God is only one part.'[40] Those voicing a call for more attention to an ecclesial spirituality reflect a concern about the separation occurring between spirituality and ecclesial existence, and the possible shortcomings involved in the adoption of a 'generic' spirituality. Indeed, there is a request for 'a new phase' in the conversation between an ecclesial Christian faith and the broadening realm of spirituality, contending that 'the institutional component is necessary if Christian witness is to have a presence, a voice and a witness in the groaning, conflictual reality of world history.'[41] In explaining how this dialogue might be conducted, Australian theologian Fr Anthony Kelly CSsR believes the recovery of 'the full panoply of modes of understanding'[42] is needed in communicating the rich reality of the Christian beliefs and ecclesial understandings within the Australian culture.

The argument that this dialogue is unachievable contends that there is no possibility for a bridge with the present ecclesial direction and that a new language and paradigm ought to be embraced.[43] The Church continues to rapidly lose credibility and relevance exacerbated by the worldwide abuse scandals. Amid this, the sense of spirituality to be found within the Church community has diminished:

> *Within the Catholic community in Australia there has been a deep, dark hole for a long time now, which amounts to a lack of genuine spirituality. By 'spiritual' ... [I mean] something that can live at the very centre of the human dilemma. Religion can become the possession of an elitist group, whose power reinforces the power of all the other institutional forces in society. Its language then becomes spiritually hollow, incapable of criticising or challenging any of those forces.*[44]

Rather than condemning the secularity of Australian culture and the absence of a particular expression of traditional spirituality, an authentic

---

38   Morwood, 2007; Tacey, 2006, 2016.
39   Kelly, 2004.
40   Rufus Black, quoted in Quillinan, J, 2012.
41   Kelly, 2004.
42   Kelly, 2004. Also for an exploration of how this might be applied, see Kelly, 2008.
43   Tacey, 2003; Morwood, 2007.
44   Fr. Ted Kennedy, ABC, 2004.

response to the present context is finding the sacred in the reality of the now, however that presents itself.

I am convinced that this is the way forward for religion: a movement from creed and proposition to receptivity and listening. It is a move away from moralism to mysticism, away from religious instruction to the encouragement of spirituality.[45]

Staff in Catholic schools, as members of an ecclesial community and the broader Australian culture, experience these very tensions in both their personal and professional lives.

Generational Shifts in Worldview

Currently, senior leadership in Catholic schools and diocesan organisations is the responsibility of those belonging to the Baby Boomers generation (including a large number of ex-religious). In contrast, teachers and administration are predominantly from Gen X and Gen Y. It is they who are Catholic education's future leaders.

Gen X, Gen Y and the Baby Boomer generation are each characterised by distinctly different experiences with Church, religion and culture.[46] Many of the Baby Boomer generation are increasingly disaffected from the Church, but carry a corporate Catholic memory from direct experience in Catholic parish culture during their formative years. Gen X are the first post-conciliar generation with little knowledge and connection to the cohesive pre-Vatican II Catholic culture with its strong experiential indicators (fasting; benediction; devotional practices).[47] Gen Y are the first 'post-church generation'[48] – *children of children* who have not had a childhood imbued with Catholic parish cultural experience. Church attendance research indicates that most current Catholic school parents and students do not have a connective experience with parish and its culture.[49] Any experience of Church they have is school related, and they bring with them to this community their own perspective and experience of the world.[50]

---

45 Tacey, 2006.
46 Beare, 2003.
47 Rymarz, 2004.
48 Rolheiser, 2008.
49 Other Australian diocesan surveys amplify the 2009 findings in the Archdiocese of Brisbane BCE survey, Who's Coming to School.
50 McLaughlin, 2002; Rymarz, 2004.

Table 5.1 illustrates key features of the generational demographics that constitute the staff, parents and students in present school communities.

TABLE 5.1: GENERATIONAL DEMOGRAPHICS[51]

Year Born	Known as ...	Key Features ...
1927-1945	Silent Generation	Generous, conformist, parents affected by the Depression, disciplined, like consistency, still providing the backbone of support in parish life
1946-1954 1955-1965	Baby Boomers Phase I and II	Peacetime generation, the first divorce generation, loyal, economically comfortable, expectant of a full and healthy life, carrying the current leadership of the church with ex-religious providing a significant role in this
1966-1976	Generation X	Predominantly single, rapid rise in divorce rates, rapid rise in women in a paid workforce, post-feminist generation where inclusion and equality need to be authentic, acute drop in Church attendance and involvement, rise in use and accessibility of illegal drugs, deferral in marriage and raising children, greater reluctance to leave the family home, decline in home ownership.
1977-1994	Generation Y (also known as Gen Net; Gen Next; Millennials or Echo Boomers)	Children within rising divorce rate, raised within a technological revolution, mostly unchurched generation but tolerant of a multitude of faith pathways, education oriented, continuing deferral of marriage and children, grew up with a revolution in media, communications and digital technology – e.g. Internet, Foxtel, Global citizens.
1995-2012	Generation Z	'Digital natives', used to instant action and satisfaction, mainly the children of Gen X parents with smaller families and older mums, communicate mainly through online communities and social media like MySpace, Twitter and Facebook. These are the students in our classrooms – they are global, digital, social, mobile and visual.

The cultural influences for each generation whether student, parent, staff or grandparent, are markedly different. While it is possible to burrow further in the profile of each generation[52] there are generalisations pertaining to both Gen Y and Gen X. These include:

- They are suspicious of authority, institutions and ideology, reactive to orthodoxy and absolutism and prefer to build their own conceptions of reality.
- They identify liminal experiences but do not connect them to 'Catholicity'.

---

51 Source: McKay, 1997; Schroer, 2016; McCrindle, 2015.
52 Rymarz for example identifies three different cultures within Gen X Catholics.

- They have engaged with the world in ways that often give stronger meaning to them than their engagement with church.
- Voluntary commitments tend to be short-term with visible and local outcomes.[53]

In addition, Gen X and Y adopt a more informal and non-traditional approach to any and all community involvement.[54] Faith is expressed in highly personal and informal ways, and social networks are integrated and diverse. At the same time, relationships, however they are formed, shaped and maintained, remain central to Gen X, Y and Z. And parallel to their fierce independence is a strong respect for parents as role models.[55]

The conclusion that can be drawn is that loyalty, community, commitment and spiritual seeking are not extinct in the post-modern Australian generations. Rather, these things are expressed in manifestly different ways than by their predecessors. Spirituality remains predicated on a distinct culture and special context influenced by the individual's value system.[56] Therefore if the goal of organised religion is to facilitate connectedness with the sacred,[57] then the primary challenge must lie in the ability of institutional Christianity to connect meaningfully with the context of the contemporary individual.

The Influence of Indigenous Spirituality

Indigenous art and spirituality have found a place in popular Australian culture, and the syncretism that marks the faith expression of indigenous Australians who have embraced Catholic Christianity is an important part of the current Australian Catholic spiritual landscape. The difficulties in this relationship are real and complex and reflect the painful and fractured history between indigenous and white Australians. The collector's mentality already identified in the broader culture (where the non-indigenous gather indigenous 'artefacts') is apparent in the mainstream appropriation of Aboriginal and Torres Strait Islander art and spirituality. In challenging this consumerist mentality, Tacey contends that 'we have not only stolen Aboriginal land, destroyed the tribal culture, raped the women and the environment, but we now ask for their spirituality as well'.[58] A different consciousness is called for:

---

53   See Hughes, 2007, 2010; McQuillan, 2002; 2004; Rymarz, 2002; Tacey, 2003, 2016.
54   Donovan, 2000; Greenberg & Berktold, 2004.
55   Boiler Room Communications, 2003.
56   Johnson & Castelli, 2000.
57   King & Boyatzis, 2004.
58   Tacey, 1995, p. 132.

> *We cannot merely tack on Aboriginal spirituality to our own faulty or overly-rational consciousness, but must change our consciousness from within ... The direction we need to take is downward, into our own depths, to see what could be happening there, rather than to remain the same and move sideways by appropriating another culture's dreaming.*[59]

At the same time, there is a compelling argument for an integrous fit between indigenous spirituality and the mystic dimension of an emerging contemporary Australian Christian spirituality.[60] Aboriginal spirituality is described as 'a relationship between the Great Spirits and the heart that allows the mind to live in peace and harmony with the human'.[61] The non-indigenous person engaging with this spirituality requires the leaving of a western frame of reference, or at least an inclination to see the everyday with a different lens:

> *... Indigenous Australian peoples' experience of nature is more cosmic, more communal, more natural. It is not the ecstatic, unrepeatable experience of a chosen individual, but the ordinary, every-day, abiding experience of the sacred and interconnected unity of all beings with the earth, cosmos and ultimate reality.*[62]

It is an understanding that both challenges an individualistic consumerist culture and strikes chords of familiarity and attraction. The question of how a contemporary Christian spirituality embraces this spiritual richness, without appropriating it in a tokenistic or disjointed way, presents a challenge for us into the future.

ADULT FORMATION: THEORY AND PRAXIS

In understanding the adult spiritual journey, a range of associated disciplines has contributed valuable insights for our consideration. These combine traditional developmental theory with psycho-spiritual theory and learnings from approaches in adult faith education, as well as perspectives and praxis in the relatively new discipline of health and wellbeing. The remainder of this section addresses firstly the nature of spiritual formation, and then each associated discipline in turn, as it intersects with the formation context.

The Formation Context of Spirituality

Spiritual formation in a developmental sense has remained a rather general term referring to 'all attempts, means, instructions, and disciplines intended

---

59 Tacey, 1995, p. 134.
60 See Hendriks & Hall, 2009, 2012, for a detailed exploration of this relationship.
61 Hendriks & Hefferan, 1993, p. 31.
62 Hendriks & Hall, 2009.

towards deepening of faith and furtherance of spiritual growth, including educational endeavours as well as the more intimate concept of spiritual formation ... has carried a sense of separate reality from general human development, a product of the dualist understanding of the human condition discussed earlier.

Contemporary understandings of Christian formation remain grounded in the tradition of discipleship, while encompassing the post-modern attention to the individual. Spiritual formation and human formation are inseparable without one being reduced to the other.[63] Formation thus implies deep and experiential learning, not additional learning, that involves personal attitudes, values, commitment to particular life directions, and knowledge and skills.[64] The resulting spiritual growth constitutes a lifelong journey and occurs within a 'formation field' which includes the forming influence of memory, other people and the immediate and wider environment.[65] In the Christian tradition, spiritual growth is 'an inner journey travelled in a partnership between God's spirit and our spirits working in kinship'.[66] In being lived out, it is the 14 inch drop from the head to the heart that binds both together in a leaning into the world that can change everything.

While spiritual formation may occur independently from a religious faith tradition, the faith tradition provides a powerful conduit for meaning-making through its language, stories, beliefs and rituals. The concept of faith within a Catholic context originates singularly and directly in the Hebrew Scriptures. A useful mapping of the term through documents from the early centuries into the modern era portrays Christian faith as developmental and expressed in discipleship (mission), as well as growth in understanding:

> *Because circumstances vary and situations change, discipleship of Jesus requires more than following a set of explicit instructions. It involves willingness to learn from one's own contemporary experience, and to grow into progressively deeper understanding of the meaning and demands of the Gospel.*[67]

The journey of 'deeper understanding' of the Gospel has also been described as 'our moving into deeper and more comprehensive love'[68] and has its origins in the early Church. The Biblical words in the scriptures for

---

63 See Wolski Conn, 1999; Streeter, 2012.
64 See Gowdie, 2006.
65 See Whelan, 1994, for an explication of the 'formation field'; and Casson, 2013, for an excellent discussion of the place and space of the Catholic school in this new environment.
66 Groome, 2002, p. 325.
67 Hellwig, 1993, p. 38. Known as 'the people's theologian', Monika Hellwig's understanding of the importance of engagement with contemporary experience is as relevant today as it was in her teaching years.
68 Wolski Conn, in Thompson, 1995, p. 652.

hospitality (in both the Hebrew - הכנסת אורתים - and Greek - φιλόξενος) mean 'love of/for the stranger', and the creation of a welcoming space where guest and host encounter each other. These concepts are of course central to the Gospel.[69] Spiritual maturity was seen in early Christianity as love of God and love of neighbour. In every era, Christian tradition has interpreted spiritual growth as a gradual process of seeking integration and communion (*koinonia*), detachment and self-emptying (*kenosis*), service for others (*diakonia*) and self-transcendence (*metanoia*), as this deeper love, reflecting and engaging Godself, takes hold over one's being.[70] This context inscribes a transformational personal spiritual journey that grows attentiveness to the spirit of God in relational and connective ways, seeking

> *an existence before God and amid the created world. It is a praying and living in Jesus Christ. It is the human spirit being grasped, sustained, and transformed by the Holy Spirit. It is the search of believers for a communion that arrives as a gift.*[71]

Spiritual formation may not necessarily lead to transformation. However, formation provides the environment or catalyst in which transformation may take place. Many spiritual writers describe spiritual formation as the 'planting of seeds.'[72] The dynamic process of spiritual transformation is often sparked by moments of conflict (which can take many forms) and which happen across the life cycle. The Christian meta-narrative provides a way of framing the experience as a lifelong process informed by one's individual life and formation field, and profoundly influenced by 'the collected wisdom gathered through history relating to God, Jesus Christ, the Holy Spirit and Church'.[73]

Spiritual Formation and Developmental Theory

Seen as a developmental process alongside other human development processes, spiritual formation is a recent phenomenon.[74] The emergence of the 'spiritual' has been generally viewed in the field as an adjective that describes one's personal religious or faith orientation reflecting 'in large measure a commitment to the ideal of post-conventional claiming of authority for one's own religious and ethical orientation and practices.'[75]

The developmental psychological theorists[76] are relevant to understanding spiritual formation because they offer frameworks to explain how individuals

---

69   Nouwen, 1976.
70   Wolski Conn, 1994.
71   Wainwright, 1987, p. 452.
72   For example, Tang, 2006; Langford, 2008.
73   Bracken, 2004, p. 24.
74   See Erikson, 1994; English, Fenwick & Parsons, 2005.
75   Fowler, 2000, p. 6.
76   See Piaget, 1955; Fowler, 1981, 2000; Kohlberg, 1984.

construct meaning through experiential maturation. Building on the work of Piaget in cognitive development and Kohlberg in moral reasoning, Fowler's 'stages of faith' outlined in Part B has provided a developmental understanding equating faith with the growth of individual meaning systems: 'Faith is the process of meaning-making that is universal and relational'.[77] In relating this understanding to the journey of formation it is helpful to frame faith formation as spiritual growth within a religious tradition while not being bound or defined completely by that tradition. In other words, while a person's faith can be nourished within a religious tradition, it also transcends it and is open to change through new insights and experiences.

The identification of faith with meaning-making also reflects the influence of Richard Niebuhr's theology of radical monotheism.[78] There is an underlying 'system of transformations by which the self is constituted as it responds to questions of ultimate meaning'.[79] This nuanced model of stage theory in faith development proposes the narrative structure of life history. The stages may be viewed as a frame for weaving the tapestry of meaning for one's life – a flexible spiral of interaction between person and society. This thinking has seeded alternative approaches exploring the spiral process theories whose stages intermesh and overlap.[80]

Spiritual Formation and Adult Faith Education

Identifying a blurred distinction between education and formation, Australian research has highlighted a drift towards understanding formation as formal coursework involving lectures, assignments and accreditation. Thus, the informational dimension has gradually subjugated the formative dimension and the transformative focus.

In focussing on the gaps in the intricate journey from information to formation to transformation, prominent developmental researchers have identified sources and stages of faith change, as well as elements involved in the dynamic of transformation such as imagination, community and higher education. Where the complex interplay of these factors has been addressed,[81] the contexts of community and personal experiences are key factors, and the use of a shared praxis approach in any kind of religious

---

77   Fowler, 2000, p. 15.
78   Niebuhr, 1993. A Christian ethicist by training, Niebuhr's theological ethics can be described as relational. His theology of radical monotheism asserts that there is only one God as the value-centre. So, the community is not a closed society. Whatever participates in such a community has equal value derived from the only center of value without the presence of any privileged group. His ecumenist and egalitarian understanding resonates with the process of individual meaning-making and dialogical interaction.
79   Fowler, 2000, p. 29.
80   See Wilber, 2006; Huitt & Robbins, 2003.
81   However, Daloz & Parks, 1986, 2011; and Miller, 2005, have done excellent work in this area.

education is advocated as a way of ensuring 'an intentional space for engaging and supporting the ongoing and inseparable interplay between formation and transformation'.[82] Religious transformation is a change in the forms or structures of one's religious being[83] or a change or complex series of changes that enable movement from one state of being to another.[84] In this process, six influential factors have been identified in Australian research:

1. The importance of warm, trustful relationships in the very early part of life
2. The catalysing impact of later life experiences as major triggers
3. The practice of habits of reflectivity, meditation or prayerfulness
4. The confirming influence of being placed in a religious leadership role
5. The sustenance of contact and support with a faith community
6. The absence of the above factors adversely impacts faith development.[85]

While useful in informing adult faith education, these influences also provide insightful reference points for engagement in the contemporary adult formation journey.

Spiritual Formation and Psychotherapy

In the twentieth century, secularism became the dominant motif of psychology. The 21st century has seen a resurgent connection between psychology and spirituality in two ways:

> First, psychotherapy professions are engaged in an impressive effort to humanise their work more broadly by paying unprecedented attention to spirituality and in some cases to religion. Second, efforts to de-pathologise the mental health field have continued to grow and prosper.[86]

In particular, psychotherapy and spiritual direction have developed rich conceptual correlations. Both approaches share many common concerns in working with individuals, concerns about growth, change, development, mind, consciousness, insight and self-experience.

In addressing transformational processes and spiritual formation, psychotherapy research adopts the use of 'additive and subtractive principles of change'[87] in approaches to personality change and transformation. These

---

82   Groome, 2002, p. 279.
83   See Miller, 2005.
84   See Lawrence, 1998.
85   Leavey & Hetherton, 1988, p. 124.
86   Beck, 2003, p. 24.
87   Leffel, 2007, p. 281. Also, the kataphatic and apophatic traditions are discussed in further detail on pp. 31ff.

are derived from both the kataphatic tradition (where God is found in the external signs and created interpretations in the world) and the apophatic tradition (where God is found in the mystery of the process of an internal emptying of self) in spiritual formation. In other words, a very useful connection is identified between strategies for personal change and the innate approaches to spiritual formation in the Christian tradition:

> *The kataphatic and apophatic traditions tend to emphasise different principles of personality change, the kataphatic with the additive principle and related decisionist methods, and the apophatic with the subtractive principle and transformist methods.*[88]

The current and popular focus on cognitive behaviour strategies associated with the kataphatic approach overlooks the possibility of deep change offered by the alternative apophatic approach, with its attendant strategies of self-reflection and examination, and the development of character virtues or affective capacities.[89] While both have their place, there is an argument for a stronger focus on the latter, which 'taken to its logical conclusion, shifts the paradigm from the presently dominant cognitive rationalist moral psychology to a "cognitive intuitionist" approach that is more centrally focused on implicit more than explicit meaning-system constructs of personality.'[90] In this way, the insights and habits of the apophatic way being explored by contemporary approaches to psycho-therapy offer a deeper and possibly more sustainable change in life perspective and spiritual awakening congruent with the essence of spiritual formation.

Spiritual Formation and Health and Wellbeing Theory

One of the key developments in understanding the adult spiritual journey has been the recognition of human life formation as part of spiritual formation. The generation of values, attitudes and behaviours can no longer be seen as a separate area of development in the human being. Rather, these things emerge out of and are an expression of a person's deepest reality. The nurturing and growth of this deepest reality is the work of spiritual formation.

Disciplines related to health and medical research see spiritual wellbeing as 'a fundamental dimension of people's overall health and wellbeing',[91] and conceptualise this as the development of harmonious relationships with self, others, God and the world.[92] A number of concurrent studies confirm

---

88   Leffel, 2007, p. 282.
89   Huitt & Robbins, 2003.
90   Leffel, 2007, p. 282.
91   Fisher, 2001 p. 100.
92   National Interfaith Coalition on Aging (NICA), 1975, cited in Ellison, 1983, which reconstituted as the Forum on Religion, Spirituality and Aging (FORSA), 2010.

that a core component of internal development is 'spirituality'. Even more significantly, the spiritual dimension is identified as a contributor to core leadership capacity and, in particular, to transformative change.[93] This dimension is now attracting attention in educational leadership and is addressed in the final section of this chapter.

The Forum on Religion, Spirituality and Aging established in 2010 expanded its earlier understanding to contend that the 'fundamental' dimension of spiritual wellbeing permeated and integrated all other dimensions of health (i.e. the physical, mental, emotional, social and vocational). Four corresponding domains of spiritual wellbeing were created to integrate into the original NICA definition (Personal, Communal, Environmental and Transcendental) with the proposal that:

> *Spiritual health is a dynamic state of being, shown by the extent to which people live in harmony with:*
> * *themselves (i.e. stated meaning, purpose and values in life)*
> * *others (as expressed in the quality and depth of relationships, relating to morality, culture and religion)*
> * *the environment (beyond care and nurture for the physical and biological, to a sense of awe and wonder; for some, the notion of unity with the environment)*
> * *some-thing/some-one beyond the human level (i.e. ultimate concern; cosmic force; transcendent reality; or God – through faith).*[94]

We know that staff in Catholic schools express a consistently high level of concern for their students' wellbeing in each of these four domains, reflecting support for the holistic goal of education in Catholic schools in contemporaneous research findings. The *Who's Coming to School* research conducted in Brisbane Catholic Education school communities[95] confirmed similar findings for the Brisbane Archdiocese. (Of note are the contrasting findings from Christian independent schools involved in the Fisher study indicating considerably lower scoring in the first three domains, reflecting a more compartmentalised approach). The holistic approach that has emerged in the area of health and wellbeing aligns well with an understanding of spiritual formation which recognises both personal and communal dimensions of response to the experience of the transcendent.

---

93 Moxley, 2000; Thomson, 2004.
94 Fisher, 2001.
95 ACER, 2010.

CATHOLIC CULTURE AND THE ADULT SPIRITUAL JOURNEY

A critical element in understanding contemporary Catholic spirituality is the influence of traditional Catholic culture. In Australia, as in other Western countries, spirituality has traditionally been linked to a Christian understanding of worship and practice.[96] Many authors have written on spirituality, outlining principles of prayer, discernment, asceticism, direction, silence, solitude, reading, meditation, journal writing, contemplation, and service to guide a person's growth in the spiritual life.[97] For 'lay' people though, Mass attendance and involvement in parish ministry have been viewed by the Church as key pathways for spiritual formation, while engagement in a specific lifestyle based on the monastic or religious life tradition of the institution has been viewed as appropriate for those in religious orders or the priesthood.[98] Both these assumed pathways are energetically criticised. There are good reasons for this, as well as good reason for threads of that distinctive culture to continue.[99]

Participation and Practice – A Changing Culture

Weekly Mass attendance and parish participation have traditionally been viewed as a central built-in formative construct for 'lay' people.[100] However, since the 1970s Catholics have been drifting away from active parish involvement and Church attendance. In recent years this drift has been noticeable, even among people who were once regular Mass attenders and active parishioners for much of their adult life. This phenomenon has serious implications for how Catholic culture is transferred between generations and how community is modelled, as the current Church-going population diminishes without a new generation replacing it.[101]

The actual churchgoing demographic has changed in terms of size, age, background, country of origin, and personal attitudes and practices. The 2006 and 2011 Australian Censuses have indicated that while Catholics remain the largest religious group (25.3%) in Australia (with Anglicans following at 17%), 22% of Australians chose 'no religion' as their option. Of those who identified as Catholic, 22.7% were born overseas, with 17.6% of these born in non-English-speaking countries. In addition, Mass attendance continues to drop (15.3% in 2001; 13.8% in 2006; 12.2% in 2011) and

---

96   Rossiter, 2005.
97   See in particular Keating, 2007; Keating & Ward, 2015; Griffith & Groome, 2012; Guardini, 2013, for a contemporary overview of key approaches and prayer traditions.
98   Dixon, 2005.
99   See discussion in NCLS, 2008; Hughes, 2009.
100 Wilkinson, 2011; Dixon, 2005.
101 See Dixon, Reid & Chee, 2013, for a more detailed explanation.

the trend in the profile for Mass attendees indicates they are on average older, better educated, more likely to be female, married and born overseas than Catholics in general.[102] This trend continues in the data from the 2016 Census, with an increase expected in those choosing 'no religion' set to rival those identifying as Catholic.

Regarding the causes and profile of 'disappearing Catholics', a marked decline was identified in the attendance rate of Catholics in Australia who are 50 years of age or younger. Of this cohort, the lowest numbers of Mass-goers are in the 20-34 age group. In their 2013 report, *Mass Attendance in Australia: A Critical Moment*, Dixon, Reid and Chee make the following observations:

> *Two major factors have contributed to this decline. Firstly, people in particular age cohorts have stopped going to Mass; it is estimated, for example, that up to 26,000 Baby Boomers stopped going to Mass between 1996 and 2011. Secondly, young adult attenders are not being replaced as they age.*

They go on to say in terms of diocesan data:

> *Between 2006 and 2011, the number of dioceses with attendance rates below ten per cent rose from two to fourteen. It is not improbable that the number could increase by another nine by the time of the next national count (in 2016), and several dioceses could drop to as low as five per cent.*[103]

The most commonly expressed reason for not going to Church was the belief among those surveyed that attendance at Mass did not define a 'committed' Catholic.

> *More than half (54%) of all the infrequent or non-attenders among Catholic parents nominated as one of their reasons for non or less frequent attendance the statement, 'I no longer feel that being a committed Catholic requires attending Mass every week as frequently as I used to attend,'*[104]

Australian Catholic adults are deciding on their own parameters as to what defines a committed Catholic. This shift will continue. An additional trend sees young adult Catholics beginning to cease identifying themselves as Catholics at all by the age of 25.[105] These two trends in particular, and the overall trends in general, together provide an enormous challenge to traditional ecclesial and institutional constructs.

---

102 See Dixon, 2005; Dixon, Reid & Chee, 2013; ACBC, 2007, 2011, 2014; NCLS, 2006, 2011, 2013, for occasional papers and detailed analysis on the trends outlined here.
103 Dixon, Reid & Chee, 2013.
104 ACBC, 2007, p. 5 (and sustained in the most recent surveys).
105 Dixon, 2014.

Two particular studies concerning women and the Church and Gen Y and the Church offer nuanced insights to these broader trends in Australia which are of note:

1. The research project on the participation of women in the Catholic Church in Australia identified three specific areas of dissatisfaction among women:[106]
   a. a perceived lack of support by the Church for single women;
   b. the Church's perceived discrimination against and active exclusion of those who were divorced and remarried without an annulment;
   c. disagreement with the Church's teachings about sexuality, contraception, divorce, marriage and abortion.
2. The *Spirit of Generation Y* project[107], echoing earlier US studies,[108] reported specific reasons for not attending Church as being:
   a. disillusioned by the Churches' attitudes to moral issues;
   b. disillusioned by the restricted role of women in the Church;
   c. a feeling that the Church was unrealistic and out of step with society.

Even as churchgoing declines, there is some support for the concept that personal faith continues in society. This is described as believing without belonging. However, both the *Participation of Women* and the *Spirit of* Gen Y research confirm that there is little evidence to support this proposition in the longer term. [109] With participants indicating a sense of responsibility and capability about their own spiritual life, 'believing without belonging' is considered more likely to be an expression of 'residual religiosity':

> Participants insisted that they wanted to take responsibility for the quality
> of their own spiritual lives, leading to an eclectic approach to spirituality
> and a readiness to leave aside beliefs and practices that were not seen as
> helpful, life-giving or leading to personal fulfilment.[110]

Thus, while there remains a call from within the Catholic Church to support its current structure and practices, enormous shifts are in progress – influenced by both cultural and ecclesial issues. The traditional patterns of formation associated with participation in that structure can no longer be assumed. Neither attendance at Church nor active participation in a parish

---

106 Macdonald et al, 1999. A digital version of the resulting book Woman and Man: One in Christ Jesus was released by the ACBC in 2015.
107 Mason, Webber, Singleton & Hughes, 2007.
108 Camille & Schom, 2004; Hoge et al, 2001.
109 Voas & Crockett, 2005.
110 ACBC, 2007, p. 49.

community is considered fundamental to spiritual growth or Catholic identity.[111] Within this landscape, the risk for the Church and for those who form our leaders and teachers, is in providing designated programs that actually meet no fundamental spiritual needs and to provide answers to questions no-one is now asking.

Core Components of Catholic Practice: Prayer, Self-reflection, Outreach

In exploring Catholic practice, the range of activities can be examined in three categories: prayer, reflection and outreach. Given the changing landscape, an understanding of the essential aspects of each of these three areas of practice is helpful.

Prayer

Prayer remains a pivotal practice in all programs of spiritual formation. *The Catechism of the Catholic Church*[112] lists three expressions of prayer: vocal prayer, meditation and contemplative prayer, each having in common 'the recollection of the heart.'[113] The Church invites all its followers to participate in regular prayer: daily prayers, the Liturgy of the Hours, Sunday Eucharist, feasts of the liturgical year.[114]

However, within the broad catechism definition, the Catholic Christian tradition has a diversity of prayer practices heavily influenced by religious orders through the ages and by liturgical scholars and practitioners in Christian spirituality. This range of prayer experience and practice includes the following different types of meditative and contemplative prayer: the examen of conscience and prayer of gazing; liturgical prayer; *lectio divina* and other styles of praying with Scripture; body prayer such as labyrinth walking; and reflective prayer that includes song and movement working with spiritual texts. As interest in the spiritual life continues to develop a wider appeal, the broad assemblage of prayer practice appears to have been recovered and reinvigorated both inside and outside of the institutional context of the Church.[115]

In particular, the range of contemplative and meditative prayer forms appeal today to those searching for ways to navigate their own suffering or need for healing, whether emotional or physical. Prayer and the experience of suffering, identified as the 'dark night of the soul' by St John of the

---

111 ACBC, 2007, 2011; ACS, 1998; CCLS, 1996; NCLS, 2006, 2011.
112 John Paul II, 1997.
113 Congregation for Catholic Education CC, 1997, Part 4, Chapter 3, n. 2721.
114 Congregation for Catholic Education, 1997, n. 2720.
115 See Oliver 2004; Sheldrake, 2007; Keating & Ward, 2015; Griffith & Groome, 2012; Rolheiser, 2013.

Cross,[116] are commonly seen by Christian spiritual teachers as catalysts for the transformative spiritual journey. The capacity to be in the present moment is the very locus of contemplative prayer and the mystical tradition within the Catholic Church. Specific works of Chittister (2009, 2015); Keating (2009, 2015); Merton (1961); O'Donoghue (2011); Rohr (2015) and Silf (2011) have brought the mystical tradition into the contemporary practice of spiritual life.

Self-Reflection

Woven throughout the daily and seasonal cycles of Catholic life is a practical emphasis on self-reflection. This practice is given special focus during particular liturgical seasons of the Church year (Lent/Advent), and in particular traditional activities (the 'parish mission') and groups (e.g. Cursillo), encouraged personally and communally in the parish pastoral context. It is part of Catholic culture. There are two important aspects of this broad practice to which I draw your attention: 'theological reflection', and 'life narrative reflection'. While these have long been a part of Catholic practice, they are meeting contemporary needs in new ways.

Praxis of theological reflection

Developing the praxis of theological reflection is a core element of the Catholic tradition and spiritual discipline, and yet has been relatively underutilised. The scholarship of Robert Kinast,[117] Patricia Killeen and John DeBeer,[118] Robert Wicks[119] and James and Evelyn Whitehead[120] contribute to a body of work that constitutes the seminal thinking and development in the discipline of theological reflection.

Practitioners in this area offer a reflective method that creates a balanced conversation between the individual's experience and the Christian tradition. Pioneering work by the Whiteheads offered a model that created a dialogue between three sources of information: the faith tradition; personal and communal experience; and contemporary culture. Working with the same basic model, contemporary scholars (Kinast, Killeen and DeBeer) have turned their focus very specifically to how the tradition translates as a relevant touchstone for reflective praxis in today's world. They ask: *Is Christianity a viable wisdom tradition for the 21st century?*[121] They propose a method that

---

116 See Underhill, 2002, p. 477, For an insightful and beautiful translation of the collection of direct writings of John of the Cross, I recommend The Dark Night, Saint John of The Cross (Translated by Mirabai Starr), 2002, Riverhead Books, New York.
117 Kinast, 1999, 2000.
118 Killen & DeBeer, 1994.
119 Wicks, 2003, 2006, 2009.
120 Whitehead & Whitehead, 1997.
121 Killeen & DeBeer, 1994, p. 2.

integrates life experience and the wide heritage of the Christian tradition in a transformative dialectic that has a contemporary energy:

> *Authentic lives reflecting integral patterns grounded in religious wisdom and values, result from seeking God's presence, not apart from the world, but in the midst of it ... in this conversation, we can find ourselves called to act in new, courageous and compassionate ways. We are called to transformation.*[122]

In this way, orthodoxy (or right thinking), and orthopathy (right feeling), lead to orthopraxis (right acting). Lived experience is as important as the classic Christian texts, and the outcome of theological reflection is to be reflected in practical action, not theoretical ideas. This approach also aligns with the direction of contemporary thought with regard to the work and witness of Christians: 'Emerging Christianity is going to have to emphasise orthopraxy (walking the talk) much more than mere orthodoxy (talking the walk).'[123]

Crucially, Robert Kinast identifies three characteristics in the process of theological reflection that make it relevant and meaningful for spiritual seekers today: 'it must be *portable* so Christians can carry it into their daily lives; it must be *performable* so that they can translate their reflections into actions; and it must be *communal* so they can face today's challenges with each other.'[124] This process has real application for Catholic school leaders.

In the development of ways to engage in theological reflection, the issue of language – of how one imagines God and how one dialogues with God – is an important one. Reflecting on what he refers to as the deep *communal* nature of theological reflection, Bevans[125] stresses the dialogical nature of the process, a mode that mirrors the communal nature of the God who is at the centre of Christian faith. Australian poet Les Murray's concept of 'wholespeak'[126] offers a prototype for the kind of imaginative language needed to make spiritual dialogue more accessible. 'Wholespeak' invites an appropriate language of the imagination that 'brings together poetry and religion to express the ultimate and comprehensive realities of our lives'. It is 'the language of real conversation, of genuine prayer, of poetry and indeed all the arts'.[127] The engagement with this realm of 'wholespeak' also offers pathways for genuine connection among our Catholic school teachers and leaders, as well as our children.

---

122 Killeen & DeBeer. 1994, p. 3.
123 Rohr, 2010.
124 Kinast, 2000, p. 7.
125 Bevans, 2005.
126 See lecture delivered by Les Murray in 1998 in a defence of the role of poetry: http://www.lesmurray.org/defence.htm
127 See Kelly, 2004, for a further explanation of 'wholespeak' and 'narrowspeak'.

Praxis of life narrative reflection

A fundamental component of spiritual development is the depth with which people make sense of their life experiences. While the encouragement of self-reflection on life choices and daily living has been part of the Catholic culture and a routine homiletic focus for pastors, scholarly development in this area has both recovered and enriched its basic principles.[128]

The use of life narrative reflection is an important element in the work of practical theology. The basic questions of practical theology concern the development of a community of faith built on an engagement and understanding of the lives of its members. 'Life and faith history' refers to the narrative a person tells about her/his own life and the developments of what s/he experiences as 'faith'. The narrative is never a 'true' report of what happened; it is not a documentary of facts, but rather:

> a painting, a work of art, giving meaning to 'reality' from the narrator's point of view. Not only the knowing about God is important for a faithful life, but also the experience, just fleetingly perhaps, just sometimes, that God really has something to do with and in one's everyday life. [129]

While not always explicit, this process is a constant conversation for someone immersed in the Christian tradition – a conversation between tradition and life moment, which reveals a certain hermeneutic:

> a manner of understanding the Christian tradition in the context of the life of a concrete person, relating to a community of Christian faith in one way or another, with a certain degree of commitment.[130]

The product of a well-developed practice of life narrative reflection is the process of prayerful discernment. From the Latin *discernere*, meaning 'to sift apart', discernment as a spiritual practice refers to the process of prayerfully seeking to notice with clarity, a contemplative disposition that takes 'a long, loving look at the real.'[131] Decisions are made by sifting choices and scenarios in prayer, identifying what is spirit-led and life-giving in one's story, and what is not. Within the Christian tradition, the process of discernment is often carried out with the guidance of a mentor, companion or spiritual director. This practice has been part of the tradition since the early ascetic communities through the Middle Ages into the present. The traditional Christian model for spiritual mentoring includes developing awareness of God's presence, wholeness and healing,[132] and communion ('friendship with Christ grows

---

128   The work of Sandra Schneiders has been instrumental here – see reference list.
129   Klein, 1993, p. 59.
130   Bons-Storm, 2002, p. 27.
131   Burghardt, 1989, p. 14.
132   See Merton's 'theosis' 1960, p. 23.

deeper through human spiritual friendship').[133] The goal is transformation.

While the practice of theological reflection and the development of a narrative mode of thinking about one's life are distinct and separate practices, they are complementary. The two operate in an iterative way to grow the individual's capacity for deep reflection and integration within community.

Outreach

The third important dimension of activity in Catholic practice involves outreach. Catholics retain in their theology and church culture a strong emphasis on social justice, the common good, and community.[134] This includes service learning and participation in social justice activities. While traditionally these have been associated with Catholic organisations directly connected to the Church (St Vincent de Paul, Caritas and Catholic Mission) they now include initiatives through religious congregations, Catholic education offices, Archdiocesan services and broader independent Catholic community networks. The opportunities afforded across these providers are immense and include immersion experiences, political activism, local voluntary work on the streets and environmental protection issues, as well as fundraising and donations. This dimension of social action and outreach has a strong resonance among the students, parents and staff of Catholic schools locally and nationally, and is growing broader connections and growth points within the wider culture.[135]

In the Post-Vatican II shifts in the Church, such a development was anticipated with the hope it would have a positive impact on strengthening community through 'a growing centrality of justice as a constitutive dimension of the Gospel, having a great influence on eroding a purely privatised and individualistic spirituality; and the ecological movement.'[136]

This shift is fundamental to the authenticity of Gospel witness and by implication the relevance of the Church in today's world.[137] The dialectic of contemplation and action, an important part of spiritual work and Catholic culture, has thus been revived as an essential element of formation and ministry, and one which speaks to the world individually and communally.

THE INTERFACE WITH THEOLOGY

The development of Christian spirituality as a discipline in its own right, and its dynamic interplay with systematic theology, have made for a fertile and remarkable body of literature. It is an area still growing and characterised by boundary breaking scholarship engaged in the work of

---

133   Guenther, in Shinohara, 2002, p. 105.
134   Laser & Jones, 2010.
135   ACER, 2010; ACBC 2007.
136   Harris & Moran, 1998, p. 6.
137   For further discussion on this, see Rohr, 2010; Treston, 2015; Edwards, 2014.

translating the fundamental Christian realities into new cultural paradigms. While self-transcendence is a central aspect of spiritual development, implying internal growth, traditional theology has articulated spirituality as either a non-developmental and fixed aspect of the human experience or a mystical approach to religion and worship practice.[138] Understanding the role of theological scholarship in the independent discipline of spirituality offers important insight for future directions in spiritual formation.

Christian Spirituality as a Theological Discipline

The discipline of theology initially subsumed under itself in a seamless way all other aspects of scholarly focus concerning Christian studies, including Biblical studies and Christian spirituality. As the focus on dogmatics developed in theology, a multiplication of associated disciplines emerged. Spirituality, previously a minor area of focus in theology, then became a focus of scholarship and praxis in its own right, with a strong body of work behind it.

The development of Christian spirituality as a discrete discipline has been strongly influenced since Vatican II by the Council's inclusive call to holiness (*Lumen Gentium*, n. 40-41) and its invitation to engagement with the world which invited dialogue with other approaches and traditions (*Nostra Aetate*, n. 2). The acceptance in definition of inclusion and continuity 'between the ordinary (ascetical) and extraordinary (mystical) elements of spirituality'[139] and the recovery of the early Christian understanding of living 'in the spirit' has also seen sustained consideration in a more holistic understanding of spirituality. This has been accompanied by attention to experiential and contextual aspects, as spirituality is promoted 'as a way of being integrated into the everyday.'[140] This experiential context has been highlighted by the work of Sandra Schneiders in particular, articulating the primacy of spirituality 'as the study of lived experience, preceding theology which is a second level reflection on experience.'[141] This distinction between lived experience and theology is an important distinction for us in the work of formation.

In charting the terrain of Christian spirituality, seven useful focal points are offered. These are, Christian spirituality is concerned with the work of the Holy Spirit in individuals:

'(1) within a culture; (2) in relation to a tradition; (3) in light of contemporary events, hopes, suffering and promises; (4) in remembrance of Jesus Christ; (5) in efforts to combine elements of action and contemplation; (6) with respect to charism and community; (7) as expressed and authenticated in praxis.'[142]

---

138   Driedger, 1999; Hill, 2004.
139   Ryan, 1997, p. 13.
140   Downey, 1991, p. 271.
141   Schneiders, 2006, p. 4.
142   Downey, 1991, p. 277.

In exploring the ways these elements have integrated since Vatican II, we can see four general patterns in approach. In the first approach, spirituality is equated with an individual's personal prayer life. In the second, it is equated not just with prayer but with intense faith-filled engagement in daily activities. A third and still broader view argues that spirituality incorporates the whole of personal experience, including bodily and emotional dimensions discounted in earlier Church development. The fourth stresses relationship between Christian commitment, social and political life (particularly justice, feminist and ecological issues).[143]

The early, and still relevant, understanding of the journey in Christian spirituality was predicated on theological approaches known as the apophatic and the kataphatic ways of knowing (as introduced in the Spiritual Formation and Psychotherapy section, pp. 19). The kataphatic way of knowing (or the *via positiva*) seeks to understand God by learning what God is, with a focus on a cognitive understanding of God. This approach does not necessarily require the learner to negotiate the inner journey of self. Apophatic theology (also known as the *via negativa*) stands in contrast to the kataphatic way in that it seeks unity with God as the unknowable, through discernment and focusing on the individual experience of the Divine, often found outside institutional structures. The apophatic way is most often linked with the mystic tradition.[144]

This contemporary work in the discipline of spirituality has synchronicity with research in psychotherapy (as outlined earlier in this chapter) against the backdrop of a renewed interest in mysticism in the general culture. As noted, psychotherapists have identified the apophatic tradition as an appropriate conduit for sustaining transformational change in individuals. Theological observers of contemporary shifts in religious affiliation identify the apophatic tradition as one which needs to be recovered and respected for different reasons:

> The emphasis has been external: 'religion' is performed by good works, helping others in the world, rescuing those in need, shared rituals often practiced by rote, and community service. This is all very good, but it is only one side of religion. The other side is esoteric, and has largely been suppressed by mainstream tradition and forced to the margins. This exiled esoteric tradition, namely, the mystical tradition of finding the God within, is now the 'stone rejected by the builders', which is to become the cornerstone of the future church.[145]

---

143   See Schneiders work, 2006.
144   Beck, 2003; Leffel, 2007.
145   Tacey, 2006.

Thus, the focus on lived experience has become the defining characteristic of scholarship in Christian spirituality, influencing contemporary theological thinking in a continuing and iterative way.

Theological Perspectives for Contemporary Spiritual Formation

The heart of the spiritual journey is the realisation of personal experience of God which profoundly influences how life is lived. In the Catholic Christian tradition, this is nurtured and shaped by culture and tradition, and, within tradition, particularly by theological perspectives. Because of this, the conceptualisation of God is fundamental to the construction of meaning in the journey of spiritual formation. The pre-Vatican II 'fall-redemption' theology which informed so much of the shape of spiritual formation has been challenged by rich theological development since the sixties. Current theological thinking, as it engages with the exponential arcs in thinking in the sciences and the arts, is opening up new articulations of God and God's action in the world.

In the transition from the modern to post-modern world, there is a shift in theological models for understanding ultimate reality or God. This movement is away from a monolithic view or model to a post-modern multilithic view or model of ultimate reality.[146] The implications for systematic theology suggest an urgent need for recalibration of the language inherent in the modelling of God, from that of a closed system and machine metaphor to that of an open system and more organic metaphor.[147] The implications for spiritual formation demand a similar shift from a confessional approach to an experiential and mystical approach. This mystico-prophetic perspective finds resonance in the inductive theological method of Bevans (2002), Fischer (1994), Gutierrez (1971), Lonergan (1972), O'Murchu (2004), Rahner (1963), Schillebeeckx (1990), Solle (1981), Schussler-Fiorenza (1984) and Wright (2010). The perspectives of these theologians are now examined for the unique insights they offer in formation for a contemporary context.

Incarnation and a Mystic Perspective

In a prophetic anticipation of the current direction in thinking around spiritual experience, some forty years ago the great systematic theologian Karl Rahner contended that 'the Christian of the future will be a mystic or (he/she) will not exist at all'.[148] By mysticism, Rahner explains, he does

---

146   Craig, 2010.
147   See Hartwell, 1996, for this metaphor.
148   Rahner, 1973, Theol. Invent. XX, p. 149.

not mean some esoteric phenomenon, but 'a genuine experience of God emerging from the very heart of our existence'.[149] Ultimately for Rahner, the source of spiritual conviction comes not from theology but from the personal experience of God.[150] This reflection, made late in Rahner's life, echoes a similar insight attributed to Thomas Aquinas after his own mystical experience late in life: 'All that I have written seems to me like so much straw compared to what I have seen and what has been revealed to me.'[151]

An analysis of Rahner's own theological journey as a systematic theologian suggests a trajectory that encompassed a comprehensive paradigm that always had its primary model in the 'heart'. Out of this paradigm, Rahner offered projections about the shape of Christian spirituality into the future. Six important indicators are identified in Rahner's work – Christian spirituality in the future will have to:

- engage the whole person: head, heart, hands, and feet
- provide a grammar that avoids false dichotomies which divide the divine and human
- focus on the original central revelation
- be humble and open
- live with diversity – and value that diversity while also patiently seeking the unity of truth and love in the pluriformity of its expressions
- be sacramental and dialogical. [152]

Christian faith therefore calls for a spirituality that integrates orthodoxy and orthopraxis, personal spirituality and social responsibility, intellectual and affective dimensions. Rahner insists on the Incarnation as 'the grammar' which communicates that the human is found in the divine and the divine in the human. From this original centre, the mystery of God and the self-revelation of God in the diversity of cultures, philosophies and theologies in the world-church rest easily. Despite accusations of promoting a non-kerygmatic spirituality, Rahner rather suggests a different understanding for the Church's purpose: it is not to provide another route to solidarity with God beside the life of love, but 'to reveal that the dynamism of the world is indeed rooted in love, and to reveal that the goal and culmination of that dynamism is union with God through the Spirit of Christ'.[153]

---

149   Rahner, 1973, Theol. Invent. XX, p. 149.
150   Vorgrimler, 1986.
151   Bacik, 2002, p. 15.
152   Masson, 1984, p. 353.
153   Rahner, as cited in Masson, 1984, p. 354.

Conversion and a Unitive Perspective

If Karl Rahner provides a meta-view of the lived out nature of Christian spirituality and the implications for the Church, then his brother Jesuit, theologian Bernard Lonergan, offers a micro-examination of the process of transformative experience for the individual. Like Rahner, Lonergan's understanding of the conversion experience central to the spiritual journey is redolent of a deep experiential reality. He describes it as 'falling in love' and 'becoming a being in love' where God is all there is.[154] Lonergan's theology of conversion as part of the process of transformation which is at the heart of spiritual formation has three stages (intellectual, moral and religious conversion) that create a dialectic. For these three stages, each individual step requires a moment of conversion. Lonergan presents this as:

> a complex process of transformation involving various judgments, decisions and actions that move us from an established horizon, usually formed through the desires and addictions of the false self, into a new horizon of knowing, valuing and acting, informed by our true self that has its ground in the being of God.[155]

Intellectual conversion challenges and clarifies the bounds of our knowing 'to enable divine wisdom to be the only source of our knowing'. *Moral conversion* shifts the criteria for decision making 'from the satisfaction of the self as the basis of choice, to the discovery and pursuit of truth and value'. *Religious conversion* integrates all else and centres one's own centre in God. Lonergan understands this unity that occurs with and in God as 'love'.

> Then one's being becomes being in love ... It is the first principle. From it flows one's desires and fears, one's joys and sorrows, one's discernment of values, one's decisions and deeds ... cor ad cor loquitur: love speaks to love and it's speech is powerful ... faith is born of this love.[156]

Normative Experience and a Social Justice Perspective

It is well recognised that the experiential starting point in the development of theological thought has historically been male, mainstream and European.[157] This has been the dominant perspective and regarded as normative until relatively recent times. Accordingly, much of the theological literature of the tradition reflects the inherent bias of this perspective. However, new

---

154   Lonergan, 1971.
155   Hide, 2004, http://dlibrary.acu.edu.au/research/theology/ejournal/aejt_3/Hide.htm
156   Lonergan, 1971, pp. 105, 113 & 115.
157   O'Murchu, 2007; Radford Reuther, 1993.

frontiers in theological scholarship[158] have progressively explicated what it means theologically if the experiential starting point is female or Asian or poor or creation centred. In particular, this scholarship has generated a range of hermeneutical paradigms that offer more connections to the Gospel than had previously been available.

As confirmation of their validity, all these approaches have their foundation in a justice perspective drawing on the tradition itself. Both scripture (Genesis, Micah and the Gospels of Matthew and Luke in particular) and key Church documents (especially *Rerum Novarum*, 1891; *Mater et Magistra*, 1961; *Gaudium et Spes*, 1965) underpin the preferential option for the poor and vulnerable, the stewardship of creation, human rights and human dignity. These four justice dimensions are embedded in the new hermeneutics. The exploration of new boundaries has also provoked consideration of an understanding of being God-centred outside the context of the institutional Church. Soelle for example embraced mysticism as the appropriate response 'in a world reeling from consumerism, economic inequities, ecological trauma and global chaos'.[159]

> Not one to be as concerned about organised religion as about living out God in the world, Soelle's brand of radical Christianity finds connections between mystical experience and political activism, between suffering and resisting the status quo.[160]

The limitations of God language and image became an issue for Soelle as it did for Rahner and Schussler Fiorenza. The language of traditional systematic theology, where God is understood objectively, has become particularly inadequate. Authentic knowledge is intuitive, personal and ineffable, finding its expression in paradox and poetry. Thus, the experience of God, and the social response to that experience, begs a new language both to describe it and to engage with others.

Quantum Theology and a Missiological Perspective

The new boundaries in theology include a re-visioning of the Christian understanding of ecology, binding it closely to the principle of experiential knowing central in our exploration thus far. Liberation theologian Leonardo Boff integrates ecological theology into the social context, insisting that such an understanding of the nature of God requires an understanding of the world's social systems and the use and misuse of power for exploitation of nature and the world's poor. Boff offers an agenda for spirituality that

---

158   See Boff, 1993; Gutierrez, 1971; Koyama, 1980; O'Murchu, 1997; Soelle, 2001; Edwards, 2014; Schussler Fiorenza, 2014; Bingemer, 2016; Johnson, 2016.
159   Soelle, 2001, p. 210.
160   Oliver, 2006.

goes beyond any individual-centred or 'feel good' spirituality. Rather, Boff advocates for a new alliance between humankind and other beings, a new respectfulness for creation and the working-out of an ethic and mysticism of brother/sisterhood with the entire cosmic community.

Other theologians have directly explored the links between modern developments in particle physics and spirituality[161]. Irish evolutionary theologian, Diarmuid O'Murchu's work has moved beyond previous dialogues between science and religion. He explores the divine co-creativity emanating from the scientific discoveries of quantum theory through the use of metaphor, particularly the Dance, the Story, Darkness and Light.[162] Principles of quantum theology describe God and the divine in terms of 'creative energy', which is perceived to include, but also supersede, everything traditional theology attributes to God. A new paradigm is offered: 'The God of Trinitarian theology is a God of mutual and equal relations. When such a God creates a universe it is not surprising that it turns out to be a radically relational and interdependent one.'[163]

The new scholarship in cosmology interrelates with the current work of leading trinitarian theologians and missiologists (the latter being outlined in further detail in Part F). Trinitarian theology adopts a new and expanded perspective underpinned by the premise that biology and theology both point towards a view of reality in which relationships have a primary place: 'When life unfolds through the process of evolution, it emerges in patterns of interconnectedness and interdependence that 'fit' with the way God is.' [164] Citing both the early theological work of Aquinas (1245-59) and the more contemporary theological work of Elizabeth Johnson and Leonardo Boff, missiologist Stephen Bevans concludes:

> God in God's deepest identity is a relationship, a communion. This life in communion spills out into creation, healing and sanctifying, calling all of creation ... into that communion, and once in that communion, sending that creation forth to gather still more of it into communion.[165]

Finally, the gradual re-emergence of biblical theologians and liturgical scholars,[166] using the imagination as a language to explore the Scriptures within a broader setting, has encouraged the regeneration of symbolism in the tradition.

---

161 See O'Collins & Myers, 2012. also Ilia Delio (ed), 2014, for excellent overviews of this theological development. Also see Ilia Delio, 2015, for a discussion on Catholicity and this new cosmic consciousness.
162 O'Murchu, 2012.
163 Edwards, 1999, p. 28.
164 Edwards, 1999, p. 28.
165 Bevans, 2009, p. 2.
166 Byrne, 2001; Kelly, 2009; Schneiders, 2003; Stevenson, 2011; Francis, 2014; Wainwright, 2006, 2016.

Attention to the language of the Hebrew Scriptures as well as that of the New Testament assures that incorporating the imagination more fully into spirituality is not a matter of a current craze or passing fad. It is rather the recovery of a long-standing spiritual tradition, the renewing of a lost spiritual resource.[167]

In this process, traditional symbols are transformed, allowing for new ways of connecting with familiar symbols and rituals. This work advances that of Rahner, Soelle, Schussler Fiorenza, Gutierrez, Boff and Johnson, in advocating a new language to engage a deeper and more expansive perspective in Christian spiritual formation.

IMPLICATIONS

The world of adult spirituality, formation theory and praxis is undergoing considerable change. In the Australian Catholic landscape, this is amplified in the rapidly declining number of religious and clergy; the rising expectation on 'lay' educators to model authentic Catholic leadership; the growing understanding of the adult developmental journey; and the shifts in both understanding and practice around spiritual formation. The coalescence of these changes has overwhelmed traditional assumptions about appropriate spiritual formation, with the uniqueness of the individual journey now being heavily influenced by cultural context and key relationships. Existing research and experience has induced those in other faith traditions and secular environments to explore new ways of formation that address both new contexts (post-modern culture) and renewed purpose (personal transformation). We are on the same journey.

Implications for the Contemporary Context

While there is declining support for institutional religion in Australia, there is openness to spirituality. This openness is characterised by particular cultural traits. These include an indigenous perspective that embodies interconnectedness with creation; a postmodern perspective that demands personal meaningfulness; and a cultural perspective that demands its own vernacular and symbolic expression. This is our cultural context.

Implications for Contemporary Lay Formation

The traditional patterns of participation and practice which have constituted the key elements of formation for lay Catholics have been fractured for the variety of reasons outlined. Even so, essential threads of a distinctive Catholic culture appear to survive and thrive, albeit in a different way than

---

167   Fischer, 1989, p. 105.

packaged in traditional ecclesial structures of participation and practice. The challenge is how to harness these vital 'threads' in new formation pathways.

Implications for Formation Design and Praxis

A reflective analysis of personal development theory supports a more nuanced stage trajectory in individual growth and an engagement with cyclical and spiral theory. The relational contexts profiled in the development of spiritual wellbeing (self, others, nature, God/Creator) amplifies the dynamic between self-awareness, interconnectedness and a relationship with a being beyond self. Finally, in the field of psychotherapy, the understanding of individual drivers and their link to specific pathways in the spiritual journey offers insights into a contemporary approach in the engagement of individuals.

Theologically, central elements for our consideration include: the integration of a mystic perspective into everyday experience, an understanding of conversion that is centred on transformation rather than redemption, and an attentiveness to relational engagement with and in the world. The implications for language, symbol and ritual that has resonance with contemporary meaning-making, while remaining faithful to the essential revelation of the Christian tradition, is an immediate challenge.

6

EDUCATIONAL CULTURE

The world of Catholic educators and leaders is located within an educational environment which has a particular culture. This is an essential lens in our understanding of appropriate formation. The three areas of focus in this chapter canvas contemporary perspectives in three specific areas of workplace learning and adult education:

> *Professional Learning Communities and Workplace Context*
> *Adult Learning: Holistic Approaches and Reflective Praxis*
> *Transformative Learning: Change Education and Critical Mass Theory.*

Understanding these particular dimensions has quite a direct application to the development of an effective approach to staff formation. While this may challenge dualistic thinking about the role of formation and the work of education, the gold is in the discernment and integration of foundational principles and perspectives.

PROFESSIONAL LEARNING COMMUNITIES AND WORKPLACE CONTEXT

As the understanding of adult professional development has grown over the last 20 years, significant change has occurred in how staff development is conceptualised and provided. This shift recognises the primary importance of the social nature of learning, the key influences in effective professional learning, and the shared workplace as the setting for sustainable and ongoing adult learning and staff development.

From Professional Development to Learning Communities

Many policy definitions of professional development across the educational field focus teachers' knowledge and skills acquisition, and refer to measurable outcomes of teaching and learning. However, a 'skills and acquisitions' approach belies a deficit model in professional development that is about filling the gaps.[168] The understanding that is now prevalent acknowledges the nurturing of strengths and renewal of what is already present, and the many ways and places learning and growth occur.[169] This shift in understanding is accompanied at the micro-level with two further clarifications:

- In regard to the difference between, and roles of, in-service and professional development: 'In-service is characterised by short bursts focusing on aspects of curriculum, while professional development refers to long-term sustained learning.'[170]
- There has been a move to using the term 'professional learning' (which will be the term used here) rather than 'professional development' to reflect the growth in conceptualisation of the adult as both a lifelong and life-wide learner.

In Australian 2014 meta-analysis research in professional learning, five global trends were identified, as educating authorities search for the best balance between flexibility and personalised professional learning, and systemic goals. These trends are for learning that is:

1. *Integrated*: closely connected to performance and development and embedded within organisational culture and practice
2. *Immersive*: intensive, holistic experiences that challenge beliefs and values, and radically alter practice
3. *Design-led*: where disciplined, problem-solving processes require deep understanding of and engagement with users
4. *Market-led*: in that new providers (e.g. schools) stimulate demand and grow the market for new products and services
5. *Open:* ideas and resources are freely exchanged in unregulated online spaces.[171]

On the surface these trends and strategies appear mismatched, yet the researchers found 'some of the most powerful professional learning we came across were ones where features that should be in tension, instead were complementary and mutually reinforcing.' [172] It is instructive to reflect on how these trends might find important adaptation for strategies in the area of adult formation at both school and system level.

---

168 Bellanca, 1996.
169 Garvin, 1993; Hough, 2004; Senge, 2000; AITSL, 2014. Consequently, a more helpful definition of professional development, complex and career long, is 'the sum of all activities both formal and informal carried out by the individual or system to promote staff growth and renewal.' (Connors, 1991, p. 54.)
170 O'Brien, with reference to Bellanca's research, 2004, p. 10.
171 See AITSL research: Global trends in professional learning and performance & development: some implications and ideas for the Australian education system, 2014.
172 AITSL, 2014, p. 15.

As the concept of lifelong learning has developed, so too has the contextual nature of adult life-long, life-wide learning.[173] Research concerning 'learning communities' whose norms emphasise lifelong learning and the communal nature of learning (first given recognition by Dewey in 1938) maintains momentum in current educational, social, economic and religious contexts.[174] While the individualist culture remains strong, there is a contemporary movement away from the 'age of the individual to the era of community':

> *Learning communities are a manifestation of this movement and aim to strike a balance between individuality and social connectedness ... [as we begin to] see the essential role that relationship, participation, reciprocity, membership, and collaboration must play in any theory of human development that aspires to guide us ...* [175]

As an organisational arrangement, the professional learning community is a powerful staff development approach and a potent strategy for school change and improvement. A learning community is one that learns continuously and transforms itself. School leadership seeking to operate in this way must share 'an understanding that constant learning is central to the current and future success of the school, and will assume that parents, students and the wider community are partners with teachers in a learning community based around the school organisation'.[176] The fundamental principle of operation is an assumption that the whole community shares a common purpose and vision in order for the partnership to be realised:

> *Learning communities are made up of people who share a common purpose. They collaborate to draw on individual strengths, respect a variety of perspectives, and actively promote learning opportunities. The outcomes are the creation of a vibrant, synergistic environment, enhanced potential for all members, and the possibility that new knowledge will be created.* [177]

---

173   Day, 1999; Carter, 2009; Jarvis, 2007.
174   See DuFour, Eaker & DuFour, 2005; DuFour & Eaker, 1998; Fullan, 2010; Senge, 1990; 2008; Sergiovanni, 1994b; Turkington, 2004.
175   Feldman, 2000, p. xiii.
176   Hough, 2004, p. 26.
177   Kilpatrick, Barrett & Jones, 2003, p. 11.

Key Elements in Fostering Professional Learning Communities

Five attributes are commonly ascribed to successful professional learning communities:

1. Supportive and shared leadership – the style is collegial and facilitative, fostering staff input into decision making
2. Collective creativity – developing new ways through one another's insights and skills
3. Shared values and vision – that are consistently articulated and referenced
4. Supportive conditions – both physical and human to support initiatives
5. Shared personal practice – peer mentoring and sharing.[178]

Two drivers are critical to the establishment of these attributes:

a. A **leadership that drives** the re-culturing of a common vision
b. A community that is characterised by **a culture of trust**.

These attributes, and in particular these two drivers, leadership and trust, are also fundamental in growing the soul and the spiritual capital of a Catholic school.

School change and educational leadership literature continues to stress the pivotal role and influence of the administrator (i.e. the principal and school leadership team) in determining whether authentic change occurs in the school.[179] And there is consistent argument for a particular model of leadership that does this best. While both the transformational and transactional models of leadership have been critiqued for their shortcomings in providing a framework for change in the contemporary context,[180] they offer useful insights. Transformative leadership understands the role of good communication in inspiring trust and articulating vision. At the same time, there is recognition of the goal orientation of transactional leadership, and its capacity to be an intercepting catalyst in the learning process.

The capacity to drive vision in the creation of professional learning communities also involves the work of 're-culturing.'[181] Sharing vision is not just about agreeing with a good idea; it is a particular mental image of what is important to an individual and to the whole. In such a community, the relationships between individuals are described as caring. Such caring

---

178   Hord, 1997; Mullen 2009.
179   See Fullan, 2002, 2012; Gronn, 2002; Dimmock, 2012; Tomal, Schilling & Trybus, 2013.
180   See Evers & Laskomski, 1996; Gurr, 2001; McLaughlin, 1997; Rshaid, 2009.
181   Fullan, 2001; 2010.

is supported by open communication and made possible by trust, resulting in a dynamic where the individual staff member is responsible for his/her actions, and the common good is valued equally with personal ambition. It is the growing and embedding of this understanding within the whole community that constitutes the work of re-culturing.

The development of a culture of trust has to recognise and incorporate the life world of the teacher.[182] As the understanding of the dynamics of professional learning communities has deepened, the important role of other dimensions of the teacher (and leader) outside of classroom skilling has come into focus:

> *Teachers teach in the way that they do not just because of the skills that they have or have not learned. The ways they teach are also grounded in their background, their biographies, in the kinds of teachers they have become. Their careers – their hopes and dreams, their opportunities and aspirations, or the frustration of these things – are also important for teachers' commitment enthusiasm and morale.*[183]

Attention to this wider context is reflected in the perspectives of leading educationalists about the purpose of education itself. 'Education is a profoundly moral work which calls on the full humanity of teachers and students.'[184] The implication for leadership is the need to respect and harness that 'full humanity' in a collective, collaborative way: 'An enabling presence starts with this premise; I can't do it alone; you can't do it alone; only *we* can do it.'[185]

This aspect of 'collaborative enabling' in leadership, also highlighted by Fullan, is underscored by the work of Heifetz on 'adaptive leadership,'[186] identified as the real need in leadership in a time of unprecedented change.

> *Adaptive work is required when our deeply held beliefs are challenged, when the values that made us successful become less relevant, and when legitimate yet competing perspectives emerge ... solutions to adaptive challenges reside not in the executive suite but in the collective intelligence of employees at all levels.*[187]

Thus, we know that transforming a school organisation is orchestrated with the intentional support of leadership that understands the power of collective wisdom, uses this understanding to shape the culture and ownership of it,

---

182   Gilligan, Spencer, Weinberg & Bertch, 2003.
183   Maguire & Dillon, p. 4 in Czerniawski, 2011.
184   Starratt, 2004, p. 2.
185   Starratt, 2004, p. 99.
186   Fullan & Quinn, 2015; Heifetz & Laurie, 2010.
187   Heifetz & Laurie, 2001, p. 6.

and does so through the active nurturing of the entire staff's development as a community. The management skills of the school leader are a perennial requirement, and the inspirational skills of the school leader are critical in articulating shared vision. However, it is the capacity to develop a pervasive culture which captures a resonance in thinking and belonging between the individual and the community that is emerging as the pre-eminent task of leadership. The development of a culture of trust which is built on the principles of collaborative enabling and adaptive leadership is fundamental to this general task. Authentic leadership is at the core of this.

The Workplace Context

The school workplace context is influenced by the staff individually and collectively, and it is in this setting that the work of re-culturing and en-culturing is undertaken. With the recognition that most learning, formal and informal, occurs in the workplace setting, the term 'workplace learning' has been established to mean:

> the way individuals/groups acquire, interpret, re-organise, change or assimilate a related cluster of information, skills and feelings. It is also primary to the way in which people construct meaning in their personal and shared organisational lives.[188]

Three main dimensions can be identified in workplace learning: instrumental learning, dialogic learning and self-reflective learning.[189] These take on a particular shape in the Catholic educational setting:

- Instrumental learning is that which gives focus to isolating skill development and improving individual productivity.
- Dialogic learning relates to how the individual learns about the organisation and gives focus to team relationships, coaching, mentoring and understanding the mission of the organisation.
- Self-reflective learning gives focus to extending the individual's own understanding of themselves, their beliefs, and their values in orientation and in their workplace.[190]

Instrumental learning, dialogical learning and reflective learning are part of the daily activities of the school workplace setting. However, the evidence for these kinds of learning does not on its own guarantee an authentic professional learning community. Most recent research points not

---

188   Marsick, 1987, p. 4.
189   Marsick & Watkins, 1990, 2015.
190   O'Brien, 2004, p. 15.

only to the importance of workplace based professional learning, but within that to the need for differentiated learning for staff.[191]

Professional Learning Models in the Workplace

Numerous models can be identified in the literature for the application of professional learning in the educational workplace. In general, there are three kinds of approach: outside-in models; inside-in models and inside-outside models.[192]

Outside-in models draw upon the knowledge of others (expert outsiders) for teachers to use. The most common example of the outside-in approach is the 'training staff' model. Inside-in models draw on the expertise and drive of the teachers themselves, recognising the previous knowledge and experience of staff in the learning community. Examples of this model include staff working in pairs or small groups for the development of school based curriculum plans, classroom practice evaluation or curriculum modification. The inside-outside models make use of the knowledge and experience that teachers have as well as the knowledge and experience of the broader educational community. This model attempts to integrate theory and practice in order to maximise application in the workplace context. Indeed, the research indicates that the dimensions of workplace learning identified by Marsick and Watkins operate in different ways in each of the models. Nor is it surprising, given the indicators of best practice in professional learning communities we have already identified, that the inside-outside models are the most instructive in nurturing staff professional learning.

A detailed analysis of these models and associated approaches identifies four areas that strongly influence effectiveness:

1. School factors
2. Structure and content of the program
3. Post professional development (learning) follow-up
4. School based follow-up.[193]

Figure 6.1 offers a useful contemporary model which integrates the characteristics of effective professional learning and the attributes arising from the model analysis.

---

191   See research of Bowgen & Sever, 2014.
192   Hoban, 2002.
193   O'Brien, 2004, p. 129.

FIGURE 6.1: PROFESSIONAL LEARNING MODEL[194]

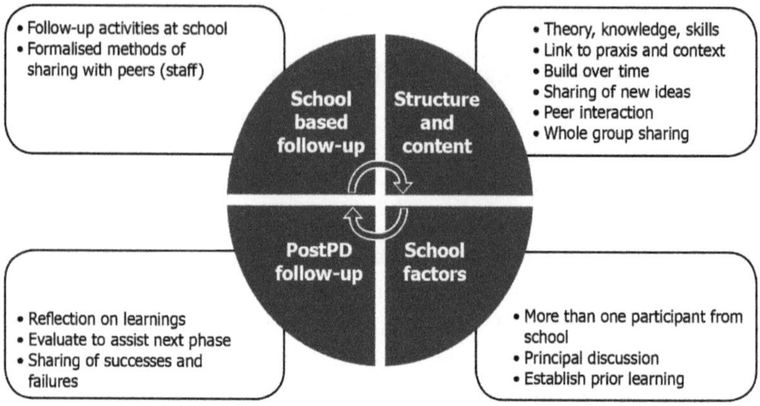

This model also highlights key factors in professional learning that we can see are equally relevant to the strategic embedding of spiritual formation into the school community culture. In the research supporting the development of this model, peer sharing, reflective time and follow-up emerged as key elements regarding good process in professional learning in the workplace. There was further evidence that 'where more than one teacher went to a professional learning program, and where this could be shared back in the school workplace context, there was greater effective implementation and follow-up'.[195]

While these elements are found to be highly valuable, the difficulties of building in any kind of reflective sharing time in the school routine are well documented.[196]Research on work intensification further confirms the challenge in integrating reflective praxis.[197]

Paradoxically, research conducted on spirituality in the workplace is providing both insight and empirical data on the positive, even critical, role of personal reflectivity and sharing for sustainability and meaning-making. These are also key elements in two of the three key dimensions (dialogic learning and self-reflective learning) discussed above.

Communities of Practice

Within the workplace, an important form of experiential learning is in the emergence of communities of practice. Less structured than organised workplace learning, a community of practice does not need to have a formal social structure, nor charter, manager, or executive officer. Shared expertise

---

194 O'Brien, 2004, p. 130.
195 O'Brien, 2004, p. 153.
196 Carotta, 2003; Downey, 2006; Simone, 2004.
197 Jarvis, 2004; McMahon, 2003; Simone, 2004.

and passion for practice connect members. Figure 6.2 illustrates the varying levels of participation that can be identified in a community of practice.

FIGURE 6.2 LEVELS OF PARTICIPATION IN A COMMUNITY OF PRACTICE[198]

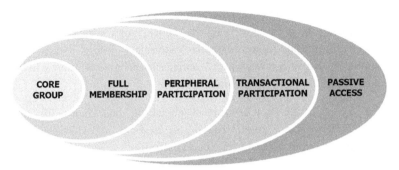

Each of these levels of participation represent different groups and can be described in terms of distinctive functionality:

> *The core group is a small, energizing group called masters who establish ideals, enhance practice standards, and are highly respected by the community. Full membership describes members possessing the explicit and tacit knowledge needed to practice within the community. They are often called upon to function in the role of mentors to those new to the practice. Peripheral membership belongs to newcomers, the apprentices, with casual practice in the community's body of knowledge. Transactional participation describes outsiders who occasionally interact with the community or provide a needed service. Passive access includes people who value artefacts produced (e.g. websites, publications, standards, recordings, or art objects).*[199]

Within the culture of a learning community, where enabling leadership and trust is present, the development of communities of practice reflects a dynamic and energising response within the whole community to improve educational outcomes. Identifiable as an organic way of working in the school context, this dynamic remains relatively fluid, responsive to changing needs and foci within a school context from term to term and year to year. When this dynamic works well, its strength comes from the grounding of recognised expertise within and outside the school community itself. This creates a sustaining capacity for ongoing collaborative learning. It gives energy to workplace learning and reflects key characteristics in an inside-outside model of effective growth (prior learning, team participation, reflection praxis sharing and celebrating).

---

198 Wegner, 2000, in Carlson, 2003, p. 30.
199 Carlson, 2003, p 18.

Spirituality in the Workplace

The spiritual dimension of the workplace is being given increased attention in developing commitment to vision, organisational trust and personal and corporate productivity,[200] with many corporations identifying spirituality as an important part of professional learning. This is scaffolded by a growing body of evidence in understanding the influence of a spiritual dimension in the workplace and its connection to leadership.[201] Janet Groen in work spanning the last fifteen years, has identified a surprising consistency in key tenets of a spirituality-infused organisation:

- People have a sense of vocation and passion about their work.
- The workplace culture encourages creativity and risk taking through training and career development.
- The workplace balances both work and home by having supports and programs in place which foster outside commitments.
- Base line wages and benefits are in place, which demonstrate the organisation's willingness to invest in its workforce.
- There is a sense of community both within and beyond the workplace, which is reflected in its operational and decision-making practices.
- The articulated values of the organisation are infused into its day-to-day practice.[202]

The spiritual dimensions of the workplace apply to all of its aspects. Also apparent is an alignment between the characteristics required for the development of a culture of trust in a learning community and the characteristics noted above which feature in a spiritually infused organisation. In addition to this, there is specific research on how teachers might best strategise to recognise, incorporate and develop the spiritual dimension of their practice.[203]

Addressing the fundamental and deeper dimensions of workplace culture requires both organisational and personal spiritual leadership. More particularly, the strength of spiritual formation in the leadership role is found to be pivotal in addressing the spiritual dimensions of the workplace: 'In order for it [the workplace] to become "spiritually infused", the leadership … must also be "spiritually infused".'[204]

---

200   English, Fenwick & Parsons, 2005.
201   Neal, 2015.
202   Groen, 2001, p. 20. See also Janet Groen's further work: 2008, 2013.
203   English, Fenwick & Parsons, 2005.
204   Groen, 2001, p. 21.

ADULT LEARNING: HOLISTIC APPROACHES AND REFLECTIVE PRAXIS

Having traversed the perspectives concerning professional learning communities and the shared workplace as the setting for sustainable staff growth, we now turn to adult learning. In a lifelong and life-wide adult learning paradigm, learning is assumed to be an inclusive engagement that happens in a variety of ways.[205] Within this understanding, the principles of holistic education have gained currency, with experiential learning taking its place as a central component. Of particular relevance is the role of reflective praxis in adult learning, in both personal and communal forms, along with the functions of mentoring and coaching.

Holistic Education

Holistic education has developed a strong following over the last 50 years in educative methodology and curriculum. The word holistic comes from the Greek word *holon* and refers to 'an understanding of the universe as made up of integrated wholes that cannot simply be reduced to the sum of its parts'.[206] Researchers and educators attracted to this theory are vitally interested in an integrated approach to learning, and in systems where they see the trend has been and continues toward silo learning. Such educators are attuned to the understanding of the variety of ways of knowing and engaging, made popular by Howard Gardner's seminal work on intelligences:

> *Seven kinds of intelligence would allow seven ways to teach, rather than one. And powerful constraints that exist in the mind can be mobilised to introduce a particular concept (or whole system of thinking) ... Paradoxically, constraints can be suggestive and ultimately freeing.*[207]

The roots of holistic education are found in the expression of 'a core wisdom underlying various spiritual traditions and teachings'.[208] There are five essential elements in developing this way of knowing:

1. There is an interconnected mysterious unity in the universe (Huxley's 'divine reality').
2. There is a connectivity between this mysterious unity and the individual's intimate self/soul.
3. Knowledge of the mysterious unity develops through various contemplative practices.

---

205   Kalantzis & Cope, 2008.
206   Miller, 2007, p. 6.
207   Gardner, 1993, p. xxiii.
208   Miller, 2007, p. 16.

4. Values are derived from seeing/realising the interconnectedness of reality.

5. This realisation leads to social action to counter injustice and suffering[209]

Holistic education thus seeks to underpin learning with a sense of balance, inclusion and connectedness. Catholic educators have long been encouraged to see the connections between holistic learning and the field of spirituality. Examination of the five elements defined in holistic education indicates the intersection of three dimensions when situated within a Christian approach to spiritual formation:

1. An engagement with the world – others and all creation
2. An inner engagement with deep self – internal God space
3. An imperative to make a difference (social action) based on 1 and 2.

Specific practices encouraged in the holistic approach correlate with similar key practices in the Christian tradition. These include varieties of meditation and contemplative practice. Finally, there is a general alignment identified in this educational approach with current understandings in spiritual growth and theology already identified and discussed.

Engaging the Aesthetic

An understanding of the aesthetic and the psycho-spiritual dimensions of learning provide more specific scholarship in the areas of holistic learning. This has been an important contribution in the development of religious education, at the forefront of praxis in the Catholic educational setting of lifelong learning and teaching as a holistic journey demanding new pathways.

If we remain wedded to the way education is currently provided we cannot imagine other ways ... we need some imagination, some fantasy, some new ways of thinking – some magic in fact.[210]

While there had been proponents for an aesthetic dimension in early educational research,[211] the aesthetic as a way of knowing gained sustained attention in the 1970s, building further on the well-developed 'ways of knowing' theory which identified three pathways: cognitive, interpretive and self-reflective.[212] The aesthetic dimension of religious education, introduced

---

209 Miller, 2007, pp. 17-18.
210 Beare, 2001.
211 Dewey, 1934; Kant, 1760; Rosenblatt, 1938; Sparshott, 1963.
212 Habermas, 1972, 1974.

and promoted by Maria Harris in the 1980s and 1990s, placed a focus on the imaginary and an embodied approach to learning in religious education that was, at the time, revolutionary. Harris's work (1989, 1996) in the aesthetic imagination remains ground-breaking. Both she and Gabriel Moran (1983; 2000) expanded the understanding of the purpose and process in religious education, with their scholarship regarded as a touchstone for best practice teaching and learning in religious education. Their contribution has been about re-shaping an understanding of religious learning that draws on multiple ways of knowing (much like Gardner's intelligences), is outward in its dialogue with the world, at the same time drawing directly on the content, symbolism and insights of the Catholic Christian tradition.

Harris connected Moran's work on forms of educational curriculum with the four themes of Church ministry: koinonia, leitourgia, diakonia and kerygma.[213] In pursuing an understanding of these in relation to community, literate knowledge, work and wisdom, recognisable links are made to the symbolic and metaphorical language of the tradition in understanding and naming God as 'Trinity', 'Logos', 'Creator' and 'Sophia'.

The aesthetic dimensions of learning in religious education have been developed by Groome in his work on the sacramental imagination as part of a shared praxis approach and 'wisdom way of knowing'[214] that engages both tradition and experience. Engaging the aesthetic is and must continue to be a vital element of learning in any Catholic educational context.

Experiential Learning

Also critical to holistic education is the integration of experiential learning in pedagogical practice. The term 'experiential learning' is used in different ways, but a helpful categorisation of experiential learning differentiates the area into four 'villages' of interest:

1. Assessing and accrediting learning from life and work experience
2. Bringing change in the structures ... of post-school education
3. Providing a basis for group consciousness raising
4. Having concern for personal growth/self-awareness.[215]

Areas 3 and 4 are of particular relevance for us, and have contributed to the development of experiential models of learning over the last thirty years. A foundational model for experiential learning provided by David Kolb (1976, 1981, 1984) has been central to the scholarly conversation around the theory and practice of adult learning, informal education and lifelong learning. Kolb's

---

213   Harris, 1998, p. 19.
214   Groome, 1998.
215   Weil & McGill, 1989, p. 3.

model has four elements, predicated on the argument that 'effective learning entails the possession of four different abilities'.[216] These abilities generate four distinct learning styles: the Converger, the Diverger, the Assimilator and the Accommodator. The model is represented in Figure 6.3.

FIGURE 6.3: KOLB'S CIRCULAR MODEL OF ADULT LEARNING

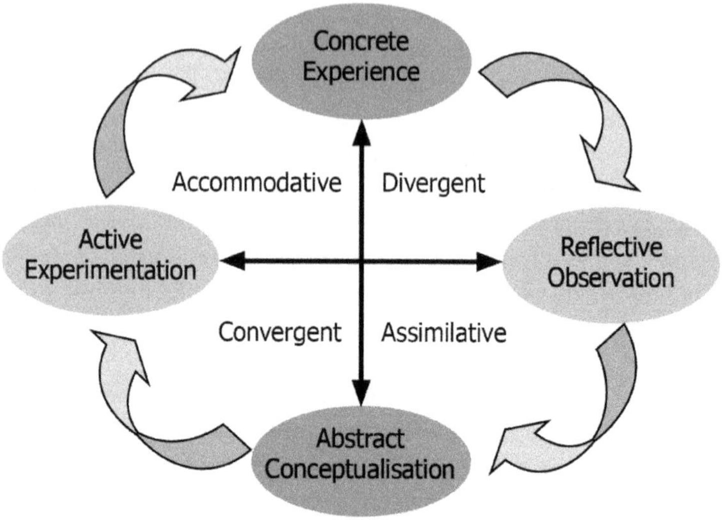

Kolb Experiential Learning

The four elements are represented in an 'experiential learning circle' that involves:

- concrete experience, followed by
- observation and reflection, followed by
- forming abstract concepts, followed by
- testing in new situations.

While its strength is in understanding the role of experiential learning, the weaknesses in this model lie in a lack of recognition of the importance of reflective praxis in adult learning, and a lack of recognition of the differing contexts of learning and the role of community in individual learning. Even as the model expounds a view that knowledge is a result of 'grasping experience and transforming it',[217] the focus is on knowledge rather than praxis.[218]

Recognising both the insight and the limitation of Kolb's model, others have drawn more intentionally on the work of Paulo Freire and

216 Kolb & Fry, 1975, pp. 35-6.
217 Kolb, 1984, p. 41.
218 Jarvis, 2004.

John Dewey to validate the experiential aspects wherein the role of the learner's psychological history is part of the interpretive processing of any experience.[219] Experiential learning, particularly as it both connects with and stretches the lifeworld of the learner, is now privileged in adult learning approaches, even as it continues to contrast with the classic philosophies of learning which use didactic methods to teach facts and principles.[220] This is the formative ground of the adult learner.

Service Learning

Service learning is an area of experiential learning that has particular interest for those in Catholic education, as it finds a place in the curriculum of schools and universities. Best defined as 'a form of experiential learning that connects meaningful community service with academic instruction while emphasizing student learning through reflective thinking and analysis'[221], service learning as a child of experiential education draws on Dewey's theory of experiential learning (1933), and the further research of other field practitioners (Kolb, 1984; Jarvis, 2004). Education is authentic when, through repeated and thoughtful reflection on an experience, a student is informed to take action because of their meaning-making. Finally, continuity as a criterion for experiential education is seen as vital for real learning.

In the context of Catholic education, the 1980s saw the emergence of education for justice re-surfacing a long tradition embedded in Catholicism. The trend toward the inclusion of outreach and service programs in religious education curricula was viewed by educationalists as a positive sign where students would experience and reflect on real life and learn that they could make a difference in the world.[222] In the last decade, service learning has been linked with the increasing interest in 'values' programs (for Catholic high schools, pre-service and continuing staff), the underpinning view being that service learning also 'affords a unique and valuable opportunity for student (participant) value exploration and development.'[223] Consequently, a focus in service learning research has been the measurable differences in values development in participants, with a number of findings confirming the efficacy and potential values growth for participants.[224]

It is important to note that the provision of service learning in itself is not necessarily a catalyst in promoting deep levels of experiential learning. It might initiate experiential learning, but unless there are structures and

219   Jarvis, 2004.
220   Billig, 2004; Mezirow, 2000.
221   Bailey, Carpenter & Harrington, 2002, p. 433.
222   Hecht, 2003; Harris, 1998; Meyers, 1999.
223   Chapdelaine, Ruiz, Warchal & Wells, 2005, p. 7.
224   Kenary, 2009; Price, 2008.

processes in place that purposively nurture reflection with participants, including an intentional use of mentorship, structured supportive frameworks and prolonged period of time in engagement, then its impact can be limited.[225]

Reflective Praxis

The role of reflective practice in the context of growing and sustaining teacher excellence is well documented.[226] In the sphere of Catholic education, research in both teaching and leading confirms its central place.[227] Reflective practice has both an outward and an inward dimension: situating the reflective practitioner in both a global context and an inner self context. Broad research highlights the importance of the reflective practitioner having an awareness of their contemporary global context, as well as confirming the role of inner reflection in teachers' initial and ongoing professional learning.[228]

In the exploration of reflective practice in the spiritual domain, systematic and personal reflection about teaching in a Catholic school both nurtures and sustains the teaching vocation itself.[229] More than this, reflective practice in the spiritual dimension, in and of itself, can have an observed and measurable influence on the wider community culture.[230] Further research into preferred teaching practices demonstrates that teachers who are highly spiritual are more likely to use student centred pedagogy, with accompanying stronger outcomes for students personally and educatively.[231] These kinds of findings have implications for enhancing pedagogical practice as well as staff formation.

Mentoring

The importance of a significant person or experience in the formation of leaders is a common finding in the research on companioning and mentoring, regardless of the context. Inspiring human connections with others is identified as a key formation element.[232]

Within the research on lifelong learning and the role of the learning community context, the reflective exercise of naming and discussing helpful mentor relationships appears itself to be instructional in learning and growth.

---

225 Fowler, 2009; Price, 2008. Debra Fowler's research concerning nursing students generates conclusions which show a failure of service learning participation in influencing the nurturing of professional values among the participants. Damien Price's research in contrast demonstrates the power of service learning when there are embedded in it well-structured support processes.
226 Schon, 1983; Carter & Francis, 2001.
227 See Branson, 2004, and particularly his 2009 book, Leadership for an Age of Wisdom.
228 For example, Hanifin, 2000
229 Downey, 2006; Jackson, 2006; Neal, 2000; Rolph, 1991; Simone, 2004.
230 Kauanui & Bradley, 2003.
231 Lindholm & Astin, 2008.
232 Moore, 1999; Newby & Hyde, 1992.

Authentic relationships are understood as transformational in the lives of participants. Consequently, the literature identifies the need for quality reflection processes to be a non-negotiable part of mentoring relationships.[233]

Responding to these trends in the literature, organisations have widely committed to formally structured mentoring relationships for staff.[234] Yet the lived experience is that people 'perceive more benefit from an unstructured mentoring alliance.'[235] Continuing research on informal mentoring has led to recommendations that organisations should '... identify, recognise, acknowledge and legitimise [mentoring] where it exists, and thereby create a climate for its existence, rather than constrain it by formal structures within the organisation'.[236] The rationale is that such an approach has potential to build a culture of empathic respect, rather than legislated mentor structures, as a community-changing strategy.

Intentional and systematic ways are needed for teachers to reflect upon their practice. Such reflection needs to take account of the pivotal role of teachers and all that they bring, influenced by their lives, their histories and experience as well as their skills and expertise.[237] This is the inner terrain or world of the teacher and leader.[238] The reflective praxis thus developed gives focus both to the self as mentor and the community as mentor, and is aimed at sustained development centred on the personal growth of the teacher and their spiritual dimension, within a community of colleagues.

Coaching

Alongside mentoring, coaching has become a dominant methodology in professional learning. Highly goal-focused and increasingly strength-based in approach,[239] coaching is proving to be a widely-used tool in building competence and a wide range of skills. Coaching most often involves 'integrating new or alternative approaches into the professional's existing repertoire of skills and strategies'.[240] In this way, both the inner and outer world of the professional expands. It is also apparent that coaching is central in negotiating change in the workplace and supporting productivity while living and working in uncertain times.[241]

The education context provides a very specific landscape for the practice of coaching. The 2013 Hay Report identified four models within the education

233   Bennet, 2001; Green, 2006; Fletcher & Mullen (eds), 2012.
234   See Manternach, 2002, for the beginning of this trend.
235   Blackwell & McLean, 1996, p. 26.
236   Lyons & Scroggins, cited in Bennetts, 2001, p. 284.
237   Senge, 1990; Starratt, 2004.
238   Palmer, 2000, 2004.
239   See Growth Coaching International http://www.growthcoaching.com.au: a highly recommended group.
240   AITSL, Hay Group Report, 2013.
241   Creasy & Paterson, 2005; Grant, 2016.

sector: peer coaching, specialist coaching, instructional coaching and in-class coaching.[242] In all of these, coaching focuses on outcomes with a systematic approach in building capacity in the individual and learning community to attain those outcomes. It is thus future-focussed and change-oriented.

Some of the key coaching processes have strong resonance with both mentoring and the reflective practices in spiritual companioning. All are learner or person-centred, and are most effective when the holistic nature of individual learning and growth is recognised and worked with. Given the growing profile of coaching practices within the field of education, and in particular within the life of professional learning communities, these are commonalities to be affirmed and leveraged in any culture change initiative.

TRANSFORMATIVE LEARNING: CHANGE EDUCATION AND CRITICAL MASS THEORY

Transformative learning theory is of interest to educationalists because it offers them authentic strategies to examine meaningful engagement that is learner centred. Spiritual formation in the context of education is richly informed by scholarship in transformative learning that leads to deep change in a community setting.

Transformative Learning

Because the goal of spiritual formation is transformation, and the context for our work is an educational one, the adult educational theory in this area is instructive. Transformational or transformative learning is about change, 'dramatic, fundamental change in the way we see ourselves and the world in which we live'.[243] Accordingly, there are three concepts in transformative learning that contribute to the change process:

- Experience
- Critical Reflection
- Development of New Understandings.[244]

Transformative learning theory is built largely on the work of Jack Mezirow. His theory suggests such change occurs in one of four ways: 'by elaborating existing frames of reference; by learning new frames of reference; by transforming points of view; or by transforming habits of mind.'[245] When transformative learning theory is applied to adult professional learning[246]

---

242 AITSL, 2013, pp. 7-9. See also Showers & Joyce, 1996; Annenburg Institute for School Reform, 2004; Department for Education and Skills, 2005.
243 Merriam, 2007, p. 123.
244 Merriam & Caffarella, 1999.
245 Mezirow, 2000, p. 19.
246 Cranton, 2005; Hansman, Kimble, Hildreth & Bourbon, 2008.

the life context and personal developmental dimensions of the adult learner are highlighted. Mazirow identifies five principles of androgogy[247]:

1. Self-Concept: As a person matures, they move from dependency to self-direction.
2. Experience: Adults possess personal histories which define their identities and are a source for their experiential learning.
3. Readiness: The learning readiness of adults is closely related to socially relevant learning.
4. Orientation: As an adult learns new knowledge, they want to apply it immediately.
5. Motivation: As a person matures, motivation to learn comes from internal factors.

Perspectives in developmental and organisational theory have further contributed contextual and multiple learning dimensions to the highly cognitive method of early transformational learning theory.[248] Laurent Daloz, in particular, contributed a re-framing with emphasis on a developmental, intuitive, holistic and contextually based approach to adult transformative learning. Sharon Daloz Parks explored this further within a spiritual and faith dimension, revealing a powerful role for mentoring in the developmental process. Knud Illeris's work supports the multiple dimensions of learning within an integrated relational dynamic. But it has been the work of John Dirkx and Suzanne Prenger that has grounded the contextual framing and, for the first time, advocated in the process approach 'the inclusion of the spiritual dimension, along with the intellectual, emotional and moral dimensions of being.'[249]

When learners undergo transformative learning, they experience a deep shift in how they understand and interpret the world, a re-setting of their inner mapping. This occurs within the context of their own lives, and through an integrated and holistic process that draws on the intellectual, emotional, moral and spiritual dimensions of being in the world. This process influences behaviour. Importantly for our focus on formation, a meta-analysis of the empirical research in transformative learning has identified contextual conditions essential for an effective transformative learning experience.[250]

---

247 Knowles, 1980, p. 43. (Androgogy is a term introduced to specifically refer today to 'the art and science of helping adults learn'. It actually comes from the Greek derivation 'man-leading'.)

248 See Daloz, 1999; Dirkx & Prenger, 1997, 2006; Illeris, 2003, 2004; Daloz Parks, 2000, 2011.

249 Dirkx & Prenger, 1997, p. 1250.

250 Taylor, 2007. Among other findings about context, Taylor asserts that research needs to continue into the nature of and relationship between critical reflection and other ways of knowing.

These include establishment of relationships, engagement in dialogue, self-disclosure, careful listening and the accessing of alternative understandings.

Higher order qualities of leadership that contribute to transformative change continue to be explored. Consistently, the nature of reflective praxis for deep learning is highlighted. It is here that the concept of 'presence' as a conduit for that 'deep learning' has gained attention.[251] While 'presence' is not a new concept, it has gained currency over the last ten years as a significant component in leadership literature[252] and parallels the broad and growing interest in the spirituality of leadership. While not widely used with explicit reference to the Catholic leadership context, the connections have been explored in the context of authentic leadership.[253]

Change Facilitation

All professional learning involves change education.[254] A focus on change facilitation that precipitates transformational learning has captured the interest of organisational scholars around the world. Generally, three types of change are identified – the implementation of new materials and resources; changing behaviour and practices; and changing professional beliefs and understandings.[255] A fourth type of change is proposed as underpinning other types of change in the Catholic education context of the teacher and leader: 'a sense of spiritual growth and transformation through experiences that are generative of new learning.'[256]

The following principles are identified as influential in the process of change facilitation:

- Change is a process, not an event, and therefore requires time, energy and resourcing.
- Change is accomplished by individuals first and then by institutions.
- Change is a highly personal experience.
- Change entails growth in both feelings about and skills in using new programs/ways.
- Interventions can be designed to support the individual's implementation of innovation. As this is done, consideration is given to the systemic nature of the organisation.
- The change facilitator needs to adapt to the differing needs of individuals and to their changing needs over time.[257]

---

251   Senge, Scharmer & Flowers, 2005.
252   Starratt, 2004, 2005.
253   Bezzina, Burford & Duignan, 2007; Duignan, 2002, 2007; Horner, 2008.
254   Fullan, 2002.
255   Johnson, 1998.
256   Healy, 2005, p. 29.
257   Hall & Hord, 2015.

The role of the educational leader as a change facilitator building a learning community is well documented in the work of Michael Fullan.[258] Linked with leadership development,[259] change facilitation also highlights the internal growth and inner learning journey of the individual leader where vision and reflective practice are given priority. In exploring how leaders might usefully conceptualise their leadership, Fullan[260] generates five 'conceptions': moral purpose, relationship building, knowledge generation, understanding the change process and coherence building. It is the development of these belief systems, rather than management techniques alone, that creates influential leadership.

> *Leaders who are effective operate from powerful conceptions, not from a set of techniques. The key, then, is to build up leaders' conceptions of what it means to be a leader ... These conceptions can be fostered, but they must be fostered through a socialization process that develops leaders as reflective practitioners.*[261]

Fullan writes for a broad audience in education. In Catholic education, 'moral purpose', 'relationship building' and 'coherence building' sit within a much more resonant worldview that goes beyond the meaning confines of this kind of language. In particular, Catholic educators are called to a deeper summons than the term 'moral purpose' can encompass. Ours is a view into eternity, with our eye on the whole being of each child growing into the fullness of their lives long after they finish schooling. More than educating being the right thing to do, for the Catholic educator educating is soul work and, as Pope Francis says, the work of love. However, while Fullan's five conceptions might be recalibrated, all studies in leadership sustainability support his basic premise of the need to grow leaders through a long term sustained process.[262] Ongoing or lifelong learning for both principal and staff must be prioritised and shared.[263]

These insights and change facilitation principles have been applied to whole system reform. The term 'collective capacity' in a group or organisation 'implies a level of trust and collaboration essential to whole system reform'.[264] Where this exists, there is the opportunity to maximise high impact strategies in the everyday context. In such a paradigm, connection, coherence and collective capacity-building characterise the entire system from classroom to school to cluster to organisation. A

---

258   Fullan, 2007, 2008, 2010.
259   Fullan & Fink, 2003; Senge, Scharmer, Jaworsk & Flowers, 2005; Starratt, 2005.
260   Fullan, 2010.
261   Fullan, 2010, p. 12.
262   Shimbakuro, 1998; Hargreaves, 2007.
263   Hallinger & Heck, 1997.
264   Fullan, 2010, p. 5.

collaborative competition develops (lateral capacity building) as schools and clusters learn from each other in a robust and positive process where leadership 'is central in promoting collective capacity and ownership'. [265]

Change facilitation requires commitment to a shared vision and individual meaning-making that demands a radically new way of approaching learning – one that guides the individual mind through the process of many minds working together.[266] Within this, the focus on the deeply human dimension of change[267] has overtaken the structural dimension as the key to facilitating the ongoing complexity of change in community. There is recognition that expertise and wisdom, and the commitment that comes with them, lies within the community, though not exclusively. In the endeavours of whole system reform or change, as with micro-change at the individual school level, everything points to the critical role of leadership. A relevant model of leadership for Catholic school communities is one that accompanies staff, builds a culture of trust, applies personal reflective praxis, nurtures other leaders and is clear about the primary purpose of leadership in the midst of change.

Critical Mass Theory

To understand and identify the process and space in which transformative change occurs in a group or community, critical mass theory offers rich analysis. The term 'critical mass' was originally borrowed from nuclear physics where it refers to 'the quantity needed to start a chain reaction, a qualitative shift or turning point.'[268] Critical mass models found their genesis in game theory[269] becoming popular as the generalised term for a wide variety of phenomena.[270] Following this, critical mass models became a major stream of the theoretical sociology literature on crowd behaviour and collective action.

The earliest research[271] suggested that critical mass could be quantified as a percentage point. This research was applied to exploring how minorities could begin to influence the dominant culture of an organisation and suggested that 'when the numbers reached about 35 percent, the shift would occur'. [272] Social science researchers have since applied the critical mass concept to explain the diffusion of innovations and ideas, although with a more cautious approach to quantifying the shift.

---

265   Fullan, 2010, p. 13.
266   Hammonds, 2002.
267   Sergiovanni, 2000.
268   Dahlerup, 2005, pp. 275-6.
269   Schelling, 1978.
270   Granovetter, 1978.
271   Kanter, 1977, cited in Dahlerup, 2005.
272   Kanter, 1977, p. 239, in Dahlerup, 2005.

In the area of Christian studies, critical mass models have been used to analyse church growth and community membership.[273] In particular, exploration of the phenomenon of Christian conversion of communities has used the principles of critical mass to argue that social networks, along with other variables, provide adequate insights to explain growth:

Most new religious movements fail because they quickly become closed or semi-closed networks ... they fail to keep forming and sustaining attachments to outsiders and thereby lose the capacity to grow.[274]

This more sophisticated application of the threshold or critical mass model illuminates how, at a particular point, a shift can occur in movements of a spiritual nature, as well as political or social (though it can be argued these elements interlink in any group) which creates a qualitative change in the wider group or community. In this dynamic, the critical mass is most likely to lead to maximum movement, when a small core of the most interested people begin contributing to draw in the other, less interested members of the population.[275] Both resourcing support and community environment influence the depth and efficacy of the movement.[276]

More recent work on critical mass theory and threshold or tipping point modelling offers 'species' or different kinds of group models.[277] The type most relevant to our context is the 'influence' model. Key factors in developing critical mass in this setting are:

1. The reach of the strategy (the total number of direct participants)
2. The selectivity of the strategy (the degree to which it focuses 'member' efforts on those with the greatest interest and resource levels)
3. Inter-dependence (how direct participants take into account the effect of their actions on those of others)
4. The production function (the relationship between the total amount participants contribute to the strategy and the amount of the collective good obtained.[278]

The learning in critical mass modelling, as part of change facilitation and culture growth, offers important possibilities in the strategic work of system-wide staff formation.

---

273   Land, Deane & Blau, 1991.
274   Stark, 1996, p. 20.
275   Oliver & Marwell, 1988.
276   Oliver, Marwell & Teixeira, 1985.
277   Oliver & Marwell, 2002.
278   Prahl, Marwell & Oliver, 1991.

IMPLICATIONS

As educators and leaders, you will be making the connections between the fundamental elements of an authentic learning community and the feel of an authentic Catholic school and staff community. Here are some further thoughts for your ongoing reflection.

Implications for Adult Learning in a Catholic Educational Setting

Holistic education is focussed on contemporary dialogical pedagogy that supports a learner-centred rather than an instruction-centred approach, an inquiry culture rather than a testing culture, and which is also welcoming of digital modes of learning that are grounded and integrated into the learning process.[279]

Using a comprehensive philosophical underpinning we see how holistic educational approaches are well placed to navigate the post-modern terrain in a constructive and positive way.[280] It is no coincidence that holistic education is gaining more and more traction at a time when many cultures are becoming identified as increasingly disconnected – the 'fragmentation which permeates everything'[281] identified in Part A. 'Education has done much to sever the relationship between head and heart. As a result, in industrialised societies we live in our heads, denying our deeper knowing and intuitions.'[282]

Holistic educative approaches, privileging the aesthetic, experiential and service dimensions of the learning process, seek to redress the balance. Important features for maximum efficacy include a well-structured framework, a form of mentor accompaniment, and a sustained process, within which direct experience and full engagement can occur.[283] This pedagogical approach presents a strong conceptual alignment with spiritual formation design and praxis.

Implications for Formation and the Workplace Context

A focus on spiritual leadership in the workplace comes at a time when people are increasingly looking for meaning in their work, a time when they highly value recognition, appreciation and a sense of ownership.[284]

---

279   Miller, 2007.
280   Forbes, 2003.
281   Senge, Scharmer, Jaworski & Flowers, 2005, p. 190.
282   Miller, 2007, p. 4.
283   Price, 2008.
284   Pink, 2015.

Teachers have a stronger morale and are more personally invested in their work when it has meaning and significance in contributing to a higher purpose or goal. Influential leaders know this and know how to do it, prioritising professional and personal support and challenge for staff. Where an authentic culture of trust is fostered, communities of practice flourish, exhibiting the best features of professional learning that maximise both the skills within and expertise outside the school community.

Implications for Formation in the School Community and Systemic Context

There are two points of note here for our work in formation. Firstly, while the precise point at which qualitative change might occur in a community can be debated, critical mass theory verifies that it involves numbers of people.[285] One person is unlikely to affect a qualitative shift in the whole community. Thus, critical mass theory suggests an effective formation strategy ought to involve the targeting and resourcing of a small group of staff in each school community to engender wider influence and culture change. Secondly, critical mass theory depends upon the identification of underlying differences in the values, attitudes and behaviour of the group concerned.[286] In ascertaining effectiveness of any formation strategy, we would need to identify a discernible change in development of attitudes and behaviour in staff. That comes with specific and nuanced challenges for systems and governance.

285   Oliver & Marwell, 2002.
286   Norris & Lovenduski, 2001.

7

THE FAITH TRADITION

Catholic schools also exist within an ecclesial environment. And in the changing landscape of Catholic schooling, the spiritual formation of staff is closely connected to and influenced by the shifts in the ecclesial landscape. Once again, three inter-related areas emerge as relevant to our discussion:

Mission, Evangelisation and the Catholic School
Catholic School Ethos and Culture
Ministry, Vocation and Formation

Let us consider these in turn.

MISSION, EVANGELISATION AND THE CATHOLIC SCHOOL

Prior to the Second Vatican Council (1961-65), apart from the papal encyclical on Christian Education in 1929 (*Divini Illius Magistri*), the articulation of the purpose and identity of the Catholic school attracted little attention. There was little need. Until the sixties, there was an ecclesial and cultural correlation in which the Catholic school was seen and experienced as an extension of the home and the parish.

> *It was a milieu that supported the religious faith and practices of the Catholic family that also belonged to and actively participated in, a local parish under the leadership of the clergy and the authority of the local bishop. The school was the cultural agent of the Church, entrusted with the task of handing on the Catholic faith, its beliefs, traditions and practices to the next generation. Such an environment provided a strong sense of identity and purpose for members of the Church and school.[287]*

This correlation has weakened and has consequent ramifications for shared understandings in the work of Catholic educators.

---

287   Belmonte, Cranston & Limerick, 2006, p. 2.

In particular, and for a variety of reasons, the term evangelisation as the focus for mission has not had an easy reception among Catholic school teachers and leaders, and this is reflected in the findings generated in a range of Australian studies over the last decade or more.[288]

Today, the individual Catholic school is a community which is still bound together ecclesially and communally with the local Church community and the worldwide Catholic community. A shared and monitored vision and mission continues to be espoused which ought to afford the local and global organisation a strong sense of its purpose and identity[289] with considerable potential for influence. However, from this same place of powerful potential has risen a powerful concern – precisely because the sense of a shared understanding among the stakeholders of the key elements of the role of the Catholic school appears increasingly fractured. Let us explore how this dissonance has developed.

Understanding Mission Now

Prior to Vatican II, that which constituted the nature of mission was clear and simple and shared by Protestants and Catholics alike. But this understanding of mission has collapsed amid the reality of political, geographical, cultural and ecclesial shifts. The twin purposes of 'saving souls' and 'church extension'[290] are now being supplanted by a new and energetic theology of mission that responds to the questions about purpose quite differently. This has consequences for how contemporary spiritual formation for mission is constructed and delivered. Table 7.1 summarises the change in understanding.[291]

TABLE 7.1: SUMMARY OF SHIFT IN UNDERSTANDING OF MISSION

	Prior to Vatican II, Mission is:		Post-Vatican II, Mission is:
1	the church's work for the salvation of souls	1	for the reign of God
2	carried out for the benefit of the pagans abroad	2	to the world
3	mainly by priests, religious brothers, nuns, and specially-commissioned lay folk, mostly from Europe and America	3	by the whole community of believers, in God and the Spirit
4	with the financial and spiritual support of the laity back home	4	with cross-collaboration by all Catholics and Christians
5	by planting the church in these 'mission fields'	5	in dialogue

---

288 Graham, 2006; McLaughlin, 2000, 2002; Tinsey, 1998.
289 See Turkington, 2004.
290 Bosch, 1991.
291 See Phan, 2002, and Bevans, 2009, for a detailed exploration of these shifts.

In light of the Post-Vatican II directions in mission, four useful insights emerge from current thinking. These are, the Church: helps realise God's mission, which is not confined to the institutional or historical tradition; requires a new and different language for understanding and dialogue; invites an inclusive approach to other denominations and faiths in a common search and calling, and: demands a genuine and collaborative appreciation of the role of non-ordained members. Each of these points is now briefly explained.

The heart and energy of Mission has its source in God, not the Church. Mission is what God does, through the church and in the world. In other words, it is not that God's Church has a mission but rather that God's mission has a church:

> *Imagine what our church would be like if Christians really understood this and took this seriously. What it means is, first, that the church is not about the church. It is about what Jesus called the Reign of God. We are ... [mostly a] church not when we are building up the church, but when we are outside of it: being good parents, being loving spouses, being diligent and honest in our workplace, treating our patients with care if we are health workers, going the extra mile with our students if we are teachers, living lives responsible to the environment, being responsible citizens, sharing our resources with the needy, standing up for social justice, consciously using inclusive language, treating immigrants fairly, trying to understand people of other faiths, etc. etc. What we realise too is that people in the church don't have a monopoly on working for the Reign of God.*[292]

The implications for such a redefinition of mission are that the signs and indicators of effective missioning are not necessarily or even probably found in traditional measures such as church attendance or priestly vocations.

This understanding of mission, with its origins in the theology reflected in the Vatican II documents, is moving toward a dialogue around church where new language plays a central role. It is best described as a *prophetic dialogue*[293] and is accompanied by the development of a missiological imagination.[294] A missiological imagination stretches thinking, reflection and perspective on mission and generates an understanding of how what those within the Catholic Church do, contributes to what God does, and is, in the world. In so doing, there is a more intentional drawing on the Vatican II language that sees Church as a sign of grace, as sacrament, and as a sign and instrument of God's grace in the world.[295] It is a direction

---

292   Bevans, 2009, p. 11.
293   Bevans, 2006; Kirk, 2000; Lakeland, 2003.
294   Bevans, 2005; Bevans & Schroeder, 2010, D'Orsa & D'Orsa, 2013.
295   See in particular these sections in the following Vatican documents: Lumen Gentium, 1964, n. 1, 5; Dei Verbum, 1965, n. 7, Sacrosanctum Concilium, 1963, n. 6; Gaudium et

supported by the work of scholars from related disciplines interested in the re-shaping and re-contextualising of how God, Church and Jesus function in authentic meaning-making within the diversity of the current culture.[296] It also signals a shift from making traditional ecclesial language the conduit for the dialogue, to instead allowing that to underpin a new language that finds traction within the culture.

In the contemporary context of Catholic schools, Church and culture interact in a variety of different modes. Thus, an ecumenical orientation is encouraged. It is a paradigm that sees 'mission in many modes'[297], where signs of grace are recognised in other religions and in the general culture. This offers a new way of thinking into the future.

> *Mission still is ... about crossing boundaries. Like Jesus, whose ministry crossed the boundaries that religion, culture and class had set up, the early community crossed boundaries that even Jesus could not have imagined when it admitted Gentiles and respected their customs. Indeed, I believe that it was in this willingness to move beyond itself under the guidance of the Holy Spirit which allowed the early community to become aware of itself as something clearly distinct from its Jewish roots, as a discrete ekklesia or church.*[298]

In exploring ecclesial history to recover and develop a robust understanding of mission, we can discover ambiguities and a misappropriation of ecclesial 'traditions'. For example, the origins of the separation of 'clergy' and 'laity' are not found in the scriptures, but rather in a later organisational development that has grown into 'a tradition'.[299] A critique of Council documents (*Decree on the Apostolate of the Laity; Ad Gentes; Gaudium et Spes*) exposes ambiguities in the attempt to define the lay vocation and the church-world relationship. There is a danger, inherent in the documents themselves, of the lay vocation being perceived and grown as 'the apostolate of the second string'[300], and based on a deficit understanding of what the laity *cannot* do in ministry. The implications of this in terms of the development of a formation for mission are discussed further in a later section of this chapter.

The tension that has emerged in theological discussion around mission can be explained by two contrasting models of church.[301] The 'citadel'

Spes, 1965, n. 3, Apostolicam Actuositatem, 1965, n. 2; Nostra Aetate, 1965, n. 2.

296   Leading thinkers here have been Johnson, 1994; LaCugna, 1993; Phan, 2000; Schreiter, 1996.

297   Bosch, 1991, p. 511.

298   Bevans, 2005, p. 8.

299   See Lakeland, 2003.

300   Lakeland, 2002, p. 95.

301   See Gerald Grace, writing from 1997, especially with reference to the 'citadel' and 'web' models of church and the growing concern for the building of spiritual capital within Catholic schools .

approach, where the church is protected and extended in the process of evangelisation, has its energy invested in maintenance and measurement, and quite specific outcomes. The 'web' approach, where the church sees itself as part of, rather than owning or being the origin of God's mission, has its energy invested in recognising and contributing to the wider reign of God in the world, with outcomes far more difficult to measure. The movement from a citadel approach to a web approach represents a paradigm shift in conceptual understanding:

> *If the motive for mission is the creation and maintenance of the church, mission will be essentially concerned with baptism and church-extension. But if the focus is the kingdom or realm or God, then without compromising the significance of either [sic] neither the gift of baptism nor the importance of visible communities of baptized people, there is less likelihood of restricting mission to church-extension.*[302]

There is a movement among leaders in theology and Catholic education across the globe (including Australia) to develop a new collaborative sense of meaning-making. Czech philosopher and parish priest Tomas Halik points to understanding mission in the twenty-first century as 'accompanying the seekers' of our post-Christian societies. This was well expressed in the document *The Common Call* which emerged from the 2010 conference on mission and which was promulgated by representatives of World Christianity:

> *Recognising the need to shape a new generation of leaders with authenticity for mission in a world of diversities in the twenty-first century, we are called to work together in new forms of theological education. Because we are all made in the image of God, these will draw on one another's unique charisms, challenge each other to grow in faith and understanding, share resources equitably worldwide, involve the entire human being and the whole family of God, and respect the wisdom of our elders while also fostering the participation of children.*[303]

Understanding Evangelisation

The term evangelisation is translated from the Greek (*evangelion*) and Latin (*evangelium*) as 'good news' or 'Gospel'. Church teaching on evangelisation as the fundamental mission of the Church developed under the enthusiastic patronage of both Popes Paul VI and John Paul II. While Paul VI re-centred evangelisation as the baptismal responsibility of all Christians[304], the concept

---

302   Gittins, 1993, p. 38.
303   Bevans et al. (2015), p. XIV.
304   Evangelii Nuntiandi, 1975.

of 'a new evangelisation' gained currency under John Paul II. Recognising the need for new ways, strategies and commitment, he promoted the Holy Spirit as the 'principal agent of the new evangelisation'.[305] In 2005, the publication of Pope Benedict's XVI'S first encyclical (*Deus Caritas Est*) provided a further lens for the present ecclesial understanding of evangelisation drawing on key terms from the Church's earliest times: *leitourgia* (worship), *marturia* (witness), *kerygma* (proclamation) and *diakonia* (service). Two other functions to be included in this framework are *didache* (teaching) and *koinonia* (community).

However, while there can be a tendency to prescribe evangelising activities when using the term evangelisation, it has always had a broader understanding:

> *In the church's work of evangelisation there are undoubtedly certain elements and aspects which are deserving of special attention. Some of these are indeed of such importance that they may at times be regarded as constituting in themselves the whole of evangelisation ... But no such defective and incomplete definition can be accepted for that complex, rich and dynamic reality which is called evangelisation without the risk of weakening or even distorting its real meaning.*[306]

Even as these efforts to anchor terminology continue, their application to the current local and global context remains complex. New understandings shape and are shaped by the historical-cultural context, or movements of culture, and the corresponding theological knowledge of particular figures, times and places.[307] This means that while evangelisation is understood as 'the church's proper grace and vocation – its deepest identity'[308], and the school has a role in this, there is need to embrace the reality of what it means 'to evangelise human culture and cultures not in a purely decorative way, but in a vital way, in depth and right to its roots'.[309] At no time has the impact of a particular figure, time and place been more obvious than during the early years of the pontificate of Pope Francis who has sought in word and deed to open up understanding:

> *Proselytism is solemn nonsense, it makes no sense. We need to get to know each other, listen to each other and improve our knowledge of the world around us. Sometimes after a meeting I want to arrange another one because new ideas are born and I discover new needs. This is important: to get to*

---

305   Tertio Millennio Adveniente 1994, n. 45.
306   Evangelii Nuntiandi, 1975, n. 17-18.
307   Knights, 2005.
308   Evangelii Nuntiandi, 1975, n. 14.
309   Evangelii Nuntiandi, 1975, n. 20.

know people, listen, expand the circle of ideas. The world is crisscrossed by roads that come closer together and move apart, but the important thing is that they lead towards the Good.[310]

Thus, the understanding has now moved far beyond the idea of evangelisation as conversion to 'the faith' or developing 'the faithful' to preserve and strengthen the Church:

Evangelization is not a call to restore Christendom, a kind of solid, well-integrated, cultural complex, directed and dominated by the Church. It is not an activity set in motion because the Church is endangered, a nervous activity to save the remnants of a time now irrevocably past. It is not a winning back of those people who have become a prey to sin in such a way that the organised Church no longer reaches them.[311]

Further, the shift from a citadel model of church to the web or connective model outlined earlier is further extended in an understanding of evangelisation under Pope Francis to a living in, with, for and through a world shot through with goodness: 'All that is good, all that is true, all that is beautiful brings us to God. Because God is good, God is beautiful, God is the truth.'[312]

Thus, the Post-Vatican II understanding of a synthesis of faith, culture and life is being recovered and re-directed in a quite unambiguous manner, reflecting an approach that 'must not only be organic, but also critical and evaluative, historical and dynamic'[313] and where 'in the process of evangelisation, culture makes the Gospel understandable, and dialogue possible'.[314] The critique of contemporary trends (Church as counter-culture) is giving way to a more iterative dialogue with culture (inculturation). This is nowhere more evident than in the shift in language used: while Pope Benedict XVI appeared to give emphasis to the Church itself as giver and 'the culture' as recipient,[315] Pope Francis consistently emphasises a dialogical approach where all involved have something to learn.[316]

---

310   Pope Francis. quoted by Curran, 2015 p.144.
311   Donovan, 1997, cited in Tinsey, 2002, p. 190.
312   Pope Francis, Address in Cuba, September, 2015.
313   Congregation for Catholic Education, 1982, n. 20.
314   Donovan, 1990, cited in Tinsey, 2002, p. 115.
315   See Knights, 2005, pp. 13-14: 'Emphasis is on fidelity and the discipline of those who communicate the Gospel and the content of the Gospel communicated, and little weight [is] given to those by whom this communication is to be received.'
316   See Pope Francis, 2013 Q and A Session: '... with our faith we must create a "culture of encounter", a culture of friendship, a culture in which we find brothers and sisters, in which we can also speak with those who think differently, as well as those who hold other beliefs, who do not have the same faith. They all have something in common with us: they are images of God, they are children of God. Going out to meet everyone, without losing sight of our own position.'

Evangelisation in the Australian Context of Catholic Schools

In ecclesial terms, the purpose of the Catholic school remains intrinsically linked to the mission of the Church. Education is perceived as a dynamic and transformative process,[317] and the work of teachers in a Catholic school, linked with mission, is profoundly concerned with the formation (and transformation) of human persons.[318] This is expressed as transformational on a personal, communal, local and global level, 'bringing the good news into all strata of humanity from within and making it new'.[319]

In Australia, evangelisation has become a more mainstream term in Catholic culture in general over the last fifteen years. In some dioceses, the implications of a broader and deeper understanding of 'the complex, rich and dynamic reality'[320] of evangelisation has been explored in preference to a narrower interpretation usually associated with (and often confused with) the direct witness modes of 'evangelism.'[321] The publication of the *General Directory of Catechesis* (1997) and the accompanying adaptation for Australian Catholic schools provided by the Australian Bishops[322] has supported this broader perspective. The implications extend beyond catechesis and religious education to encompass the identity, ethos and culture of the school, including its whole curriculum, structures and processes.

The post-synodal apostolic exhortation *Ecclesia in Oceania* (2001) re-iterated Pope John Paul II's call for a 'new evangelisation' and cited the strengthening of the identity of Catholic schools as a critical way in which to action this. *Evangelii Gaudium,* Pope Francis' first apostolic exhortation, frames evangelisation specifically in academic settings as a kind of dialogue. The Pope calls for 'an encounter between faith, reason and the sciences with a view to developing new approaches and arguments on the issue of credibility, a creative apologetics'.[323] For Pope Francis, the best image of evangelisation in a Catholic school 'is of a well-spring where we use tradition to generate new ideas, re-launch our identity as new ways of being missionaries, new meanings of being a school'.[324]

---

317 Congregation for Catholic Education, 1988.
318 Congregation for Catholic Education, 1982, n. 16.
319 Paul VI, 1975.
320 Evangelii Nuntiandi, n. 17, 18.
321 See in particular the impact of the Archdiocese of Brisbane's national Hearts on Fire Conference on Evangelisation, 1999, and Let Your Light Shine, 2004.
322 Holohan, 2009.
323 Curran, 2015, p. 144, Quoting the Pope in Evangelii Gaudium, n. 132.
324 Professor Fiorin from LUMSA in Rome during the first General Assembly of the Congress reported this interpretation quoted by Joseph Curran, 2015, http://www.accunet.org/files/public/Rome%20Seminar/Curran%20Teaching%20and%20Leading.pdf

So, although the Catholic school as an agent of evangelisation has become a focal point for renewed discussion in the Australian context over the last fifteen years, the understanding of what that means has been nuanced under successive popes. The most recent reading suggests a shift toward language that conveys a deeply human sensibility and a broad canvas as implied in the spirit of Vatican II documents:

> ... *evangelisation is to be achieved, not from without as though by adding some decoration or applying a coat of colour, but in depth, going to the very centre and roots of life. The Gospel must impregnate the culture and the whole way of life of man (sic), taking these words in the widest and fullest sense which they are given in the constitution Gaudium et Spes (Evangelii Nuntiandi, 1975, n. 20).*

This direction is predicated on the assumption that God is already active in the world, and that the church is part of the world. Evangelisation is understood as being conducted through word and action and made visible in personal, communal and organisational ways. It involves deep listening as well as dialogue at a communal level with other traditions and faiths, thus respecting the Spirit's movements throughout humankind. It need not be said that the task of realising the missiological vision embedded in the Vatican II documents remains challenging for all stakeholders!

Australian Catholic schools may be a setting where primary proclamation is a pre-dominant need.[325] However, the means and mode of 'sharing the Gospel' is more varied, more complex and more integrated into the life and rhythms of the school community and its operation than has often been understood or affirmed. Evangelisation involves an outreach to students in the formal curriculum and the general culture of the school. It also involves outreach through the processes, values, relationships, structures and curriculum of the school, as well as in corporate witness, in communion with all those who stand in the Catholic Christian tradition. This implies an outward looking, inclusive, and more seamless approach to the place of evangelisation in the Catholic school. It signals a process that is better described as intrinsic in all that occurs, rather than a discrete action that happens.[326]

The work of Australian researchers continues to accentuate the need for new ways of connection with stakeholders, as the data continues to indicate the dissonance between the official rhetoric about Catholic schools and the worldviews of students and parents (and some staff). Yet those who

---

325   Holohan, 2009.
326   For an interesting way of discussing this perspective, see Bryk et al, 1993, pp. 334–5, and his explanation of this process as 'Openness with roots'.

are searching for bridges to be made between the ecclesial call to mission and the lived reality of Catholic schools have found very useful connecting points in the current missiological literature.[327] This has generated four emerging principles:

1. The always contextualised nature of evangelisation
2. The centrality of dialogue in all contexts
3. Respect for the range of forms of authentic responses (which may or may not include joining a worshipping community)
4. The deep engagement of in-culturation.[328]

These four principles find a resonance with the inclinations of Pope Francis. An address to the Congregation of Catholic Education in 2014, again calling for schools to be a place of dialogue and encounter, summarises his position neatly:

> Effectively, Catholic schools and universities are attended by many students who are not Christian or do not believe. Catholic educational institutions offer to all an approach to education that has as its aim the full development of the person, which responds to the right of every person to access to knowledge. However, they are also called upon to offer, with full respect for the freedom of each person and using the methods appropriate to the scholastic environment, the Christian belief, that is, to present Jesus Christ as the meaning of life, the cosmos and history. Jesus began to proclaim the good news of the 'Galilee of the people', a crossroads of people, diverse in terms of race, culture and religion. This context resembles today's world, in certain respects. The profound changes that have led to the ever wider diffusion of multicultural societies require those who work in the school or university sector to be involved in educational itineraries involving comparison and dialogue, with a courageous and innovative fidelity that enables Catholic identity to encounter the various 'souls' of multicultural society.[329]

Yet, the end point of this trajectory of course is uncharted territory. While inspiring and boldly inclusive in the spirit of the Gospel, embracing a new missiology as a most authentic and appropriate platform for the complex context of Catholic schools today may well have profound ramifications. The issue of Church membership highlights this:

---

327   See especially D'Orsa & D'Orsa, 2008, 2012, 2013; Bevans, 2010.
328   Although these principles were identified by Wayne Tinsey in 2002, they have remained reliable guideposts.
329   Pope Francis, February 13, 2014, http://www.catholicworldreport.com/Blog/2929/pope_francis_offers_three_proposals_for_improving_catholic_education.aspx

Church membership defined in terms of regular association with a worshipping community, is a desired but not indispensable response to evangelisation and can be envisioned in more than one way. As Panikkar argues: 'If it be true that "outside the Church there is no salvation", this "Church" should not be identified with a concrete organisation, or even with adherence to Christianity.'[330]

CATHOLIC SCHOOL ETHOS AND CULTURE

We can describe 'culture' as the lived beliefs and values of an organisation expressed in policies, practices, ritual and ceremony.[331] Ethos refers to the deeply embedded matrix of values, ideology and philosophy that drives the dominant spirit or character of a place.[332]

The culture of the Catholic school then, is the lived expression of its ethos. It expresses:

core beliefs, values, traditions, symbols and patterns of behaviour which provide meaning to the school community and which help to shape the lives of students, teachers and parents. In short, culture is 'the way we do things around here'.[333]

The ethos of a Catholic school is a complex mix of tradition and context, where the core values of Catholic education 'are distinctive insofar as they are explicit and predetermined by the religious tradition of the Catholic Church.'[334] In this way, the iterative relationship between school ethos and culture determines the authentic continuity of mission and purpose.

The role of culture in the Catholic school has become a critical frontier. Church documents since Vatican II have reflected a concern to re-establish the ecclesial identity of the school in the face of the 'complexity of the modern world'.[335] However, the disengagement among parents in recognising the elements of Catholic ethos is quite apparent. While the Vatican has been concerned about the increasing secularisation in schools, and encouraging a stronger evangelising thrust, the challenge is not just for stronger promotion of core business: evangelisation, ethos, spiritual formation and Catholic education.[336] The challenge appears rather in relation to a re-articulation that connects with all stakeholders, including parents, students and staff. The language of ecclesial authorities and scholars might resonate with educational authorities, but this understanding of

---

330 Tinsey, 1998.
331 Treston, 1992.
332 Beare, Caldwell & Millikan, 1993; Williams, 1997.
333 Deal & Kennedy, 1982, p. 4.
334 O'Donnell, 2001, p. 25.
335 Congregation for Catholic Education, 1998, n. 11.
336 Crotty, 2002; Holohan, 2009; McLaughlin, 2000.

Catholic education and Catholic ethos does not appear to be in the mindset of parents and students.[337]

In this interplay, while affirming the engagement with culture, the ecclesial perspective has been nuanced. At the same time, we face the challenge of a disappearing ethos where Catholic schools risk becoming 'too expensive for the children of the poor, not posh enough for the children of the rich, but just right for those who want a cheap private education'.[338]

Again, Pope Francis has been unequivocal in his challenge to Catholic school authorities to ensure Catholic schools are open to all, especially the poor and the marginalised:

> Education has become too selective and elitist. It seems that only those people or persons who are at a certain level or have a certain capacity have the right to an education. This is shameful. It is a reality which takes us in a direction of human selectivity. Instead of bridging the gap between people, it widens it. It creates a barrier between poor and rich ... The greatest failure for an education is to educate within the walls: the walls of selective culture, the walls of a culture of security, the walls of a social class ... We cannot go on like this with a selective type of education. No one should be denied. We must leave the places where we are as educators and go to the outskirts, to the poor.[339]

At the same time as the Pope exhorts a quality education to be the right of all children and for Catholic schools to be radically inclusive in ensuring this, he raises the deep concern that, 'Educating that is too focused on the tangible and closes off the spiritual dimension of existence is "the biggest crisis" facing Christian education.' He goes further to affirm a holistic approach to Catholic education: 'There are three languages: the language of the head, the language of the heart, and the language of the hands; education must go forward by these three ways.'[340]

The concerns to which Pope Francis has given voice have been echoed by writers and scholars in the field for some time, and given rise to the terms 'mission integrity' and 'spiritual capital' in naming these priorities.[341]

---

337 ACER, 2010; McLaughlin, 2000 .

338 Fisher, 2006, p. 7.

339 These quotes are taken from an impromptu question-and-answer session by the Pope, Nov. 21, 2015, during an audience with more than 2,000 participants in the World Congress, as related in Educating Today and Tomorrow: A renewing passion (marking the 50th anniversary of the Second Vatican Council's Declaration on Christian Education and the 25th anniversary of 'Ex Corde Ecclesiae).

340 Pope Francis, 2015, http://en.radiovaticana.va/news/2015/11/21/pope_francis_educate_openness_to_transcendence

341 See in particular the work of Gerald Grace: Faith, Mission and Challenge in Catholic Education: 2015. Grace has been a leader in this research field, and his name is synonymous with these two terms.

Mission Integrity and Spiritual Capital

Mission integrity is a 'fidelity in practice and not just in public rhetoric to the distinctive and authentic principles of Catholic education'.[342] Mission Integrity is the compass which constantly directs and redirects teachers, leaders, parents and students.[343] The true north in the purpose of Catholic education reverberates for the common good of all humanity. This is the true measure for Catholic school culture.

Spiritual capital is well described as 'an informed, reflective and personal commitment to religious and spiritual values'.[344] It is a powerful personal resource because it provides a perspective for a larger reality that can give deeper guidance to both judgement and action in the everyday. 'Those within education whose own formation has involved the acquisition of spiritual capital do not act simply as professionals but as professionals and witnesses.'[345] Within the energy invested over the last 20 years in Australia, England, America and Canada to cultivate what we might call 'spiritual capital', two areas deserve special note. These are the areas of charism development and theological literacy.[346]

Charism Development

The Greek χαρις means grace. In this sense charism is the gift of grace to the whole church. And the Greek use of χαρισμα refers to the exceptional gift of the Holy Spirit given in grace by God to certain individuals (charisma) to inspire others in a particular way.[347] Many religious congregations ministering in education from the 1500s onward were founded by impressive charismatic leaders. In the last 20 years much work has been done in the name of those founders to transmit their charism to lay people as religious congregational numbers rapidly decrease. Interestingly, in discussing the effectiveness of the plethora of formation programs built around a charism, Gerald Grace makes a useful observation:

> *If charism is an exceptional gift of the Holy Spirit to certain individuals, it cannot easily be transmitted in a formation program. There is a case for saying that what these programs are attempting to do is to renew the resources for spiritual capital.*[348]

---

342 Grace, in Leithwood & Hallinger, 2002. p. 343.

343 Finlay, 2015, https://webclasscommunity.wordpress.com/category/mission-integrity/

344 Grace, in Leithwood & Hallinger, 2002. p. 447. Grace found during research for this 2002 book that Catholic principals were drawing on a personal spiritual and religious resource which gave them a sustained sense of mission, purpose and hope in their work. He named this spiritual capital, building on the work of social theorist Pierre Bordeau.

345 Grace, 2002 a, p. 236.

346 See Weeks and Grace, Theological Literacy and Catholic Schools 2007, for a full explication of this.

347 See Lydon, 2009.

348 Grace, 2012, p. 17.

The original gift to the individual is now a gift to the whole. Formation programs seek to grow the influence of that gift, not replicate it, because that is by definition not possible.

Theological literacy

This kind of literacy is concerned with the learner's understanding of transcendent reality itself – the ability to think, feel, act and communicate wisely about God.[349] In the 12th and 13th century expansion of universities, the study of theology developed as a discipline combining the wisdom of the Scriptures with the best of the philosophical traditions of the Greek world. Yet while grounded in experience, theology is any form of reasoned discussion about the principles of our religious tradition embodied in its stories, and theological literacy is the capacity to understand both its song-lines and intellectual logic. It reflects, one might say, both rigour and vigour!

In this sense, Grace sees that both experiential witness and theological literacy are elements of what needs to be nurtured in the growing of spiritual capital. Historically, religious orders with ministries in education have been the initial transmitters of charism within the confines of their own tradition and story, but now there is need for:

> a new form of spirituality which needs to be reconstituted in lay school leaders and teachers by formation programs which help them to be Catholic witnesses for Christ and not simply professional deliverers of knowledge and skills as required by the secular state and the secular market.[350]

This concept of spiritual capital articulated by Grace is regarded as 'a major insight or thesis in the context of maintaining the mission and integrity of Catholic schooling'.[351] In the context of Grace's work in general, the efficacy of such capital will be tested most rigorously by the extent to which schools are able to sustain a distinctively Catholic culture within the broader contemporary educational and secular culture.

Distinctive Elements in Catholic School Culture

The foundational feature of the Catholic school is 'to create for the school community an atmosphere enlivened by the Gospel spirit of freedom and charity.'[352] It is argued that there is a distinctiveness in Catholic education that is found in the distinctiveness of Catholicism itself, and which is accessible and faithful. The five key characteristics identified by Tom

---

349 Wright, in Iversen, Mitchell & Pollard, 2009, p. 170.
350 Grace, 2012, p.16.
351 See James Arthur, 2002.
352 Congregation for Catholic Education, 1982, n. 38.

Groome to describe this distinctiveness have been widely used among Australian dioceses as reference points for Catholic school culture:[353]

1. a positive anthropology
2. a sacramentality of life
3. a communal emphasis
4. a commitment to tradition as a source of story and vision
5. an appreciation of rationality and learning.

In developing this picture, Groome argues that effective schools have a characteristic set of ideals[354]: they value people; they are optimistic about people and society; they promote community and relationships; they help to develop spirituality; they emphasise issues of justice and peace; they respect diversity, and they teach critical thinking. For Groome, these embodied values arise out of the 'depth structures' or 'core convictions' of Christianity which lie below institutional expression and which are embedded deeply in the 'ethos and style' (the total culture) of the school.[355]

In an educational culture or discourse in which 'improvement', 'quality assurance', 'stakeholder confidence', 'performativity', 'effectiveness' and 'excellence' are dominant considerations in the making of public judgements, the depth-structures of Catholicism resonant in the writing of both Groome and Grace seem a difficult fit. Such a sense of deeply embodied values, symbols and meanings lived out by a group in everyday and varied expression needs to be profoundly held. The challenge is how this is grown, sustained and made to flourish in the midst of the pressures of the current educational culture as well as within the range of meaning-making options and ambivalence that characterise broader post-modern culture today.

A Focus on Social Justice and Holistic Education after Vatican II

As explained earlier, Vatican II heralded a radical extension of outlook and outreach. This renewal found expression in the activities of Catholic schools, significantly shaping school culture. There have been two specific areas of note in Australian Catholic schools:

• a strong social justice orientation
• a holistic Catholic curriculum.

Social justice as an expression of Catholicity experienced a re-emergence after Vatican II and has gained renewed momentum since the beginning

---

353   Groome, 1996. has been a leading teacher and writer in this area over the last 40 years.
354   Groome, 1998.
355   Groome, 1998, p. 56.

of Pope Francis' pontificate. The pre-Vatican II emphasis on classical study and development of human reason and morals has been enriched by the Post-Vatican II emphasis on social justice in the teachings of Jesus.

> First and foremost, the Church offers its educational service to the poor or those who are deprived of family help and affection or those who are far from the faith. Since education is an important means of improving the social and economic condition of individuals and of peoples if the Catholic school was to turn attention exclusively or predominantly to those from wealthier social classes it could be contributing towards maintaining their privileged position and could thereby continue to favour a society which is unjust.[356]

The implications are challenging at both the school and system level. Post-Vatican II Catholic education documents continued to proclaim to be 'at the service of the economic poor, the family poor and the faith poor (the latter including lapsed Catholics) and those of other faiths and no faith'.[357] The principle of Catholic schooling being for the service of the community and the common good was especially highlighted later in *The Catholic School* (1977):

> Knowledge is not to be considered as a means of material prosperity and success, but as a call to serve and to be responsible for others ... a policy of working for the common good is undertaken seriously as working for the building up of the kingdom of God.[358]

This focus is evident in successive church documents through the next 30 years[359], and in almost every address with regard to mission, culture and Catholic schooling that Pope Francis has delivered since his pontificate began in 2013. At the same time, the premise that this remains part of the core purpose of Catholic schooling is one that is now strongly contested in the current culture by both the changing demographics of Catholic schools, and the increasing focus on performativity identified across Catholic schools research.[360]

Holistic Catholic Curriculum

The social justice perspective gained momentum with the re-iteration in Vatican II documents of the value and centrality of the person in education,

---

356 Bryk, Lee & Holland, 1993, p. 44–45.
357 Grace & O'Keefe, 2007, p. 5.
358 Congregation for Catholic Education, 1977, n. 56 and n. 60.
359 See especially Solicitudo Rei Socialis (On Social Concern), 1987; Deus Caritas Est (God is Love), 2005; Sacramentum Caritatis (Apostolic Exhortation on the Eucharist), 2007.
360 Grace, 2000; Mulligan 2005; Cook, 2008; Lavery, 2012.

and of the underpinning of the whole curriculum with Gospel values. Curriculum was to originate from the mission and not the mission from the curriculum. Thus the Catholic school:

> is not simply a place where lessons are taught; rather it has an operative educational philosophy illuminated by the Gospel message, a philosophy which is attentive to the needs of its students in their search for meaning and life.[361]

It follows that Catholic education authorities therefore must seek to ensure the provision of

> an authentic educational environment, where the value of the human person is affirmed, where knowledge is integrated for the sake of ultimate truths and where the relationship of the human person with God is modelled, as well as taught.[362]

With the 2007 publication of *Educating Together in Catholic Schools: A Shared Mission*, the holistic purpose of education was further developed by outlining what such a task required of the educator.[363] In 2014, *Educating Today and Tomorrow: A Renewing Passion*, reiterated the holistic purpose of education, naming current challenges for all levels of education.

The more recent focus on the identification of a 'Catholic curriculum'[364] attempts to recapture the spirit and substance of this holistic purpose in response to the view that Catholic school curriculums are becoming more aligned to a performance and production culture.[365] Catholic educational authorities around Australia have responded by articulating parameters for this kind of perspective. For example, The QCEC *Queensland Catholic Schools Curriculum Paper*[366] grounds the renewed focus for a holistic approach in Queensland Catholic schools by articulating foundational themes in a Catholic theology and philosophy of curriculum.

The contemporary Catholic school continues to be called to provide a curriculum shaped and informed by Gospel values and appropriate to

---

361 Congregation for Catholic Education, 1988, n. 22.
362 McLaughlin, 2000b, p. 91.
363 The Sacred Congregation for Catholic Education, 2007, particularly focused on the broader purpose of Catholic education and what that requires of the educator. N. 24: 'Catholic educators must attain a special sensitivity with regard to the person to be educated in order to grasp not only the request for growth in knowledge and skills, but also the need for growth in humanity. Thus educators must dedicate themselves to others with heartfelt concern, enabling them to experience the richness of their humanity.'
364 See especially D'Orsa & D'Orsa, 2008.
365 Grace, 2010.
366 Queensland Catholic Education Commission, 2008. This Paper was commissioned by QCEC and developed by Dr Kevin Treston. In this paper a Catholic theology and philosophy of curriculum is examined under four headings: anthropology; epistemology; Cosmology and Catholic Christian story and tradition (Treston, 2008, p. 6).

the needs of its students, providing quality learning and teaching that is relevant, challenging, Christ-centred and values based. Within the broader curriculum, religious education as a discrete part of the whole curriculum has a defined role. *The Religious Dimension of Education in a Catholic School* published in 1988 promulgated six goals for the Catholic school. Again, the pre-eminence of Gospel values within course content, the explicit naming of Gospel values as the inspiration of the school, and the 'precise description of the pedagogical, educational and cultural aims of the school'[367] reflected the new thrust in a total education.

Modelling and Measuring School Culture

The trends outlined above have emerged as specific drivers in shaping Catholic school culture into the present time. Efforts to develop frameworks and instruments to measure the efficacy of Catholic school culture attempt to take account of these factors. These efforts include models and typologies common to all school environments.

Development of Typologies in School Culture

One of the first models developed to explore school culture consists of four typologies, each accompanied by an image to represent its structured relationships:

1. the *club* culture (spider's web – with principal in the centre)
2. the *role* culture (pyramid – with principal at the top)
3. the *task* culture (grid – outlining connections via role)
4. the *person* culture (cluster – illustrating person centred relationships).[368]

In contrast to the focus on principal and staff relationships, a similar style of typology is offered with descriptors of four different cultures focussing on school atmosphere:

1. *Formal* culture: perception of a traditional school espousing traditional values
2. *Welfar-ist* culture: work pressure is low and social cohesion displaces academic goals
3. *Hothouse* culture: focus is on personal enjoyment, involvement and success in the school community
4. *Survivalist* culture: teachers strive to maintain control at the expense of academic expectations and social relations are poor.[369]

---

367 Congregation for Catholic Education, 1988, n. 100.
368 Handy & Aitken, 1986.
369 Hargreaves, 1994.

The development of these typologies in studying school culture in general, amplifies themes concerning the building of learning communities discussed in Chapter 6. Within the context of mission in a contemporary Catholic school community, the language of 're-culturing' acquires a particular resonance. The nature of the school environment and the influencing relationship of leadership are key elements. Let us look at each.

Symbol and Ritual in the Catholic School Environment

In the process of en-culturing and re-culturing in the Catholic school, the place of symbol and ritual is influential. In looking to the future and how the contemporary Catholic school shapes its culture, Timothy Cook, American Professor in Catholic School Identity and Culture, defines Catholic school culture as:

> a way of life' rooted in Christ, a Gospel-based creed and code, and a Catholic vision that provides inspiration and identity, is shaped over time, and is passed from one generation to the next through devices that capture and stimulate the Catholic imagination such as symbols and traditions.[370]

In view of this, Cook[371] has proposed essential building blocks to promote the Catholic culture of the Catholic school:

1. integration of core religious beliefs and values using the school's mission statement
2. honouring of heroes and heroines who exemplify Gospel values
3. creation of a symbol reflecting Gospel values
4. rediscovering of the school's religious and historical heritage
5. socialising staff to Gospel values and mission.

Note that these building blocks offer focus to the symbolic, ritual and relational life of the school, underlining the importance of this dimension in developing culture.

Catholicism is characterised by a strong liturgical and symbolic tradition. Symbols, rituals and ceremonies reflect the ethos and core values of the school and the tradition, and the symbolic and ritual dimension is realised in a variety of ways in the Catholic school. For example, the metaphors, descriptors and language a school uses in its mission statement, parent newsletters, staff meetings and strategic goal setting reflect the culture that operates and permeates the school. Ritual and symbol present in prayer and liturgy convey a deeper meaning about a school's core beliefs and values. Participation of staff in communal prayer and liturgy provides engagement

---

370 Cook, 2001, p. 16.
371 See Cook, 2001, 2008.

at a deeper level in the domain of the spiritual. The presence of religious symbols in the school environment can also provide moments of reflective space and encourage students and staff alike in the development of a sacramental consciousness.

To the extent that culture captures the imagination of the people, it acts as both a window and a mirror in meaning-making. Besides professed truths and the values that being Catholic represents, Terrence Deal and Allan Kennedy note that people are attracted (to the Catholic Church) 'because of its soul, spirit, magic, heart, ethos, mission saga'.[372] To Greely and others,[373] Catholic identity and culture are perhaps more a function of a distinctive imagination of faith than they are a function of dogma. This dynamic operates like a door to the Divine. It finds a home with the 'aesthetic ways of knowing' and the 'ground of being' which are core to a Catholic education.

Leadership in the Catholic School Environment

Catholic leadership is about 'an influencing relationship, a collaborative process that supports a community of believers pursuing a transformational cause'.[374] This aspect of the Catholic school leader's role is variously called faith leadership, missional leadership, religious leadership, spiritual leadership, or Catholic leadership. It particularly describes the capacity to translate mission into the lived reality of the community. The faith leader recognises the influence of mission within the school and is able to build a community of faith around a vision of the Church that is shared by all members of the community.

Chapter 6 has highlighted the critical role of leadership in the broader contemporary educational setting. As leadership theory has moved from scientific management theory to influence and contingency theory, dialogue concerning school leadership has moved from viewing the principal as manager, to instructional leader, to transformational leader. In the general leadership literature, the pressures and challenges of this shift in itself are well documented. However, for Catholic school leaders, the challenges faced are compounded by the distinctly different missional role of the Catholic school leader:

---

372 Deal & Kennedy, 1982, p. 195; 2000.
373 McBrien, 1994; Hellwig, 1995; Greely, 1995; Groome, 1998.
374 Spry & Duignan, 2004. Note: all of the leadership literature is explicit about the role of the Catholic school leader in promoting Catholic faith, spirituality and culture throughout the school community (Flynn, 1993; Cook, 2007; Duignan, 2006; Moxley, 2000; Starratt, 1993).

> *The difference to other leaders however is in the overt expression of the primary motivation that shapes these values and attributes: the explicit commitment to a theocentric and Christocentric view of life ... a commitment to the reign of God in making meaning and in building the common good. Faith therefore provides 'the reason why' in that making of meaning, and it is 'this faith element frame that makes the difference' in ensuring 'the congruence of values and practice' across the whole school community.*[375]

A constant concern for Catholic school leaders over the last 15 to 20 years has been a struggle to focus the school community on values that underpin the mission of Catholic schools. Pressures emanate from increasing disengagement from the Church[376] ; a parental 'culture of performativity'[377] and academic expectations[378]; the impact of increasing numbers of non-Catholics in schools[379]; an ever-expanding list of compliance and accountability duties and expectations[380]; and the general secular culture of Australian society.[381] Thus, even when Catholic school leaders are clear and energetic about the mission of the school, there is real concern about whether this is strong enough to balance the day-to-day demands of the school as an efficient educational organisation in competition in the 'market place.' It remains a question open to vigorous debate. Many principals, for example, protesting the national 'My School' website initiative in Australia and the National Assessment Program,[382] have done so out of this very concern about market competition engulfing the essential vision of Catholic schools.

At the same time that these challenges have increased, the clarity of connection and support between school and parish has decreased. The lack of a functioning relationship between priests and principals has been repeatedly cited as a source of anxiety and confusion.[383]

In addition, Wayne Tinsey's research nearly 20 years ago found that almost half of all Australian priests in his study considered that the Catholic school agenda had little to do with partnership with the local parish. At the same

---

375   Flintham, 2007, p. 7.
376   McLaughlin, 2002; Tacey, 1998.
377   Grace, 2002, p. 141.
378   Flynn, 1993; Flynn & Mok, 2002.
379   Ryan & Malone, 2003.
380   Carlin, d'Arbon, Dorman, Duignan, & Neidhart, 2003; Duignan, 2004; Scott, 2003.
381   Flynn & Mok, 2002; McLaughlin, 2000c, 2002; Treston, 2001.
382   The National Assessment Program – Literacy and Numeracy (NAPLAN) (commenced in 2008) is an annual assessment for students in Years 3, 5, 7 and 9. The annual assessments are undertaken nationwide in the second full week in May. NAPLAN is made up of tests in the four areas (or 'domains') of: reading, writing, language conventions (spelling, grammar and punctuation), and numeracy. Debate centres around possible misuse of the system in rating schools, teachers and students via a narrow view of achievement and progress.
383   For example, Coughlan, 2010; D'Arbon, Duignan & Duncan 2001.

time, school staff in the study perceived that communication between the parish and the school was poor, and that the parish priest was responsible 'in making parish life more relevant to young people.'[384] These views have not altered dramatically since that time.[385] Rather, they have been exacerbated by other trends.

The awareness of increasing disconnection between parish and school, along with the escalating impact of a declining and aging Catholic clerical profile is deeply felt. A consequent shift has been identified in the role of the principal as a Catholic leader. There is sufficient data to argue that with a combination of dwindling clerical numbers and availability, and the continuing pain and permanent fracturing of the Church through the revelations of sexual abuse by clergy and religious, that 'the unofficial pragmatic pastoral leadership of the Australian Catholic Church has slid from clergy to Catholic lay principals and teachers.'[386]

In the last fifteen years, teacher leadership has also emerged as a focus in school leadership. Underpinning teacher leadership is the concept of 'parallelism' which claims that 'the leadership activity of principals and teacher leaders occurs simultaneously and is of equal value.'[387] There are three essential characteristics of parallel leadership: 'a sense of shared purpose; mutualism (trust and respect); and an allowance for individual expression'.[388] The application of these principles within the Catholic school context provides fertile ground for the development of a community culture that is peer driven and richly formative.

> *Teacher leaders therefore build culture by aligning their leadership with the Christian vision and Catholic tradition; they are sustained in their leadership by the trust and respect of the principal; they are encouraged to express their individuality in creative and active ways. In strengthening Catholic culture, teacher leaders create opportunities for the spiritual formation of teachers.*[389]

The power of parallel leadership is confirmed in other research findings which indicate that:

---

384 Tinsey, 1998, p. 39-40.
385 The Who's Coming to School data in Brisbane, 2009. confirms the general views expressed above.
386 McLaughlin, 2002, p. 15. McLaughlin goes on to assert: It is the principal, the Assistant Principal (Religious Education) and other approachable teachers who have been given the unofficial leadership of the local Catholic communities (McLaughlin, 2002, p 11). This view has gained broader acceptance across schools and the Church in the intervening years.
387 Andrews & Crowther, 2002, p. 155.
388 Crowther, Kaagan, Furguson & Hann, 2002, p. 38.
389 Bracken, 2004, p. 62.

the 'practice of partnering, conversing, arranging and developing shared vision' in two different schools were 'powerful re-culturing mechanisms' and 'conversations about learning, shared beliefs mission and vision, enabling leadership that reflects parallel learning relationships and enabling organisational arrangements are critical for sustainable reform.'[390]

It is therefore not surprising that there is a strong call for visionary, spiritual and authentic leadership in Catholic schools.[391] As a result, school leaders are being challenged to be the 'architects' and creators of culture rather than its guardians and defenders.[392]

Application of Typologies in the Australian Context

While Brisbane research,[393] reflective of general Australian findings, indicates that the cultural traction in Australian Catholic schools at this point remains strong, there has been proactive research to understand what it might mean to be architects and creators of Catholic school culture into the future. Of particular interest to the Australian context is the research developed out of KU Leuven Faculty of Theology (the oldest Catholic University in Europe) in looking at Catholic School Identity. [394]

Enhancing Catholic Schools' Identity Project

Australia has engaged with this research initially through *The Enhancing Catholic Schools Identity Project* (ECSIP), conducted in Australia through partnership between the Catholic Education Commission Victoria (CECV) and the Catholic University of Leuven in Belgium. It now includes a consortium of Queensland diocesan authorities, along with other diocesan educational authorities from South Australia and Western Australia. The research has gained international traction (scheduled for implementation in the UK, USA, the Netherlands, France, Germany, the Philippines and Lithuania) and gained affirmation from the Congregation for Catholic Education. In Belgium, the Catholic theologian who had done the original work in this area has been appointed by the Bishops as Director General of Flemish Catholic Education, and is overseeing the introduction of the so-called 'Catholic Dialogue Schools'. He remains a full professor of Systematic Theology while his colleague who further developed this work into ECSIP, Professor Didier Pollefeyt (who is also a full professor in Theology and now Vice Rector of Education at the University) continues with his team in overseeing the approach, support and use of the theological

---

390   Martoo, 2006, p. iii.
391   Duignan, 2004, 2007; Duignan & Cannon, 2011.
392   Cook, 2001.
393   ACER, 2010; BCE, 2009.
394   See article in The Tablet, by Didier Pollefeyt and Jan Bouwens, Feb. 13, 2016, pp. 4-5, 11.

tools in other countries. It is exciting work at the cutting edge in creating the future shape of Catholic schools.

'The normative framework of this research is the ideal of the re-contextualisation of Catholic identity, based on dialogue with plurality and a symbolic understanding of religion.'[395] It is the underlying theology, the practical tools and the future-oriented possibilities marking the distinctive strengths of the research at the heart of this 'Dialogue lens.'

It is helpful to briefly discuss here the compelling and insightful theological and philosophical lens which Lieven Boeve has applied to the current cultural shifts. [396] Boeve suggests that behind the process of secularisation, there are three cultural processes (de-traditionalisation, individualisation and pluralisation) whose interplay affects the way individuals make meaning and construct personal identity. He explains this interplay within a 'theology of interruption.'[397] In response, Boeve proposes the need for a re-contextualised catholic theology, seeing the current challenge as an opportunity to construct a new, deeper and richer relationship with God and one another. Entering into this process is to develop both roots and wings – and in so doing it calls for the capacity for radical dialogue and positive engagement with contemporary culture.

Added to this is Didier Pollefeyt's contribution to a pedagogy for this theological stance known as 'hermeneutical communicative competence'.[398] The Christian Tradition, according to this model, is not viewed as fixed and closed but rather as an open tradition. Every person can participate in and shape tradition and at the same time he or she can also learn from it. This model facilitates five theological shifts in the learner: from mono-correlation to multi-correlation, from a deductive to an inductive hermeneutics, from a closed to an open understanding of tradition, from a correlative to an anti-correlative didactical structuring, and from humanity as religious beings to humanity as hermeneutical beings. [399] The role of the teacher in this hermeneutical-communitive pedagogy involves three critical roles being: as Witness to their own faith, as Specialist in the Catholic and other religious traditions, and as Moderator of the dialogue.[400] To be a Witness means the teacher and leader need to have engaged seriously in constructing their own ideological and religious identity in dialogue

395   Pollefeyt & Bowens, 2010, p. 193.
396   Boeve, 2005, 2007, 2011.
397   For a comprehensive understanding, see Boeve, God Interrupts History, 2007.
398   Developed primarily by Herman Lombaerts, also from KU Leuven (Lombaerts, 2000; Lombaerts & Pollefeyt, 2004; Pollefeyt, 2008).
399   For a comprehensive understanding, see Pollefeyt, 'The Difference of Alterity. A Religious Pedagogy for an Interreligious and Interideological World,' in Burggraeve, Festschrift Roger, 2008, Responsibility, God and Society: Theological Ethics in Dialogue.
400   Pollefeyt, 2008, p. 16.

with the tradition. To be a Specialist means the teacher and leader need to have learned and appreciated the depth and diversity within the Christian tradition and other faith traditions. As Moderator, the teacher and leader need to be skilled in facilitating the dialogue they engender between the different worldviews held by the students, our pluralist post-modern culture, and the Catholic tradition.

Personal engagement in this dialogue is the pivotal factor in an understanding that truth lies in the future as a fruit of dialogue. The Catholic teacher is one who is skilled, confident and has engaged in their own faith-making journey to take students on a communal search for truth, goodness and beauty. The Christian tradition is an open one where our ministry to students is about helping young people discover the meaning of life in the name of a truth that is greater than the easily assumed truths of the world. It is an existential growth with an eschatological horizon rather than an educational learning process aimed at initiation into 'the tradition.' In this way, the approach itself is an interruption to traditional thinking.

Seeking to deepen and broaden the capacity to name and gauge the dimensions of Catholic school culture and identity, ECSIP is predicated on engagement in two stages:

1. *Assessing the identity of Catholic educational institutions* by means of quantitative and qualitative survey instruments.
2. *Enhancing the identity of Catholic educational institutions* by means of practical-theological instruments, promoting post-critical belief and a re-contextualisation of Catholic identity in dialogue with the cultural context.[401]

The first stage involves the profiling of the current context and a large scale empirical investigation. Three scales have been developed for this: the Post-Critical Belief scale, which describes religious coping styles; the Melbourne Scale, describing the theological stance of the school; and the Victoria Scale, which describes the pedagogical stance of the school. In particular, the Victoria scale outlines four school types, and in the mode of other typologies discussed[402] offers accompanying metaphors as descriptors:

1. The monologue school (air raid shelter – a traditional school led by Catholics for Catholics)
2. The dialogue school (the oasis – a Catholic school in the midst of cultural and religious plurality)

---

401   Pollefeyt, 2011, p. 3.
402   Handy & Aitken, 1986.

3. The colourful school (the action centre – a secularised and plural school environment where people relate to each other in a social, engaged way and in solidarity with each other and society)

4. The colourless school (the meeting place) – a secularised and plural school environment where the relation between individuals remains free of engagement or obligations.[403]

The research reports which each school receives show sophistication and complexity in their statistical analyses, and offer schematic and informative interpretations of trends.

The second stage involves the interpretation of the data to devise strategies that customise the way forward for each school or institution. This enables re-textualising into a dialogical community with a post-critical belief system made meaningful and explicit through every facet of the lived community. Within this engagement, Catholic identity is re-imagined and re-enlivened.

While the collapse of religious affiliation and observance has been considerably more advanced in Belgium than Australia, the contextual challenges of the post-modern secular culture are well documented in Australia. The indicators here are that Catholic education stakeholders are desiring to embrace a new dialogical paradigm that sees the heart of the tradition re-imagined for a new time. The data from the Australian schools participating in ECSIP show a strong register in 'second naivete' in the Post-Critical Belief scale, which profiles the role of symbolic mediation and on-going interpretation in assisting people to enter into a relationship with the transcendent reality. The application of the Melbourne scale indicates a strong support within school communities for re-contextualisation as a hermeneutic approach in sustaining Catholic vision and culture. Finally, the application of the Victoria scale indicates a shift toward a 'dialogue' school culture.

In many ways, this work continues the spirit of Vatican II and brings to life the aspirations of the Vatican II documents to read 'the signs of the times' and 'to look far ahead',[404] and many scholars and educators have contributed their energies to progressing this since then. In an age in education where the question about 'how do we know?' is critical, the contribution of the Leuven theologians provides a data-informed, point in time, theologically grounded, life-affirming way forward. At the same time as it provides both

---

403　Catholic Education Commission of Victoria (CECV), 2010.

404　Pope John XXIII (1963) stated: 'Those who have lived as long as I have ... were enabled to compare different cultures and traditions, and know that the moment has come to discern the signs of the times, to seize the opportunity and to look far ahead.' Pope John Paul II (1984) reinforced this with: '... faith will ask culture what values it promotes, what destiny it offers to life ...' Francis continues to look to this open horizon.

quantitative and qualitative data with a preferred direction, it remains profoundly grounded in an open-edged and inviting imaginary that is tethered in the tradition even as it embraces possibility. It is a perspective that finds synergy with a leaning into the world of Pope Francis:

> *Our life is not given to us like an opera libretto, in which all is written down; but it means going, walking, doing, searching, seeing ... We must enter into the adventure of the quest for meeting God.*[405]

Here in Australia, prominent theological, missiological and educational leaders are collaborating now in new ways to take this work further, harnessing the thinking and praxis within our own unique context in Catholic schools and parishes. Formation is at the heart of the way forward. The next ten years will see the potential of this work realised at the growing edge of Catholic education. It is a most exciting development.

MINISTRY, VOCATION AND FORMATION

As the challenge in sustaining an authentic culture in Catholic schools has intensified, there is a growing dependency on Catholic school staff to enliven the ethos, culture and mission. Systemic policy provisions for staff formation reflect an ecclesial certitude. This was first signalled as the Second Vatican Council finished and has maintained its veracity: 'For it is the lay teachers, and indeed all lay persons, believers or not, who will substantially determine whether or not a school realises its aims and accomplishes its objectives.'[406]

It has been no coincidence then that there has been a concomitant focus on both the laity and the mission of the Catholic school in many Church documents since Vatican II. The opening up of the church to the modern world coincided with large numbers leaving religious orders, a major decline in new recruits, and a consequent need to employ ever-greater numbers of lay teachers.[407] Many of the Australian Catholic schools of the sixties had been founded and were fully staffed by religious orders. In Australia today, the presence of members of religious sisters, brothers and priests as teachers and administrators in schools, is less than 1%.[408] For students in Catholic schools in Australia, as in many other English-speaking countries, 'their teachers are now lay teachers, the principals in their schools are lay women and men, and lay people predominate on their school boards'.[409]

---

405   Pope Francis, interview with Antonio Spadaro SJ, over three days in August 2013.
406   Paul VI, 1965, n. 8.
407   Grace, 2002.
408   See O'Donohue & Potts, 2004, p. 469.
409   O'Donoghue, 2004, p. 11.

Consequent to this, there has developed a growing and explicit expectation that the laity assume a more active role in the life of the Church, and this has been realised in Catholic education more than in any other arena.

There are three particular areas of focus in the formation of Catholic educators, and we shall consider each in turn:

Teacher formation
Leader formation
Whole of staff formation.

Teacher Formation

The Second Vatican Council gave particular emphasis to the role of the teacher in a Catholic school. The *Declaration on Christian Education* (1965) defined the ecclesial understanding of this role as a vocation, 'requiring special qualities of mind and heart, careful preparation, and readiness to accept new ideas and to adapt to the old'.[410] *Apostolicam Actuositatem* acknowledged that the spirituality of the laity is shaped by the conditions of one's life.[411] Documents since then have continued to reinforce connection between the personal and the professional:

> The concrete living out of a vocation as rich and profound as that of the lay Catholic in a school requires an appropriate formation, both on the professional plane and on the religious plane. Most especially, it requires the educator to have a mature spiritual personality, expressed in a profound Christian life. 'This calling' says the Second Vatican Council, speaking about educators, requires 'extremely careful preparation'.[412]

Further, formation occurs through interpersonal relationships within an educational community that has a theological as well as a sociological foundation.[413]

Adult spiritual formation for Catholic educators is therefore central to the professional life of the workplace. It is personal and it is professional, tapping into the adult learner's own experience and living that out professionally as part of a Catholic education community. This in turn ultimately determines the effectiveness and credibility of Catholic schools with respect to their mission.[414]

---

410 1965, n. 8.
411 1965, n. 4.
412 Congregation for Catholic Education, 1982, n. 60.
413 Congregation for Catholic Education, 1998, n. 18.
414 See Gloria Durka, 2002, for an excellent introduction to understanding the teacher's vocation.

Teaching as a Ministry

The origins of the term ministry derive from the Greek word *diakonia*, meaning 'table service'. This was the word chosen by the early church to express the New Testament understanding of both ministry and leadership.[415] In the last twenty years, there has been a trend to express the vocational role of the lay teacher in terms of 'ministry'. The understanding behind this is that 'the teacher is called to serve in a special way (through the Catholic school and Catholic education) in furthering the mission of the church'.[416] The ministry of teaching in a Catholic school is thus recognised as a participation in the evangelising mission of the Church. To teach in Catholic schools therefore is to give witness to the community's understanding of its heritage, its culture and its tradition, its teaching and belief.[417]

While the use of the term ministry has gained increasing currency since Vatican II, and it is now common usage to speak of 'lay ministry' and 'ordained ministry', scripture scholars and theologians point to the fact that the terms 'lay' and 'clerical' are historically determined categories, with no basis in the Hebrew or Christian scriptures.[418] John Stott's scholarship details how in the earliest communities the word *apostolos* (messenger) was used for all the disciples indiscriminately: 'In this sense we are all messengers of Christ, and we are the message.'[419] Indeed, Vatican II championed the recovery of a 'total ecclesiology'[420] where the separation of a theology of clergy and laity would be discarded and the original sense of the early community of disciples recovered.

While contemporary scholarship has developed a constructive ecclesiology moving the conversation beyond the thinking of Yves Congar, Vatican II and the two Popes previous to Pope Francis, the re-emergence and persistence of a dualist approach to ministry has been apparent in general perceptions.[421] The sense persists that lay ministry is 'a second string ministry'[422] considered as a lesser status than priests, brothers and nuns, even among a generation who are more theologically literate than ever.[423] This is identified in a new sensitivity to the ecclesial rhetoric about ministry in the Catholic school that proclaims it as distinctive and varied (lay, priestly, religious, professional) with a sense of 'mutual and complementary presence' that ensures 'the character of the Catholic school'[424] and yet at the same

415   Adair, 2001.
416   Mulligan, 1994, p. 120.
417   Refer to Congregation for Catholic Education, 1982, n. 23, 24.
418   See the work of Australian scripture scholar, Mary Coloe, 2010, and Australian theologian Richard Lennan, 1995, 2013.
419   Stott, 2002, p. 18.
420   See especially the work of Yves Congar, cited in Beal, 2009.
421   Lakeland, 2008; Beal, 2009.
422   See Lakeland, 2003, for a full explication of this.
423   See O'Donoghue & Potts, 2004, for research on this.
424   Congregation for Catholic Education, 1982, n. 44.

time appears to lament this reality.[425] Among lay Catholics, this sensitivity exacerbates a strong current of disillusionment with clergy already amid a rising distrust of the institution.[426]

In response, there is a growing interest for either a re-alignment or a re-development of lay ministry with recognition of the centrality of the school community. In recovering Post-Vatican II theological thinking of Yves Congar (1965) and Leonardo Boff (1986), James Mulligan revives the term '*laos*', used by Boff to describe a de-clericalised community, interpreting Pope Paul VI's inclusive call to mission as one where gifts and talents are richly distributed by all members of the community:

> *The new ecclesial reality is that the Catholic school for many is the primary place where young people will encounter Jesus and his teaching, and it is Catholic educators, the laity, who are the evangelisers.*[427]

While there have been notable formal ecclesial initiatives to reframe lay ministry within the existing reference points (e.g. *Co-workers in the Vineyard of the Lord*, USCCB, 2005), there is growing appeal for a completely new ecclesial conceptual structure that takes account of the new ecclesial reality. In other words, the contemporary situation is such that:

> *given the enhanced role of the People of God in the Post-Vatican II Church and the decline of the clergy in numbers and credibility, Catholic education should be reconfigured as a ministry of the laity and new models of leadership are necessary.*[428]

Teaching as a Vocation

Derived from the Latin word *vocare* (to call), 'vocation' has religious origins used in the Christian tradition to refer to the decision to enter a monastic order. The reformation expanded this understanding to apply to all people, with each of us having a vocation that could be enacted in everyday life. Ecclesial documents affirm for lay people the integrative nature of the spiritual life in the everyday:

> *In discovering and living their proper vocation and mission ... [there] cannot be two parallel lives in their existence: on the one hand, the so-called 'spiritual life', with its values and demands; and on the other, the so-called secular life; that is, life in a family, at work, in social relationships, in the responsibilities of public life and in culture.*[429]

---

425 Congregation for Catholic Education, 1982, n. 45.
426 This is a current evident as well across Europe and the US – see Mulligan, 1994; 2005.
427 Mulligan, 1994, p 76.
428 O'Keefe, 1996, p. 178 .
429 Christifideles Laici, 1989, n. 59.

Translated into a teacher's life, this requires an underlying spirituality within a humanising and holistic vision, educating not only for character[430] but also for life.[431] In such a setting, every teacher has a vocation to be a 'humanising educator, to teach with a spiritual vision.'[432] This calling (*vocatus*) is heard within one's being and comes from beyond one's self. 'My vocation (to use the poet's term) is the spiritual life, the quest for God, which relies on the eye of the heart.'[433]

In exploring vocation in the context of a spirituality for teachers today, renowned educator Gloria Durka outlines five characteristics of a teacher's calling. These characteristics of a teacher's calling are that it:

- presumes a sense of adventure to engage the world
- is more than selfless devotion
- is more than a personal matter
- is active and compelling
- is unique in every individual as the inner work of the person leads to the outer journey of the teacher.[434]

And so, vocation is always embodied, unique and individual for each person: 'Such a way of looking at life is a result of our character that has been formed over time. It flows from our soul.'[435]

The emphasis on the outward expression of the inner journey resonates across educators and human well-being practitioners and practical theologians.[436] For both Sharon Daloz-Parks and Parker Palmer for example, vocation involves commitment to others as well as personal fulfilment. This is a process of 'personal and social transformation, venturing and abiding' where engagement with others is grounded by turning 'deep into self'.[437]

The 'deepening into self' influences growth from the inside out since the 'spiritual journey of the teacher is the peeling away of loose outer layers of teaching beliefs and diving deeper into the centre of what calls us into the classroom'.[438] The disciplines of philosophy and psychology offer the learning that one's deepest identity will be found in 'finding and following your bliss'.[439] More than this, the journey in vocation is a spiritual one because 'it is all about your life but still not about a life that is all yours'.[440]

---

430   See Lickona, 1991.
431   See Groome, 2002, for a full understanding of this.
432   Groome, 1998, p. 37.
433   Palmer, 1993, p. xxiv.
434   Durka, 2002.
435   Durka, 2002, p. 10.
436   See especially Buechner, 1973; Palmer, 2007; Daloz-Parks, 2000.
437   Daloz-Parks, 2000, p. 11.
438   Michalec, cited in Simone, 2004, p. 5.
439   Joseph Campbell, cited in Flowers, 1988, p. 120.
440   Carotta & Carotta, 2005, p. 14.

This is such an important perspective. The meeting place of the work one is called to and which is responsive to the world, is framed in spiritual terms: 'The place God calls you to is the place where your deep gladness and the world's deep hunger meet.'[441]

In examining the adult Christian vocation, James Fowler (2000), who similarly defines vocation as 'a purpose for one's life that is part of the purposes of God', brings a psycho-spiritual perspective to the subject of vocation, and critiques it within the changes and tensions apparent in the Post-Vatican II Catholic church:

> ... with Vatican II we beheld the spectacle – truly remarkable – of an international communion of faith solemnly and publicly going through the anguish of fundamentally altering its self-definition and its structures of authority. From a church defined by the hierarchy and its solemn control of scripture and tradition we saw a move towards a church defined as 'the people of God.' The normative images of Christian adulthood fostered by the church became more pluralistic.[442]

This critique spoke to a generation of highly educated, faithful laity, in whom extensive research has confirmed 'a growing disillusionment with the official church.'[443] Fowler's view is that the efforts of popes since Vatican II to re-institute a hierarchical authority has been superseded by a community that has simply grown up and out. Speaking of John Paul II:

> While he (the Pope) has had some success in re-establishing centralised authority and maintaining a male dominated church, this has not been accomplished without the alienation of millions of thoughtful and faithful Catholics around the world whose faith had developed to the individuative-reflective stage or beyond.[444]

This perception has begun to show a shift under the current Pope (Francis). It has nonetheless compounded the challenge for those charged with providing appropriate spiritual formation for staff today: the hierarchical Church's position is viewed as an additional layer of requirements and expectations for a generation with a mistrust of institutional values and authority, and an emphasis on a personal spirituality rather than an imposed religion.[445]

Recognising the current alienation of Australian people from the Church, Australian theologians are concerned with recapturing the relationship

---

441 Buechner, 1973, p. 95.
442 Fowler, 2000, p. 5.
443 Mulligan, 1994, p. 59.
444 Fowler, 2000, p. 5.
445 Treston, 2000.

between the deepest reality of mission in the Church and the deepest reality of everyday lives:

> And yet this 'other thing', this Church-thing, is just what is essential to Catholic identity. Indeed to be Church is essential to the Catholic vocation – to be called to mediate the mystery of salvation, in word, sacrament, personal witness, to the world of suffering. It is sent as a promise of healing into those dark zones of guilt, despair and absurdity, and to offer the bread of life to the deepest hungers of the heart – even if a vocabulary for our deepest needs and longings now scarcely exists.[446]

The question is whether the shift in ecclesial perceptions and response is too late to have any impact on those who remain within the Church or those who work within our schools.

Developments in Teacher Formation

The *Catechism of the Catholic Church* recognises that spirituality arises in the context of an individual's work, life and circumstances.[447] So it is the teacher's work and person which must be the starting point in tending the formation of a teacher's spirituality.

Despite this, relatively little has been done to probe the experience of what it means to be a teacher in an Australian Catholic school. There is, however, a common concern as to the formation of teachers 'with appropriate knowledge, values and commitment'[448].[449] In explicating an understanding of evangelisation, West Australian Catholic Bishop, Gerard Holohan, defined the place of initiatory catechesis in the school as 'an apprenticeship in how to enter into the beliefs, celebrations, life and prayer of the faith community so as to experience Christ. It enables the 'apprentice in the faith' to enter into each experience.' [450]

> Initiatory catechesis is needed by those who say 'I can be a good Christian without going to church'; 'I feel closer to God on the beach than at mass in church'; 'A good Christian is someone who just loves their neighbour. Nothing else is necessary.' I gave up Christian faith because its teachings are too hard'. 'I am a spiritual person, but do not feel a need to belong to a church' – and so on.[451]

Concern for the relationship between the individual's experience and the life of the Church is also evident in the 2007 Vatican document, *Educating*

---

446   See Australian theologian Tony Kelly for a spirited discussion on this (Kelly, 2009, p. 7).
447   Congregation for Catholic Education, 1994, n. 2684.
448   Croke, 2007, p. 823.
449   Croke, 2007; Holohan, 2009; NCEC, 2005.
450   Holohan, 2009, p. 23.
451   Holohan, 2009, p. 22.

Together in Catholic Schools. It includes a call for formation that is holistic and of the heart rather than solely knowledge based:

> *Catholic educators need a 'formation of the heart': they need to be led to that encounter with God in Christ which awakens this love and opens their spirits to others, so that their educational commitment becomes a consequence deriving from their faith, a faith which becomes active through love.*[452]

The focus on the formation of the Catholic school educator is further developed in the Vatican document published recently, *Educating Today and Tomorrow: A Renewing Passion* (2014). Here, again is the call for a holistic, integrated education in a context where 'contemporary educators have a renewed mission, which has the ambitious aim of offering young people an integral education as well as assistance in discovering their personal freedom, which is a gift from God'.[453]

The concept of the vocation of teaching as essentially a spiritual calling nurtured in the reflective self-awareness of the teacher is most vibrant in the methodology of Parker Palmer[454], who is attracting widespread international interest in educational circles.

Central to Palmer's work in teacher formation, and predicated on the belief that 'good teaching comes from the identity and integrity of the teacher'[455], is the development of trust in the individual's own story and inner wisdom. In contrast to the predominant focus on technique and skills in the educational literature, Palmer illuminates the personal dimension of the individual teacher and its central place in the teaching-learning dynamic.

> *The question we most commonly ask is the 'what' question – what subjects shall we teach? When the conversation goes a bit deeper, we ask the 'how' question – what methods and techniques are required to teach well? Occasionally, when it goes deeper still, we ask the 'why' question – for what purposes and to what ends do we teach? But seldom, if ever, do we ask the 'who' question – who is the self that teaches? How does the quality of my selfhood form – or deform – the way I relate to my students, my subject, my colleagues, my world? How can educational institutions sustain and deepen the selfhood from which good teaching comes?*[456]

Formation involves an encouragement of 'creative conversation' around these things. Palmer suggests centring this reflection on four themes: '*critical moments* in teaching and learning; the *human condition* of teachers and

---

452 Congregation for Catholic Education, 2007, n. 25.
453 Congregation for Catholic Education, 2014.
454 See all works of Parker Palmer, but especially: 1997, 2000, 2004, 2007.
455 Palmer, 2000, p. 11.
456 Palmer, 2007, p. 4.

learners; *metaphors and images* of what we are doing when we teach; and *autobiographical reflection* on our great teachers, and ourselves.'[457]

In his approach to formation, Palmer draws a strong demarcation of the 'inner' and 'outer' worlds of the individual. This individualised and bounded understanding of selfhood has been soundly critiqued by those who recognise how it can unintentionally feed into the post-modern focus on the self.[458] Yet, his process of narrative reflection is different from the self-focus associated with the plethora of social networking tools (e.g. Facebook, MySpace). As such it intersects well with the narrative and reflective practices within the Catholic spiritual tradition, providing a valuable way to understand the story of one's life and the shaping of that narrative.

Leader Formation

The Church has given voice to what it sees as foundational in nature of Catholic leaders. It is evident in papal reflections:

> What the world needs now are heralds of the Gospel, who are experts in humanity, who know the depth of the human heart, who can share the joys and hopes, the agonies and distress of people, but who are, at the same time, contemplatives who have fallen in love with God.[459]

It is also evident at the more local level in the voice of the Australian bishops:

> If Catholic schools are to succeed in the mission ... it will be essential that: all those appointed as Principals, Assistant Principals and Religious Education Co-ordinators are faithful Catholics who are ready to embrace the mission of the Catholic school today and to lead and inspire their staff and parents accordingly.[460]

Yet, as aspirational as the conversation is around the spiritual heart of Catholic leadership, there is identified an inherent conundrum for lay Catholics moving into leadership with traditional religious formation models inappropriate for them and little provided in its place to prepare them for such lofty aims:

> In a society increasingly marked by secularism, consumerism and market forces, the need for strong spiritual leadership in Catholic schools is very clear. But it is a daunting challenge. The Vatican document of 1982, Lay Catholics in Schools: Witnesses to Faith, presented some high aspirations when it said that 'the Catholic educator must be a source of spiritual

---

457   Palmer, 1993b, p. 10.
458   Burkitt, 1990; Sampson, 1993; Smith, 2005.
459   John Paul II, 1984.
460   Bishops of NSW & ACT, Catholic Schools at a Crossroads, 2007, n. 16.

inspiration'. Being a personal faith witness is one thing but being a source of spiritual inspiration is quite another. Many professional and highly competent teachers may feel less confident of leading in this area and articulating persuasively the fundamental spiritual purposes.[461]

In an ecclesial sense, religious leadership begins with a profound sense of Mission and an understanding that the Mission originates in God. This reflects the development in the understanding of evangelisation we've already traversed. The responsibility around school leadership and mission is also emphasised in diocesan and inter-diocesan systemic policy documents also previously noted. These spiritual and religious responsibilities are not to be thought of as an overlay but rather as integral to the exercise of leadership within a faith community.

Developing this further, it is the integral spiritual sensibility which comes first; that principals in Catholic schools are *called*; that they are in fact spiritual persons who become Catholic school principals and not the other way round.[462] These attributes brought to leadership 'are influenced and grown through the individual's personal lived faith experience'.[463]

The Catholic school principal of today must be a person who recognises the sacredness of their call, how their task is to develop community and challenge for excellence, and are people who respect their role as being a servant of Christ in the mission of educating children. It is a vocation described by Cardinal Thomas Williams as the most widespread and effective ministry in the church today.[464]

It is clear that this process is highly individualistic, and so the way spiritual and religious leadership is interpreted in an individual Catholic school has much to do with the individual vision and attributes developed in the principal.[465]

While there is considerable variance in expression in terms of whole school identity, there is a conceptual commonality in terms of their translation of mission. In British research, a concurrence of three interrelated aspects of the predominant view of Catholic leaders regarding the special mission of Catholic schools is identified: 'Gospel values, the teachings of Christ, and the nurture of community.'[466] This concurs with similar research in Australia[467]

---

461 Grace, 2000 p. 16.

462 This understanding was first discussed by Cappel, 1989.

463 Drahmann & Stenger, 1989, p. 191.

464 Lacey, 2003, p. 2. It can be argued that this view has become more strongly held since this time.

465 Barth, 2004; Lingard, Hayes, Mills & Christie, 2003; McGilp, 2000.

466 Grace, 1997, p. 162.

467 Lavery, 2012; Neidhart & Lamb, 2013.

but remains at odds with the more prescriptive and static pre-Vatican II understanding of the mission of the Catholic school as 'institutionalising Catholic traditions and doctrinal emphasis'.[468] The existence of these dual approaches remains an ongoing cause of tension in the formation of Catholic school leaders. And we must manage that.

Understanding the Spiritual Dimension of Leadership

Until the fifties and sixties, the Catholic school was seen as a doctrinal and social teaching agent in the mission of the Church.[469] What was offered by the Catholic school was a tightly defined spiritual and educational 'package deal'. The principal was part of a religious order on site; the local parish fulfilled the role of ongoing support and solidarity for schools[470] and parish priests supported the local Catholic school by their words, presence and actions.[471]

> ... this was a clear Catholic identity compounded of Friday fish, Saturday confession, Sunday Mass in universal Latin, strong authority, answers for all questions and rules for almost everything. To a child it seemed that most things were either forbidden or compulsory, and that everyone in your world, from your parents to the Pope, was unanimous about which was which. There was a very definite world that you belonged to, and an equally definite, faintly hostile world outside it.

With ecclesial, cultural and theological changes, Catholic school leadership now constitutes much more than being part of a chain of 'handing on the doctrine' or 'passing on the torch to the next generation.'[472] Catholic leadership today involves a broader desire and capacity to develop a sense and experience of the Transcendent in the lives of staff and students, and an awareness of the presence of a 'beneficent watchfulness' in their lives.[473] Identified as 'spiritual leadership', it is only since 2000 that there has emerged the need to consider deeply and specifically what 'spiritual leadership' is as a discrete function, and how institutions might educate for spiritual leadership. Consideration of the day-to-day school context, and the often nebulous language used to define what such a leader, begs the question:

---

468   Heft, 1990, cited in Joseph, 2002, p. 3.
469   Congregation for Catholic Education, 1988, n. 11, 33, 34; Reck, 1991.
470   Congregation for Catholic Education, 1988, n. 44.
471   Code of Canon Law, 1983, Canons 805, 806.
472   Prendergast & Monahan, 2003, p. 13.
473   Hicks, 2004, p. 2.

> *But what do the less specific descriptions actually mean? 'Leads the school community in prayer' is specific but, 'Integrates Christian social principles into the curriculum and life of the school'?? When the bell goes at 8 a.m. how do you observe spiritual leadership?*[474]

In this milieu it can be helpful, as Marjorie Thompson has done, to identify what spiritual leadership in a Catholic school context is *not*: 'It is not holier than thou, head in the clouds, mysterious, unaccountable, ethereal, pious, jargon-thick syrup.'[475]

Even as principals find it difficult to articulate the essence of spiritual leadership, nonetheless they have confidence and commitment in this area of leadership. There is evidence in American research to demonstrate a common understanding of what it means to be a Catholic school principal and spiritual leader.[476] Findings in Alan Flintham's Australian and British research[477] identified a similar cogency: 'When asked to describe the foundations of their faith, the spiritual bases on which their school leadership stands, two words summed up the responses from principals – "inclusion" and "invitation".'[478] The research of Theodore Wallace also identified a high level of self-belief among principals about their spiritual leadership role. This finding has been confirmed in other research[479] showing that principals tend not only to have a strong self-perception regarding their spiritual role in schools, they also express strong commitment to spiritual mission in taking up leadership positions.

There is a far more uneven understanding around spiritual leadership among the broader staff population, though its importance is recognised. Participants in Kathleen O'Hara's study[480] consistently referred to the significance of the principal being a spiritual role model, visible through participating in and leading prayer and liturgical services, and acting toward others in ways consistent with the teaching of Jesus. However, in another prominent American study to determine how effectively teachers could identify more closely with the Church's mission,[481] it was found that none of the school staff were able to agree on or articulate the mission of evangelisation and the role of teachers in this. Wherever they are though, teachers are more likely to emulate the same behaviours as their leaders in

---

474 O'Hara, 2000, p. 3.
475 Thompson, 2005, p. 4.
476 Ciriello, 1994; O'Hara, 2000; Schuttloffel, 2007.
477 Flintham, 2007, 2010.
478 Flintham 2007, p. 6.
479 Wallace's original research was undertaken in 1998, followed by Compagnone, 1999; Rieckhoff, 2014.
480 O'Hara, 2000.
481 Cioppi, 2000.

this area, even without articulation of it. And this reinforces how influential spiritual formation for leaders is.

Missional Leadership

Missional leadership lies at the juncture of contemporary missiology and contemporary leadership theory. The transformational imperative in Catholic education means that the nexus between personal meaning-making and mission shaping is explicit and transparent in the Catholic school leader. There are a variety of ways to describe dimensions of this area of leadership.[482] This is because in addition to the work in missiology and spirituality, the general development in this area has been heavily influenced by leadership literature on servant leadership, transformational leadership and values-led leadership.

Servant leadership[483] has a natural alignment with leadership in a Catholic context with its strong Gospel connotations. The blending of this with the dominant model of leadership since 1990 – transformational leadership – has provided the theoretical bedrock for the development of missional/spiritual leadership. Thomas Sergiovanni's seminal research on leadership[484] demonstrated that while educational leadership ensures competence, it is the dimensions of symbolic leadership (giving vision, communicating deep purpose, and leading beyond management issues) and cultural leadership (articulating vision, supported by systems, symbols and rituals) that are necessary for excellence in leadership. Research exploring the spiritual role of the Catholic school principal has confirmed the closest links between general and educational leadership theory and the spiritual leadership role of the Catholic school principal lie in the cultural and symbolic, transformational and servant leadership theories.[485]

In the construct of transformational leadership theory,[486] transformational qualities associated with the domain of spirituality have a link to effective capacities for organisational change.

> *The transformational leader creates a compelling narrative about the mission of her/his organisation ... embodies the narrative in her/his own life; and is able through persuasion and personal example, to change the thoughts, feelings and behaviours of those whom she/he seeks to lead.*[487]

---

482   Cardona, 2000; Duignan, 2004; Hjalmarson & Helland, 2011; McLaughlin, 2002; Vaill, 1998; Wheatley, 2002; Woods, 2002.
483   Associated with the seminal work of Greenleaf, 1977.
484   Sergiovanni, 1987.
485   See O'Hara, 2000; also Chambers (ed.), 2016.
486   See Bass, 1985; Frost & Egri, 1994; Moxley, 2000.
487   Gardner, 2006, p. 100.

More recently, the term 'post-transformational leadership' has emerged. It is a values-led leadership construct that emphasises vision, integrity, context, reflection and continuing personal professional development.[488]Aligned with the Australian work on authentic leadership,[489] values–led leadership research gives direct focus to spiritual leadership capacity. Accordingly, an essential characteristic of authenticity in leadership for principals is their own spirituality, a sense of deep meaning from an awareness of a transcendent presence and a sense of unity and relatedness to one another.[490] Modelling authenticity is argued as the most important role a principal has in building school culture and community, and this is supported by the research already noted. The disciplines of self-reflective practice are critical in developing authentic self. These include reflective practice in both personal disciplines (meditation, silence, prayer journaling) as well as interpersonal disciplines (sharing of life stories, deep listening).[491]

These principles and capacities grown through attention to the heart and soul of one's own narrative in leadership and modelled authentically in community, are at the growing edge of current explorations in leader development.

Preparation for Catholic Leadership

Another identifiable trend associates the spirituality of the leader as vital in the maintenance of direction and the sustaining of purpose in the life and culture of the school.[492] Such studies have identified the need for the implementation of personal faith formation plans for principals to strengthen their role as spiritual leaders.[493] Despite what strategies and tools alluded to in the Catholic leadership programs (e.g. reflective practice), a lack of relevant, integrated and systematic formation for the challenges of leadership is a common finding across Australian, American, Canadian and English research.[494] This is apparent both from the voices of principals themselves as well as from those in diocesan positions overseeing the development of principals.

Attributes and competencies required in the Catholic school leader generally span two areas:

488   Day & Harris, 2000; Branson, 2004.
489   Duignan & Bhindi, 1997; Treston, 2010; Striepe, 2014.
490   Duignan, 2004.
491   See Moxley, 2000, for an outline of these elements.
492   The earliest discussions began around 2000 with Kelleher.
493   See Crotty, 2005.
494   Bezzina, 2008; Flintham, 2007; Grace, 2002; Moore, 1999; Mulligan, 2005; Wallace, 1998.

> *... the spiritual attributes that a person brings to the job through a personal faith experience, and the pastoral competencies to create a prayer environment, develop a sense of community service, witness to the faith, and integrate the Gospel message into the curriculum.*[495]

The gap in formation crosses both the knowledge and experiential domains, and is identified by principals as an issue prior to appointment and through continuing principalship.[496] The perceived lack of theological understanding to underpin their leadership is also cited in a number of studies. Australian research in principals' experience and perceptions found there was 'a significant dearth of adequate support for them especially in the religious matters of their responsibilities'.[497] Participants identified this 'failure to assist their on-going religious growth'[498] as a major challenge and anxiety for them. In particular, principals voiced that they had need for continuing personal growth in faith and vision, and were frustrated in the lack of provision for this. These findings are consistent with other Australian research.[499]

In exploring strategies of support, a 2007 study involving principals from 12 dioceses in Australia and England identified self-sustaining strategies that included support from peer networks and parish, renewal through retreat programs and sabbatical opportunities, and the development of reflective space and capacity. The most valued of the support structures were spiritual development opportunities, which were usually accessed individually with little provision by the system or employing authority. Significantly, the opportunity for 'time-out' reflective space in the presence of like-minded colleagues, 'giving an away-experience of spiritual discussion at an adult level'[500] was perceived as more important than the content of preparatory or ongoing study.

> *There was a cri de coeur for the provision of such 'events with a spiritual heart' with 'the opportunity to talk about the role of principalship in the context of the distinctive nature of Catholic schools' (p5). In this, the opportunity for structured retreats and sabbaticals ... was highly valued, particularly in creating space 'to set the problems of school in the perspective of eternity.'*[501]

---

495   Drahmann & Stenger, 1989.
496   Graham, 2006.
497   Belmonte, Cranston & Limerick, 2006, p 11
498   Belmonte, Cranston & Limerick, 2006, p 11
499   Duignan, 2004; Duignan, Burford, d'Arbon, Ikin, & Walsh, 2003; Flintham, 2007
500   Flintham, 2007, p. 14.
501   Flintham, 2007, p. 7.

Importantly, principals have cited their own lived faith experience (as childhood Catholics), their personal and professional experiences in Catholic schools, and their mentors – many of whom were vowed religious – as foundational to their capacity as spiritual leaders. They also believe they are 'more intentional about this aspect of their leadership than vowed religious may have been in the past.'[502] Consequently, while principals perceive their leadership preparation as lacking, they also believe that contemporary Catholic schools are 'as successful as schools in the 1950s in establishing and maintaining Catholic identity even though those 1950s schools were predominantly staffed by vowed religious'.[503] Allan Flintham's findings neatly sum up the need for spiritual formation in growing leaders:

> Their (participant principals) vision is of an alternative paradigm which places the development of leadership capabilities above competencies, 'being' above 'doing', relationships above results, and Christ at the centre of all things, rooted and grounded in faith in Him.[504]

Whole of Staff Formation

While what we do know about the efficacy of staff development programs is not extensive, our understanding to date includes the following:

1. Staff development programs need to be designed according to the backgrounds, experiences and needs of the participants.
2. Teachers as adult learners are autonomous in nature and will have a tendency to resist staff development programs that are mandated rather than those that give them the freedom of choice.
3. Teachers who are engaged in staff development activities need to have the support and guidance from local school principals and/or coaches.
4. Staff development programs designed for Catholic school teachers need to focus more on the contemporary concerns that the laity have in relation to their individual daily lived experiences and levels of faith development.
5. Catholic school lay teachers have a strong sense of mission and dedication to the ideals of *Catholic education* and see themselves as very important in carrying out the mission of the Catholic Church.[505]

---

502 Flintham, 2007, p. 192. This view was echoed in Belmonte, Cranston & Limerick's findings, 2006.
503 Wallace, 1998, cited in Joseph, 2002, p. 7.
504 Flintham, 2007, p. 13.
505 DiPaola, 1990.

Additional research into models for staff formation offers a useful five step framework for ongoing staff development. This framework (below) attempts to make spiritual formation part of the core staff development agenda rather than an addendum.

1. View all interactions with staff as having staff development implications.
2. Make a clear distinction between informal and formal staff development.
3. Build a strong informal staff development program.
4. Set the stage for a strong formal program.
5. Consider specific program priorities in both professional development and spiritual formation.[506]

The importance in prioritising a place for spiritual formation in staff development that is integrated, and at the same time quite distinct from other professional learning, is echoed in the work of Gabriel Rshaid:

> The key to the success of any personal growth initiative is to understand that it must be approached differently from other types of training or professional development. For example, the effectiveness of such activities is almost impossible to measure quantitatively (which is flagrantly countercultural in this accountability era).[507]

Attention to dimensions of growth associated with spiritual formation is also critical in developing effective learning communities: 'Most schools have the goal of becoming professional learning communities. Staff meetings centreed solely on pedagogy and technique, however, do not enable teachers to form the emotional bonds that can truly cement such communities'.[508]

These observations emphasise a holistic imperative in the approach. Importantly, the holistic nature of the experience in Rshaid's study uncovered potential leaders – an unexpected and illuminating result!

> ... the alternate environment of the retreats gave us a different starting point for discovering leaders. It opened our eyes to the fact that the academic and intellectual traits that are conventionally regarded as the preeminent indicators of leadership potential sometimes emerge only after the person has been given the chance to exhibit those traits in a different environment.[509]

---

506 Rogus and Wildenhaus, 2000, p. 159.
507 Rshaid, 2009, p. 74.
508 Rshaid, 2009, p. 75.
509 Rshaid, 2009, p. 76.

So, what we know of staff development programs and ongoing formation confirms the importance of context and holistic learning as the philosophical learning construct for spiritual formation. Moreover, we see confirmation of key themes already canvassed: recognising and supporting teaching as ministry; remaining attentive to the life questions in the teaching vocation; enacting leadership through witness and example; and the nurturing of rich authentic community relationships.[510]

Formation in Pre-service, Service and Succession Planning

Following this, the view has grown over the last ten years that formation needs to extend to teacher pre-service preparation into the future. In 2009, Australian Bishop Holohan reflected:

> To date, our focus has been mostly on accreditation and professional development. As employers, we need to be much clearer in what we ask of our Catholic universities, and of our Catholic tertiary institutes that work in other universities.[511]

Of course, this implies a responsibility for education in employing authorities and teacher training institutions:

> Catholic Education Offices have a responsibility to ensure that all school staff, but especially young teachers, yet to mature in their faith journey, have access to appropriate professional education aimed at nurturing faith 'in an educational, personal and pastoral environment designed for its promotion'.[512]

We continue to be on a journey of addressing how these particular concerns might be met. For continuing teachers, accreditation has been the strategy adopted by most Australian dioceses to ensure that teachers in Catholic schools undertake regular in-service of a religious nature. This generally involves a minimum number of hours of professional and spiritual development per year. There is currently inter-diocesan conversation across Australia about the efficacy of the current accreditation practice. A number of dioceses are currently developing a more intentional approach to what is offered systemically for accreditation in the area of spiritual formation.[513]

---

510 Derbyshire, 2005.
511 Holohan, 2009, p. 37.
512 McLaughlin, 2000a, p. 73.
513 An example of this has been diocesan research undertaken in Wollongong diocese by Suz Marden in 2009 with a view to developing planning on a needs-based survey of staff. This survey highlighted different self-perceived needs between male and female staff and between age demographics. 19–25 year old female staff reported as highly interested in immersion and inter-personal activities while their male counterparts reported preference for course work in theology and e-learning opportunities. As the age demographic increases, across both male and female cohorts the perceived need

The challenge here is in recognising the diverse needs and experience of staff reflected in their life-world, and the need to acknowledge this diversity of starting points in any accredited programming of formation during continuing service.

With regard to leadership succession planning, we can identify a particular set of issues with implications for spiritual formation. confirms other studies in Canada, England and America about an apparent 'global crisis' in relation to the lack of teachers exploring opportunities for principalship.[514],[515] The 2003 *Australian Journal of Education* symposium on the problem of principal shortages gave international focus to available research evidence.[516] The wide and disparate expectations among principals has been identified as a key contributing factor, along with burgeoning expectations and intrusion into family life.[517] Prominent educator Michael Bezzina re-visited all of these issues in 2010, drawing out foundational recommendations to support aspiring leaders and sustain early career principals in the 21st century.[518]

In particular, the challenge of religious leadership has also been identified as a disincentive for Catholic school leadership aspirations.[519] This is particularly illuminated by research indicating that current principals draw heavily on relationships with members of religious congregations for their formation. As these 'cradle Catholic' principals diminish and religious congregations contract, a new generation of teachers and leaders who have had little meaningful connection with parish and no affiliation at all with living out the norms of religious orders, are unlikely to benefit from the 'matrix of sources for spiritual capital'.[520] Flintham notes this as a major conclusion in his research. It is a significant concern that can also be insinuated from the research of Wallace.[521]

---

for reflective retreat time increased and a desire for wide and diverse opportunities for encounter in their formation was expressed. Negotiating grief and loss figured prominently in the 26-65+ female and the 36-65+ male cohort.

514 ACU Leadership Succession Project, D'Arbon, Duignan & Duncan, 2001; ACSP Leadership Succession Survey, Lacey, 2003.
515 Lacey coined this term in 2003, p. 2. The view remains a prevalent one.
516 D'Arbon, Duignan & Duncan, 2002; Carlin, d'Arbon, Dorman, Duignan, & Neidhart, 2003; Scott, 2003.
517 Barty, Blackmore, Sachs & Thomson, 2005.
518 Bezzina, 2010. The 3 key recommendations involve mentoring and role modelling by experienced principals, the collaboration of all stakeholders in removing obstacles and structural impediments; and the introduction of specific programs to include elements that address current perceptions of impediments.
519 Crotty, 2005.
520 Grace, 2003, p. 237.
521 See Wallace, 1998: Crotty, 2006 & Belmonte, 2006 .

There is a major conflict in a system of schooling that exists to nurture the faith of young people, yet it fails to realise and address the fact that the traditional spiritual capital of Catholic school leadership is likely to decline. The renewal of spiritual capital therefore becomes a critical question for the continuance of the distinctive purpose of Catholic schools in the future.[522]

In addressing this concern, we can identify three areas for strategic focus:

- broader opportunities for spiritual (and theological) development;
- early identification and spiritual mentoring of aspiring leaders;
- and the development of new Catholic school leadership constructs.

Noting the need for growing the 'soul' of leadership, there is an appetite for broader strategies than formalised accredited programs in the selection, screening and training of future Catholic school principals.[523] Educator and researcher Leonie Crotty calls for more diverse opportunities for religious and theological development, and 'expanded processes and strategies that constitute accreditation for all teachers to teach in the Catholic school'.[524] This suggestion is relevant in the current environment in that it reflects a long-term, organisationally contextual recommendation responsive to both vision and reality.

The active identification and spiritual mentoring of potential leaders is also an avenue attracting interest, as research mounts around the importance of the inner capacities of the principal for promoting both the Catholic ethos and culture of the school, and the embedding of spiritual formation in staff.[525] Successful leadership in Catholic schools is strongly influenced by the cultural and spiritual capital that a principal brings to a school. It signifies the fundamental importance of appointing principals who are not only professionally competent, but spiritually mature also.

So the strategy of early mentoring is seen as a way of building in this spiritual capital, and the issue continues to have energy at significant Catholic leadership gatherings around the country.

If school leadership is going to assume wider religious leadership then persons need to be identified who, alongside possessing administrative capacity, are also grounded in faith, possessing spiritual maturity, a vocational sensibility and the awareness of ecclesial responsibility. Such persons obviously don't come ready packaged! Such persons, identified by potential, require

---

522 Belmonte, Cranston & Limerick 2006, p. 9.
523 Bolman & Deal, 2001; Killeen, 1997.
524 Crotty, 2006, p. 793.
525 Bracken, 2004; Flintham, 2007; Bezzina, 2010.

sustained formation and requisite education. Both focussed theological and spiritual formation are required.[526]

This has stirred recommendations from principals' feedback which bear serious reflection:

Potential principals should be spotted young, grown, nurtured and affirmed by the school and diocese. National preparation programs should be 'translated' into the language and context of faith. The increasingly shallow pool of candidates secure in the background of faith and its expression should be addressed by 'remedial opportunities' for spiritual formation and development prior to taking up principalship. Selection processes should focus more upon 'being' rather than 'doing': 'the heart as well as the hoops of headship'.[527]

Finally, we see the need to explore different future scenarios for Catholic leadership. These include shifting to a new paradigm of leadership integrating formation into professional learning at all stages and giving the development of spiritual leadership high priority in the identifying of future leaders and their preparation.[528] While the shape of new leadership constructs is not defined, the need for new paradigms of leadership development is part of the broad conversation during a period of recognised change:

Within this current 'liminality' new styles of leadership for the Church in Australia will emerge, and these new styles will have direct implication for the way in which leadership of our schools is imagined ... School leadership will, more and more, need to be seen as religious leadership. This will demand persons who are deeply conscious not only of their own vocation for leadership but also highly aware of the vocation of the Catholic school community, and yet, at the same time, of the relative and participative place of the school community in the wider evangelical mission.[529]

Integrating formation into professional learning programs at all levels is a strategy that invites a range of possibilities. 'Regular strategic planning' in spiritual development, and the provision of more structured, targeted, protected and even mandated opportunities for principal spiritual formation and growth, are two areas of focus. Another is the integration of the three aspects of the spiritual role identified in our exploration (being, knowing and doing) into any planned framework for spiritual leadership. This has strong advocacy. Building on research by James Sarros for example, Patrick

---

526   Ranson, 2006, p. 421.
527   Flintham, 2007, p. 3.
528   See Ranson, 2006; Spry & Duignan, 2004; Branson, 2004, Gowdie, 2012, 2016.
529   Ranson, quoted in NCEC, 2005, p. 9.

Duignan declares that 'formation programs for leaders in catholic schools need to focus on the heart and soul of leadership as well as on its cognitive and intellectual aspects'.[530] The outcome is the development of authentic witness. This kind of formation is highly valued by school leaders:

> *Of more importance to us as Principals of Catholic schools is the spiritual, moral and ethical framework that underpins the use of these types of skills ... What we really value is transparent not in the good times but in the bad. That is when we act from a heart informed by an integrated faith/ spirituality.*[531]

And there is rising interest in pursuing new understandings of leadership that give a much stronger focus to the spiritual heart of leadership. Moreover, this is recognised as fundamental to sustainability of authentic Catholic schools into the future:

> *If Catholic schools are to continue to be distinguished by their strong faith communities and not become private schools characterised as schools of academic excellence and a religious memory, attention must be given to faith leadership and how it is being developed in school leadership.*[532]

Within the changing landscape of Catholic schooling, then, the spiritual formation of staff is intimately connected to and influenced by shifts in the ecclesial, theological and cultural landscape which influence understandings of mission, ethos and vocation. In an era of unprecedented change, the greatest challenge lies is imagining and undertaking the preservation and enhancement of the school's Catholic mission and culture for future generations. Everything points to the need for intentional and conscious approaches to staff formation for mission. While a range of strategies and directives have emerged, perhaps the essential challenge is to design formation that is rooted in tradition, future oriented, responsive to the present, and thus able to make sense of the 'mixed signals emanating from our social and ecclesial context'.[533]

---

530 Duignan, 2002, p.176.
531 Spry, 2004, p. 21.
532 Wallace, 2000, cited in Earl, 2005, p. 513.
533 Mulligan, 1994, p. 106.

CONCLUSION TO PART C

We have plumbed rich and diverse sources of insight across multiple disciplines in Part C. It is clear that the spiritual journey is always contexted, relational and experiential. Australian culture, and in particular the characteristics of that culture in the demographic profile of our school communities, presents a unique challenge for engagement. The post-modern search that demands individual meaningfulness is undergirded in Australian culture by a fierce independence and value for authenticity. Australian spirituality, influenced by the country's unique history, landscape and indigenous identity, demands a spiritual vocabulary that speaks to its context and experience. Such a lexicon is not found in religious institutions, and while the adults in Catholic school communities appreciate the spirit of the Catholic tradition they encounter in the school, they do not connect readily with the reality of the tradition they encounter in the institutional Church. This is a fundamental challenge for contemporary engagement.

Best practice across associated disciplines, contributing to the challenges of engaging new contexts (post-modern culture) with renewed purpose (personal transformation) illustrate just how paramount is the personal experiential foundation, with current theological thought framing the transformative dimension of formation in new ways. Through every lens – cultural, religious, cross-disciplinary and theological – the need for recovery and development of a new language of symbol and metaphor around God and Christian spirituality is amplified. Diverse disciplines, in the ways identified here, influence contemporary approaches to formation design and praxis that add a depth and vigour previously untapped in the processes of guiding individual and communal spiritual journeys.

Underlying this is a changed and diverse background in the personal and faith context of contemporary staff and in the ecclesial and contemporary spiritual context of their Catholic school setting. The absence of a shared meta-narrative in contemporary culture means that general assumptions about shared meaning are improbable and that the process of individual meaning-making in this setting is complex and varied.

The broad and deep work in adult education illuminates the strategic factors in growing and implementing spiritual formation in a systemic setting. These include the professional and community dynamics of adult learning and staff development; the importance of the connection to the workplace; the aesthetic, experiential and service learning dimensions of holistic adult learning approaches; and the integration of characteristics of change education in adult learning and how this interplays with critical mass theory to effect transformative and sustainable change. The role of leadership in providing witness, purpose and generating a culture of trust within a group of learners or staff has emerged as central. Moreover, the life-wide, life-long context of all adult learners presents opportunity and challenge for the development of appropriate formation experiences. Finally, developments in reflective practice and the dynamics of group culture also point to a strong interface with key aspects of spiritual formation in the religious context.

Finally, the fragmenting of the ecclesial and cultural fabric challenges traditional assumptions about purpose and identity for those involved in all Catholic ministries, with understanding around the core lexis of mission and evangelisation having wide variance across key stakeholders. But the same thinking and research also indicates a strong and positive alignment between leadership, vocation and the role of the Catholic school as a place of transformative vision. The developing language and imagining that underpins a contemporary missional vision of Catholic schools is a rich resource for staff formation.

Formation needs to be both integrated into the everyday school context and separated for specific attention. There is advocacy for the connective and integrative holistic approach embraced by those exploring appropriate formation in contemporary settings: for a meaning-making around formation for mission that echoes a head, heart and hands approach.

Finally, the urgency of leadership formation is apparent. The close links evident between the general leadership literature, the educational leadership literature and the spiritual leadership role of the Catholic school principal lie in the cultural and symbolic, transformational, and servant leadership theories. The importance of leadership context and integration intersect across the arc of our ruminations to create a fertile environment for addressing the challenge of spiritual formation for Catholic school educators. The harnessing of best practice in holistic education, staff development and learning communities has the potential to maximise strategic influence in the school context. An appreciation of emerging thinking in understanding mission, purpose and vocation has the potential to re-imagine ways of integrating formation into the professional and personal context of staff. And an understanding of the role of leadership in creating environments of learning, Catholic ethos and community, has the potential to develop an intentionality around formation that animates the self who leads, as well as the community who is led.

In Part D, we build on our learnings and the key levers emerging from the range of models and approaches to formation described in Part B. In adding to this from the diverse scholarship at the intersection of the life work and faith worlds of the Catholic educator (in Part C), we turn our attention to the presentation of a formative and transformative new model for staff formation today.

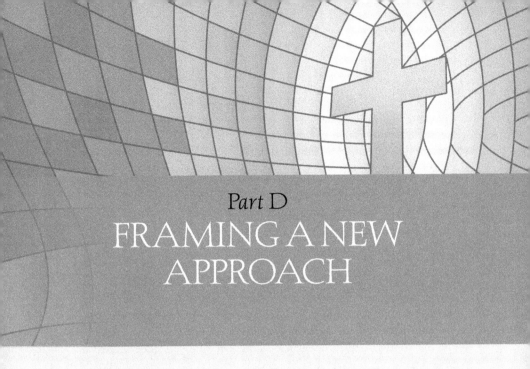

Part D

FRAMING A NEW APPROACH

'*Were not our hearts gradually catching fire within us ...*'

(Luke 24:32)

INTRODUCTION TO PART D

Part D presents the harvest of the multi-disciplinary scholarship, best practice and range of current models explored in Parts B and C. The result is the offering of a contemporary model of mission formation for Catholic educators and leaders, along with design principles for implementation, that meet the three fundamental criteria for authentic and effective formation in any systemic setting:

- To be personally meaningful
- To be ecclesially faithful
- To be strategically effective.

Embedded in the frame of this new Model are the five levers emerging from the models discussed in Part B. More than this, however, the generation of this model offers a cohesive response to meet the challenge of a formation model at the intersection of the life, work and faith worlds in the contemporary Australian Catholic educational context explored in Part C.

Part D has three chapters. Chapter 8 outlines the Model and its key elements. Chapter 9 identifies and explains the Principles of Implementation that are key in applying the Model to the Catholic educational context. Chapter 10 provides a snapshot of this new model applied in a real-life context.

8

TRANSFORMING ENCOUNTERS: MISSION FORMATION FOR CATHOLIC EDUCATORS

Here we harness the valuable learnings and strong elements that we have seen emerge. The religious life model of formation for example, while no longer an appropriate, sustainable framework in its traditional form, nevertheless offers valuable foundational design elements to be considered for a new context. Similarly, elements of approach and structure from the other models make useful contributions to our current setting. The theory and praxis in educational leadership and professional learning also offers important perspectives for how we might effectively implement formation in the Catholic school setting. The theological scholarship points the way to how we underpin formation to grow faithfully and imaginatively in a post-modern and post-ecclesial world.

Let us now look at the new Model and its key features.

A NEW MISSION FORMATION MODEL

Transforming Encounters, this new Mission Formation Model, contemporises core elements of the religious life model along with learnings from other current approaches. It also reflects the convergence of theological and missiological thinking, conceptual understanding and best practice to provide both alignment with the tradition, and a new framing of the formation journey that resonates with the context of Catholic school staff today.

Figure 8.1 presents the Model in graphic form. It highlights the strong theological base which must underpin the work of formation today. This is named as a contemporary Christology and Missiology and is currently opening up a new imaginary and a new language of God and the spiritual life.

You will also recognise in the Defining Features of the Model (and footnotes) key learnings from the scholars, practitioners and discussions in Parts B and C.

FIGURE 8.1: TRANSFORMING ENCOUNTERS:
A MISSION FORMATION MODEL FOR CATHOLIC EDUCATORS (GOWDIE, 2012)

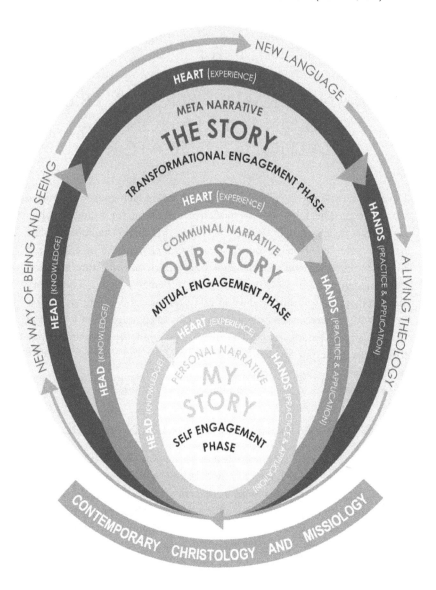

Story as a metaphor becomes the unifying motif, reflective of the holistic and narrative dimensions of the spiritual journey referred to by key writers in the field, in the Catholic Christian tradition, and in the contemporary world.[1]

---

1   O'Murchu, 1997; Palmer, 1999; Rohr, 2008.

While it is a staged model, it adopts the dynamic of the spiral models[2] in an organic process of development. This methodology acknowledges the starting point of the individual (My Story), connects to the communal story (Our Story) and into the God narrative (The Story). In doing so, it accommodates the iterative nature of the spiritual journey as the self-engagement phase is constantly re-visited and re-calibrated. Finally, the model signals an approach that is holistic in intention, operative at each phase, and cognisant of individual difference and the unique journey for each person.

DEFINING FEATURES OF THE TRANSFORMING ENCOUNTERS MODEL

The narrative frame of the Model embraces ten key features that weave together in a way that provides both coherent direction and respectfulness of individual journey.

1. The model allows for, but does not prescribe developmental steps or set pathways. There is flexibility in the process accommodating points of catalyst and points of rest.[3]
2. It is a theologically-based and person-centred model. The theological underpinning cascades through meaning-making, while the meaning-making remains centred on the person and the process, rather than content or outcome. This is about respecting people where they are, and making that place the beginning place, and ensuring there is a line of sight between their personal meaning-making and their formative pathway.
3. The model begins with the participants' engagement with their own stories (My Story). This recognises that participants come to the process with their own story, community and personal spirituality. This self-engagement phase allows participants in the spiritual journey to 'know their own story'.
4. The mutual engagement phase (Our Story) recognises the importance of community in how learning and growth takes place. This is apparent across the educational literature, as well as being a primary tenet of Christian spirituality.[4]

---

2 Korthagen, 2004; Wilber, 2006.
3 Shultz & Sandage, 2006.
4 See Rosov, 2001, for learning in community; Senge, 1990, for educational literature; Schneiders, 2000 for Christian spirituality.

5. The transformative engagement phase reflects the experience of the unitive or Oneing,[5] universalising,[6] deep connection,[7] or the opening[8] phase for the individual. Here, 'the pieces fall together' in an experience of conversion[9] or mystery.[10] Theologians recognise the heart of this moment as an experience of profound love. It is a connection to the God meta-narrative (The Story) that signifies a self-identified inner change or shift, reflected in behaviour and outlook. This nurtures a new way of being and seeing – a new language – and because of this, a living theology (transformation, integration, recreation). It is in this phase that the individual realises a sense of being 'the fifth gospel.'[11]

6. The three narrative or 'Story' phases operate in an iterative manner. Thus the narrative builds in a developmental way from self-engagement (My Story)[12] through mutual engagement (Our Story) to transformative engagement (The Story), always revisiting and re-framing the ground of being in self-engagement within a constant dynamic of individual growth.

7. In each phase, the core elements of the formation process operate in a holistic way: a 'head, heart and hands' engagement,[13] allowing for diverse ways of encounter and learning in adults.[14] This approach draws on traditional elements of spiritual formation. At the same time, it reflects the literature on holistic learning and the primacy of experiential learning in formation, acknowledging different points of entry and different ways of learning. Giving value to experience as well as knowledge in the formation process, and the discipline of practice in everyday life, the steps of practice/application take the inner journey out into the world: a core element in traditional Christian formation[15]: 'Formation must be more than just an intellectual exercise of the head. It must be of the heart and hands as well: prayer, contemplation, activity leading to justice and a love for the poor.'[16]

---

5   Hide, 2004.
6   Fowler, 1981.
7   Kessler, 2000.
8   Wilber, 2006.
9   Lonergan, 1972.
10 Rahner, 1973.
11 Schillebeekx, 1990.
12 Remembering Westerhoff, 1980.
13 Groome, 2002; USCCB, 2005.
14 Huitt & Robbins 2003; Kessler, 2000.
15 Hide, 2004; O'Donoghue & Potts, 2004; Schneiders, 2000.
16 Mulligan, 2005, p. 240.

8. The formation process is dynamic and ongoing as the 'lifelong learner' grows in engagement with the 'lifelong Creator'. This is indicated in the Model by the wraparound process of 'learning to be and see with new eyes', understanding 'a new language' and articulating it and living a new theology as relationship with God creates a re-imagined understanding.[17] Thus, change, subtle or dramatic, occurs as the transformative insight impacts upon self-engagement and mutual engagement.

9. The vocational connection to Catholic education is woven through the phases from the beginning – it is part of participants' own stories.[18] Participants situate their work and calling in the wider story of school community and Church, and in the wider mission of God.[19]

10. Finally, this new narrative Model structures reflective praxis as an inbuilt dimension. Theological reflection or 'doing theology' is the pre-eminent practice here.[20] This is built developmentally on the skills of self – reflection (learning how to self-companion), as well as the practices of peer companioning and leader companioning.[21] The Model would therefore appropriately utilise, in part, a group retreat context[22] where the process dynamics of the individual, small group and whole group can be applied. These practices are then applied in a systematic way back in the everyday life and responsibilities of the school setting.

Conclusion to Chapter 8

The *Transforming Encounters* Model responds to the complex challenges of staff formation in our contemporary context. But it also maintains the dynamism of the authentic formation process and illuminates one of our most powerful and formative Gospel narratives – the Emmaus 'way': a journey that still asks for a head, heart and hands response; a journey where we only make sense of the bigger story through our own story; and as disciples of Jesus, a journey where we learn who we are through the eyes of each other. And in a sacred company that will take us all the way home.

---

17   Doherty, 2008; Hide, 2004; Lonergan, 1972.
18   Shimabukuro, 2001.
19   Brookfield, 1995; Earl, 2007.
20   See D'Orsas, 2013, pp. 232-43, for a review of basic process and approach.
21   Kinast, 1996; Mulligan, 2005; Zanzig, 2004; Gowdie, 2012.
22   Palmer, 1999.

9

PRINCIPLES OF IMPLEMENTATION

It is helpful to have a model that crystalises relevant perspectives into a new and cohesive way of understanding. And I hope the *Transforming Encounters* Model resonates for you in your own work and experience in that way. However, just as important is the way a model and approach is implemented!

The external conditions in which we find ourselves today demands that the approach to implementation also meets other critical criteria besides a cohesive personal meaning-making. In particular, implementation needs to develop ongoing sustainability in order that spiritual capital is not just maintained, but grown. Further, the organisational sophistication of Australian Catholic education demands any implementation of mission formation to be mindful of strategies for systemic effectiveness as well as individual growth. Let us examine the design principles for implementation. Once again, you will recognise the line of sight from scholarship and practice explored in Parts B and C.

Effective implementation of staff formation for Catholic educators and leaders and their school communities is fostered most strongly by:

1. A Culture of Participation
Formation is fostered through a sustained invitational approach that develops a culture of participation.

2. Connection to Vocational Context
Formation is most effective and sustained when it is contexted in the everyday personal and professional vocational reality of the Catholic educator and leader.

3. A Holistic Design
Formation is powerfully facilitated by a 'head, heart and hands' experiential and holistic approach predicated on a positive anthropology of the human person. A contemporary holistic design is therefore person-centred, purposeful and inclusive of different engagement pathways.

4. Time

Spiritual formation requires inclusion of chronological time away from the school/office/ work environment, facilitating a unique qualitative experience of time. This 'kairos' time experience is fundamental to growth and sustainability.

5. Connecting with Tradition

In the current context, the contemporising or re-contextualisation of key elements of traditional Catholic formation creates a powerful conduit for connection and meaning-making. These ways of connecting are multi-targeted, multi-layered and multi-modal.

6. Companioning

Formation has greater sustainable influence when individual confidence and capacity is supported by a core group sharing vision and praxis. This involves companioning – of self and others, reflective of best practice in spiritual direction, adult learning and change facilitation.

7. Modelling in Community

Authentic modelling of individual learnings and shared experience in formation is a transparent and powerful catalyst within community.

8. Strategic Alignment

Spiritual formation has sustained influence when it is connected to the language, structures and processes of mission and vision, annual goal setting and strategic renewal.

9. Engagement of School Leadership

School leadership that reflects an authentic engagement in spiritual formation is critical for the effective embedding of staff formation, and the growing of spiritual capital and mission integrity in the school culture.

10. Theological Underpinning

Formation that is anchored in a clear theological foundation reflecting a sound re-contextualist and Post-Vatican II stance captures a strong alignment in communal meaning-making.

We can also group these Principles of Engagement in terms of those that maximise individual spiritual growth and those that maximise community engagement. Let us examine them as such.

PRINCIPLES OF IMPLEMENTATION THAT MAXIMISE INDIVIDUAL GROWTH

Implementation Principle 1: A Culture of Participation

Formation is fostered through a sustained invitational approach that develops a culture of participation.

Catholic educators today enter the formation journey from a range of personal points of perspective and experience. The general understanding that spiritual formation must be invitational is now well accepted.[23] Findings with regard to a sustained sense of invitation are less well documented, but the most specific studies point to this aspect in the ongoing process of formation being pivotal rather than incidental.[24]

The variety of research in adult learning theory and practice underlines the influence of situational factors on the type of instruction an adult learner seeks.[25] Thus, an adult learner may relinquish control over the learning situation to the 'session leader', and still remain a responsible and self-directed learner because the decision to do so for a particular kind of learning has remained theirs to make.

Three aspects can be identified which contribute to sustained individual commitment.

- Clarity of boundaries
  As well as providing some simple and direct rules of engagement, the effect of 'boundary markers' invites participants to move into a 'performance free' space. While it is the encouragement to do the inner work of negotiating the personal and structural landscapes of self and school that embeds change, the reality is that teachers faced with any kind of professional learning are likely to implement only what they absolutely have to and 'once their classroom door swings shut they tend to return to their own ways'.[26] Thinking and reflecting in deep personal and systematic ways about the teacher's spiritual perspective as an

---

23 Bevans, 2006; Crotty, 2005; Mulligan, 1994; Treston, 2001; Wright, 2002; Hughes, 2009, 2016.

24 See Gowdie, 2012, and Mulligan, 1994. These studies reveal a lack of familiarity among school staffs with a sustained and integrated experience of formation, since their common experience had been in-service and workshop style professional learning. Gowdie's 2012 research demonstrated the impact of the 'invitation' at every step in formation, not just the initial phase. While trialling a somewhat different model of teacher formation, Mulligan was alerted to the reticence of beginning teachers as his program progressed. To address this, one of the 'experienced' participant teachers was given the strategic role of being the supporter of the beginning teachers in the group.

25 For example, see Brockett & Hiemstra, 1991.

26 Simone, 2004, p. 3.

educator in a Catholic school is not part of the fabric of school culture.[27] The clarity of articulated boundaries from the outset helps participants move into the kind of space that promotes this deep reflection.

• Individual acceptance
This refers to the perception of genuine acceptance of the individual's experience on the spiritual journey. While the regard and experience of the Church is often enough characterised as one of coercion and compliance[28], Catholic theology and the Church documents themselves consider such a position as the antithesis of the Gospel imperative: 'The church strictly forbids that anyone be forced to accept the faith, or be induced or enticed by unworthy devices.'[29] More than simply being non-coercive, the implementation approach progressed here reflects a positive anthropology[30] and a recognition of different pathways into the spiritual journey.[31] The acceptance of individual reality and meaning-making as the starting point, and as a continuing principle for their individual journey, paradoxically acts as a catalyst for deeper engagement in the spiritual formation process.

• Sense of welcome
From an ecclesial perspective, a sense of welcome is foundational to the atmosphere of the school community: 'Before all else, lay people should find in a Catholic school an atmosphere of sincere respect and cordiality.'[32] And from a theological perspective, it is identified as central to spiritual formation: hospitality is not part of the gospel; hospitality IS the gospel. It is not to change people but 'to offer them space where change can take place'.[33] Finally, from a practitioner's perspective, 'Hospitality means receiving each other, our struggles, our newborn ideas, with openness and care ... the classroom where truth is central will be a place where every stranger and every strange utterance is met with welcome.'[34]

These experiences of exchange, sharing and mutual recognition are reflected in the term *commensality*, coming from Latin

---

27 Cole and Knowles 2000; Maynes 2002.
28 Knights, 2005.
29 Ad Gentes, 1965, n. 13.
30 Groome, 2002, 2011.
31 Kessler, 2000.
32 CCD, 1982, Part IV, n. 77.
33 Nouwen, 1976, p. 201.
34 Palmer, 1993, p. 74.

(*com,* 'together', and *mensa,* 'a table') and incorporate the concepts of guest (linked to the notion of receiving), and hospitality (linked to the host notion of sharing a table). Allowing staff to understand 'welcome' experientially as well as exploring it conceptually through the tradition in the gospels, and the Acts, and in the fabric of Christian community, also facilitates them to be highly attuned to its presence (or absence) in the culture of their school community.

Implementation Principle 2:
Connection to Vocational Context

Formation is most effective and sustained when it is contexted in the everyday personal and professional vocational reality of the Catholic educator and leader.

One of the key messages in professional learning literature is that adult professional development is most effective when connected to the work or professional context of the learner.[35] The fundamental principles of a professional learning community apply to the context of spiritual formation: an inclusive group of people, motivated by a shared learning vision, who support and work with each other, finding ways to review and reflect on their values, processes, structures and practices.[36] Within this community setting, the vocational contexting allows for three conceptual messages to grow: spiritual formation is hinged on life and system worlds; it is explicitly linked to mission and ministry in the Catholic context; and it involves all staff, through their role and membership of the community.

Systemic surveys and anecdotal evidence in Australian dioceses have indicated that where retreats and formation programs are offered to catholic education school staffs, principals and teachers are generally reluctant to participate. Time poverty and the lack of a sense of perceived relevance are the two key reasons given for non-attendance.[37] Assuming the veracity of the research findings is as applicable for spiritual formation as it is to adult professional learning, contemporary formation must be structured to target the vocational and role context of the school staff community. This allows participants to explore their own identity and story in relation to their role and vocational context, not split from their life context. It can make the shifts from the 'my story' stage to the 'our story' stage, and the meta-narrative, full of sense and immediacy.

---

35   Carlson, 2003; Sparks, 2003; Hough, 2004; Kilpatrick, Barrett & Jones, 2003; Kwakman, 2003.
36   Preedy, Glatter & Wise, 2003.
37   Crotty, 2003.

The correlation between spiritual formation and transformative learning theory and practice[38] is strong. Senge's concept of 'deep learning' as the key to transformational change, and Fullan's work on educators as change facilitators in their professional learning communities, are most applicable in the work of formation in the Catholic education context. The deep learning in participants operates as the catalyst for change facilitation in their school communities.

Implementation Principle 3: Holistic Design

Formation is powerfully facilitated by a 'head, heart and hands' experiential and holistic approach predicated on a positive anthropology of the human person. A contemporary holistic design is therefore, person-centred, purposeful and inclusive of different engagement pathways.

This is a critical design principle when the range of outlook and presenting perspective is so diverse as is currently the case among Catholic school staffs.[39] The head, heart and hands design signals an approach that is holistic in intention, and this has deep roots in the Catholic tradition, reflecting a 'positive anthropology of humanity' and 'epistemology of being'[40] firmly rejecting dualist understandings developed at particular times in the tradition.[41] Further, since the goal of spiritual formation in the Christian tradition is transformation,[42] the holistic program structure, design and process show strong evidence of being an effective conduit for sustained transformative experience, making it more likely for participants to embrace each phase of the formation journey while strengthening their personal spirituality.

Whilst their own teaching practices use a variety of skills, many Catholic school staff (and leaders) retain a 'jug-mug' preconception of content and process in this area of adult learning, with an assumption that the individual's experience and story will be of little focus or relevance and anticipating that the formation process will be information based and doctrinal. Yet an authentic contemporary approach recognises that each person has a different gateway to the spiritual journey that is as unique as they are. This recognition of different entry points into the dynamic of 'head, heart and hands' is very important in the process of effective spiritual formation. There are different ways individuals engage in their spiritual journey[43], and within this the experiential dimension is pivotal in sustaining development.

---

38 Dirkx & Prenger, 1997; Mezirow, 1990.
39 McLaughlin, 2002; Mason, 2007; ACBC, 2007; Hughes, 2009, 2016.
40 Groome, 1998, p. 285.
41 Schussler Fiorenza, 1984.
42 Hide, 2004.
43 Kessler, 2000; Wilber, 2006.

This is not a haphazard approach – it requires both intention and rigour in design and method. The 'head, heart hands' process must underpin each phase of the 'my story', 'our story', 'the story' formation journey. *Head, Heart and Hands* also reflects four steps identified[44] as being fundamental to the formation process – knowledge (Head), experience (Heart), practice and application (Hands). And authentic formation is ongoing, developmental and sequential.

Particular elements of the *Head, Heart and Hands* approach include facets of reflective praxis[45], narrative method[46] and experiential and service learning.[47] This last step, a service element, is intentionally connected to the social justice imperative of the Catholic tradition[48], and is identified in ecclesial documents pertaining to the Catholic school educator:

> The vocation of every Catholic educator includes the work of ongoing social development: to form men and women who will be ready to take their place in society, preparing them in such a way that they will make the kind of social commitment which will enable them to work for the improvement of social structures, making these structures more conformed to the principles of the Gospel ... All of this demands that Catholic educators develop in themselves ... a keen social awareness and a profound sense of civic and political responsibility (CCE, 1982, n. 19).

The being 'for the other' and for the 'common good' reflects the Catholic Christian awareness that formation involves understandings and experiences which promote a personal transformation involving a passion for serving the community. It also demonstrates the uniqueness of this approach in contrast to many contemporary spirituality opportunities that maintain a focus on personal and individual satisfaction and wellbeing. The latter approach is more amenable to the prevailing cultural discourses operating in the reality of Catholic school communities. Integrating the former as a key element of formation for Catholic school leaders. In fact it can strengthen their internal resolve to adopt a social justice lens which, while personally challenging, functions as a potent catalyst for the deepening of their reflective praxis in a variety of aspects from enrolment decisions, to expressions of mission

---

44 Brookfield, 1998; Groome, 2002; Mulligan, 2004; Gowdie, 2012.
45 D'Orsa & D'Orsa, 2013; Kinast, 2000.
46 Johnson, 2002; Kinast, 2000; Rahner, cited in Masson, 1984; Rosov, 2001.
47 Jarvis, 2004; Kenary, 2009; Price, 2008. The importance of this is amplified in the 2012 study (Gowdie) showing the response of participants to the experience of theological reflection confirming the primacy of the integration of orthodoxy and orthopathy in developing authentic orthopraxis (Rohr, 2010).
48 Rolheiser, 1998.

integrity and commitment to a Catholic community culture.[49] This constitutes the renewal of heart advocated in Church documents:

> But education demands a renewal of heart ... It will also inculcate a truly and entirely human way of life in justice, love and simplicity. It will likewise awaken a critical sense, which will lead us to reflect on the society in which we live and on its values; it will make men (sic) ready to renounce these values when they cease to promote justice in all men (sic) (Justicia in Mundo, 1971, n. 51).

The recovery and exploration of a holistic approach is congruent with the contemporary context of staff where a postmodern sensibility demands a primacy of experiential encounter for the individual in their meaning-making.[50] At the same time, Catholic educators will be attentive for what they perceive to be any quality educative approach in the *Head, Heart and Hands* elements, aligning with their own understanding of best practice. This balance is critical for a positive inclination at their initial entry point into formation and in their sustained application within the school setting.

Applying the new Model with its spiral narrative dynamic, three insights are prominent:

- Recognising there are many 'gateways' into the spiritual journey affirms participants in their own journey and sustains their engagement.
- Being able to enter the journey through a particular personal 'gateway' encourages the individual to negotiate all steps of the formation process in each phase.
- Affirming the spiritual journey honours the whole person, and their integration and re-creation allows a way for both the apophatic and kataphatic pathways of the tradition to be absorbed into the approach.[51]

---

49 Crotty, 2005, and Flintham, 2007, confirm in their studies that the demands of the social justice imperative so fundamental to authentic Catholic leadership can prove too challenging for the current Catholic school context. However, Gowdie's 2012 research confirms the deep impact of the justice experiential dimension when integrated into leadership formation programs.

50 Hughes, 2010; Tacey, 2003.

51 This illuminates the efficacy of the approach generated from adult learning theory (Feldman, 2000; Heifitz & Laurie, 2001; O'Brien, 2004; Oliver & Marwell, 2002; Starratt, 2004) and theology (Bevans, 2009; Fischer, 1989; Hide, 2004; Kelly, 2009; Lonergan, 1971; Rahner, 1973; Schneiders, 2003) for spiritual formation.

Implementation Principle 4: Time

Spiritual formation requires inclusion of chronological time away from the school/ office/ work environment, facilitating a unique qualitative experience of time. This 'kairos' time experience is fundamental to growth and sustainability.

One of the main concerns expressed by all stakeholders in Catholic education in the provision of professional learning is the issue of 'time'. There are two aspects of this issue: the quantity and the quality of time. Both are pivotal for the efficacy of formation for individuals and in the sustainable impact within the school community.

When discussing the issues around time in the context of formation, it is helpful to borrow descriptors from the discipline of spirituality to further understand the dynamic at work here.

The ancient Greeks had two words for time, *Chronos* and *Kairos. Chronos* refers to chronological or sequential time, and is measured by the clock or calendar. It is quantitative, rhythmic, and predictable. It best describes the pace and measure of the school day and school year for educators. The other word for time from the ancient Greeks is *Kairos.* There is no equivalent word in English. This is a qualitative understanding of time – an 'in between time' or liminal time that is almost outside chronological time. It is to make a space for something unique and significant to happen that would not be able to happen in the normal pattern of *chronos* time.[52]

Quantity of Time

The social history literature gives focus to the concept of a post-modern 'time-poor' culture[53] and schools operate within and reflect the pressures of this culture. All schools are constantly busy places, with new curriculum initiatives, compliance audits and support programs. Staff generally carry responsibility for at least one other area of school life or curriculum in addition to their teaching role. Furthermore, the majority of staff has outside commitments including family. This cultural reality, discussed in Part B as the 'system world' and 'lifeworld', is characterised by the attendant issues of professionalisation, work intensification and overbusyness.[54] Yet even in anecdotal evidence across schools, the pressure of any perceived extra time commitment has been a constant one, and is a predictable challenge for commitment to any formation program.

Some of the concerns about overbusyness are connected to self-identity questions separate from the system world and lifeworld issues. In particular, the educator's self-expectations are identified as a major contributing factor

---

52 Nouwen, 1975.
53 McMahon, 2003; Senge, Scharmer, Jaworski & Flowers, 2005.
54 Branson, 2004.

on busyness and intensification, regardless of how much time they are given for preparation and planning. Other research confirms that the nature and substance of that time is indeed critical to the outcomes[55] Through a different lens on busyness, Thomson, researching the experience of principal leadership, gives voice to the loss of personal and even professional identity for principals, in the pressures of a task oriented culture: 'The change goes to the core of who the principal actually is, their identity, that is their self-narrative. It is hard to maintain a view of oneself as a teacher if one spends most of the time engaged in managerial tasks.'[56]

Indeed, the provision of reflective non-classroom time given to educators is pivotal not only in changing the sense of intensification, but in the development of world class delivery of best outcomes for students. Investment in resources and time for teachers' development has become a key indicator. And for all educators there are dangers to the professional core calling of the teacher in *not* scheduling in reflective time: 'The constant busyness and overbusyness of teachers' lives can divert them from the initial vocational engagement, or "epiphany of recruitment".'[57]

Quality of Time

Hand in hand with the amount of time prioritised for teacher and leader formation is the quality of time experienced. Knowing that 'kairos' time does not happen easily in a day or a half-day session, the structuring in of retreat time as a part of any formation program acts as a catalyst space to maximise the prospective shift into kairos time.[58] Particular processes within sessions further help this,[59] and intentional scaffolding and skilled direction must be constant.

The intentional fostering of kairos time creates a fertile space for the reframing of self-understanding and theological reflection or 'making faith sense.' The honest self-reflection allows for the generation of a more

---

55 Intrator & Scribnor, 2000; Simone 2004; English, Fenwick & Parsons, 2005; Flintham, 2007.
56 Thomson, 2004, p. 8.
57 Mahan 2002, p. 20.
58 In particular, for women with families, the taking of time away in itself launches them into a different space, precisely because it is so atypical for them: 'I don't even remember when I have ever been on my own like this, where I am just focusing on me. I found it very hard to begin with just because of that. I'm not used to really thinking about me.' The sense of leaving responsibility behind can be powerful for teachers in a different way: 'I couldn't do any more at home or school to plan for the time I was away. Once I stopped fighting this, and let myself be "present" as we were asked, things changed. We quickly gave up thinking about what we would be doing now or what our classes would be doing now. We were there! Some parts of the day just flew incredibly — we couldn't believe that we had no idea of the time; and other moments seemed so forever in the lasting feeling.'
59 Examples of this are having no pre-circulated program outline; having participants leave a symbol of their work life at the door on arrival, and bringing a personal symbol of their life into the prayer space of the first gathering. There would be no expectation to share about this: the action is enough in itself.

authentic and adult connection with participants' personal narrative, while the kairos experience facilitates encounter with a more mature and 'present' relationship with God. This latter description of the experiential connection with God is what philosopher Ken Wilber refers to as expressive of the esoteric religious tradition. This connection with God is 'the ultimate reality that traditional science can't touch'.[60] It is what the mystics describe as 'the identity of the interior soul with the ultimate ground of being.'[61]

Quality processes will often mean that in the kairos time, the 'shadows of life' experience or 'via negativa' can surface for participants.[62] This must be carefully contexted and monitored. The great teachers, mystics and writers have always emphasised how critical the facing of the shadow is to spiritual growth. The 'dark and hidden part' chronicled by John of the Cross may open and flourish in ways no other path can offer. This is a critical way of knowing, and for a Catholic leader, the capacity to at some point take the inner and downward journey into self is part of the authentic shaping of self. When this isn't done, the great risk is that the untransformed shadows are transferred or projected onto those around the leader. This is never healthy, life-giving nor reflective of the mature Catholic teacher or leader.

Implementation Principle 5:
Connecting with Tradition

In the current context, the contemporising or re-contextualisation of key elements of traditional Catholic formation creates a powerful conduit for connection and meaning-making. These ways of connecting are multi-targeted, multi-layered and multi-modal.

The term 'contemporising tradition' or 're-contextualising' refers to an intentional approach that seeks to faithfully hold the essence of Catholic identity in new and imaginative ways for a contemporary audience. There has grown an assumed understanding among many practitioners that the traditional monastic and religious life models of Catholic formation are not a fit for the contemporary lifestyle and demographic of those now in various ministries of the Church. In addition to this, one of the key indicators from the literature concerning the current dissonance between members of Catholic school communities and 'church', is the lack of connection and attendant meaning-making of traditional symbols, concepts, rituals and other expressions of Catholic culture.[63] In response, the appeal is

---

60 See interview by Steve Paulson, 2008.
61 Paulson, 2008; O'Murchu, 2004, 2007.
62 Keating, 2009; Merton, 1961; Palmer, 2000; Underhill, 2002.
63 McLaughlin, 2000, 2005.

for a re-inflaming of the imagination[64] that embodies a vision of Church, Christianity, discipleship and leadership that inspires and expresses what the Catholic community holds close to its heart, how it engages others, and how it uses its resources. This involves rediscovering the gold that lies at the heart of Catholic culture and practice.

Contemporising or re-contextualising the tradition therefore refers to the enlivening of key elements of traditional catholic formation in concept, symbol, ritual, prayer and scripture. This means the recovery of older principles and practices in the tradition and bringing them into the present, as well as re-imagining new ways of doing past practice and engaging the layered world of the Catholic imagination.

It also means that strategic resourcing of formation needs to be multi-targeted, multi-modal and multi-layered in order to engage staff in their own context. This in turn means that in addition to formation initiatives that build in a re-contextualised worldview in face-t- face modes with specific groups, school-based resourcing and on-line methods that embrace new modes of educational technology[65] are part of a contemporary approach.

There are three particular reasons for engaging tradition in this way:

A Response to the Contemporary Reality

As we now understand, the homogenous culture of 'being Catholic' is no longer the reality. The current adult population is a generation whose parents have progressively ceased regular attendance at Mass and participation in parish life. So, while the parents of the current generation have a memory of the culture of Catholicism from direct childhood experience, the current generation itself does not, apart from exposure through Catholic schooling. In consequence, the experiential thread that holds ritual and meaning is stretched thin. With it, the assumed understanding and connection to traditional elements is contracted and fragile, and the engagement has become informational rather than formational.

An Appreciation of the Power of Aesthetic Ways of Knowing

The second reason for pursuing this process of 'contemporising the tradition' is the role of experiential praxis in the individual and communal journeys of spiritual formation. In exploring aesthetic ways of knowing, the senses provide a powerful means of engaging in ritual. A different way of knowing is accessed through hearing, feeling, touching, sensing and seeing. More than this, this aesthetic dimension is engaged when a particular experience becomes transformational. At a time when the cultural rituals of Catholic life are anecdotally described by Gen X-ers and Gen Y-ers as variously

---

64 Kelly, 2004; Rolheiser, 2006; Gowdie, 2009.
65 Refer again to O'Brien, 2004.

mind-numbingly boring and/or irrelevant[66], the rise in appreciation of aesthetic ways of knowing remind us of how critical this dimension is to human growth. Greene quotes Dewey in explaining how the opposite of 'aesthetic' is 'anaesthetic': for her, the aesthetic is about 'awakening people into fullness of life'.[67] Thus, the promise and the challenge is that in connecting and re-connecting with some of the Catholic tradition's key symbols and rituals, it would be necessary to recover the original aesthetic experiential influence and its meaning.

A Recognition of the Richness of the Tradition

Finally, the traditional monastic models of formation, identified so closely with religious teaching orders and 'religious life' in general, presented a daily reality and routine so markedly different from 'lay' teachers' lives. Now that these are in decline, the assumption has naturally developed that the Religious Life model itself is irrelevant in today's landscape and has nothing to offer. However, there are significant learnings and principles in formation to be recovered in examining the traditional models. As outlined in part B, the Religious Life model of development through postulancy, novitiate, juniorate and final profession highlights formation as being developmental and taking time. Further, within this overall staged growth model, the traditional approach was characterised by three things, an explicit commitment to calling, to the community, and to service. Thus, spiritual formation in this context involved a community experiential immersion approach with distinct stages. These aspects are wisely integrated into structures and processes of formation, albeit in new ways. Where this has been done, it has been enthusiastically embraced.

Re-traditioning Dynamics

Two important dynamics can be identified in the re-traditioning or re-contextualising approach. These are retrieval interpretation (pulling things out of the storehouse of tradition), and creative interpretation (going into new spaces, which, in turn, become tradition).[68] The premise is that that those who live now are 'the fifth gospel'[69] and that Catholic Christian identity is not static and thus its potentiality can never be exhausted:

> A deep Catholic conviction is that God's revelation did not end with the Apostolic era and is not limited to the Bible's pages. Rather, by the presence of God's Spirit, tradition continues to unfold throughout human experience.[70]

---

66 See Parts A and B.
67 Greene, 1999, p. 13.
68 Groome, 2002.
69 Schillebeekx in Harvey, 2003, p. 2.
70 Groome, 2002, p. 152.

The 're-traditioning' or 're-contextualising' approach is integrated in the overall structure of this contemporary approach to formation through the principle of staged growth, through fundamental skilling in theological reflection and praxis, through specific expression in prayer and ritual, and in engagement with scripture and the Jesus narrative. The recovery of traditional elements of spiritual practice can include attention to physical sacred space with specific symbols in that space that reflect the tradition and speak to the current community. A new way of engagement with scripture includes the use of psycho-spiritual tools to help participants understand scripture personally and theologically. This approach does not truncate other scriptural approaches, but rather intensifies and integrates reader response and historical critical techniques. The experience and the teaching of this approach are named again and again in the 2012 findings as life changing, leading to a re-connection with the Jesus narrative in a way that is immediate, personal and challenging.[71]

Re-traditioning therefore has emerged as a critical element in the personal connection of staff to practices that have become for them a veneer of adherence with little bearing on their lives and vocation. More than simply a useful addition to the process and experience within formation programs and resources, the influence of this approach for individuals and for the community is central and profound. It is an approach that offers a large enough understanding of the authentic spiritual journey to both hold the core of Christian belief and acknowledge the individual's unique experience and varied entry-points.

Let us now turn to those principles of implementation that maximise community engagement.

PRINCIPLES OF IMPLEMENTATION THAT MAXIMISE COMMUNITY ENGAGEMENT

Implementation Principle 6: Companioning

Spiritual Formation has greater sustainable influence in community when individual confidence and capacity is supported in partnership by a core group sharing vision and praxis.

---

71 For example: 'I have never understood scripture like this. I listen I guess at Mass, but it just flows over me like a nice fairytale while I really think about how I'll sort out a family issue or how I'll plan the next few weeks' work, or what needs to be done with the shopping. I know that sounds bad but that's the truth. Now it's so real to me we have all said how personally challenged we are in our thoughts and our lives' (SFPGFB).

Companioning refers to a range of ways or modes of personal and inter-personal mentoring or accompaniment. In our context, this involves companioning of self, each other and the community; and reflective of best practice in spiritual direction, adult learning and change facilitation. The concept of 'companioning' embraces the first steps of the individual's self-companioning to the development and influence of a critical mass within the school community. The word 'companion' comes from two Latin words – cum meaning 'with' and panis meaning 'bread.' A companion is in the fullest sense of the word, one who breaks bread – shares a meal – with another. 'To share food with a person is to share life with them.'[72] Embedding this understanding of companioning in both the structure and the processes of contemporary formation approaches reflects both a strong practice in the Christian tradition as well as best practice in professional learning,[73] and includes self-companioning, peer-companioning, leader companioning and facilitator modelling.

A Companioning Construct for Facilitators

Co-facilitation in delivery of formation programs has a number of benefits. It is an explicit way to model and embed the concept of companioning. It shares the responsibility for facilitation and also models collaborative skills and a shared respectfulness of skills and processes. It speaks of authentic witness and servant leadership where the focus is on the process and the participants, not the presenters themselves. In a time where a performance culture is strong and individualism is normative, this kind of modelling can be a new experience to see. In addition to this, skills of facilitation adopting both professional learning theory and spiritual formation principles modelled then practised in incremental ways as part of formation processes, are ways of working that participants can then re-produce and adapt in their school communities.

Companioning in Formation Program Processes

Companioning can be both implicit and explicit within formation processes. The first step in learning how to 'companion self' involves practising self-reflective skills and an introduction to particular styles of personal prayer. These might include journaling, walking prayer, meditation and lectio divina, using a variety of focus pieces – music, art, poetry, psalms, scripture. Learning to be with oneself in this way, and building it into everyday life, is one of the sustainable tools to be learnt and applied. This is about learning first to be one's own companion – or anam cara (soul friend) in one's own story before moving to the wider community story and learning how to be an anam cara with and for others.

---

72 Chittister, 2001, pp. 98, 99.
73 See O'Brien, 2004.

The next step is to learn the skills to companion the other. These skills will include the art of attentive listening supported by a theology of presence and an understanding of being both guest and host to each other.[74] These are challenging skills to learn. They seem counter to the skills most used in the school and in the classroom (making judgements; fixing problems; leading discussion and giving direction). They require instead silent listening and attentive presence to the other; reminding oneself not to reflect back your own experience or to fix another's situation. The power of being listened to and listening deeply to another can be one of the most moving experiences. As Catholic educators and leaders, we are called to this.

The opportunity for sharing between principals of both honesty about the demands, and inspiration about the calling, has been a recommendation in Australian and British studies. The importance of the influence of significant mentors – whether identified as such or not – in the spiritual growth of leaders, with the capacity to inspire human connection with others as a key element, is another factor noted in a variety of studies.[75] Critical here is the selection and skill of the companions and the mentoring dynamic where mentoring is explicit rather than organic.[76] Flexibility in the structure and the content focus of the companioning is critical to the success, in keeping with the literature around successful mentoring and coaching practice.

Companioning, Adult Learning and Christian Community

The efficacy of the companioning component is of importance for two reasons. These have to do with both the educative and the spiritual perspectives reflected in the literature and the Formation Model.

Firstly, the companioning strategy is supported by the educational literature around adult professional learning and professional learning communities particularly in the school context.[77] At a time when the cultural milieu is characterised by a sense of fragmentation and a lack of shared meaning [78] the effect of 'companioning' that is apparent in studies is remarkable. A shared meaning-making develops, and a communal sense of meaning is built that stretches the community beyond its current patterns. In educational terms, what is being generated is a professional learning community[79] operating at

---

74   Nouwen, 1976, 1991.
75   Gowdie, 2005, 2012; Moore, 1999; Newby & Hyde, 1992.
76   Where this does not work as well, it is the calibre of the Mentor/Leader Companion that appears to be at issue. This disconfirming data underlines how important it is to be discerning in the choice of those invited to be involved as Mentors/Leader Companions in the catholic educational context.
77   Hord, 1997; O'Brien, 2004; Starratt, 2004.
78   Taylor, 2015; Senge, Scharmer, Jaworski & Flowers, 2005.
79   Groen, 2001; Hord, 1997; O'Brien, 2004.

a high level of functionality, doing the work of re-culturing[80] that grows out of the emergence of a powerful culture of trust.[81] The culture of trust is the product of the companioning experience and skilling of a small group who constitute a critical mass in animating their school community. The efficacy of this strategy would indicate that in terms of the four factors critical to the effectiveness of the 'influence' model of critical mass[82], the reach, selectivity, interdependence and production functions[83] are adequate enough to effect change. When this happens, change is transformative.

Secondly, as the understanding around adult professional learning continues to shift in focus away from a gathered information paradigm and into a lifelong learning paradigm, the application of the principles of adult learning as a life-wide and lifelong process in community has a deep correlation with fundamental principles in Christian spiritual formation.[84] The concept of companioning is deeply embedded in the Christian tradition.[85] The Christian tradition is a tradition of companions in discipleship, and the twin pillars of divine presence and communal wisdom are fundamental to how the journey of spiritual formation is understood.[86] For example, disciples were sent out in company, two by two; the early communities had a brother or sister mentor or confessor whose earliest understanding was as a companion in the spiritual journey; and pilgrimages were made to anchorites by wise sisters and brothers, seen again as learned companions among the great communion of saints. Further down the ages, two giants of Christian spirituality, Thomas Aquinas and Teresa of Avila, advocated and modelled what educationalists might now call professional learning communities for individual and systemic growth – Thomas of Aquinas in his advocacy that the whole Christian community become teachers and learners together, and Teresa of Avila in the creation of her active mentoring network in the re-shaping of the Carmelite order. In Australian adult faith education, adult learning is situated in a community context, having long moved from a 'jug and mug' model of learning to a 'shared wisdom' model.[87] Thus, this contemporary embedding of companioning across the variety of modes of formation, while reflecting solid pedagogy for adult learning and change principles, also recovers the deep theological and spiritual practice wisdom in the history of the Christian tradition.

---

80   Fullan, 2001.
81   Gilligan, Spencer, Weinberg & Bertch, 2003.
82   Oliver & Marwell 2002.
83   Prahl, Marwell & Oliver, 1991.
84   Groome, 2002; Kinast, 2000; Miller, 2000; Whitehead & Whitehead, 1997.
85   Shinohara, 2002.
86   Wolski Conn, 1999; Groome, 2002; Rolheiser, 1998; Rosov, 2001.
87   Benet McKinney, 1987.

The confluence of principles of contemporary practice in adult education and spiritual formation is predicated on the movement that occurs within the individual because of the community dynamic in which they are placed. While 'reality is a web of communal relationships, and we can know reality only by being in community with it,'[88] at the same time, 'anyone engaged in education must, in preserving their integrity, seek to make sense of their work in terms of the rest of their outlook on life.'[89] Any internal shifts need to be authentic to be sustained. It is apparent that reflective praxis and the companioning work in story with 'self' and the 'other' helps this process of meaning-making.

Thus, the fruits of the variety of modes of self-companioning and peer companioning help teacher and leader participants develop a strengthened personal commitment and vigour for their life and work, and a deeper and more satisfying understanding of and relationship to God and questions of ultimate meaning. This in turn has a wider influence on the community as they transmit a new awareness among each other and with each other. It results in the nurturing of rich authentic community relationships[90] and, in fact, emerges as a key to sustainability in the community.

Implementation Principle 7:
Walking the Talk

The authentic modelling of individual learnings and shared experience in formation is a transparent and powerful catalyst within community.

Formation in the Catholic Christian tradition recognises deeply the place of the community in the individual journey in a relational culture modelled on Jesus. Church documents repeatedly call attention to the importance to the school community of teachers in relating a transformative vision of life (CCE 1977; 1982; 1988; 1998).

However, Tony Kelly observed from his research that for some teachers at least, the ecclesial reality of the church has undergone 'a form of sociological reduction which leaves it with only its most imperfect and limited institutional form'[91], and other Australian diocesan research shows no shift in perspectives towards the ecclesial community as a result of in-service. Other findings however indicate a different possibility, where formation content and processes can indeed shift the perspective of individual teachers about church and about the relevance of the God meta-narrative in a personal and meaningful way. Such subtle change in perspective can ripple into

---

88 Palmer, 2007, p. 95.
89 Hull, 1997, p.18.
90 See Derbyshire, 2005.
91 2002, p. 312.

the staffroom and the classroom precisely because it is borne of personal meaning-making.[92]

The enabling factor in the wider community influence develops from a shared confidence and capacity among a critical mass of formation participants who model the learned processes and practice in everyday school and family life. This constitutes a pivotal factor in the influence of staff formation in whole community growth and life. There are two aspects of this – firstly the intensely personal growth in the formation programs that leads to a desire and capacity to be a change maker on staff; and secondly, the practical reality of having other colleagues model action and behaviour on staff.

A more recent document from the Vatican expresses this in more metaphorical language:

> Catholic educators need a 'formation of the heart': they need to be led to that encounter with God in Christ which awakens their love and opens their spirits to others, so that the education commitment becomes a consequence deriving from their faith, a faith which becomes active through love.'[93]

This concept of a 'formation of the heart' is more the language of contemporary spiritual writers. Joan Chittister echoes Parker Palmer's attention to the heart of the teacher – 'What you are, your students will be.'[94] And Marcus Borg, Ron Rolheiser, Richard Rohr and Margaret Silf, in explaining what is essential in following Jesus' vision, use the language of transformative imagery. These perspectives have traction with Catholic educators in their own meaning-making.

The bridge between the personal journey of individuals and the communal journey of change is a difficult one to build, particularly in the context of large education systems. The literature shows that individual staff most often find themselves buried under the pace and weight of school routine and demands, and that best intentions are soon forgotten despite the strength of the experience.[95] The personal everyday integration of formative practices and a formative approach in school life is pivotal to modelling change, and the collegial support for this modelling is therefore very important. Using Nancy Carlson's terminology[96] in developing

---

92 This sensibility for authenticity or 'being real' is a strong Australian characteristic: In the 2003 survey Exploring What Australians Value by Philip Hughes, Sharon Bond, John Bellamy and Alan Black, the results demonstrate that the overriding concern among Australians is for the depth and authenticity of their relationships. This is amplified in Hugh Mackay's 2016 research.
93 Congregation for Catholic Education, 2008, n. 25.
94 Chittister, 2003, p. 9.
95 Groen, 2001; O'Brien, 2004.
96 Carlson, 2003

communities of practice, the modelling of a core group acts as an energising group on staff, drawing in peripheral members, and creating an atmosphere of ongoing collaborative learning grounded in the staff themselves. This is critical in bridging the personal and the communal, and paramount where successful strategic implementation has been identified.

Despite pressures of time and workload, the clearer teachers are about their purpose, reflected in daily actions, the more likely they are to become committed to it.[97] More importantly, as Parker Palmer reiterates, teachers teach who they are,[98] and the deeper the clarity they have about their own story and its connection to purpose and vocation and a broader story, the more powerful will be their influence in what they do and how they do it among staff, students and parents. When this is supported by a core group of peer support, applied behaviour and peer modelling, it has the potential to become a self-sustaining reality.

Implementation Principle 8:
Strategic Alignment

Spiritual formation has sustained influence when it is connected to the language, structures and processes of annual goal setting and strategic renewal in schools and systems.

One of the emerging understandings about spiritual formation within Catholic organisations is the need for it to be connected more strategically to the broader system structure and perceived as a core engagement for teachers and leaders. For those Australian Catholic schooling authorities grappling with this in their organisational vision and structure, the issue of where formation is best placed has become a key challenge. A number of different options are being pursued. One of the observable developments is to move away from the structuring of formation services as addendums or adjuncts to other areas and move towards integrating spiritual and faith formation into wider professional learning and leadership programs. Among senior system leadership, this still constitutes a major paradigm shift from thinking about formation as a time-out/retreat option or religious in-service, to thinking about formation as *the* core foundation in teaching and leadership development. The former mindset provides a fast track to formation becoming a soft option irrelevancy. The continuing corporatisation of education makes this a dangerous continuing mindset and mission risk. The latter mindset demands that system authorities meet the confronting realisation that authentic Catholic education is deeply

---

97   Deal & Peterson, 2003
98   Palmer, 2007.

personal and radically communal in its understanding of both educators and students. That carries with it responsibility, maturity and courage to step into the space of personal meaning-making with every graduate teacher and every aspiring leader.

Understanding how to implement formation across a community of schools requires a system level strategic vision and purpose with all staff as its target audience. Organisationally, the placement of the team overseeing formation needs to signal that it is core strategic business for all staff across the organisation, and not an adjunct of any particular area. Locally, each school needs to connect formation into their strategic school renewal plan and annual goal setting, and engage with a system-wide shared language and approach. Thus, the organisational intention ought to be to provide strategic leadership and grow local capacity. This is built on the premise that shared responsibility at the local school level will not grow without strategic system leadership, and that central systemic leadership on its own will not grow local capacity. Both are needed.

The practical 'knitting in' of spiritual formation to the key structures and processes of the organisation is a new frontier for contemporary Catholic education systems. In general, very little research has been done about the 'how' of this shift. The most reliable research indicates maximum effectiveness through strategic alignment of the following:

- A shared framework
- Practical connection with the organisation's Strategic Renewal and Leadership frameworks
- Support through systemic resourcing
- An expectation of practical goal setting and annual planning
- Centralised provision of targeted formation programs
- Key messaging from system leadership.

Dialogue at every level is critical in bringing life and practical reality to this alignment. The starting point conversation between school leadership and staff requires a simultaneous dialogue between system leadership and school leadership, so that school leadership is able to facilitate their staff conversation with a sense of shared clarity and confidence. When a system can formulate and communicate its purpose, it is likely that school principals can better lead an agenda for spiritual formation that is appropriate for their context.

Without system level dialogue, individual schools can develop an ad hoc approach to formation predicated on diverse personal interests, and with a limited cohesive strategy. The risk in this approach is that formation becomes no-one's responsibility and is sidelined and buried under multiple and pressing responsibilities. When formation becomes a localised negotiation with a general but un-focussed shared responsibility, there is the possibility of a reactive and piecemeal approach lacking a strong driver for overall responsibility.

In addition, while on the face of it a localised collaborative approach in creating the agenda for spiritual formation reflects the operating principle of the primacy of learner experience and direction in adult education, the learner's context mitigates against the effectiveness of this. In the post-modern context, learner experience in the area of spiritual formation for mission has been limited; the provision of system led formation has been inconsistent (until the last ten years); and the consequential shared recollection and understanding of what might constitute appropriate formation had therefore become nebulous. This was an emerging reality across catholic schools in Australia noted in the early 2000s:

> *Another common phenomenon is that spiritual and faith formation becomes defined by whomever or whatever is on offer to deliver a formation experience, without reference to any broader understanding of what spiritual and faith formation entails. This gives rise to situations where 'spirituality' morphs into anything that somehow connects with people; where facilitators are often put in the difficult position of having no brief but to 'do something about spirituality'; where excellent programs are dropped – or not offered – because there are 'no takers'; and where very little is offered at all because formation is an adjunct to someone's area where there are always more immediately pressing issues to address.*[99]

The issue of strategic capacity when addressing the sustainability of spiritual capital and the provision of formation can no longer be left to chance.

Implementation Principle 9:
School Leadership

School leadership that reflects an authentic engagement in spiritual formation is critical for the effective embedding of staff formation, and the growing of spiritual capital and mission integrity in the school culture.

In Part C we identified the role of leaders, both formal and informal, as crucial to the effective development and nurturing of culture within a school community.[100] Within this task of nurturing culture, the capacity for

---

99 Queensland Catholic Education Commission Report, 2005, p. 7. This had been further apparent in the literature on contemporary Catholic school staff and leadership cohorts, Bracken, 2004; Downey, 2006; Hughes, 2009.
100 Chittister, 2003; Deal & Peterson, 1999; Starratt, 2004.

the principal to build community relationships has become pre-eminent. This is because for many parents, students and staff who now constitute a post-ecclesial community[101], the school is the only place that provides a sense of connectedness to Church. For reasons of both expectation and success in this, the Catholic school is seen as the 'new church'[102]. In this context, the role of the leader that is emerging is as one who builds school community based on principles and values that govern judgements and direction within the cultural context of the school.[103] Because 'principals bring themselves, including their deepest convictions, beliefs and values to their work'[104], a capacity to understand their deepest identity and convictions and to grasp the power of their own shadow and light[105] is a crucial element in building authentic community.

Catholic school principals know the importance of community in their school culture. They work hard to develop a sense of belonging and inclusion in their schools.[106] An important difference between this generation and previous generations for those who seek to influence the spiritual life of the contemporary Catholic school community through their witness is that each person will make up his or her own mind about its value. Relationships and friendships are the mainstay of life and demonstrating commitment in relationships may be very significant in communicating what the Christian faith is all about.[107] The principal must provide what Palmer calls 'the permissions and excuses for teachers, parents and students to realise their full potential'. [108]

Also consistent with the literature, these Principals today share the strain of maintaining authentic ecclesial relationships parallel to their emergent role as pastoral leaders for the school families, thus displacing the priest and parish.[109] Formation for leaders must provide in an open, direct and dialogical manner a space in which they can explore and process these issues.

The Australian research identifying the role of principals, particularly in the area of spiritual formation within their school communities, is small and relatively recent. However, as this area emerges as a focus in the field of leadership, there is indication that the growing of spirituality in the leader is vital to the maintenance of direction, and the sustaining of mission, in the life and culture of the school. Central to this is the need for personal faith

---

101   Rolheiser, 2007.
102   McLaughlin, 2002; 2005.
103   Meyer & Macmillan, 2001.
104   Starratt, 2004, p.65.
105   Palmer, 2000.
106   Belmonte et al, 2006; Flintham, 2007; Fullan, 2010; Sergiovanni, 2005.
107   Hughes, 2009.
108   Palmer, 2007, p. 111.
109   McLaughlin, 2002, 2005, 2008; Kelly, 2007.

formation to strengthen the role of principals as spiritual leaders.[110] 2012 research clearly showed that the impact of formation strategies and programs are weakest in those schools where the leadership is correspondingly non-committal.[111] Conversely, strategic engagement in formation has greater traction in those schools where one can characterise the principal's leadership as collaborative and directly enabling with staff, and with clear, committed key messaging to students and parents. While some studies indicate that principals see their responsibility in providing spiritual formation for staff summed up as to 'put things in front of people'[112], the same research indicates that the hit and miss approach is becoming more and more fractured and dangerous, as the veneer of Catholic culture becomes thinner. While staff members have a degree of responsibility for their own formation, it is also true that leadership is called to be more personally committed, strategic and targeted in the planning and provision of formation. Further, although teacher leadership can exist without principal support, where teacher leadership flourishes, principals have actively supported and encouraged it.[113] A strong commitment to strategic planning and culture building appears to correlate highly with an active and tangible personal commitment to the spiritual life and reflective praxis of the Christian leader.

Leadership and self-engagement

Visible engagement of school leadership (especially principals) has influence in itself. For principals, the peer mentoring that occurs organically during formation programs is a gift for the younger and newer principals. The paradigm of principal-ship, as management in overseeing the religious/spiritual (and other) dimensions of school life, is now challenged by a paradigm that sees principal-ship as 'walking the talk' of the religious and spiritual heart of leadership through all the dimensions of leadership.[114] This represents a profound shift because it is personal — it is about the person and the 'who' of their leadership.

In Christian churches where a more assertive approach to formation exists other than is the accepted norm in mainstream Catholic culture (for example, the Uniting Church, the Christian Outreach churches and the Pentecostal Churches), the nurturing of personal spiritual charisms for leadership is the major focus of attention. The other capabilities of leadership are built around this core which forms the centre of integrated leadership programs. With a strong grasp of this concept, a number of Christian ministry centres in Australia (for example, Barnabas Ministries, the Potter's House, Christian Churches

---

110   Crotty, 2005.
111   Gowdie, 2012.
112   Bracken, 2004, p 148.
113   Crowther, Kaagan, Furguson & Hann, 2002.
114   O'Hara, 2000; Thompson, 2005; Wallace, 2000.

Australia) have put extensive resources into integrated leadership programs that combine the formal study in the faith tradition and personal spiritual formation with the other elements of management and responsibility.[115] This is a strength-based approach where value is placed in leaders being able to identify and explore their particular gifts. New Catholic leadership programs will heed the importance of growing leaders who have learned who they are and what they bring to the table in leadership.

Spiritual formation and leadership preparation

Over the last decade there has been ongoing concern within Catholic educational authorities about the nature, process and content of current pathways to Catholic leadership. There are two issues arising out of this concern: one is in relation to the place of formation in existing and future leadership programs. The other is in relation to the nature of the required study pathways themselves.

The place of spiritual formation in leadership programs presents a challenge for as long as it remains fundamentally perceived as an optional extra outside of required preparation for aspiring and current leaders. While it is perceived by some as a soft option or a 'soft skill', the research indicates the centrality of spiritual formation to deep leadership growth. The broader leadership literature is recognising this, even as Catholic educational leadership development shows signs of moving away from this and towards a corporate approach.

Researchers and writers in the field[116] now strongly contend that effective leadership requires something beyond experience and competence and is 'much more a matter of who the leader is than how the leader applies leadership principles or adopts leadership style'.[117] However, the place and nature of spiritual formation for this development is given scant attention. Yet, in the Catholic context, it is spiritual formation that is at the heart of the kind of leadership described above, and which grows that authentic, inner, values driven leadership so prevalent in professional leadership conversation.

Those at the cutting edge will in fact move to integrate formation more tightly and explicitly into leadership development from induction to senior leadership. Formation will become part of the mandatory developmental pathway for leadership positions.[118]

If the connection between the human and the divine, and between personal leadership development and spiritual formation, is not made, then

---

115   Miedema, 1995; Dowson & McInerney, 2005.
116   Bezzina, Burford & Duignan, 2007; Duignan, 2002; O'Hara, 2000.
117   Starratt, 2004.
118   Not surprisingly, aspiring school leaders appear to be more open to spiritual and faith formation initiatives where they see these programs directly connected to their career path and/or school context.

the Jesus story and the God meta-narrative will indeed become no more than a vague religious memory: 'If the principal is not able to lead his or her community to a realisation and celebration of the divine in the human then he or she might as well create a secular non-religious school.'[119] And if it is not in the leadership of Catholic schools and systems, it is most unlikely it will survive in the 'follow-ship' of either.

The current construction of leadership pathways

The general concern that has emerged around the structure of leadership pathways is about a mentality of 'paper-chasing' and a culture of 'box-ticking' among teachers and leaders. The issue around the structure of leadership programs also goes to the heart of the effectiveness of the organisation in its mission. General organisational research indicates that it is a collective passion and mission at the core of an organisation that assures enduring success, as opposed to being an organisation that is merely 'good'.[120] The emergence of the core ideology that inspires its members in a flourishing organisation cannot be left to chance:

> It is intentionally cultivated by making it the centrepiece of regular professional development activities and serves as the driving purpose and inspiration behind decision making, employee development, and resource allocation.[121]

At present, Catholic education systems struggle to integrate their core ideology in a concrete way, and this is reflected in the corporatisation of approaches to leadership and employee management under the pressure of a culture of performativity and measurable productivity. The consequence is the depletion of spiritual capital, an impoverished understanding of what a Catholic education is, and significant mission risk into the future. While it appears imperative that school leadership understands and is committed to the core place of formation within staff and in the community, this needs to be supported, encouraged and underpinned in the system leadership. The challenge therefore is to develop such a systemic culture.

Implementation Principle 10: Strong Theological Underpinning

Formation that is anchored in a clear theological foundation reflecting a sound re-contextualist and Post-Vatican II stance captures a strong alignment in communal meaning-making.

---

119   Lacey, 2003, p 3.
120   Collins & Porras, 2004.
121   Intrator & Kunzman, 2006, p. 39.

The current generations of Catholic educational leaders have grown amidst enormous ecclesial upheaval and enormous theological growth. The change to a predominantly lay led Catholic schooling system in Australia began to happen in the mid-sixties[122] and initial research into the impact of this development on 'religious' staff followed.[123] However, research into the life perspectives of the 'lay' teachers and leaders in Australian Catholic schools has only gained serious momentum in the last two decades.[124] The work of these researchers has been instrumental in identifying the fractures and fault-lines in 'lay' teachers' reception of church doctrine and belief, and increasing understanding of the unique stressors for those who choose a vocation to teach or lead in a Catholic school.[125] This has been complemented by other research on the increasing recognition of the role of 'spirituality' in leadership and in 'work' in general.[126] The result has been the generation of interest in a bigger picture approach, more encompassing than the task and management focus for leadership in the eighties and nineties.[127]

However, while the difficulties become clearer and the importance of the spiritual dimension becomes sharper, the precise shape of learning in the area of spiritual formation has remained an elusive area for thorough exploration. The challenge involves creating an approach to formation that addresses the fractures and gives a concrete, strategic and cohesive approach for growing a spiritual core perspective for all staff in Catholic school communities. Just as the research on the role of principals in the area of spiritual formation within their school communities is small and relatively recent, so too the Australian research on spiritual formation for Catholic educators in general is relatively slim, although gathering increasing attention. The accumulated work giving focus to formation for 'lay staff' in response to the post-conciliar reality still gives little direction outside of general guidelines and suggested discussion strategies. One of the challenges appears to be how to effectively engage with the theological elements of the Catholic tradition in formation.

Anecdotal experience of various programs developed as 'spiritual formation' in Australian dioceses has indicated that where the focus remains heavily on the personal dimension, and ambivalent or 'light' on the theological dimension, programs risk remaining at the level of a 'holistic personal experience'. Where the focus leans heavily on theological input, and

---

122 Grace, 2002; O'Donoghue, 2004.
123 Kyle, 1986; Trimingham-Jack, 2003.
124 Burley, 2001; McLaughlin, 1997, 1998, 2005, 2008; O'Donoghue & Potts, 2004.
125 Branson, 2004; Carotta & Carotta, 2005; Downey, 2006; Jarvis, 2004; McMahon, 2003.
126 Bolman & Deal, 2001; Conger, 1994; Duignan, 1997, 2002, 2003; Holmes, 2005; Starratt, 2004.
127 See Millán, 2013, Leadership and Management: what we can learn from the founders, pp.70-75.

is light on the holistic and experiential elements, programs risk remaining a cerebral exercise. In developing efficacy, the theological component is best incorporated in three ways:

1. In the conceptual underpinning of a shared framework
2. In the developmental skills and praxis of 'doing theology' within every program
3. In a consistency of approach and in the articulation of key theological concepts.

1. Conceptual underpinning of a shared framework

A framework provides a way of understanding the main elements and connections in complex concepts. In the formation of Catholic educators, a framework will reflect the underlying theological foundation of that understanding. It is a way of seeing the world and living in it that constitutes a core belief system of reality that is shared and nurtured.

In this sense alone, the theological foundation underpinning contemporary formation for Catholic educators and leaders presents a counter-cultural challenge to a post-modern time. For, while our post-modern culture tends to reject universal narratives, the reign of God is the transforming vision for those who choose to stand in the Catholic Christian tradition. And while the individual path to this reality is acknowledged and respected, the vision itself is a non-negotiable touchstone for all those choosing to be involved in the educational mission of the church. This theological vision is founded on a sacramental view of the world, nurtured in the cradle of community, strengthened by pathways of prayer, challenged in the world to do what must be done for justice sake, and reflected in the compassionate hospitality that is the hallmark of all followers of Jesus.[128]

2. The practice of 'doing theology'

Theological reflection provides the praxis with which to build meaning between personal experience, the cultural context and the faith tradition. The skill of 'doing theology' is a critical practice in a post-modern environment for Catholic educators. This praxis needs to be *portable* so leaders in particular can carry it into their daily lives; *performable* so that they can translate their reflections into actions; and *communal* so they can address issues together.[129]

The process of deep engagement and responsive action embedded in the practice of 'doing theology' requires disciplined skilling. The temptation to take individual experience to the tradition in a way that reinforces prior interpretation and habitual thinking is intentionally backgrounded, so that a space for genuine conversation can occur. Such praxis aims at practical

---

128   Gowdie, 2006, 2009, p. 7.
129   See Wicks, 2009, and Kinast, 1996.

action rather than theoretical or abstract ideas. It requires immersion in a stepped process of experience with prayer practices, scriptural engagement, deep listening, orthodoxy (right thinking), orthopraxis (right acting) and orthopathy (right feeling)[130], before becoming an organic part of processing and action. This process opens up a different way for Catholic educators and leaders to approach issues. It enables us to walk the talk of a Catholic worldview. It fires the hard work of giving witness now to the heart of Jesus' vision. It trains us to remain true to the authentic belief that in this dialogue, we may be surprised by what emerges in the encounter – it is not a closed reflective praxis.[131]

'Doing theology' encourages people to move 'beyond knowing *about* Jesus' or '*about* scripture' or '*about* tradition' to a point where they become 'disciples' of the 'way.'[132] It is an approach that emphasises inner transformation over external behaviour[133] rather than external practice over internal beliefs (even as its outer practice can begin to facilitate inner change). It facilitates an authentic engagement between a solid theological foundation and the Catholic educator and leader's lived experience, ensuring that the missional meta-narrative of 'The Story' is always grounded in the praxis and lived experience of 'My Story'. This journey moving from 'My Story' through to the transformative phase of 'The Story', and being profoundly changed by that encounter, is at the very heart of the formation journey.

3. Consistency in approach and articulation

A consistency of language, messaging, and core components particulary around Scripture, Christology, Ecclesiology and Mission is critical to the efficacy of theological underpinning and in growing a shared understanding of formation for mission. In doing so, the focus and beginning point is firmly on the *experience* of incarnation; the *experience* of the living community; the *experience* of scripture made relevant in the present life; and the *experience* of a sacramental reality. In this way, the intellectual meaning-making of the tradition takes on a perspective that speaks to the experience. The vocation of the Catholic educator is thus framed and understood as being animated by a spirituality that is:

- Incarnational, accompanying the 'joys and hopes, the grief and anxieties of the people'[134]

---

130   Rohr, 2010.
131   In genuine dialogue, space is made for something new yet to be known: 'In this process of theological reflection, we bring our experience to the tradition so that a surprising encounter can emerge' (Killen & De Beer, 1994, p. 64).
132   Groome, 1996, p. 118.
133   Kelly, 2009.
134   Gaudium et Spes, 1965, n. 1.

- Paschal, affirming the promise of a bigger, deeper, everlasting reality of life even in the face of pain, diminishment and dying
- Ecclesial, nurturing the bonds of communion and community
- Gospel, deepening relationship with the one whose way sets our principles and actions.
- Sacramental, developing a sacramental imagination that sees that all is sacred
- Missional, being in the world to bring a transformative difference.

Framing an ecclesial identity into the future

The connection of this theological heart to ecclesial reality is critical into the future for an authentic missional trajectory. The importance of the experiential pathway into such a reality is highlighted eloquently by key figures in the Catholic tradition, both past and present. Speaking of his own transforming journey in ministry, Daniel O'Leary, priest and spiritual writer, explains:

> *After decades of clerical ministry, I began to realise that what people were yearning for, much more than information about the Church and its doctrines, was the actual redeeming reassurance of God in their daily lives. They wanted the experience of God more than knowledge about him. They longed for in the here and now, light in their darkness, hope in their despair, courage in their fear ... the inner journey preceding [sic] the outer one.*[135]

This personal narrative animates the prediction of Karl Rahner, made in the late sixites, that 'The Christian of the future will be a mystic or will not exist at all.'[136] A decade earlier than O'Leary, and three decades after Rahner, John Paul II expressed the same essential insight:

> *What the world needs now are heralds of the Gospel, who are experts in humanity, who know the depth of the human heart, who can share the joys and hopes, the agonies and distress of people, but who are, at the same time, contemplatives who have fallen in love with God. (John Paul II, 1984.)*

The great line of mystics in the Christian Catholic tradition have always advocated this transformative pathway, seeing the model and person of Jesus as the key. Teresa of Avila, in the fourteenth century, referred to Jesus as the doorway to the Godhead, and urged all those true seekers to follow this way: 'We must look at his life – that is our best pattern.'[137] In doing so, language, symbol and the new imagining advocated by the foremost

---

135   O'Leary, 2011, p. 41.
136   Rahner, 1973, p. 149.
137   Peers, 2002, p. 139.

theologians and practitioners in the literature, is a key to linking the reality of Jesus to followers in a new time.

> *Jesus invited his followers to see in a radically new way. The appeal is to the imagination, to that place within us in which resides our images of reality and our images of life itself; the invitation is to a different way of seeing, to different images for shaping our understanding of life.*[138]

The insitutional Church itself has been perceived to be complicit in blocking or damaging this kind of connectivity. The Australian theologian, Tony Kelly, sums it up well in his 2009 Aquinas lecture: 'There is a general sense that the Church's stance on many issues is not a genuine search for understanding and answers, rather 'a mere flexing of institutional power.'[139] Other Australian research in the last ten years has highlighted that principals and employing authorities themselves struggle trying to separate 'an authentic search for a liveable theology from the strictures of official Church policy'. In addition, there is concern that Catholic school leaders (principals) lack the sophisticated spiritual awareness and theological literacy to adequately fulfil the role of religious leadership.[140]

A well-grounded contemporary theological and ecclesial foundation assists participants to re-frame their experience in a way that allows them to hold the challenges and short-comings of the institutional Church firmly enough to claim an active place in the wider Catholic community.

Situating a Values Approach

As discussed in Part A, some Australian dioceses are embracing values education as an entry point to Catholic theological belief and ecclesial teaching. This development reflects increasing interest in this approach in England, Scotland and the U.S.[141] Such an approach finds support in the literature. However, the focus on values as a conduit for spiritual formation also carries a mission risk, and the risk is two-fold:

1. Firstly, the 'values' espoused can present as a generalised and reductionist mix of biblical and sociological concepts (e.g. terms from current Australian diocesan documents using the Values approach include: 'search for wisdom and truth'; 'community and common good'; 'freedom from oppression'). These risk being largely indistinguishable from the general values focus promoted across all Australian schools with the establishment

---

138 Borg, 1994, p. 74.
139 Kelly, 2009.
140 Gowdie, QCEC Report, 2005.
141 For example, Values for Life, Scotland, 2007; Virtues Seminars: U.S., Earl, 2008.

of a *National Framework for Values Education in Australian Schools* in 2005. (The values in the National Framework include 'care and compassion'; 'a fair go'; 'freedom'; 'integrity' and 'tolerance and inclusion'.)

2. Secondly, the deeper theological concepts underpinning the values risk being lost in an unbridgeable void between the more generic nature of the stated values and the more complex and rich theological and scriptural base. In more recent research on the ethos of Australian Edmund Rice schools, Kerry Tuite's findings[142] name this very concern around clarity, direction and connection of values, ethos and formation.

Cognisant of the risk and the concerns, the practice wisdom suggests the better choice is to embrace a more direct, though still integrated, theological underpinning within formation program process and structure. Moreover, the 'story' Formation Model reflects and is couched in a theological framework that provides a 'system of ideas'[143] which can leverage terms and concepts already familiar to Australian Catholic school educators and leaders. To some degree, the use of this theological framework assumed enough participant acceptance of the reality of God, the person and vision of Jesus and the continuing presence of the Spirit. It is very probable that a more severely eroded culture, which is the reality in some European countries, would create a significantly greater challenge for this formative work.

Conclusion to Chapter 9

These ten design principles are the influencing markers that make the 'mission field' of Catholic educators more likely rather than less likely to be a space in which personal growth and transformation occur and community witness to the Gospel flourishes.

The interlocking dynamic of these markers in the application of the Formation Model cumulatively creates a context where the experience of the individuals, and their influence in the school community, reaches a 'critical mass' phase of genuine transformative impact. These markers constitute pivotal elements, or triggers, that either channel participants more deeply into the formation journey (as they move from self-engagement to mutual engagement to transformative engagement), and/or trigger a stronger influence in the community experience.

Amplifying the depth and power of narrative, the journey design resonates with both the core of Catholic tradition and with a post-modern, individualistic, experiential context. It applies and extends learning theory

---

142   Tuite, 2007, unpublished thesis.
143   Erikson, 1994.

to the development of a contemporary approach to spiritual formation in a Catholic education setting. You see how the couching of spiritual formation in the language of lifelong learning and transformation has a natural alignment with key messages in the professional understanding of Catholic educational staff. In this way, the personal and professional meaning-making happen in an iterative way, each fostering the other. The adoption of principles and best practice in professional learning also provides an authentic framework for workplace change and culture shaping. Figure 9.1 below visually illustrates the 10 design principles for the strategic embedding of spiritual formation around this new Formation Model.

FIGURE 9.1: MISSION FORMATION MODEL FOR CATHOLIC EDUCATORS WITH PRINCIPLES OF IMPLEMENTATION IN A SCHOOL AND SYSTEM SETTING (GOWDIE, 2012)

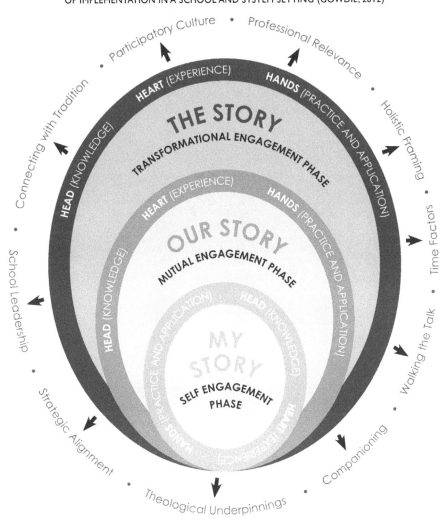

10

THE *TRANSFORMING ENCOUNTERS* MODEL IN A REAL-LIFE SETTING: CATHOLIC EDUCATION, ARCHDIOCESE OF BRISBANE: *CATCHING FIRE!*

THE CONTEXT

In the Australian Archdiocese of Brisbane, the *Catching Fire* initiative[144] is the lived expression of the new mission formation model outlined in Chapter 8. This initiative has been in operation for the last ten years. Having explored the complexities of the mission field and the best thinking and practice in the disciplines across the fields of spirituality, theology, andragogy, missiology and organisational culture, the intention was to apply the formative conditions for a deep and rich conversation between life, culture and faith that would be transformative for individuals and communities, and sustainable into the future.

THE INITIATIVE: CATCHING FIRE

Applying the new model, *Catching Fire* reflects the Catholic educator and leader's formation journey as personal and professional, individual and communal. The participant is seen as a lifelong, life-wide learner, who has a unique story, context, experience and way of knowing. The formation 'curriculum' is based on an approach to learning that understands spiritual formation as holistic, enlivened by engagement with multiple learning strategies, and most effective when priority is given to the experiential dimension. In this way, the approach is designed to be person and process-centred. Finally, the approach is congruent with the contextual religious and evangelising priorities of the system and the Archdiocese. And so, spiritual formation remains a transformative journey in the context of

---

144   *Catching Fire* Staff with Spirit Formation framework for the Mission of Catholic Education, 2009. See the appendices for the complete framework, including the Matrix. Also see Gowdie, 2012, unpublished thesis http://researchbank.acu.edu.au/theses/356/

Catholic education that influences a way of being in the world in both personal and professional contexts.

The formation framework is shown in Figure 10.1 below. Together with an accompanying 'Curriculum Matrix' it provides a framework for staff formation across the system. All programs and resources are developed out of this framework. Taking the translation of the early Aramaic text of Luke 24:32[145], the aspiration was to develop a genuinely formative and transformative strategy for staff formation that fulfilled the three criteria: to be personally meaningful, ecclesially faithful, and (in a large system) strategically effective.

FIGURE 10.1 *CATCHING FIRE* FORMATION FRAMEWORK

---

145   The early Aramaic translation of the Emmaus story suggested the wording, 'Were not our hearts gradually catching fire within us as he spoke to us on the road?' evoking a sense of growing of deep understanding that was transformative. This reflected the aspiration of the program itself.

KEY ELEMENTS

Strategically, the aims of the initiative have been threefold:

1. To support and nurture the spiritual culture in all schools each year through the provision of centrally prepared formation processes and resources for local implementation by school staffs
2. To provide a set of coordinated and targeted staff formation programs for selected staff to influence school culture in each school
3. To build capacity across the system by growing 'formation facilitators' among school staff.

Strategic Parameters

At systemic and school levels, *Catching Fire* is premised on the belief that spiritual formation is a shared responsibility between the individual staff member, the individual school and the systemic authority. In addition to strategic planning and goal setting using the Formation Framework as a touchstone, those schools accepting the invitation to engage in *Catching Fire* undertake to discern and invite staff to be involved in the formation programs. The strategic purpose in engaging a number of staff from the same school in the three formation programs is to build a core of shared experiences, shared understanding and shared praxis – a critical mass – in order to influence the wider culture in the school. Targeting a cross-section of staff that includes leadership, classroom teachers and support staff has the strategic intention of capitalising on the influence of leadership as well as generating broader staff ownership. Accreditation and funding for participation and teacher release are part of the strategic organisation, shared between the individual school and the central Catholic Education Office.

Participating schools are expected to engage in four ways over the three years of the program:

1. **The *Catching Fire* Formation for Mission Framework:** Familiarising all staff with the approach and language of the *Catching Fire* Framework Model and Matrix
2. **Planning and Goal Setting:** Ensuring formation planning and goal setting occur for staff individually and the school, linked to school and system annual goals and strategic renewal
3. **General Systemic Initiatives and Resources:** Using the range of systemic resources provided to all schools, including resources made available for planning.

4. *Catching Fire* **Staff Formation Programs:** Sponsoring particular staff to participate in the three staff formation programs.

Figure 10.2 illustrates the commitments of participating schools. The way in which schools engage with each of these strategic parameters remains a choice for each school, allowing flexibility to shape and integrate formation to meet the needs and context of the staff and school community. Staff members are encouraged to think outside of set programs, to critically analyse through the 'lens' of the framework what is already happening in their school, and to include appropriate strategies that integrate easily into staff life. Contact is maintained with each school community involved in *Catching Fire*, thereby supporting work with the whole staff and the leadership team in annual goal setting and renewal. Throughout, intentional connections are made with concurrent Brisbane Catholic Education developments in the broader priority areas of school renewal, leadership, succession planning and induction.

FIGURE 10.2 STRATEGIC PARAMETERS FOR COMMITMENT OF
EACH SCHOOL TO CATCHING FIRE

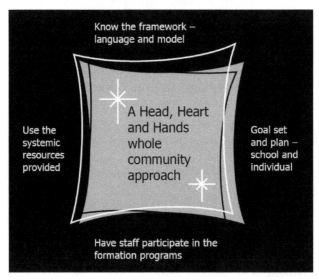

Systemic Resources

Intentional in formation and resource design, *Catching Fire* is about recovering key elements of tradition in a way that is faithful to the tradition, and at the same time experiential and connective for a new time. A comprehensive and growing hub of resources is provided for all school and office communities across the system, accessible on the *Catching Fire* website. These resources offer a broad range of spiritual formation activities and support resourcing. This extensive and multi-modal resourcing includes:

- The *Light a Prayer Candle* website[146]
- *Staff Prayer Fire* – a growing collection of resources for staff prayer[147]
- The Spiritual Formators Local and National Network
- A planning and goal setting resource
- A guide for facilitation
- *MusicFire* and *ArtsFire* resources and networks
- DIY (Do It Yourself) formation resources, prayer cards, and web guides.

The Light a Prayer Candle website has become popular farther afield than the archdioceses within Australia and overseas. While it contemporises a traditional ritual of prayer, embracing new modes of educational technology, it has gained approval for also being perceived as remaining faithful to the heart of the tradition.[148]

---

146 The site includes a brief introduction with an invitation to light a candle, and the long history of this ritual in the Christian tradition and in other faiths. The site was launched on All Saints Day, making the link to the communion of saints – part of the unseen reality that is a key element of the Catholic imagination (Wright, 2013). The online mode was well embraced by Gen–Xers as well as the Baby Boomers: 'Hello, I just wanted to congratulate [you] ... on the lovely idea enabling people to light a candle online for their special intentions. I wondered if it is possible to load the page as a screen saver or desktop background?' (Parish Secretary)

147 This resource provided eight different prayer experiences for Catholic school staff drawing on the variety of prayer styles found in the Catholic tradition. The purpose was three-fold:
- To develop a culture of expectation within staffs for communal prayer and personal prayer
- To provide a formative experience of prayer styles to help staff find and practice a sustainable prayer style
- To support leadership in the commitment to and engagement in the facilitation of staff prayer.
The following responses reflect the resonance of the *Staff PrayerFire* initiative across diverse communities.
'I actually had too many volunteers and had to put them into weekly teams!!!!! We have extended our staff prayer time to 30 minutes and changed the day so that more people (part-time staff) can be involved. I think we will finally have the school officers joining us for prayer and that has been a goal I haven't been able to achieve up to now.' (Systemic APRE, at a country primary school).

148 'I too have heard great things about the prayer candle site. At a meeting in Sydney

- The *Staff PrayerFire* initiative generated a sense of inclusion with an understanding that prayer life (like any other kind of learning) needs to fit the learner rather than the learner needing to fit the learning. This changed the spirit in which staff prayer was held.[149]

Overview of *Catching Fire* Staff Formation Programs

All schools access the goal setting, framework and systemic resources. And each year, in a strategic roll-out, 12 additional school communities are invited to be part of a *Catching Fire* Staff Formation Program. This program is carried out in a school-based, and systemically supported, whole school community approach. It is a targeted, developmental and sequential three-year program. It focuses on up to twelve staff from each school who engage with specific programs related to their role and context. The *Catching Fire* three core staff formation programs each explore the framework's three theological dimensions:

- The *Keepers of the Flame* program is designed for class-room teachers
- The *Guiding Lights* program is designed for school leadership personnel
- The *SpiritFire* program is designed for staff 'animators' and includes support staff.

All programs occur simultaneously and over a three-year period. During this time, each program reflects and explores the contemporary theological underpinnings of mission, aligning with the developmental formation journey of *My Story, Our Story, The Story* through the pedagogical lens of *Head, Heart, and Hands.*[150]

The *Keepers of the Flame Teacher's Program* is designed for classroom teachers to reflect on their life journeys and teaching vocations over a three year period. Each year there is a two and a half day live-in retreat, with follow-up days and contact. In the second year of the school's involvement, another three classroom teachers are invited to begin their three-year program.

---

yesterday I told the Bishops ... and they were most impressed. It is a great way of teaching people in this brave new world to pray.' (Brisbane Archbishop, John Bathersby.)

149   'Staff prayer has been great for us. It has been a revelation for our staff that the Catholic church actually had these different kinds of prayer in the vault! A bit more than the Our Father, Hail Mary and a bit of Christian meditation, which is about the limit of what I think most staff think Catholic prayer is, to be completely honest! And they love it. And they're doing the QuickFire prayer themselves through the week.' (Principal, outer metro primary school.)

150   The three programs share common principles and skills applied appropriately in differing contexts.

Participants must have at least five years' experience in the classroom. *The Guiding Lights Leadership Program* is designed for those on the school leadership team. The principal begins in the first year; other members of the leadership team begin their program in the second year. The focus is on the development of a strong spiritual base to their Catholic school leadership, their theological understanding, their developing of an integrated leadership style, all while engaging within the context of their school and church and developing a big picture understanding of mission. *The SpiritFire Program* is designed for those staff who are identified as animators – who already have spirit and interest in this area. The APRE and any other two staff members are targeted in this program (including finance officers, tuckshop convenors and secretaries). During this three-year program, which has a strong scripture and skills base, participants learn formation group facilitation and accompaniment skills for use in their school communities.[151] Figure 10.3 illustrates the three program banners.

FIGURE 10.3 THE THREE KEY *CATCHING FIRE* STAFF FORMATION PROGRAM BANNERS

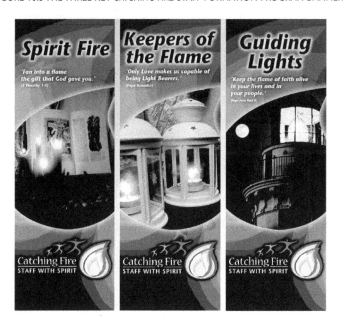

---

151 See link for Principles of Change Facilitation integrated into implementation: http://www.bne.catholic.edu.au/formationandleadership/Mission and Formation docs/Part E – About Adult Learning.pdf

Building Sustainable Systemic Capacity

Quite different from a retreat team approach or a service delivery approach, the aim of the *Catching Fire* strategic approach is to build powerful confidence and capacity across the 155 school communities that make up the Archdiocese. In this way, a 'discipleship' of staff is grown 'on the ground' who can co-facilitate formation in their own schools and clusters and other initiatives.

Those who complete one of the three-year programs are invited to discern a calling to become a Staff Formation Facilitator. They then complete a program which runs over one year. The purpose is to build system-wide capacity into the future among staff by growing a band of skilled formation facilitators across the system. This program is central to building strategic capacity across the system. (A more detailed outline of each of the programs is provided in the appendices for those who would like to explore further).

The Facilitators Formation Program

The program is accredited at Masters level at the Australian Catholic University and BBI – The Australian Institute of Theological Education (BBI – TAITE), key providers of graduate study for Catholic educators. The transference of experiences and skills from the program back into the classroom and school community context is a strong feature of development.

The focus of this program includes the following:

- Scriptural exegesis, prayer practices, group spiritual discernment and psycho-spirituality, tools in exploring and reflecting on the spiritual journey in a Christo-centric context
- Learning new tools with which to lead and facilitate groups
- Planning and practising formation processes during and between gathering days
- Opportunities to co-facilitate with 'seasoned' facilitators
- Explicit emphasis on how to 'do theology' and teaching others this skill

- Explicit emphasis on vocation and Catholic educational ministry
- Skills in presentation and articulation of faith story, catholic education story, and Christ story.

Principles of Practice for Facilitators

The work of formation for mission is a constant process of companioning people, and deepening understanding in reaching out, in transformation, in building community and in sending forth to be a difference in the world. The way Jesus built his community can be broken into those four steps:

1. He continually encountered others however and wherever they were in their lives [e.g. Mark 1:16, 38; Luke 4:43].
2. He opened a door to personal transformation/conversion [e.g. Mark 1:15].
3. He taught a vision of how Christian community grows and what it looks like [e.g. John 15:12; Matthew 18:15-18].
4. He empowered his followers to continue in living into this reality [Matthew 28:20; John 20:21].

Key Principles of Practice for facilitators of *Catching Fire* staff formation programs are also included in the Appendices (See Appendix 2).

Core Formation Elements and Community Capacities

Both the process reflected in the four core formation elements, and the nine capacities seen as missional outcomes of engagement in *Catching Fire*, reflect the new Model and its principles.

Core Formation Elements

Embedded in the formation approach itself are four core formation steps that embrace a Head, Heart and Hands approach, namely[152]:

1. **Experience** – engagement and reflective praxis with personal experience/story or stories of others who model particular ways of being
2. **Knowledge** – information about and conceptual understandings of key theological, scriptural and spiritual content
3. **Practice** – skills, practices and disciplines that will deepen the formative journey in an ongoing way

---

152   Such was the traction of this approach that the words Head, Heart and Hands has become the catch phrase in formation across the broader school communities. It has provided a framework educators can work with and feel confident in modelling and supporting because, in the words of one participant, 'Head, Heart and Hands speaks to everyone in a real and relevant way that makes sense for each of us separately and all of us together' (Principal, GLPGFB).

4. **Application** – application of deep learnings and skills to everyday contexts.

Core Capacities

Also embedded in the formation curriculum are associated capacities that the *Catching Fire* program seeks to develop in participants. These capacities are outcomes of their spiritual formation experience and recognisable hallmarks of Catholic Christian educators.[153] They reflect core characteristics of a Catholic school community and are the practical ways for living out the Mission of Jesus within Catholic education. The purpose is to nurture people in:

Presence	Prayer	Principle
Welcome	Ritual	Journey
Purpose	Commitment	Fidelity

These core formation elements and capacities guide content and process in each staff program and all resources. However, both program and resource implementation are designed to be experienced in different ways appropriate to the context and target group. Furthermore, while nominating core formation elements and spiritual capacities, the accompanying Framework book offers a comprehensive understanding of spiritual formation and a flexible guide for spiritual formation planning and goal-setting for renewal. Within this Framework individual staff and schools may shape programs of formation according to specific needs and contexts.

STRENGTHS

The strengths of this initiative lie in its careful construction, its context specific approach, its authentic formative experience and its comprehensive implementation. The experience of *Catching Fire* participants and school communities gives credence to the perspectives with which Bevans (2005), Borg (1994) and Wright (2002) understand the Christian meta-narrative. This way shifts the focus from dogma to relationship as the firmest pathway in recovering the 'layered universe' and 'conceptual world' of the Catholic tradition, so that those in educational ministry can live and be enlivened by what they are asked to proclaim.

In a concrete catholic educational setting, the new Model and implementation principles situate mission formation within a vocational

---

153   See link for an explication of each capacity: http://www.bne.catholic.edu.au/ formationandleadership/Mission and Formation docs/Capacities handouts.pdf

context that is both personal and professional. The process embraces reflective vocational praxis with personal journey. This becomes a powerful catalyst for those involved in Catholic educational communities where professional and personal witness are expected to converge. Further, the capacity to transfer the formative learning in programs to the classroom and community contexts embeds changes in everyday working structures and routines.

While skills and resources are part of the learning, there is a strong aspiration of authenticity evident among participants as a source reality that is sustaining. An emerging personal authentic relationship with Jesus and with the Divine not only sustains individuals, but directly influences community relationships, growing a culture perceived to align with the gospel values that underpin Catholic community. In addition, the impediments for some individuals in relation to the institutional Church appear to be reframed in a way that sees a diminishing of the negative encounters experienced. Thus, participants learn to hold the truth of their personal relationship with God, developed in community over the duration of the program, in creative tension with their reality of the variable ecclesial experience of church.

The resultant transformative phase for the individual is marked by a new way of seeing and being, with a new way of engaging with the tradition. The transformative phase for the school community is strongly characterised by the witness of the participants, self-described as 'authentic presence' in themselves and with each other.

The Model, Design Principles and Resources have now been adopted and contextualised by other dioceses and organisations in Australia and overseas. Two new staff networks have also grown out of *Catching Fire*. These are *MusicFire* who have now produced 2 CDs and offer twilight concerts for all schools, and *ArtsFire* which offers contacts and advice for contemporary artwork in schools.

CHALLENGES

There have been five main challenges:

1. While the impact of *Catching Fire* reflects the efficacy of the initiative itself in the adaptation of professional learning theory to spiritual formation,[154] it also indicates the need and receptivity for clarity and creative direction in this area. This is a continuing challenge.

---

154   O'Brien, 2004; Bellanca, 2004; Senge, 2000.

2. Unexpected changes in system-wide directions and new directives can derail the best thought-out initiatives, especially in a big system of schools where there are many competing areas of focus, and new projects to embed.

3. The longitudinal nature of this approach and of the formation process in general runs counter to the fast-paced dynamic of school life and shelf life of system projects.

4. The annual movement of staff among schools can mean a core group within a school is lost.

5. If a formation priority is not in the leadership of the system or the school, it is unlikely to have strategic traction.

CONCLUSION TO PART D

Having explored the complexities of the mission field, out of which is developed a new model of mission formation and design principles for implementation, we have also explored the application of that model in a real life system setting. We turn now to see the experience of other key practitioners across Australia in applying principles of best practice in their own contexts.

Part E
PRACTICE WISDOM: CASE STUDIES IN THE AUSTRALIAN CATHOLIC EDUCATIONAL LANDSCAPE

The feeling remains that God is on the journey, too.

(Saint Teresa of Avila)

INTRODUCTION TO PART E

Part E gives voice to the Practice Wisdom across the Catholic education landscape in Australia.

In giving shape to a formation process that engages life, faith and system worlds, the Formation Model in Part D has highlighted three key features: a 'head, heart and hands' praxis; a 'My Story – Our Story – The Story' narrative approach to authentic meaning-making; and the critical role of a communal dimension to formation. Fundamentally though, these aspects come from and go back to the heart of the Emmaus journey: a journey that asks for a head, heart and hands response; a journey where we can only make sense of the big story through our own story, and when that connection is made, 'our eyes are opened!'; and, as disciples of Jesus, a journey where we do not go alone, but learn who we are through the eyes of each other.

Part E now opens to the richness of practice wisdom in staff formation through a series of case study snapshots from those working in different Australian Catholic education settings. Here, in the chapters which follow, you will see most of all how the exciting work of these leaders responds to the mission field of Australian Catholic education in ways that powerfully resonate with the Emmaus imaginary – and you have the great privilege of hearing the wisdom of these practitioners in their own voices. Each writer reflects on the strengths and shortcomings of the work they share, and the challenges and hopes for the future of formation for Catholic educators.

Listen for your own resonances.

Have your eye on the principles at work.

11

FORMATION IN AN EARLY CAREER LEADER SETTING

Catholic Education, Armidale: Spiritual and Cultural Formation of Leaders through walking on Country – An Australian Emmaus Journey

Lee Herden leads Mission and Evangelisation for the Catholic Schools Office in the Diocese of Armidale. Here, Lee shares his reflections about 'Let's Talk Dhawunda'[155] – one of the most interesting and powerful formation experiences for new leaders that seek to deepen the understanding of the unique spiritual and cultural story of the indigenous peoples of this land. In this first piece of practice wisdom, we see in a leadership immersion program how the lens of scripture is brought to bear in the journey of listening to the story of indigenous culture, and how that process transforms the perspectives and actions of the Catholic school leaders involved.

The Context

One of the challenges with any leadership formation approach is being clear about the nature and purpose of the formation by asking the fundamental question, 'What are we forming people for?' This is a complex question which for those working in the Catholic school system in the Diocese of Armidale is answered in part quite simply: we are forming leaders who can bring the Gospel through our delivery of the curriculum in a way that is responsive to the most vulnerable and marginalised. In the Armidale Diocese many Aboriginal and Torres Strait Islander peoples fall into this category.

---

155 This is accompanied by a second program called 'Let's Talk Dhurramay'. Together these programs lead staff in diocesan Catholic Schools and national leaders in Catholic education to a deeper understanding of Aboriginal and Torres Strait Islander history and cultures from a Catholic worldview.

The Formation Initiative

The Catholic School Office formation program, 'Let's Talk Dhawunda', seeks to form leaders in Catholic schools that have high populations of Aboriginal and Torres Strait peoples enrolled, or as a significant presence in the local community. This leadership program is a partnership with the Catholic Schools Office, Armidale, and Edmund Rice Education, Australia. It deliberately sets out to challenge leaders to see the world through the eyes of the Aboriginal and Torres Strait Islander people on their terms, and in their way. It uses the Emmaus Journey as a model for developing a rich understanding of the differing spiritual and cultural perspectives that underpin issues for leadership in Armidale Diocesan Schools.

This model takes school leadership teams and general staff members on a week-long journey through time, landscape and perspective. It aims, as Jesus did in the story of the journey to Emmaus, to take people from where they are at in their understanding of the history and current circumstances of Aboriginal and Torres Strait Islander people in the Diocese, to a deeper understanding by hearing the story from a different perspective. As Our Lord did for the disciples on the way to Emmaus, the participants are given the knowledge that they need to help them on their journey of understanding. This knowledge, however, is given in a gently challenging way. It is shared 'on country' from an Aboriginal perspective. It aims to shake up existing understanding, to deliberately unsettle, and then to celebrate the 'aha' moments.

The approach was developed from the belief that if our leaders in Catholic schools are not given the opportunity to experience the place in which they live and work through the eyes, voices and lives of some of its most marginalised, then they will not be able to lead a school community that will spread the Gospel of joy.

Key Elements

The 'Let's Talk' immersion program has several key elements:

- It turns stereotypical expectations of formation on its head by having the journey led by three Aboriginal women and one white male.
- It takes small groups of staff across all areas in the school on an experiential journey.
- The facilitators walk with the participants as they hear the stories of the rich spiritual and cultural custodianship woven into the fabric of the land and the challenges alien cultures continue to have on Aboriginal culture. The untold history of

the European settlement of the area is told by local Aboriginal elders and cultural guides.

- Scripture is used throughout to link the experience of the Aboriginal people with messages of honouring the dignity of each human person as a creation made in the image and likeness of God. One of the most powerful moments for many participants is hearing of the oppression of the Brewarrina Mission where the Aboriginal people were exiled and forbidden to use their language or celebrate their culture, and to reflect on the banks of the Barwon River on the words of the Psalm 'by the rivers of Babylon where I sat down and wept when we remembered Zion. How can we sing the Lord's song in a strange land?'
- It explores the impact of colonial and Australian government decisions on the outlook of Aboriginal people today.
- It highlights the leadership of non-Aboriginal people in standing up for Aboriginal rights.
- It includes pre- and post-immersion support

Challenges

The three biggest challenges in this leadership approach are common to many such endeavours. The first is that of sustainability. The program is costly as it requires a significant budget for relief staff as well as high levels of energy by the four facilitators to be present for five days during over 2000kms of travelling in remote and challenging environments.

The second challenge is providing the ongoing spiritual and practical support to leaders at the school level and ensuring that subsequent leaders are brought into the program.

The third challenge is maintaining the commitment of the Catholic Schools Office Leadership Team to an approach where personal experiences and interior change cannot necessarily be measured by empirical data. For here we are called to look to the narrative data.

Strengths

Despite these challenges, the program has very clear intended outcomes in forming entire staffs to lead educational change that is reflective of the core Catholic value of the dignity of the human person, and in being a voice for the marginalised in their local schools and communities. Involving whole staffs has been a very successful model for achieving this aim.

Two examples of the success of this approach come from two principals in vastly different areas of the diocese. Both principals are long standing members of their respective communities. Both thought they knew it all. One came willingly onto the journey with the idea that she knew her town and the local story and couldn't see she would gain much. Her eyes were opened in a way she did not expect as she journeyed with local Aboriginal people through her own town; in this journey she saw the endemic injustices that were present and which were being perpetuated in her own school through ignorance. This principal has instituted new practices that ensure that all new staff, teaching and non-teaching, are inducted into the Aboriginal story of the area. She now approaches her work with Aboriginal families in a whole new way and with greater understanding than before.

The second principal was a reluctant participant on the journey. This principal identified fear as her barrier. She was frightened of Aboriginal people and frightened about what she might see, hear and experience. This principal, with the support of the facilitators, walked the journey and was transformed. In her own words she now sees with new eyes and hears with new ears. Her new understandings have enabled her to develop across the school an educational program that welcomes the Aboriginal story and wisdom as a part of our Catholic story. Her outlook has changed to such an extent that the Aboriginal student enrolment has significantly increased, as she has been more able to engage with the local Aboriginal community.

Using the Emmaus journey approach and walking with each staff member on their own journey of spiritual discovery is a powerful experience. It bridges the gap of ignorance and fear and replaces it with one that has a very Catholic outlook where, through dialogue and gathering at the table, we come to know each other as fully human. This approach is very successful as it relies not only on the facilitators, but more importantly on the cultural guides in each community who open their homes, stories and personal journeys to each of the participants.

While these are strengths they are also weaknesses. The success of the program relies on the cultural, social and historical knowledge of the facilitators and cultural guides and the good will of the communities we visit. Relationships have been built over time. Trust is the key in the operation of the immersion; trust that has been built with the four facilitators and the communities that share their stories. If the four facilitators were to leave it would make it difficult for the program to continue, as the program requires a deep relational connection with the communities involved.

From the experience of running this style of leadership formation for several years it has become obvious that the local context needs to have a very strong connection with Scripture. Where staff can be placed into the scripture 'on country' they are able to make better connections to the message of the Gospels and to make connections more easily with their own place of work and leading. While 'retreat' style programs of formation will always have a place, they do not always provide a real opportunity to connect with current realities.

The dream of the 'Let's Talk Dhawunda' immersion program is to shape Catholic leaders who are able to make real connections between the Gospel message and current realities. Thus they are able to create learning environments that make it possible for all in the school community to have every opportunity to learn at the highest levels, given the right resources and support. In so doing, such leaders will shape the future leaders of the country in the Catholic tradition.

12

FORMATION IN A SCHOOL
LEADERSHIP TEAMS SETTING

Catholic Education, South Australia: Growing Capacity
in School Leaders to lead Formation –
Nurturing the Mustard Seed

Mary Camilleri is Senior Education Advisor and Team Leader of Staff Spiritual and Religious Formation for Catholic Education in the Archdiocese of South Australia and the Diocese of Port Pirie. Mary shares her reflections about 'The Mustard Seed' – a systemic response to the need to grow school leaders' capacity to lead the spiritual formation of staff in their schools. In bringing the life faith and culture worlds together in dialogue, Mary, through the lens of her own extensive experience in Catholic schools and her passionate commitment to Catholic education, explains a highly creative and strategic program for school leadership teams.

The Context

Catholic Education South Australia (CESA), encompasses more than 6000 staff in 103 schools. The Catholic Education Office (CEO) supports the work of all Catholic schools in South Australia and is comprised of a number of teams, each committed to providing a cross-section of services. The Staff Spiritual and Religious Formation (SSRF) Team is one such team.

The heart of Catholic education is 'the heart'; that deep place within us where we encounter the Love that calls and sends us. A life-giving spirituality of staff in Catholic schools is a priority for the vocation of education and forming students.

> *Catholic educators need a 'formation of the heart: they need to be led to that encounter with God in Christ which awakens this love and opens their spirits to others, so that their educational commitment becomes a consequence deriving from their faith, a faith which becomes active through love* (Gal 5:6).156

---

156 Congregation for Catholic Education, 2007, Educating together in Catholic schools, viewed 10/2/11, <http://www.vatican.va/roman_curia/congregations/ccatheduc/

The SSRF team works collaboratively with school leadership teams to support the building of their religious leadership capacity. From a leadership perspective, the capacity to authentically witness to faith is seen as integral to the vocational participation in the mission of Catholic Education. School leaders are leaders in faith and are called to be role models for others.

Key Challenge

The greatest challenges for formation in the CESA context are growing the capacity of school leaders to lead the spiritual formation of staff in their schools, and the availability of resourcing both finances and personnel to fund specific pre-packaged programs. CESA's strategic focus is always on supporting and developing leaders' capacities.

In 2013, the SSRF team developed a Stimulus and Foundation paper: *Like a Mustard Seed* [157], to guide the nurturing of staff spirituality and build their capacity and confidence to witness to the gospel. *Like a Mustard Seed* articulates a shared understanding of spiritual and religious formation, and offers a vision, principles and broad strategic goals for the formation of staff in CESA. It has provided the substance for the SSRF Team's work over the past three years to develop the capacity of school leaders in their religious leadership. This has been done to enhance Catholic identity and to strengthen the spiritual and religious formation of staff in CESA schools and offices.

The Formation Initiative

Like a Mustard Seed promotes an invitation for all staff to engage in spiritual and religious formation to nurture their hearts and cultivate their vocation. Formative opportunities enable them to feel confident to participate in God's mission to enliven, engage, and educate themselves and others in order to transform the world.

Nurturing the Mustard Seed: a future full of hope is one formative experience offered by the SSRF team to build the capacity of school leaders (Principal's, Deputy Principals, and Assistant Principal Religious Identity and Mission), and to support them in the provision of a range of spiritual formation opportunities for their school staff. The program is jointly funded by the sector and each participating school. It is a two year accompaniment program where the SSRF Team consultants provide ongoing support for leaders in their Religious Leadership. This ongoing support begins with a live-in, three-day experience where school leadership teams come together to engage with their own spiritual journey, and to engage with their religious

---

documents/rc_con_ccatheduc_doc_20070908_educare-insieme_en.html
157   Catholic Education, South Australia, 2013.

leadership. Also, during this experience the SSRF team opens up a dialogue with school leaders to ensure that evangelisation and formation experiences are strategically planned and resourced throughout the school year, and do not become one-off reflection experiences or retreat days each year.

The program commences mid-morning on a Sunday and concludes on the following Tuesday afternoon. CESA does not have its own formation venue, and we hold the program in a seaside town around 75 kilometres from Adelaide, where we are far enough away to allow school leadership teams to disconnect, yet close enough to return if an emergency arises. More than half of CESA's school leadership teams have engaged with this program in four years.

Key Elements

As an invitation to participate we ask each individual to bring a symbol or artefact that represents their religious leadership, and this is shared with the group. These stories lead into prayer and scriptural reflection. As spirituality is central to what it means to be human, we commence the program with a focus on personal and communal spirituality. We draw on the resources of David Ranson's Cycle of Spirituality[158] and how it is understood within the Catholic tradition. We also engage the group with writings from Pope Francis[159] and Ron Rolheiser[160]. Throughout the three days, participants engage in a variety of activities such as journaling, group discussion, various critical thinking strategies, contemplative walking and meditation. As we move into more direct leadership capacity-building we explore the hermeneutic communicative model[161] and an understanding of Jesus' leadership as a witness, specialist and moderator. One of the after dinner activities gives focus to the importance of symbols in our tradition as participants explore their own role as witnesses, specialists and moderators. We also reflect on Pope Francis' religious leadership style and explore relevant CESA documents[162]. Engaging in stories of Pope Francis and Mary the Untyer of Knots,[163] we invite each individual to reflect on the enhancers and blockers to their own religious leadership.

Another aspect of the program is an introduction to Otto Scharmer's

158   David Ranson, The cycle of spirituality, www.spirituality-for-life.org
159   Pope Francis, 2013, Evangellii Gaudium: An apostolic exhortation of the Holy Father, Francis.
160   Richard Rolheiser, 2009, Holy Longing: The Search for Christian Spirituality, Image.
161   Didier Polleyfeyt and Jan Bouwens, Framing the identity of Catholic Schools: Empirical Methodology for Quantitative Research on the Catholic Identity of an Education Institute, International Studies in Catholic Education, 2(2).
162   Catholic Education South Australia, 2013, Like a mustard seed; Catholic Education South Australia, 2015, Religious Leadership policy; Catholic Education South Australia, 2015, Religious Leadership and the Catholic Identity of Schools.
163   Vallely, 2013, Pope Francis: Untyer of Knots, Bloomsbury Academic.

Theory U[164] which allows leaders to operate from a future space of possibility as they consider change in the culture and environment in the religious domain, and changes in their role as Catholic identity coaches. Theory U assumes leaders and institutions can experience extraordinary times of awareness or 'collective presence' that can lead to cultural change. Our world is a living system and all of its parts are deeply interconnected, and our actions are interrelated. This is not a new thought for those who belong to the Christian tradition. We recognise an extraordinary time of awareness to be an act of revelation, or receipt of grace, where the boundaries between ourselves and our world dissipate. To grow in our spirituality we must listen to 'the call' in order to let go of the old and to open to transformation.

FIGURE 14.1 THEORY U

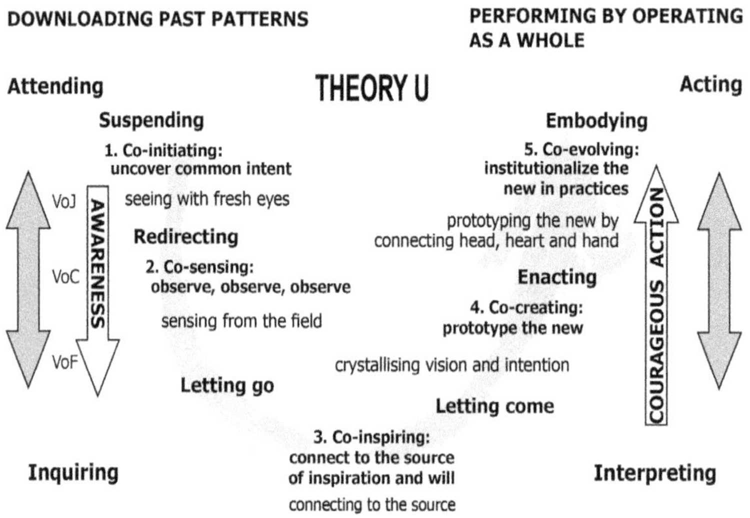

Theory U implies five movements to bring about change. Co-initiating, when we stop and listen to ourselves and others and then dialogue, is the first movement. This relates to the awakening phase of the cycle of spirituality. The second movement is one of co-sensing. This movement occurs when with a common intent we open our hearts and minds to listen and let go of personal agendas. This movement equates to the inquiring phase of the cycle of spirituality. At the bottom of the U is the presencing movement, that moment of deep connection when we can be fully present to self and others, and be in a state of being where we allow a new future to emerge from us and through us. This allows us to move into a state of readiness where we can

---

164   C. Otto Scharmer: Addressing the blind spot of our time: An executive summary of the new book by Otto Scharmer, Theory U: Leading from the Future as It Emerges https://www.presencing.com/theoryu

move from a personal spirituality (my story), to the communal (our story) and the story akin to the interpreting phase of the cycle of spirituality. On the upside of the U, the fourth movement is that time when we have allowed our new future to begin to take concrete shape and we explore new ways to having a go and exploring by doing, similar to the acting phase of the cycle of spirituality. This movement may or may not be the final emergent action. On evaluation of the prototype idea we may have to move back through these first four movements to iterate a new idea. In the fifth movement, co-evolving, we see a new flourishing of our faith in action.

It is through making the links between the cycle of spirituality and Theory U that participants have discovered a new and effective approach to spiritual formation.[165] Having linked the presencing theory and cycle of spirituality, participants embark on a more pragmatic engagement with staff formation and it is always done within their school groups, whereas early in the program we encourage participants to work with colleagues from other schools. We commence the school based section of the program with a study of Roberto's[166] quadrants of a faith community. This is done as a way of knowing their school staff community in order to understand the need for appropriate and differentiated spiritual and religious formation. With this knowledge and CESA's *continuous improvement framework*[167], we engage school leaders in the initial stages of strategic planning for the formation of their staff. The challenge for us at this point is to return the focus to staff formation, as the school leaders quickly drift to a focus on formation of students. It is often difficult for them to focus on what staff spiritual and religious formation is.

This time together to plan and reflect as a leadership team is highly regarded by participants.

Over these three days leaders are engaged with a variety of prayer styles and join together in a celebration of the Eucharist. During the penitential rite, the priest engages them with 'play of life' figurines as a way to explore mercy and forgiveness in their lives. They reflect on who is the 'other' for them. This is a powerful experience of reconciliation for participants.

A major feature of *Nurturing the Mustard Seed: a future full of hope* is the ongoing companioning of school leadership teams after the three day experience in the context of their schools. An SSRF consultant meets with the leadership team at least once a term for the next two years. Companioning takes the shape of listening in a supportive and resourceful

---

165 With thanks to Otto Scharmer and David Ranson, the SSRF team have joined these two 'theories' together as a model to engage in staff faith formation.

166 John Roberto, New Approaches to Parish Evangelisation, www.21stcenturyfaithformation. com

167 Catholic Education, South Australia, 2014.

way, acting as a sounding board as teams rediscover and sift through their school-based experiences of staff spiritual and religious formation. In our companioning we use appreciative inquiry questioning and have adapted the WDEP[168] formula from Choice Theory into a series of questions to mentor leadership teams. The companion allows them to keep perspective and maintain focus as schools explore different ideas about spirituality and religious formation. The SSRF team believes we are wiser together.

Strengths

Since the inception of *nurturing the mustard seed,* during our companioning visits the SSRF Team now notice leadership teams taking a more strategic approach to staff formation. We are also aware of an increased variety of approaches to formation and a greater connection to daily life at school in retreat and in reflection day experiences. Many schools are spending more time involving staff in formation processes and taking greater consideration of the experiences and capabilities of staff to ensure more engaging formation experiences. Both leaders and teachers are increasingly taking up opportunities to grow their scriptural and theological knowledge.

The *Nurturing the Mustard Seed* experience has evolved and we, as system support, need to be adaptable during the experience to meet the needs of participants. We gather participants together once a year to share their faith formation stories and from such gatherings two new system programs have emerged in 2016 – one, an engagement in the school leader's personal faith journey, *Come to the Water,* and the other, *Nurturing the Mustard Seed Stage Two,* known as *Making Nests in the Mustard Tree,* where we further build capacity in religious leadership.

As a Church, we are in a liminal period where school leaders are being called into new responsibilities of religious leadership. They are called to be grounded in their faith, to possess a spiritual maturity and to engage in ongoing formation not only for themselves but for their staff as well. If the capacity of leaders and staff to engage in spiritual and religious formation is to be achieved, then it is necessary to cultivate and nurture staff from the 'ground up'.[169] The capacity building principle embedded in *Nurturing the Mustard Seed* assists school leaders to help staff come to the knowledge that they are loved by God who invites them into a relationship.

---

168 Robert Wubbolding, 2002.
169 School leaders need to be mindful of the Catholic church's 'principle of subsidiarity' which is essential to any model of inclusive leadership. Religious leadership is a guiding process achieved through authentic relationships. Subsidiarity requires leadership to be spread across the school community, and hence all staff spiritual and religious formation needs to be in a trusting and collaborative environment.

13

FORMATION IN A FOUNDING CHARISM SETTING

Good Samaritan Education, Australia: Mission Formation through Immersion – The Lens of Charism in the Faith Life and Culture Dialogue

Monica Dutton and Sr Meg Kahler are leaders in the Good Samaritan Education Mission Team responsible for serving all Good Samaritan Schools across Australia. Highly experienced, they facilitate formation immersion programs for staff and for students. In sharing their practice wisdom, they provide insight into a religious institute context for Catholic education. We see how the founding story and charism of this religious order finds expression in and provides 'a way in' to the dialogue between faith, life and culture.

The Context

Education in the Good Samaritan Benedictine tradition has been a vibrant and dynamic part of the fabric of Catholic education in Australia for almost 160 years. Until very recently, Australian Good Samaritan schools were established, staffed and governed by the Sisters of the Good Samaritan of the Order of St Benedict[170], and formation in the tradition was ensured by their highly visible and influential presence in the schools. The transfer of leadership and governance from the Good Samaritan sisters to their lay counterparts in the current Good Samaritan educational context sees, since 2011, ten schools across five dioceses and three states which comprise the public juridic person (PJP) known as *Good Samaritan Education (GSE)*.[171]

---

170 The Sisters of the Good Samaritan of the Order of St Benedict were founded by Benedictine Archbishop John Bede Polding and Mother Scholastica Gibbons rsc in 1857.

171 With the agreement of the Archbishops of Brisbane, Melbourne and Sydney and the Bishops of Broken Bay and Wollongong, GSE was constituted as a collegial PJP in 2011 and 'assumed the Congregation's rights and obligations pertaining to the ministry of Catholic education'. In the transfer of governance from the congregation to GSE, the sisters were aware of 'the responsibility of reading the signs of the times and of interpreting them in the light of the Gospel' and sought to remain very closely involved with the ten schools. The work of GSE is predominantly in secondary education for girls. There are two co-educational schools, one of which meets the wide-ranging needs of students with mild to moderate intellectual disability. As a collegial PJP, GSE is

A PJP is 'established by ecclesial authority with an apostolic purpose; it is perpetual in nature; it has canonical rights and obligations and has its own internal statutes'.[172] This shift in governance models towards the PJP in the mission of education is a relatively recent trend.

The charism of *Good Samaritan Education* is centred on the person of Jesus Christ. Enriched and inspired by the Parable of the Good Samaritan, the Rule of Benedict and the tradition of the Sisters of the Good Samaritan Benedictine tradition, the mission of *Good Samaritan Education* is to sustain and nurture communities of learning in the Catholic tradition.

Challenges in Staff Formation

Maintaining staff formation as a priority is one of the many challenges faced by leadership teams in Catholic schools. Programs require a significant investment of time, energy and resources, both human and financial. Budgetary restraints and competing demands for limited financial means in the school setting, makes it increasingly difficult to allocate the necessary funds to maintain authentic, relevant and high quality opportunities. In the context of accreditation and increasing accountability, the complexity of aligning staff formation and spirituality programs to the Australian Institute for Teaching and School Leadership professional teacher standards (AITSL), provides both challenge and opportunity for leaders.

The increasing difficulty of recruiting staff members who share in the life of the Church is also a challenge. Expertise in pedagogy is not always matched by a willingness to engage with the mission and values of the Catholic school. Juxtaposed with this challenge is the question of 'mandatory versus invitational' formation experiences. While most staff members agree to participate in induction programs in the initial stages of their employment, they do not always avail themselves of opportunities to deepen their understanding in their particular school setting. After the induction process, many staff members actively (or more frequently, passively) resist engagement in formation opportunities. While, in some schools, participation in formation programs is linked to goal setting and appraisal processes; in other schools, staff more commonly self-identify professional learning opportunities.

In addition, a range of complexities arise for members of newly emerging governance structures in congregational schools. Responsibility for ensuring ongoing formation in the Good Samaritan Benedictine tradition now lies with the *GSE* Governing Council, and the imperative is clear: 'All who accept the invitation to join *Good Samaritan Education* will

---

committed to communion and to discernment as fundamental to life.
172 Date (2008).

participate in formation experiences to assist them to grow in understanding of their ministry as part of the mission of the Catholic Church'[173]. Within this structure, the *GSE* Mission Team provides a range of formation and immersion opportunities, for all school communities to 'become inspired by the charism to respond to the Gospel call to bring about the reign of God.'[174] Sustaining strong Catholic leaders, and maintaining the centrality of the Church's identity and mission at the heart of all is, however, becoming increasingly complex.

Essential Elements

In the *GSE* context, formation for mission is Christ-centred, with a focus on prayer, community and mission. Formation opportunities typically include targeted workshops, conferences, retreats and immersion experiences. The design and delivery of programs is informed by the Good Samaritan Philosophy of Education, the *GSE* Formation for Mission Framework and the *GSE* Formation for Mission Handbook.[175] *GSE* formation programs are intentional, progressive, targeted and reflective, and aim to engage staff and governance personnel in 'knowing the story, entering the story and shaping the story'.[176] Formation opportunities are designed to be developmental, ecclesial and vocationally contextualised.[177] The understanding of charism is adopted from Augustinian Claude Maréchal's description of charism as 'giving structure, being and action, and involves a story to enter, a language to speak, a group to which to belong, a way to pray, a work to undertake, a face of God to see'.[178]

The programs are empirically based and draw upon the principles of adult learning. The design elements focus on engaging participants in aspects of experience, knowledge and application, relevant to their professional role and personal spiritual journey, and the delivery method is facilitative rather than didactic. The language used in all *GSE* programs is inclusive and reflects a contemporary theology.[179] Preconceived notions or prescribed levels of assumed knowledge or practice are avoided, and the unique diversity of the Australian context and its inherent challenges are recognised. Various ways of prayer are developed and nurtured and the belief that all are called to engage in God's mission is clearly articulated.

---

173 Good Samaritan Education, 2011a, section 6.
174 Good Samaritan Education, 2011a, section 6.
175 Good Samaritan Education, 2011a.
176 Good Samaritan Education, 2011a.
177 Good Samaritan Education, 2011a, section 9.
178 Maréchal, 1999.
179 Examples of contemporary theologians who have influenced the development of GSE formation programs include (but are not limited to) Dr Elizabeth Johnson CSJ, Dr Rosemary Radford Ruether and Dr Elisabeth Schüssler Fiorenza.

Hoped-for Outcomes

It is hoped that through participation in *GSE* formation and immersion programs, staff members will come to a deeper understanding of their own personal spirituality, discover ways to prayer, appreciate the value of communion within and across *GSE* schools, and become aware of discernment as being fundamental to life. Using a reflective process grounded in the *GSE* tradition – *Listen, Learn, Live*[180], it is also hoped participants will develop a sense of their spiritual selves, and their role in their school and within the wider educational endeavour of *GSE*. It is hoped participants will develop and strengthen partnerships with other Good Samaritan schools and ministries, and that they will explore ways to apply their experience and knowledge within their sphere of influence in their school communities. In the formation process it is hoped staff members will come to see that the Good Samaritan Benedictine tradition is not an 'add-on', but rather a seamless integration of charism, pedagogy, pastoral care and mission.

Indicators of Change – Staff Immersion

An area in which *GSE* has clear evidence of change as a result of formation is staff immersion. The immersion experiences are firmly grounded in the Catholic tradition, and the Gospel message as expressed in the Parable of the Good Samaritan is central to the structure and purpose of the trips. Catholic identity and mission as expressed in Catholic Social Teaching through the concepts of human dignity, the common good, solidarity and subsidiarity, are foundational to the philosophy and rationale of the trips, and are articulated through the charism of the Sisters of the Good Samaritan[181]. During their immersion experience, participants engage with people in Catholic communities, participate in Catholic worship, and the itinerary includes visits to places of religious significance in the host community.

After their immersion experience staff members have reported higher levels of understanding of, and engagement with, the mission life of their school, including social justice initiatives, student retreats and reflection days. A significant shift in perspective in this area is common:

> *Before the trip the work of mission in the school had no connection to me, it was just, in one ear and out the other. Social Justice Day and social justice activities and Reflection Days were ... annoyances because they kept me from what I perceived to be my job, as being a deliverer of content and skills in Science. Whereas when it came around this year, I thought, 'I am a part of Social Justice Day'. I am not the teacher complaining, 'I am missing a*

---

180   Good Samaritan Education, 2011b.
181   Good Samaritan Education, 2012.

Science lesson with my Year 12s.' Now I have realised that curriculum sits side by side with my job of delivering a social justice message. It also gave me a new appreciation of teachers of Religion and the work of the Social Justice team. Yes, so I am a convert! (Chris)[182].

That was the 'aha' thing, I came back realising that charism and school should be such a natural fit and not something that just gets rolled out a couple of times a year. (Alex).

The Catholic context of their immersion trip also provides participants with the opportunity to reflect on the place of the Catholic tradition in their lives. The following comments offer an insight into their experiences.

I feel that I am not a deeply spiritual person. Raised a Catholic, I am probably a lapsed Catholic. I do not go to church every Sunday, and I have not ... [gone at all] for a long time, but for me, the immersion trip re-established that I am a Catholic. It just cemented it back (Chris).

Staff members participating in immersion trips also believe the experience changed them as teachers, and that they had developed more positive attitudes towards students. Many expressed the view that there had been a realignment of their personal and professional perspectives.

Over time, the cumulative effect of staff participation in our Immersion programs is that some schools have had over 20 staff members who have participated in the program. From a wider school perspective, opportunities for building support for social justice and mission activities within the school community are enhanced if there is broad base of people who have experienced a shift in perspective due to such transformative formation experiences.

Strengths and Limitations

A notable strength of GSE formation programs is evidence of a broad cultural shift as our school communities have become more familiar with the Good Samaritan Benedictine values. A focus on staff formation has enabled a clear articulation of the values as they are applied to teaching and learning, pastoral care, and mission programs. The development of a three-year plan using a cyclical approach to highlight Good Samaritan values has facilitated a greater familiarity with, and deeper understanding of, aspects of the tradition and their application.

GSE formation programs are progressive and intentionally target participants in different roles in schools. Programs are designed to be inclusive

---

182   All participant names are pseudonyms.

of people in leadership and governance, and teaching and non-teaching positions. Good Samaritan Benedictine values resonate with people from a range of backgrounds, enabling them to integrate values into the real-world context.

The invitational nature of *GSE* formation programs may be viewed as both a strength and a limitation. While invitational opportunities are embraced by those who share in the story and have a clear understanding of the tradition, it may enable those less committed to the ethos of the school to avoid participating in opportunities on offer. Other limitations due to timetabling and budgetary pressures constrain the number of staff members that schools can release to attend formation programs. Also, where a limited theological understanding of participants exists, the risk is that the values and context of the Good Samaritan Benedictine tradition may be adapted in ways that dilute or distort its meaning, or ignore its broader context.

Changing to Meet Needs

GSE has moved away from the 'one size fits all' staff spirituality day. It is recognised that staff members have specific and individual formation needs in the area of spirituality, Catholic identity and mission, and the Good Samaritan Benedictine tradition. A range of programs is therefore offered to meet participant needs at various stages and phases of their growth.

The design elements of GSE formation programs now prioritise sessions which draw on the personal experiences of participants relevant to their spiritual lives and include opportunities for dialogue, processing, reflection and integration. Programs also challenge on a professional level providing opportunity to explore application of learning in the wider school context.

Our Hope for Catholic Educators of the Future

Our hope for Catholic educators of the future is that they continue to have, and engage in, ongoing opportunities for formation and spiritual development. The need is clear, as 'staff formation is acknowledged as a priority area for professional learning and is argued to be the ultimate basis by which teachers are empowered to pursue the mission of Catholic education'[183].

Through deep and intensive formation experiences for those in governance, leadership and on staff, it is hoped Catholic educators of the future come to truly understand the gift of their tradition. It is hoped they come to appreciate that formation experiences are an effective way of making sense of our shared legacy, touching the heart and soul of what it means to be a Catholic educator.

---

183   Lay Catholics in Schools: Witnesses to Faith #22.

14

FORMATION IN A PEDAGOGICAL SETTING

Catholic Education, Tasmania: Catholic Curriculum as a Means of Formation – A Wisdom Pedagogy

*John Mula is the Executive Director, Tasmania Catholic Education (TCE). Here, John and co-contributors **Sandra Harvey** (Head of Education Services, TCE Office) and **Drasko Dizdar** (Project Officer Mission & Religious Education, TCE Office) share reflections on their innovative work in embedding a set of 'skills' into the broader school curriculum that seeks the flourishing of the Catholic education community through an integration of life and faith. We see how the curriculum provides 'the Way' in the Emmaus journey.*

Our Context

Catholic education in Tasmania today is a community of thirty-eight schools and colleges serving over 16,000 students and their families. Our schools aim to be quality Catholic schools where students are offered opportunities to fully develop and learn to integrate their gifts of head, heart and hands in a challenging learning environment within a caring community – a community based on Gospel values.

In many ways our history has shaped our approach to formation. Until 1821, the Catholic residents of the colony, both convicts and free settlers, had no priest. In that year Father Philip Conolly arrived and until 1835 Father Conolly laboured alone. In that year, the Most Rev John Bede Polding arrived at Hobart on his way to Sydney to take up his appointment as Bishop. The Holy See had appointed him Vicar-Apostolic of all Australia, and Tasmania remained part of his Vicariate until the coming of the first Bishop of Hobart, the Most Rev Robert William Willson, who landed in May 1844.

Catholic schools have been a vital expression of the mission of the Church in Tasmania since the founding of the first Catholic school in Richmond in 1825. Initially staffed by lay people and the Sisters of Charity, Tasmanian Catholic schools, like their mainland colleagues, have relied heavily on the dedication of religious orders and local parishes for more than 125 years.

From those early beginnings there are now 27 parishes in Tasmania and out of a total Tasmanian population of approximately 508,000, some 87,691, or 18.4%, are Catholics. This remains the lowest ratio in any Australian state or territory. Our Catholic schools and colleges reflect these demographics, with Catholic enrolments making up on average 45% of all student enrolments. Likewise, Catholic staff make up, on average, 55% of all teaching employees.

It is in this context that our approach to formation has been developed.

Our Approach to Formation

With no Catholic university in Tasmania, most graduates are recruited from the University of Tasmania (UTAS). More recently, partnerships with other institutions such as BBI – The Australian Institute of Theological Education (BBI – TAITE) have offered undergraduate units at UTAS. The Tasmanian Catholic Education Office (TCEO) supports a range of opportunities. This includes heavily subsidised scholarships to teachers who undertake Religious Education (RE) studies at postgraduate level. Reflecting the current nature of school and college governance, school-based spirituality programs have been offered in the past but have been ad hoc in their approach. Systemic programs have included staff retreat programs; however, for a relatively small system there has been no sequential program differentiating for individual needs (e.g. Catholic/non-Catholic, age, employment position, career stage, family commitments).

The challenge of a relatively low Tasmanian Catholic population, Catholic staff and Catholic enrolments, and the absence of a local tertiary Catholic presence, have shaped our approach to formation. We view formation as a particular aspect or quality of 'professional learning' that is distinct from the acquisition of knowledge and skills. In this sense we use the term 'formation' in its broadest sense as a broad, inclusive process of guidance, education, nurturing and shaping of a person – intellectually, physically, emotionally, socially and spiritually – such that their living and learning in our school communities enables their wellbeing and flourishing for life. Ultimately it is about the personal and professional formation offered for each and all in the Catholic education community, enabling one's relationship with God to flourish and thereby empowering us for the Mission of Catholic education.

Formation opportunities are an invitation to both personal enrichment and personal transformation, and as such these opportunities are a free domain open to the grace of the Holy Spirit. The essential aspects of our approach to formation are such that specific opportunities for formation, including all programs that are offered:

- Be invitational, respectful of the needs and uniqueness of each person
- Involve each person's autonomous response
- Draw from the rich traditions of the Church
- Be grounded in contemporary scholarship
- Be connected to the vocational context of each person
- Include participation opportunities at a school level and at a System level.

Like most Formation programs, Tasmania Catholic Education offers a range of differentiated approaches including:

- Whole staff school-based opportunities on an annual basis
- A range of retreat programs including
  - in school
  - overnight
  - career stage cohorts
- Formal postgraduate studies in theology
- Pilgrimage opportunities.

Perhaps our most 'broad brush' approach to formation is our school-based action research projects, specifically the exploration of Wisdom Pedagogy as a cross curriculum priority of Catholicity, and the development of a 'catholic curriculum.'

A Wisdom Pedagogy

Based on the 'Seven Gifts of the Holy Spirit' (awe, reverence, courage, knowledge, understanding, discernment, and wisdom), 'wisdom pedagogy' is an opportunity for a planning and learning methodology for Catholic education.

Formation in a culture marked by 'Catholicity' is touched by awe for God's presence and a reverent universality of vision for all humanity and all creation. Its purpose is to nurture a heartfelt commitment to the Gospel, and human integrity grounded in a relationship of faith in God. The process of formation within the dynamics of schooling is often contained in curriculum and syllabus statements that focus on the acquisition of knowledge, skills and understanding. It is important to recognise that these gifts of the Holy Spirit are part of a greater whole that culminates in the ultimate gift of the Holy Spirit, namely wisdom, and that this involves a life-long process of conversion and transformation of the whole person.

Without the prior platform of the Spirit's gifts of awe, reverence and courage, the learner will often not be personally engaged in the pursuit of knowledge, understanding and discernment, and will be impeded in their formation in wisdom as a human being fully alive (John 10:10). The TCE Learning and Teaching Platform, with its balanced focus on the learner, curriculum, pedagogy and the learning environment, is a recent expression of these principles.

TABLE 14.1 TCE LEARNING AND TEACHING PLATFORM

Wisdom Capability	Elements of a Learning Continuum Seeking wisdom ...		
Awe and Wonder	In self	In others	In God
Reverence and Courage	In self	In others	In God
Knowledge and Understanding	In self	In others	In God
Discernment	In self	In others	In God

A Catholic Curriculum

A holistic Catholic approach to the curriculum enables the Catholic education community to flourish through an integration of life and faith. It does so by developing a set of 'skills' that are contemplative, compassionate, critical and celebratory; and then integrates them into the boarder school curriculum.

Contemplative: The radically human capacity for **awe** and **wonder** before the Mystery that grounds our being gives rise to a need to express deepest **respect** and **reverence** for that Mystery and to do so with a whole-hearted commitment. To be contemplative is to be as fully present and engaged in the presence of the Divine Mystery, God. To be contemplative, then, is to dwell in that space of encounter with God. For us as Christians that space is 'salvific', a space of freedom and of liberation. The task of our Catholic curriculum is to make us ever more capable of this contemplative way of being by nurturing our natural human capacity for God, for the life-giving Spirit whose temples we are as whole human beings – body, mind, heart. To be contemplative, then, is to abide in God.

Compassionate: As contemplatives who abide in God we find our hearts begin to expand and our capacity for compassion grows. 'Be compassionate,' said Jesus, 'as your Father is compassionate' (Luke 6:36) – which is Luke's way of throwing light on what Matthew means when he has Jesus say what amounts to the same thing: 'You must therefore be perfect, just as your heavenly Father is perfect' (Mt 5:48). The task of the Catholic curriculum is to present human beings as being created for love by Love itself, capable of seeing ourselves as loved *and* capable of loving, able to *be* loved and able *to* love. Love then gives us the **courage** to be 'love-able'. In essence the Catholic curriculum provides an alternative view to a world of suffering, injustice and evil.

Critical: It takes courage to be compassionate because it takes compassion to ask the critical question: But why is there suffering? 'Courage' means to act with heart. The human heart is made for compassion; and compassion must have enough courage, enough 'heart', to ask: Why is there suffering? What are its causes? And how do we overcome them, and to ask these questions deeply, unrelentingly, comprehensively.

The Catholic curriculum offers a 'critical capacity' to question radically when grounded in love as contemplative compassion and compassionate contemplation. It wants to **know** all that can be known, to **understand** what it knows, and so to act with **wisdom** born of careful and just **discernment**. An intelligent, mature and sound Christian sensibility shapes and is itself shaped by the honing of this critical capacity and ultimately seeks deeper meaning.

Celebratory: Jesus, 'filled with joy by the Holy Spirit, said, 'I bless you, Father, Lord of heaven and of earth, for hiding these things from the learned and the clever and revealing them to little children' (Luke 10:21). Children, who are still very much in love with Mystery and abide in its embrace, have an astonishing capacity for joy and celebration. The Catholic community most frequently and pointedly calls itself a 'Eucharistic community' – a people who know how to give joyful thanks to the Giver of all good gifts, and of the greatest gift of all: life in God, which is to say the very Spirit and Self of God that we receive through Christ. The Catholic curriculum promotes life, as God's loving gift of God's very Self. It is the source of our hope for which our capacity for celebration is our most eloquent answer to any who may wonder at it (1 Peter 3:15).

Curriculum as Journey

Our entire curriculum is a course in the sense of a *journey* (the literal meaning of *curriculum*), that begins in God as Love loving us into being and ends in God as the communion of Love we call Trinity: the One Who Is Loving, the One Who Is Beloved, and the One Who Is the Love that unites us as the One-Who-Is. To be united with one another, with all creation, in a eucharistic/thankful community of celebration is the 'source and summit' of what an authentically and thoroughly Catholic Curriculum is here to serve, promote and enable. In other words, a truly *Catholic* Curriculum is one that belongs to the One Who Is and who loves us into being.

Challenge and Opportunity

The concept of Wisdom Pedagogy as a cross-curriculum priority and the development of a Catholic curriculum as opportunities for formation, is not without its challenges. Both approaches are still at the 'developing' stage with trials taking place, action research projects at a school level, retreat programs for groups/individuals/whole staff, and staff engaged in various other professional learning opportunities. System resourcing and schools being 'time poor' have hampered the work of transforming the theory into practice. Ultimately the formation of staff needs to be a strategic intent, at both a system and school level. This also requires us to challenge the culture and understanding of formation, ensuring that it is 'what we do and who we are' rather that a program or series of programs or courses.

Despite these challenges it remains our intention that formation invites each staff member on a personal journey of conversion or transformation through the imitation of Christ, which is the journey and work of a lifetime. This can be achieved:

1. *Practically* by developing skills and a knowledge base to meet the challenge of being part of Catholic education
2. *Personally* by knowing and understanding more about what it means for them individually and as members of a community to be part of Catholic education
3. *Professionally* by exploring openly, intelligently, and deeply the spiritual, philosophical and theological foundations of Catholic education and its rich tradition.

Our Hope

Our ultimate aim for formation is to see staff who are flourishing, who are focused on Jesus' mission for our schools, staff who bear witness to Christ and the Gospel in their own lives and in their teaching and dealings with young people and each other.

It is our belief that the strength of this approach to formation is its comprehensiveness and the opportunity to build capacity in all. It is daunting if we believe that it depends on just 'us'. Formation is what *God* does – it is the work of God and we are invited to co-operate in that work. While we are limited by our own ability (we cannot do this on our own), God is the unlimited and infinite source of strength and grace who not only 'can' but will bring us to that fullness of life Jesus came to give us.

15

FORMATION IN AN ONLINE SETTING

National Centre for Evangelisation (NCE) Teaching Theology to Adults: The Journey From Informing to Forming

Shane Dwyer is Director of the new National Centre for Evangelisation. Shane's reflections are distilled from his experience in adult faith education and spiritual formation in two dioceses as well as his work as an academic dean for BBI – TAITE and Director of Academic Resources at the Sydney College of Divinity. Shane has pioneered work in the online space, and here he shares his practice wisdom in this area and his insights on its gift and limitations in the wider field of formation. Dialogue, with its possibilities for the heart to gradually 'catch fire' in the recognition of Jesus in the midst of life, is fundamental to this mission field.

Setting the Context

In the broader context, I identify five current challenges:

1. The tendency to believe that knowledge is a substitute for experience

2. The tendency to regard formation as being of use only to the degree that it provides material to assist with a teacher's class preparation

3. The tendency to believe that it is possible to teach children about the Catholic faith while having little or no commitment to that faith oneself

4. The tendency to refuse to engage with objective teachings about the Catholic faith if it is perceived to be not in accord with one's current subjective experience

5. A degree of cynicism for anything to do with the Catholic faith as part of the fall out associated with the Royal Commission into Institutional Responses to Child Sexual Abuse.

Different Times, Different Needs ... a Flexible Approach

The degree to which postmodernists will happily wander between various Christian denominations, and will avail themselves of a wide variety of alternative spiritual influences, tells us something. As a culture we are not too worried about where the truth we find comes from. Instead, we are more interested in whether or not it happens to ring true *for us* and whether or not it is useful *to us*. Truth is no longer true in its own right: it is true to the degree to which it makes sense to me and contributes to the obvious improvement of my life. This context informs the faith formation work in which I have been engaged for the last few years. I have noted there are at least three groups of people who undertake theological study:

1. Those who are studying theology for a variety of reasons but who do not feel called to personally appropriate what they are discovering in the course of that study

2. Those who are on a personal spiritual quest and undertake the study of theology because they hope that it will take them further on that quest

3. Those who are on a personal spiritual quest and, while they understand the study of theology will not address their need for spiritual authenticity, they see it as useful and have other strategies in place to assist them to integrate what they are learning.

How we can address the legitimate needs of the people in each of these groups takes considerable thought. What is required is a means of communication and engagement that is flexible enough to address the diverse needs of participants. It is in this context that I began to experiment with a modified form of online learning. In recent years I have trialled three different types of online formation experiences, each with different objectives:

1. Daily prayer reflections via email, text or podcast around a particular theme.

2. Facebook closed groups for the sharing of reflections and resources for people involved in a particular ministry. The latest is for teachers who attend my staff formation days.

3. A Certificate IV in Theology and Ministry consisting of four introductory modules: Catholic theology, Scripture, sacraments and liturgy, and mission.

Essential Aspects of an Emerging Mode

In the movement from distance learning via paper and post to online learning, the emerging method of course provision brought with it a number of benefits:

1. In an age where getting to classes across busy cities is increasingly hard to do, being able to stay at home to study is very attractive. Tertiary institutions tend to be in cities.
2. In an environment where people go online to do much of their information gathering and social interaction, participating in online courses is a comfortable experience.
3. In the midst of a busy work, home and social life, being able to attend to course requirements in one's own time is very attractive.
4. Given that people learn at different rates and in different ways, the flexibility afforded by online learning can work very well.

Modified Online Learning

Despite the obvious advantages of participating in courses online, I soon became aware of an ongoing problem: the study of theology must be about more than imparting information, writing assignments and passing exams. This is especially so if the person undertaking the study is intended to be someone whose role will be to impart the practice of the Catholic faith to others. Unlike the study of theology on campus, online learning allows for little opportunity to provide the experience of support, discussion, prayer, liturgy, avenues for spiritual direction, and mission that a well-functioning Catholic campus (ideally) provides.

It is the desire to attend to this problem that has influenced my work in the online environment in the last few years. It has involved replacing the question, 'How do I best impart the information that participants need to pass this course?' with, 'How do I best engage participants in the experience of reflecting on their own relationship with God, while providing them with the vocabulary and tools needed to do that?' The provision of information is at the service of reflection on experience. For this reason I find the Vocational Education and Training sector, with its emphasis on experience-based learning, much more conducive than the tertiary sector.

This two-part question drives everything and I must admit that attending to it is not always easy. The complicating factor is that everyone's experience is different. As a result, their needs are different too. The interactive component of the course then becomes essential. Because extensive one-on-one contact with the course presenter is neither practical nor desirable, the task becomes one of facilitating and monitoring the online interaction between participants themselves. In much the same way as happens between course participants in class and then perhaps over a coffee afterwards, online course participants are asked to share their responses to the various discussion stimuli with which they have been provided. The role of the course provider becomes one of gently monitoring the participant conversations, stepping in to help resolve any tricky questions that arise, and following up with anyone who seems a bit lost.

The second element I have introduced to the study of theology online is a journal component. This is an attempt to address the need for the study of theology to be more than just an academic discipline. The current journal offers a series of 52 scripturally-based reflections on topics related to a typical course providing an introduction to Catholic faith and theology, Scripture, sacraments and liturgy, and mission. The journal is structured in such a way that it allows for participants to record the results of their prayer and reflection. No one is required to share their responses with anyone else, much less with the course facilitator. However, they are asked to verify that they have attempted to spend time with each of the reflections. So far everyone I have worked with has attempted to give them a good go. I also note that in the course of group discussions and presentations many participants choose to refer to the content of their journals. And, while not everyone is comfortable with being asked to pray, no one is uncomfortable with being asked to reflect. I have also discovered there are participants who continue with their journal well after the course has concluded, returning to the reflections again and again.

Anticipated Outcomes of Formation in the Online Approach

1. Participants will experience themselves as being on a spiritual journey.
2. The experience will be truly formational rather than simply informational.
3. Participants will experience themselves as being able to engage with the course material and activities, no matter where they happen to be on the journey of faith.
4. The experience will be one of faith from 'the inside out' rather than from 'the outside in'.

Strengths: A New Way to use
Theological Education in Mission Formation

I sincerely believe that theological education, in the context of forming people for mission, is better served if thought of as an art and not as an academic discipline. Either the theology we read is our attempt to search out an answer to a question that we are living at the very centre of our beings, or it becomes a dead letter and is perhaps even dangerous. Yes, occasionally the reading of theology 'cold' will provoke its own questions irrespective of what has been happening in us, in which case the process seems to be in reverse. But these are 'sower and seed moments' and the words that seemed so real to us as we read get lost in the hubbub of daily life if we are not taught how to reflect on them, and how to follow their meaning ever more deeply into our experience-grounded pilgrimage. Encountering the things of God in our heads can be interesting, but to those who stay there it is not life-changing. The Word of God is primarily about changing lives. So the strengths of this approach – of seeing theological education as an art – are:

1. Anyone can engage with the formation process. It does not assume that we all start from the same place.
2. It provides for a healthy interplay between subjective experience and the integration of objective information.
3. Once mastered, it is a stress-free way to enter into study and reflection.

Limitations

The limitations of the approach are:

1. People often study online believing that they will have less to do than would be the case if they were attending lectures etc. Those who take the minimalist approach tend to get less out of it.
2. Monitoring participant engagement and responding to the individual requirements of each participant is time consuming and requires a subtlety of approach modified to individual needs.
3. Not everyone instinctively knows how to operate in an online environment. We have become used to engaging in short bursts via text or on social media. That does not work well as an approach to online course requirements.

Indications of Transformation

The primary benefit I have seen over the years from viewing theological education as an art lies in the willingness of staff to engage in an ongoing conversation with one another around matters to do with faith and spirituality, and the significance of both for their ministry within a school. This ongoing engagement provides:

1. A deepened awareness that they are part of something that is bigger than themselves, that their experience of teaching others about the Catholic faith is one of participating in the mission Jesus Christ has entrusted to his people

2. The knowledge that to be a teacher in the Catholic context is to be someone who is on a journey to find and live by all that is true, good and authentic – however a person considers that to be

3. The experience that everyone has a contribution to make to the spiritual and pastoral life of a school, as long as they are open to the fact that their contribution needs to be measured against key aspects of Catholic faith and identity.

My Hope into the Future

In response to the call to the New Evangelisation, the time has come to focus on a way of learning that is at once new and ancient: one in which the experience of the individual is at the heart of the learning and into which any academic work is linked. Where we breathe what we are learning – we become it and it becomes part of who we are.

Concluding Remarks

Have you ever noticed that we often seek to explain our faith from the outside in, rather than from the inside out? I understand why we do this – I do it myself. After all, that's what people ask us to do. We get questions – why do you believe in God? Who's this Jesus person? Why listen to the Church? Why's the Church against this or for that? On and on go the questions that we do our best to answer. Consequently, the various elements of our faith get talked about and dissected in isolation. Sometimes the explanations we give make sense and sometimes (often depending on the experience and openness of those listening) they do not.

As members of the Church we hope that we can give a good account of the elements of our faith, and we also hope that if what we say makes sense to people they'll begin to think about what lies at the heart of it all.

That is to say, we hope they'll move from the outside (the questions about the various aspects of our faith) to the inside (the experience of falling in love with the God who loves them). Our faith is best understood from the inside out. What does that mean? The experience of being in love with God – Father, Son & Holy Spirit – is our faith from the inside out. The heart of our faith is not primarily about arguing the rights and wrongs of different aspects of what we believe (although there is a place for that). It begins with an experience – an encounter with Jesus Christ. Without the awareness of God at work in our personal and communal experience, the teachings of our faith become just burdens to carry. For this reason, the experience of loving and being loved is the only context in which the teachings of the Church make sense.

16

FORMATION IN AN EARLY CAREER TEACHER'S SETTING

Catholic Education, Parramatta: Formation for Early Career Teachers – Walking the Path Together, An Intentional Journey of Mutual Awakening

Ursuline Patty Andrew pioneered an innovative formation approach for early career teachers while working for the Catholic Education Office, Parramatta. Bringing her considerable professional and vocational experience to the creation of this program, Patty shares her practice wisdom in this critical·area. Of note is the dialogical approach making meaningful links between the teacher's personal spirituality and the wisdom of faith, a process often overlooked or assumed in the past. We see how her journey with young teachers in an intentional, developmental way offers an authentic contemporary expression of the path to Emmaus in the mission field of Catholic education.

The Context

With the population of the Diocese in Western Sydney rapidly growing, the principals in the 78 schools in the region employ a significant number of new teachers each year, many of whom are in the early stages of teaching. Although many of these teachers, graduating from either the Australian Catholic University or the University of Notre Dame, complete units of study in Religion, they can feel daunted when beginning to articulate their faith and spirituality to their students and colleagues. Furthermore, as Mason, Singleton & Webber[184] showed in their 2007 study, a significant proportion of these young people are not strongly connected to institutional Church. This lack of regular participation in the life of the Church can sometimes be seen as a visible marker which defines young teachers' levels of faith and spirituality.

During my forty years of working in Catholic schools, with most of these years at the leadership level, I interacted and shared at depth with many young teachers. My own spirituality was awakened and nurtured by

---

184   Mason et al. 2007

their compassion and sense of personal presence especially in relating to their students. I often experienced a disconnection between the way they were in tune with and open to the movement of God's spirit in their hearts, and the meaning they found in the practices of institutional Church. This was consistent with the compelling evidence across many countries in the Western World of an increasing disjunction between religious institutions and personal experience.[185]

David Ranson in his book *Across the Great Divide*[186] clarified some reasons for the split between spirituality and religion. It also challenged me to take steps to understand the causes and find ways to heal the unhealthy rift which weakens both these interdependent realities of religion and spirituality. Furthermore, the program was grounded in the belief that spirituality is intrinsic to being human. Research studies regarding spirituality over the last 50 years support the fact that there is a biological basis for spiritual awareness that is 'essentially part of human awareness and not an element planted through culture and education'.[187]

The Program

The program, *Walking the Path Together*, was pioneered in the Diocese of Parramatta in 2008. Specifically focused on early career teachers, it involved an initial in-depth conversation with teachers in their second year of classroom practice. This particular year was chosen in order to give teachers a sense of distance from their first year of teaching which provided them with experiences for reflection. As one young teacher said, 'The first year of teaching seems like panic while the second year unfolds with a greater sense of peace.'

Listening to Lived Reality

The starting point was to listen to the lived reality of teachers in their second year of teaching. Beginning this way provided the necessary openness which is essential for good learning in general, and in particular for personal formation for the heart and mind. It also enabled the learning conversation to begin on equal footing. Despite the fact that many of these young teachers had both their primary and secondary education in Catholic schools, immersed in the Catholic culture, they were not confident in initiating or leading faith practices, prayer or ritual. Possibly because of the doctrines and dogma which shape and define religion, young people project a sense of not getting it right, especially in terms of the specialised language,

---

185   Hay, 2006.
186   Ranson, 2002.
187   King, 2008, p. 87.

or that someone else is the expert in matters of faith and spirituality. Hence it was important to begin with an area of personal expertise – one's own life.

Engaging in Conversation

Engaging with the method of a one-to-one conversation ensured mutuality and generated the experience of being teachers and learners together.

The following four broad focus questions guided the conversation:

- What is your understanding of spirituality?
- What is your understanding of religion?
- How would you describe the relationship and connection between spirituality and religion?
- How do you see spirituality manifested in the young people you teach?

These individual conversations of about 30-45 minutes took place often during the regular school time while teachers had some release from their face to face teaching. If suitable times could not be found, meeting times were arranged either before or after school teaching hours. Because teachers were assured that the prime purpose of each conversation was 'to let their voices be heard' by listening to their understanding regarding matters of the heart, faith and spirituality, a climate of trust was built which encouraged each one to speak their own truth.

From the conversations it was obvious that all teachers were clear about the difference between religion and spirituality. Expressing this difference in a range of ways they noted:

- 'Religion provides us with the structure behind our understanding of the meaning of existence whereas spirituality is very personal and can't be defined by structure. It provides a sense of the knowing connected with an unknown.'
- 'Religion is something we all have in common, e.g. communal prayer, the sacraments. Spirituality is how you interpret religion.'
- 'Religion has a structure, an order and defined literary sources. Spirituality is more individual. It is an ongoing process, personal and private.'
- 'Religion is something that has been constructed and gives meaning to life. Spirituality is the development of the non-physical parts of our selves; our conscience and soul.'
- 'Religion is about what we teach and believe. Spirituality is feeling the truths as an innate belief in a higher power.'

- 'Religion is the teaching upon which we place our spirituality. Spirituality comes from within. One can be spiritual without being religious.'
- 'Religion is the teaching of the Church. Spirituality is more personal and is about internal beliefs.'
- 'Religion is the product of upbringing; a culture into which we are born. Spirituality doesn't mean the same to everyone. It is internal and can be expressed in prayer'
- 'Religion holds our beliefs; gives comfort and support; has a conservative and traditional face. Spirituality is about being in touch with something other.'

Deepening Dialogue

For the most part, teachers' insights regarding spirituality were 'grounded in the experience of sensibility.'[188] Enabling them to articulate these experiences in the context of a conversation, awakened and identified the feelings. This allowed the teachers to be present to their heightened awareness. The process of attending to personal experience has the possibility of leading to what Ranson terms 'the religious moment.'[189] Here the Christian narrative, liturgy and articulated wisdom provide a framework for interpreting experience.

The process of drawing on this interpretive framework was evident in particular in teachers who were working towards gaining the required accreditation for the teaching of Religious Education. Some of these early career teachers were enrolled in the program, *Foundations in Theology*.[190] The program was conducted through correspondence and provided a series of readings in each module. Teachers studying in this way were assigned to small groups led by a mentor. This provided them with the opportunity to articulate learnings and discuss their faith.

Knowledge and language gained from their study of the foundations of theology, was often referred to and integrated into the initial conversation of *Walking the Path Together*. It was good to see these teachers making connections with prior learnings in their faith. Furthermore, it was obvious that the readings from *Foundations in Theology* provided meaning and gave them a framework with which to interpret their spiritual awakening, and a language to express and discuss their faith and matters of the heart. It also showed that the method of one-to-one conversation enabled teachers to begin to weave together many strands of their learnings both incidental and intentional, leading to a personal integration of their faith and spirituality.

---

188   Ranson, 2002, p. 24.
189   Ranson, 2002, p. 27.
190   This programme is offered by the Institute of Faith Education, based in Brisbane.

New Perspectives on Student Spirituality

The final focus of the conversation asked teachers to share their observations on ways that spirituality was manifested in their students. Some ways in which teachers observed spirituality manifested in the students grouped around the experiences of participating. 'It is in their appreciation of what is going on and the excitement they show in learning new things; it is in the way they sing songs. Music gives them feeling; it is an all over body experience.' In addition, they observed that, 'by keeping everything open-ended; exploring abstract concepts like infinity, wonder and curiosity and having the capacity to share', all manifested the spirituality of the young people they were teaching. Capacity for relationships was also seen as an indicator of the students' spirituality. This was evident in 'their caring nature and the way they interacted with each other; treating each other with respect; their ability to socialise; being tolerant of each other and the ways they work through conflict'. The students showed an ability to 'voice what is in their hearts'. Finally, it was the other centred activities the young people were involved in, including volunteer work, which provided a manifestation of spirituality.

Walking together

It is envisaged that the next stage of this program for the early career teachers will move from the one-to-one conversations, to teachers forming into small groups. The following diagram presents some possible components of this ongoing way.

FIGURE 16.1 THE TREASURE WITHIN

The diagram is titled the *Treasure Within* to emphasise the fact that the starting point in authentic formation begins with the heart.[191] During the anticipated group gatherings it is important to continue nurturing spiritual awakening as in the one-to-one conversation, but to also add the dimension of the Christian religious framework.

Belonging to Networks and Wider Culture

One of the main benefits of this approach to formation is that it presents the possibility for early career teachers to experience a sense of belonging to the networks of Catholic education that is wider than the individual school. This reflects an approach that is Catholic in the true sense of being universal, expansive and inclusive. It also means that when beginning formation programs at such an early stage in one's career, teachers are more likely to grow as integral members of the Catholic education community. Furthermore, the initial one-to-one conversations provide good and essential insights to inform the shaping of ongoing programs.

My Hope into the Future

My hope for our Catholic educators of the future is that they will respond to opportunities to grow into greater spiritual awareness. As they interpret this spiritual awakening in the context of the Catholic tradition it is hoped that they will continue to nurture the religious tradition which has been planted within the institution of the Catholic school. I believe they will do this best by strengthening and deepening their embodiment of the God and the faith they proclaim. Hence, they will not only speak about what it means to be merciful, just and compassionate, but they will witness to these defining features of Christianity in their very own being.

Thomas Groome understands spirituality as 'faith at work'.[192] He noted that it is in the classroom that teachers have the opportunity 'to allow their faith commitments to shape the whole curriculum – what and how and who and why they teach. In doing this their teaching becomes their faith at work and its foundation is their own spirituality'.[193]

---

191   O'Leary, 2008.
192   Groome, TH, 2003.
193   Groome, TH, 2003.

17

FORMATION IN A SOCIAL JUSTICE IMMERSION SETTING

Caritas Australia: Global Education and Social Justice Formation programs – An expression of Catholic faith in action

Susan Bentley is the Justice Educator, Queensland, for Caritas Australia. Here Susan, a passionate teacher and activist, shares her reflections on the work she does on behalf of Caritas. We see how Catholic Social Teaching provides the lens for Catholic educators, in both their teaching and in their lived witness, to make sense of the encounter with and shape of a response to inequality, injustice and suffering in the world.

Our Context

Caritas Australia (CA) is the international aid and development agency of the Australian Catholic Church. We envisage a world in which children, women and others most vulnerable to extreme poverty and injustice, are agents of their own change and architects of their own development. Our organisation is part of Caritas Internationalis, an international confederation of 165 Catholic relief, development and social service organisations working to build a better world for the poorest of the poor in over 200 countries and territories. Our national education team consists of state-based Justice Educators who offer a quality and diverse program to the Catholic tertiary sector and 1,731 Catholic Schools across 28 dioceses.

Our Approach

There are three main drivers that shape our approach.

Gospel Imperative: Theologically and ecclesially grounded, CA's global programs are framed by the key Gospel values of compassion, empathy and understanding, and the Gospel imperative to pursue justice and help those suffering from poverty and disadvantage.

The Social Mission of the Church: The social mission of the Catholic Church is one of the three central tenets of the faith along with celebrating the sacraments and the preaching of the Word of God.[194] The framework for that mission is found in Catholic Social Teaching (CST) principles. These principles for reflection 'provide a moral framework for viewing society which ensures that the good of the individual and the common good of humanity coalesce'.[195] In our education programs we prioritise personhood at the heart of learning and teaching.

Global Trends: In a globalised and interdependent 21st century world, a plethora of global social, economic, cultural and political trends pose increasingly significant challenges. Some examples of this include environmental concerns, the increasing inequalities regarding access to information technologies, the economic gap among countries and between people within countries, and the migration of displaced peoples. The multiplicities of such injustices, in an increasingly fast-paced world, inform CA's educational rationale. Themes such as interdependence and sustainability are embedded into CA's resources and formation programs.

A Partnership Model in our Catholic Education Strategy

Each Justice Educator works in partnership with our key stakeholders in the formal Catholic Education sector in their respective states. Hence, our key strategic relationships lay in building our engagement with:

- Australian Catholic Schools
- Australian Catholic Education Offices (CEOs) in the dioceses
- Tertiary institutions such as the Australian Catholic University (ACU) and the
- University of Notre Dame Australia (UNDA – Fremantle campus).

Essential Aspects

'Let us not develop an education that creates in the mind of the student a hope of becoming rich and having the power to dominate. That does not correspond to the time that we live in. Let us form in the heart of the child and the young person the lofty ideal of loving, of preparing oneself to serve and to give oneself to others. Anything else would be education for selfishness' (Archbishop Oscar Romero).

The CA Education Team contributes to the mission field of Catholic education in its work to end poverty, uphold justice and promote dignity by transforming hearts and minds in the Australian community.

---

194 MacLaren, 2000.
195 Paul VI, Apostolic Letter of the Supreme Pontiff, June 30, 1968.

CA offers four main pathways to engage students and educators: 1. Student Engagement programs; 2. Education resources; 3. Teacher Formation programs, and 4. Adult Immersion programs. The development of these pathways has been heavily influenced by Ronald Krietemeyer's 'Vision for A Catholic Graduate.'[196] In this reflection, I will focus on the Practice Wisdom of our work in pathways 3 and 4.

Teacher Formation Pathway

We offer a number of diverse opportunities for teacher formation:

a. **Professional Development** (PD): The CA team present accredited workshops where the core audiences include CEO leadership teams, networks of school principals and vice-principals, assistant principals of Religious Education, primary and secondary teachers, campus Ministers and pre-service education students. Our PD options include twilight sessions, cluster workshops and full day workshops (for either full school staff, year level or faculty staff). Examples of our PD topics include 'Laudato Si, Our Common Home', 'Learning Service planning with Caritas' and 'Integrating Catholic Social Teachings into the curriculum.'

b. **Conferences**: Our presentations at conferences are another way of forming Catholic educators. This is often a prophetic role, calling educators back to the heart of the Gospel.

c. **Tertiary programs:** Justice Educators deliver lectures in undergraduate and postgraduate courses for pre-service teacher formation at ACU campuses (Brisbane, Melbourne and Sydney) and UNDA (Fremantle campus) in the Faculties of Theology, Philosophy, Arts and Education.

Adult Immersion Programs Pathway

The Global Justice Accredited Program in NSW, Queensland, Victoria and South Australia incorporates stand-alone coursework and optional immersion travel. The three-phase program is designed for adult and university student audiences.

Phase 1: The 'Global Justice' course offers 25-30 hours of accredited PD. It aims to deepen participants' appreciation of the centrality of Catholic Social Teachings and IHD principles in the work of the Church and Caritas Australia. Through an interactive mode of delivery, guest speakers, panel discussions and the use of multi-media, a diverse range of themes

---

196   Krietemeyer, 2000.

are explored. These themes include Justice Tradition and CST principles, the work of Caritas Australia, Poverty, Aid and Development, Charity and Justice, Learning Service, Advocacy, Changing Attitudes in Australia, Fair Trade and Ethical Consumerism, Climate Justice and Pope Francis' Encyclical, 'Laudato Si' and Catholic Identity, as well as cross-curricular case studies. Impact statements from participants include:

- 'I am now more conscious of walking gently in my students' lives, particularly those who are in need at a local community level.'
- 'Fantastic course. Should be mandatory for all teachers seeking their accreditation to teach in a Catholic school.'

Phase 2: Participants who complete the entire Global Justice course are eligible to apply for an encounter experience through our immersion program. The immersion component (10-12 days) was developed to deepen and strengthen participants' understanding of Caritas's aid and development work. It offers unique first-hand insight into the IHD model supported by CA and our other partner staff on the ground in vulnerable and marginalised communities. The program also aims to deepen teachers' understanding of CST principles founded in justice within our scriptures and tradition. In recent years immersions have included Cambodia, Nepal, Fiji and Bolivia.

Phase 3: Upon return from the immersion, participants complete a one day de-brief. They are encouraged to critically reflect on their experience and to partner with Caritas to achieve deep learning about social justice in their school and parish communities. The immersion program articulates, through a lived experience, Pope Francis' reflection that we need to:

> *stop seeing it (extreme poverty) as a statistic rather than a reality. Why? Because poverty has a face! It has the face of a child; it has the face of a family; it has the face of people, young and old. It has the face of widespread unemployment and lack of opportunity. It has the face of forced migrations, and of empty or destroyed homes.'*[197]

Between May and August 2012, the Christian Research Association conducted an evaluation of the Caritas educational programs. The feedback overall was very positive and highly affirmed the immersion program. Some examples of staff post-immersion change/formation/transformation include:

---

197 http://www.lastampa.it/2016/06/13/vaticaninsider/eng/news/pope- arms-circulate-freely-while-development-aid-does-not u4SSx0a1jyzqCmVsGjFbtL/pagina.html?utm_source=dlvr.it&utm_mediu m=twitter Accessed 16/06/16

- A Brisbane teacher evaluated her Year 9 Business course to explicitly integrate CST principles.
- A Principal evaluated her school's behaviour management policies and practices so they aligned with CST principles and a 'Strength-based' approach.

A teacher, Julieann Caffery, from Southern Cross College, Dalby, shared:

'CA's adult formation opportunities have impacted greatly on my professional and personal life ... After my immersion I became a volunteer for Caritas Australia, in the role of advocacy, to promote the important work of CA to teachers, students and church communities ... My involvement in CA has given me a rigorous understanding and appreciation of the quality and depth of CA's work as an international aid and development agency.'

The Strengths of our Approach

- A moral framework and CST principles help to amplify the voices of the poor and the marginalised, so that Catholic educators not only hear those living in poverty, but learn from and with them.
- The language of a Strength-Based Approach empowers teachers to engage in teaching aligned with foundational beliefs, and fosters a Catholic vision of life.
- The authentic voice of CA's lived knowledge and the breadth and depth of our education programs gives power to our work that is grounded in reality.
- Catholic pedagogy and the transformative process of learning and teaching is articulated in CA's programs. The programs are not just focused on knowledge and skills, but on embedding gospel values such as compassion, empathy and mercy. Our programs reflect the Catholic narrative and challenge perceptions, empowering people to act as agents for change.
- The centrality of our partnership strategy is fundamental to the development of strong and sustainable relationships and CAs mandate.
- We continue to be focused on development and deployment of curriculum, methodologies, and resources which promote high levels of Catholic religious literacy across the broader Catholic education sector, and which equip educators for their critical role.

And some Limitations ...

- Staffing capacity imposes limitations on our engagement with key stakeholders whilst challenging us to discern best practice re strategic reach, which partnerships and relationships need to be nurtured, and how to enhance learning and reciprocal benefits.
- Authentic evaluation can be difficult. With a vision to transform hearts and minds (i.e., behaviours, attitudes and values) it is difficult to discern appropriate methodologies for gathering quantitative data which can inform a program of qualitative reporting.

Challenges

My experience indicates three main challenges:

1. **The intersection between compliance issues, governance, bureaucratic imperatives and authentic Catholic Identity**: The Australian Curriculum and the National Safe School Framework is an example of this. Pope Francis' reflection that 'Bureaucracies shuffle papers; compassion deals with people'[198] cuts to the heart of this challenge. Diocesan authorities face incessant demands of the school as being a 'system' resulting in tension between the 'outer-directed esteems' and 'inner directed' school culture in the Christian tradition.[199] Social Justice Agendas are often marginalised in both school curriculum and the religious life of the school community, resulting in insufficient resources (i.e. time allocation, budgets) for teacher formation. This is not necessarily happening due to complacency or lack of concern, but is more a reflection of the 'time poverty' experienced by educators across the country.

2. **Logistical issues:** The CA Education team works across large geographical locations and some are often on the road and away from home for weeks at a time.

3. **Changing patterns of school enrolments, as well as changes in the educational and cultural context:** These pose unique challenges for the CA Education team. The school is becoming the new parish with students often receiving no formation from either the parish or the home. The role of

---

198 http://www.lastampa.it/2016/06/13/vaticaninsider/eng/news/pope-arms-circulate-freely-while-development-aid-does-notu4SSx0a1jyzqCmVsGjFbtL/pagina.html?utm_source=dlvr.it&utm_mediu m=twitter, accessed 16/06/16.
199 Ibid, accessed 16/06/16.

schools is being radically contested and this is placing huge demands on school resources and can challenge a school's capacity to prioritise teacher formation and relationships with external education providers. Our challenge is to continue to offer the formal Catholic sector robust, creative and participatory opportunities to engage, while respecting a pluralistic context regarding staff cultural traditions.

A Hope for Catholic Educators for the Future

My hope for Catholic educators is that they continue to nurture men and women who are empathetic and resilient, cognisant of the wider world with a strong sense of their own roles as global citizens. I hope Catholic educators, in shaping multi-dimensional young people, nurture students to be compassionate advocates for justice at local, national and international levels. I hope our schools remain steadfast in their commitment to offering Catholic educators rich formation programs which empower teachers to enhance their capacity to discern and integrate authentic, diverse and challenging perspectives through the lens of faith. Pivotal to my hope for Catholic educators is that they continue to journey on pathways to replace indifference with solidarity, compassion and responsibility; individualism with respect for the common good; exclusion with inclusivity; environmental degradation with stewardship; pre-occupation with compliance with justice for the poor; authoritarian decision-making with respect for the voice of all members of the school community, and marginalisation with respect for human dignity.

18

FORMATION IN A SYSTEM-WIDE SCHOOL-BASED STAFF SETTING

Catholic Education, Wollongong: Lighting the Way – Formation for School-based Leadership Teams

Suz Marden is the Team Leader, Staff Spiritual Formation for Catholic Education in the Diocese of Wollongong. Suz has extensive experience in Catholic education and adult spiritual formation. Appointed to this position to develop a system perspective in staff spiritual formation, Suz shares her learnings, practice wisdom and hopes in working with whole school staffs. The transformative journey together within the school setting is illuminated by the skill and authentic witness that Suz brings to this work. Specifically, Suz describes the development of Lamplighter Spiritual Formation Leadership through four core 'Stances' or viewpoints. These she believes have been and are still critical in translating the Emmaus journey into mission, therefore transforming and shaping the Catholic school context.

The Context

Providing Spiritual Formation for staff involved in the 39 Catholic schools of the Wollongong Diocese has been given a high priority. This intentional focus is reflected in the Catholic Education Office Vision and Strategic Direction and in the number of opportunities available to staff. The approach taken in Staff Spiritual Formation, is outlined in the *Lighting the Way Spiritual Formation Framework*. The development of this framework and subsequent spiritual formation programs is the result of an extensive 'ground-up' consultation process within and beyond the diocese. This led to the adoption of the systemic approach and resources for developing school-based spiritual formation (*Catching Fire*) established by the Catholic Education Office in the Archdiocese of Brisbane.

The *Lighting the Way* framework, based on the Emmaus Paradigm, articulates the key principles and aims of adult spiritual formation, and is linked to the Diocesan core curriculum document on RE. From the Emmaus story in Luke's Gospel (Lk 24:13-35), the paradigm has four interconnected elements that provide a clear framework for staff spiritual formation.

Adapting the Brisbane *Catching Fire* programs, the two-school based programs developed were the *Lamplighter Spiritual Formation Leadership Program* and the *Shining Lights Retreat Program*. These programs align the four movements of the Emmaus paradigm – Making Sense, Gaining Access, Celebrating and Responding – to the nine formation capacities of Archdiocese of Brisbane, Catholic Education's *Catching Fire*. This alignment is illustrated below:

Making Sense	Gaining Access	Celebration	Responding
Presence	Purpose	Welcome	Commitment
Prayer	Principle	Ritual	Fidelity
Journey			

The System Formation Initiative

The Lamplighter Spiritual Formation Leadership Program

This program is one of a number of successful and continuing programs that emanate from the *Lighting the Way* Spiritual Formation Framework. The Lamplighter program runs in conjunction with the Shining Lights program.[200] Schools commit to both programs for a period of three years. The Lamplighter Spiritual Formation Leadership Program is aimed at further developing staff communities by forming school 'Lamplighter Teams' that have the confidence and capacity to lead staff spiritual formation.

The Lamplighter program has a two-fold focus: *to offer personal spiritual formation* and *to develop skills for formation of staff within school communities*. The key objective is that schools are led and staffed by individuals who are committed to the mission of Catholic education, and to continue to develop strong Catholic identity within their communities.

Specific aims of the program are:

- To provide a sequential and developmental spiritual formation program that sits within a larger spiritual formation framework for adults employed in Catholic education
- To develop a deeper understanding and practical application of the Lighting the Way Spiritual Formation Framework
- To continue growing Catholic identity in both primary and secondary schools through the formation of staff led by Lamplighter Teams
- To develop the confidence and competence of these teams to initiate and lead spiritual formation within the Catholic Faith Tradition.

---

200 The Shining Lights program is a three-year program where three teachers from a school attend a series of two-day overnight retreats. In effect, there are seven people from each school entering into formation that are then sharing that experience. A third and important program is the Alight for the World Early Career Program that is a four-year program for teachers in their first years of teaching.

The Structure and Process

The principal and three members of staff drawn from across teaching or non-teaching roles, who have been identified as having an interest in being and the potential to be leaders in the area of Staff Spiritual Formation, form a core 'Lamplighter Team'. This team attends nine days of formation over three years: four days in the first year, three in the second and a two-day overnight retreat in the third year. Prayer and Scripture form the foundation of these days. Each day builds on the day(s) before, with teams acquiring skills and resources to form other staff.

Each day of formation is based on one of the following Formation Capacities that sit within the Framework: *Presence, Prayer, Journey, Purpose, Principle, Ritual, Welcome, Commitment* and *Fidelity*. These nine formation capacities reflect core characteristics of a Catholic school community and are the practical ways for living out the Mission of Jesus within Catholic education. The aim of these days 'is to put people not only in touch but in communion, in intimacy, with Jesus Christ' (Catechesis Tradendae,1979).

Four 'Stances' that Underpin the Success of the Lamplighter Program

These are the four stances or viewpoints that I believe have been and are critical to leading formation in schools.

*1. A Stance towards the **Importance** of Staff Spiritual Formation*

Critical to the success of Staff Spiritual Formation in our Diocese has been a fundamental stance towards its *importance* which has been promoted at all levels of leadership through a shared vision. Critical features that strengthen this stance of importance include:

- The shared vision of the Bishop of Wollongong and the Director of Schools for Staff Formation has been critical, with leadership from the Director of Schools being the catalyst for this eight-year project
- The appointment of a Spiritual Formation Project Officer with responsibility for leadership, consultation, design, implementation and evaluation was initially situated in the Office of the Director, to highlight the importance of staff formation
- Involvement of a cross-section of staff and clergy at the developmental stage and the ongoing support of members of the clergy
- The importance of understanding Spiritual Formation as distinct from Professional Development and the Religious Education Curriculum

- Catholic Education Office Leaders have requested and participated in the Lamplighter Program, deepening personal understanding and support for Spiritual Formation
- In turn, C.E.O. staff have also participated in the Lamplighter Leadership Program with over 70 completed or attending the program
- Several participants in the Lamplighter Program have been appointed as principals
- Principals and Lamplighter Teams have embraced and been committed to the vision for staff spiritual formation and its importance
- There is mutual commitment and support between the system and schools for program funding
- With over 90% of our 39 schools participating in the Lamplighter Program a common language and experience is developing across the diocese. This means that when staff are employed in a new school there is a common and known focus in staff formation.

2. *A Stance towards **Listening***

The key to listening in the process of consultation regarding staff spiritual formation involved three key elements. Firstly, an *openness* to what the other had to say about their faith journey. Secondly, *prudence* in knowing the risks and challenges in discerning the way forward. Thirdly, prayerful *discernment* which requires time. This stance towards *listening* included:

- Initial and wide consultation with all stakeholders over a substantial amount of time
- Consultation and research across dioceses to inform best practice
- Continued listening through written reflections and personal communication
- Attention paid to reflective comments at the end of each Lamplighter day suggesting that participants find the program worthwhile, challenging and life-changing
- Analysis of evaluation feedback from the same participants from day one of the Lamplighter program in the first year, and retreat days 8 & 9 in the third year, which demonstrates significant development in spiritual awareness and commitment to mission
- A discernible change in whole-of-diocese culture regarding school responsibility and commitment to staff spiritual formation.

3. A stance towards **Hope**

A stance towards hope is characterised by positive expectation and requires endurance and resilience. Only through hope can we plant the seeds for the present and the future. This stance towards *hope* is reflected in:

- Formation grounded in reality, underpinned by: an awareness of its need for a new generation of teachers and leaders; an awareness of the changing demographic of staff in Catholic Schools; an awareness of the need for succession planning, and an awareness of the critical role teachers play in the ongoing effective mission of Catholic education
- The creation of a framework that provides a system approach, understanding and language, for the 'planting of seeds' for formation
- The Lamplighter program being of three-years duration, offering a nine-year formation experience for schools
- The ready adaptation of the Lamplighter program to school contexts
- The significant success of schools who have 'taken it slowly' in order to embed real cultural change and commitment to formation
- The positive change in attitude and response to staff spiritual formation across schools since the initiative has been in place. Staffs want more!
- The increased attendance of school participants
- Transformation in schools, seen in the areas of staff prayer, staff reading of scripture, staff annual retreat days, social outreach, confidence in articulating matters of faith and leading formation of staff ... which all results in developing a rich Catholic identity and commitment to the mission of the school within the wider parish.

4. A stance towards **Faith**

A stance towards faith reminds us that renewal is something God does. It is God who seeks to renew the Church and who calls us to be co-creators. We are part of a *living* history connected by threads of wisdom given and received in a wondrous flow from generation to generation.

This stance towards *faith* is reflected in:

- The guidance, facilitation and presence of experienced and skilled facilitators in the area of spiritual formation who share faith and wisdom in continuing their own formation

- The leadership, wisdom and presence of Br Bill Tarrant FMS, who has been integral to the Lamplighter Program and in guiding formation since 2011 within our diocese
- Participating staff who, by their lives, witness and share the Good News in their schools
- Lamplighter days and Shining Lights retreats which are explicitly Christ-centred and Scripture-based, offering a variety of prayer experiences and reflective processes
- Principal and Lamplighter Teams that have embraced and been committed to the program, 'taking it back' to their school environment in a variety of faith-filled and creative ways
- The many schools that have placed a greater onus on staff prayer, creating specific prayer times for staff and transforming the way staff participate in prayer[201]
- Documentation that demonstrates school annual spirituality days are well-planned, with an increasing number of school Lamplighter Teams facilitating
- The significant number of schools that have initiated a nine-year cycle of staff spiritual formation built on the nine formation capacities
- The evolution of processes to support Spiritual Direction for Principals, that has emanated from the Lamplighter Program.

Limitations/Challenges of this Approach

While this approach has been undoubtedly very successful, there are still attendant challenges:

- One limitation was the need for 'in-school' support for Lamplighter Teams. Teams in schools need qualified personnel who can continue to encourage, affirm and guide their journey where needed. This has been addressed with the employment of an Education Officer who has previously led a school Lamplighter Team and who will work with school teams.
- A significant challenge to the effectiveness of a Lamplighter Team occurs when there is movement of staff from schools. In some cases, school Lamplighter Teams have lost one or two team members. This is also where in-school support is critical.

---

201 To illustrate:'The Lamplighter program has challenged us to reflect both personally and as a Team on the experience of staff prayer in our school. From this reflection we have changed the time we devote to prayer and the way we pray. Staff have been exposed to a range of different prayer forms focusing on nurturing a practice to the faithfulness of prayer life. It is rich and meaningful. The school has been changed and transformed by the Lamplighter Journey' (Mr Andrew Heffernan, Principal, St Columbkille's, Corrimal.)

- Secondary Lamplighter Teams face their own specific challenges, one being the sheer size of their staff. Many secondary schools send a new team each year to build the capacity and support for Formation in their schools.
- In our diocese, staff have many personal opportunities for formation. Interestingly, however, Lamplighter and Shining Light participants have asked for further formation at the end of the three-year program. As a result, newly developed offerings will be provided.[202]

My Hope for Catholic Educators into the Future

My hope is that staff spiritual formation continues to be given a distinctive priority within Catholic education, and that it is seen as a significant area with its own unique identity, that it is crucial to leadership, and that it is led by those who are continually being conformed to the mind and heart of the person of Jesus for the sake of the other.

---

202 Schools have also indicated that a retreat experience for those staff who have not been in a Lamplighter or Shining Light program would be beneficial. This retreat will also be provided in the coming year.

CONCLUSION TO PART E

The case study perspectives shared here illustrate for you the range and depth of practice wisdom across Australia. This has grown significantly in the last ten years and it has been supported by the professional sharing, collaborative scholarship and collegial spirit of the National Network of Formation for Australian Catholic Educators (FACE).[203]

In the deliberate diversity of contexts and target audiences, you will be aware of patterns emerging in terms of the sophistication in approach, strategic awareness, clarity of purpose, intentionality of formation elements, and integrity of process. These aspects converge in the mission field in ways that powerfully deepen the capacity in teachers and leaders to integrate what they do and how they do it. All of this has a profound impact on their own teaching and leading and in the communities to which they belong.

In each of the case studies, you will recognise the pre-eminent place of the individual's story, context and meaning-making. You will recognise too, the ways in which each formation approach has bound that in community and facilitated a deeper movement into the God meta-narrative. In doing so, you will have appreciated the principles of implementation that sought to ensure formation was personally meaningful, ecclesially faithful and strategically effective.

Every formation approach shared here expressed a skilled discernment of how best to meet the individual's personal meaning-making in their own context and experience. The sophistication of approach is also reflected in the informed and careful shaping of formation to the context of the particular target group. This careful shaping to the specific context of the staff, as opposed to the adoption of a one-size-fits-all approach, signals a maturity in the delivery of formation to Catholic educators. Rituals and sacramental celebrations are designed to deepen personal and communal meaning-making in a Catholic worldview. Protocols operate to respect personal boundaries while the intentionality of formation elements is informed by theologies and pedagogies that affirm the varieties of ways that adults learn and experience. These are embraced in a holistic understanding of adult formation.

The priority of ensuring formation is ecclesially faithful has a strong profile in all of the case studies. There is a shared recognition that personal

---

203   The FACE network now includes people involved in formation for Catholic educators and leaders across all Australian dioceses and authorities. Discussions in the network uncovered much agreement on the principles identified in Part D and the network has been a valuable source of mutual support for formation personnel working in different contexts around the country. More recently, the NCEC has developed a Faith Formation committee, and is building further structured support on the continuing foundation of FACE.

meaning-making without an ecclesial framework may be beneficial in a personal sense but is limited in its formative impact when untethered to the great vision and horizon of the Catholic Christian God meta-narrative. Foci and content in the case studies draw strongly on Scripture and Theology, connecting to the life experience of the participants. Those who facilitate staff spirituality sessions are educators who have extended their knowledge and application of theology and scripture. In designing and presenting sessions they use an increasing range of strategies that draw on pedagogy, experience and creativity. This has challenged and strengthened rather than displaced the integrity of process.

Finally, the strategic awareness reflected in each of these case studies shows a growing understanding of formation as the mother-lode for a contemporary expression of Catholic identity, as well as mission integrity, in Catholic education. Over the last ten years there has been a slow but sure shift in thinking across Australian Catholic education authorities as the need for strategic effectiveness has been awakened. This is characterised as a change from formation being 'a good guess' in what we think will work, to gathering the best scholarship and diverse disciplines to direct and underpin what we do and how we do it in a system context, knowing why it will work, and providing a range of indicators that show its effectiveness. This has led to consonance of message, clarity of purpose, and system thinking around staff formation. It has also been characterised by a capacity to admit limitations, face challenges honestly and share in a more collegial way the best of resources and program elements.

Most of all, the work shared in Part E gives cause to recognise and give thanks for the enormous capacity, commitment and wisdom among those who are guiding and shaping the formation of Australian Catholic educators and leaders into the future. We have much to be grateful for, and I suspect we will recognise that more in hindsight than with foresight.

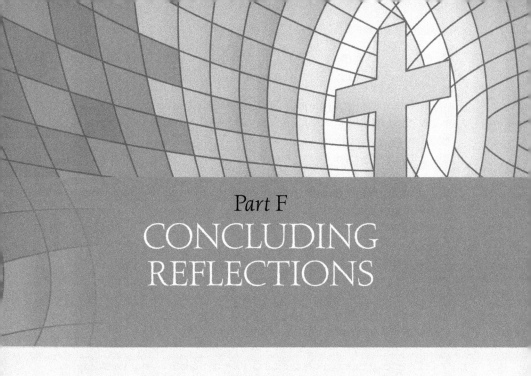

Part F
CONCLUDING REFLECTIONS

When stories collide, and eyes are opened, we know what it is to want to run to Jerusalem!

INTRODUCTION TO PART F

One of the oldest translations of the Emmaus story concludes with the words, *'And tired from walking, they ran to Jerusalem.'* Authentic formation opens us up to something so much bigger than ourselves, and which is so compelling that we can do no other than chase it.

This is because it awakens a deep knowing that our true home – our Jerusalem, in all its fierce beauty – is in God's being, and our role as Catholic educators and leaders is bound up in that being.

One word for this driving dynamic is Mission. Another word for it is Love.

In these concluding chapters, we reflect on the journey and revisit the new model that emerges from our explorations.

In Chapter 20 ,we identify critical factors that illuminate our knowledge, theory and practice in contemporary spiritual formation.

Finally, Chapter 21 outlines what this means for Policy and Strategic Practice.

19

THE JOURNEY

Let us reflect on the journey and finish where we began.

Formation is contextual. In the Catholic school context, the personal, the interpersonal and the communal come together in quite unique ways.

The educational mission of Catholic Christian schools gives witness to the gospel and the integration of faith, life and culture through both the curriculum and the people within the community itself. Spiritual formation of staff (leaders, teachers, support personnel and central office personnel) is thus central to the core work and purpose of Catholic schools. That core purpose has its rationale in an evangelising mission for the Catholic Church. This is well sourced in both ecclesial documents and systemic policy.[204]

Since 1980, the Australian Catholic Church has experienced a decline in church practice. This has been exacerbated by a decline in clergy numbers (and therefore presence and leadership among Catholic faith communities) as well as a decline in perceived authority and integrity due to the clergy abuse revelations, as well as a decline in adherence to particular Church teachings.[205] For Catholic education, the decline in religious vocations has generated the gradual disappearance of religious in schools and the accompanying increase in lay people staffing and leading Catholic schools. The particular style of 'monastic' formation which priests, sisters and brothers experienced is inappropriate to the formation needs of contemporary laity.[206] The vast majority of staff in Catholic schools now are lay people, comprising the generations of Baby Boomers, Gen X and Gen Y. These stratifications hold differing values and beliefs, personally and professionally.[207] In Australian culture in particular, there is a strongly defended egalitarian theme where one person's position and meaning-making has

---

204   As we know, this rationale is explained in successive documents from the Vatican Congregation for Catholic Education: The Catholic School,(1977); Lay Catholics in Schools:Witnesses to Faith, (1982;The Religious Dimension of Education in a Catholic School, (1988);The Catholic School on the Threshold of the Third Millennium, (1997); Ecclesia in Oceania, (2001); Educating Together in Catholic Schools: A Shared Mission Between Consecrated Persons and the Lay Faithful, (2007);Educating Today and Tomorrow:A Renewing Passion (2014).

205   Dixon, 2006; McLaughlin, 2000c, 2002, 2006.

206   Dixon, 2005; Hansen, 2000.

207   Rymarz, 2002; Dixon, 2006.

no more importance than another's 'story-choice'. This provides a robust scaffold for post-modern individualism. There is a contest between 'narratives' of post-secular society and post-religious society which calls for individuals to determine the 'orientation of the heart'[208]. Educators are finding themselves influenced in an area of 'deep change' that requires educational leaders to 're-contextualise, re-conceptualise and re-affirm their mission'.[209] In consequence, formation experiences that were appropriate at one time are no longer relevant for this contemporary context.

This contemporary context of the wider post-modern culture and ecclesial milieu presents significant challenges for Australian Catholic school educators and employing authorities. At the same time, the links to the cultural world of Catholicism through direct experience in a parish are much less strong than they were 50 years ago. The devastation wrought by the ongoing revelations of widespread institutional sexual abuse of children means this disconnection may well be terminal. For many Catholics now (adults and children), 'the face of Christ in the school is the only face of Christ they will encounter, at least the only encounter with Christ that makes any sense to them'.[210] This is an immense responsibility for a predominantly lay staff. In summary, cultural fragmentation is the societal motif against the background of an increasingly centrist Church leadership. These worlds collide in the reality of the Catholic school setting.

In addition to the pressures presented by the changing cultural and ecclesial contexts, the many competing priorities, shifting agendas and accountabilities in contemporary education can easily threaten the broader, long term planning needed to adequately address the spiritual formation of staff in Catholic schools. These include the challenge of succession planning, the need for intentional formation of a new generation of leaders, and the changing staff demographic working within Catholic education.

In this context, new ways are needed for authentic formation work to be delivered. The delivery, from a systemic point of view, is required to be strategic, cohesive and aligned with the educational setting in which staff communities exist. Many opportunities for spiritual and faith formation trialled over the last thirty years have tended to be seen as optional extras, luxuries in the day-to-day pressure of school demands. Re-framing formation as a core component of professional learning (with a solid theological underpinning connected to the ethos and mission of Catholic education) requires a shift in strategic vision and planning. Sustainability in our contemporary context is a huge challenge.

---

208 D'Orsa & D'Orsa, 1997, p. 250.
209 D'Orsa & D'Orsa, 1997, p. 50.
210 Treston, 1998, p. 70.

TRANSFORMING ENCOUNTERS:
A NEW MODEL FOR OUR TIMES

The new model is tight enough to give clarity to the complexity in understanding the process of formation, yet loose enough to accommodate diversity in role and specific context. It is simple but not simplistic, substantial yet familiar.

The phases of the model operate in an iterative rather than a linear way, so that individuals continue to re-visit their own story as they engage in the meta-narrative. Personal experience is essential for significant and sustained change in meaning-making and behaviour. Personal experience is formed in personal story, and focus on the educator's own story has proven a fundamental and deeply connective touchstone. This confirms an understanding of vocation and ministry that begins with 'the voice within calling me to be the person I was born to be, to fulfil the original selfhood given me at birth by God'.[211] The authentic call to teach comes then from 'the voice of the *teacher within*, the voice that calls me to honour the nature of my true self'.[212]

The structuring of formation according to the educator or leader's vocational setting, allows for the translation into the next phase – the mutual engagement phase – the story of the school, of Catholic education and of the broader church. Unconsciously demonstrating elements of a teacher's spirituality[213], staff take the shift in 'being' which they experience back to their class and community. The iterative nature of the journey through these two phases prepares individuals for connection to the God meta-narrative. This constitutes a transformative stage, as individuals experience connective points between their own story and this shared meta-narrative. The consequence is the unfolding realisation that their individual story is held in a deeper and wider way, giving it enhanced meaning.

The educative focus on holistic learning, and learner readiness, also reflected in the rich tradition of spiritual formation, is embedded in all processes. When the meaning-making in an authentic holistic formation process is re-framed over a period of time, and supported with strategies to embed the resultant changes in behaviour, changes can be sustained. Supporting strategies include exposure to a range of prayer styles, writers and journaling; along with ongoing contact and the use of systemic resources that reflect a head, heart and hands engagement. The educative focus on reflective practice in professional learning is used as a prior learning strategy to develop the practice of theological reflective praxis. Finally, attention to the world of language and symbol recovers its very important place in a contemporary approach.

---

211   Palmer, 2007, p. 29.
212   Palmer, 2007, p. 29.
213   Durka, 2002, and the self-transformative process identified by Daloz-Parks, 2000.

PRINCIPLES OF IMPLEMENTATION

If we know that an authentic approach to staff formation in the Catholic education setting must meet the three criteria of being personally meaningful, ecclesially faithful and strategically effective, then implementation is key. Implementation is just as important as a useful model. Several key elements in the structure and process of formation implementation create a pivotal mix for effectiveness. The presence of these elements critically influences the personal transformational experience of individuals and the strategic community influence of formation.

20

IDENTIFYING CRITICAL FACTORS

Our explorations have revealed a number of critical factors that illuminate our knowledge, theory and practice of, and policy for, effective spiritual formation.

PERSONAL AUTHENTICITY

Personal meaningfulness has far more influence in the sustainability of spiritual formation experiences than other factors such as system compliance. More than in any other era before it, the people of the post-modern era demand personal meaningfulness in experiences. Loyalty, community, commitment and spiritual seeking are not extinct in the post-modern Australian generations – they are expressed rather in distinctly different ways from their predecessors. More than ever, Gen X, Gen Y and Gen Z call for authentic witness – a person they can trust, a story they can believe in, and experience that speaks to them.

Any contemporary approach to formation must address this personal requirement for authenticity. The post-modern experience dictates that if this primacy of personal authenticity is not respected, it is highly unlikely that there will be any openness to what follows. Conversely, if personal authenticity *is* respected, there is likely to be increased openness to what is on offer.

SPIRITUAL CAPITAL

A second factor concerns the generation of spiritual capital within a community. We have seen how the growth of personal spiritual beliefs and practices can influence the spiritual capacity of the broader community culture. As Catholic education systems seek to become more mission effective, the concern for the development of spiritual capital has become intense. The approach to formation discussed in this book delivers all the elements of the 'inspirational pedagogy'[214] required for personal spiritual

---

214   Grace, 2002.

growth, practice and belief. The adoption of principles of professional learning communities and communities of practice to the nurturing of spiritual formation in the broader school culture creates an iterative dynamic between the individual and the community. This delivers both individual and cultural change that can be sustained.

PEER COMPANIONING

A third factor relevant to effective spiritual formation concerns the capability of staff to develop formation skills for both the routine context of school life, and for facilitating quality formation experiences for others. This has both cultural and educative implications. The application of skills and attitudes learned in formation, to the everyday routine of school life, influences the wider community culture. In particular, it contributes to building a culture of trust. This in turn is a critical component in creating effective professional learning communities. In addition to this flow-on effect in the educative domain, the development of participants' personal spiritual growth and their facilitation skills increases both confidence and capacity in providing spiritual formation opportunities for their peers within and across schools. This has implications for long-term sustainability in the provision of formation, with a new mode of delivery that moves away from a 'team of experts' model and towards a peer-companioning approach.

MISSIONAL LEADERSHIP

The fourth factor concerns the intersection of a theological re-imagining of mission in the contemporary world with the function of religious leadership in Catholic schools. The concept of a missional imaginary[215] provides a perspective on evangelisation that redirects it from a concern for maintenance towards a mindset for engagement. This dynamic shift signifies a tension between the ecclesial expression around mission and evangelisation and the theological scholarship in these areas. Theologically, the challenge is to embrace a missional approach that is about community, humanity and a transformative invitation to fullness of life. In the Christian framework of making a better world through witness and action, there is alignment with the concept of the contemporary learning organisation which involves transformational change or *metanoia* in the leaders and people of the community 'so that they can become who they are meant to be'.[216] Given the confluence of these elements in the Catholic school context,

---

215 Bevans, 2009; Phan, 2006.
216 Senge, 1990, p. 13.

it seems that 'the idea of a mission-ed and empower-ed people is most applicable to the Catholic education reality'.[217]

Moreover, across the leadership literature there continues to be a growing sense of the need for co-leadership to drive mission in Catholic education: '... this is best done when the partners in Catholic education, personally and collectively, live out their own vision of Catholic education in its wholeness'.[218] Thus the emerging conceptualisation around mission has resonance with leadership constructs in Catholic schools that seek to model authentic community, transformative engagement and an inclusive vision.

INTEGRATION OF LIVING

We may also conclude that personal and professional meaning-making are integrative experiences each nurturing the other. The integration of spiritual formation with lifelong learning theory offers an insight to formation participants concerning the holistic dynamics of living, where the sacred and profane are arbitrary distinctions. Spiritual formation is focussed on the nurturing of authentic human living. There is no such reality as 'work life balance' – the healthy goal is integration.

APPLICATION OF LEARNING THEORY

The diversity inherent in adult learners underlines the need for a holistic approach that honours the variety of starting points in any group of learners, and the primacy of experiential learning. Formation in the context of Catholic education must be designed such that it is directly relevant to formation participants professionally as well as personally. There also needs to be flexibility in the process that accommodates points of catalyst and points of rest. We must also recognise the importance of community in how learning and growth takes place and is sustained in practice, and leverages this to effect personal and community change.

APPLICATION OF CRITICAL MASS THEORY

Critical mass theory can be appropriately adopted to understand the dynamic of change facilitation in a Catholic school setting. There is a place for strategic thinking about the place of spiritual formation for leadership and in communities across Catholic schools, and in fostering the culture and mission of school communities.

---

217   Mulligan, 1994, p. 76.
218   Grace & O'Keefe, 2007, p. 127.

REFLECTIVE PRAXIS

Reflective praxis in a range of forms is a key component of spiritual formation that has useful application in the variety of teaching and leading contexts found in a Catholic school. In particular, the praxis of doing theology or theological reflection is foundational in formation. Accordingly, the narrative frame of the *Transforming Encounters* model integrates reflective praxis as an inbuilt dimension, involving self-companioning as well as peer companioning and leader companioning. In the school setting, theological reflection, journaling and 'circle of trust' skills offer important and innovative applications in maintaining focus, reviewing processes, and managing issues and relationships. A possible consequence of this is that these tools in reflective praxis may be more appropriate in developing leaders than the range of corporate tools that are available.

TARGETED DESIGN STRUCTURE AND STRATEGIES

Contemporary approaches to formation must be targeted and context relevant. The shaping of programs, tailor-made for the key professional or vocational roles of Catholic school staff, prove to be most effective. This means that practices learned in the formation programs are more easily adopted into work life, and the programs/processes themselves gain traction because of formation participants' perceptions of their day-t-day relevance.

STRATEGIC SUSTAINABILITY

Strategic sustainability requires an intentional focus on leadership development and staff capacity that sees spiritual formation as a joint responsibility and collaboration between the individual, the school and the system. At the level of school community, the active witness of leadership and the nurturing of a core group or critical mass among staff, offers key strategic drivers in school community sustainability. One implication of the development of staff to co-facilitate formation experiences across the system is the need for appropriate recognition of this contribution.

SCHOOL IDENTITY

One of the outcomes of authentic formation is the addressing of childhood and/or childlike understandings with a new way of seeing that reframes institutional realities and experience. There is real need for Church and Catholic educational authorities to reflect further on the decline of the parish as the primary place where Christian community is formed and experienced, and affirm the identity of the school community as such a place for many. A contemporary understanding of mission is an integrating agent in the many aspects of the Catholicity of schools – leadership, pedagogy, curriculum, pastoral care. And thus contemporary formation for mission is yeast in the bread of life!

A CULTURE OF EXPECTATION

Strategic thinking around how formation is appropriately embedded in both the professional learning continuum for Catholic school staff, and the community culture of the Catholic school context, is essential for sustainable traction. Developing a culture of expectation around formation in a systemic setting requires a re-framing that sees spiritual formation as an essential part of professional learning for all staff, in all roles, from induction to leadership extension, and as part of the strategic thinking and planning at all levels. Thus, the alignment with leadership, strategic renewal and professional learning frameworks is crucial.

21

RECOMMENDATIONS FOR POLICY AND STRATEGIC PRACTICE

The strategic integration of formation within a system requires the intentional nurturing of a culture in policy and strategy, as well as the internal coherence of programs and initiatives. In the encouragement of such a culture the following is offered in the key areas of policy and practice for Catholic education authorities:

1. The undertaking of formation programs is part of, and attracts significant recognition and accreditation for, teacher and leadership pathways.

2. Clear system policy situates formation centrally in leadership preparation and development. The policy ought to provide a shared understanding of assumptions, principles, approaches and parameters of formation for all stakeholders.

3. Formation is promoted as a joint responsibility between the individual, the school and the system. Not all formation occurs within the school context for individuals, and it is not the responsibility of the system to provide all spiritual formation opportunities for staff. Individual schools also have appropriate responsibility for the carriage of other formation initiatives.

4. Spiritual formation is regarded as mandatory for leadership preparation and ongoing development, and appropriate guidelines for this should be developed.

5. Formation is explicitly integrated into induction and succession processes, and strategic renewal and leadership frameworks.

6. Formation is re-framed as an essential part of overall professional learning for all roles.

7. Guidelines ensure all spiritual formation initiatives are underpinned by contemporary theory, reflective and experiential learning, access to best practice, and relate to the individual's professional and personal world.

8. The links evident between spiritual formation and positive psychology around meaning-making as a mechanism for well-being invite further connection and attention.

AWARENESS OF THE CHALLENGES

The introduction to this book acknowledged the multi-dimensional nature of the challenge in providing appropriate spiritual formation within contemporary Catholic education systems. These dimensions are personal, ecclesial and systemic. All three of these dimensions need to be addressed if formation is to be personally meaningful, ecclesially faithful and strategically sustainable. The major challenge for any systemic formation strategy is the task of sustainability at the individual and school community level. In moving forward, we must be mindful of key issues emerging from the Practice Wisdom. These include:

- The continuing pace and magnitude of mandated educational and organisational issues may overpower leadership priorities and staff culture.
- The maintenance of skills may be inhibited by a lack of opportunities to practice in other contexts and with other groups.
- Staff movement between schools may hinder the maintenance of a critical mass among staff and stifle the embedding of communal change.
- The natural complexity of a large organisation in the midst of ongoing structural change may mean implementation strategies are protracted.

FINAL REMARKS

In any landscape, spiritual formation is a dynamic and challenging lifelong journey. In every landscape it remains a journey of the heart – as simple and as confronting as that is. Christian spiritual formation is deeply personal and radically communal in its vision and praxis. While the shape of a spiritual life is in the end a matter of unique mystery between God and the individual, spirituality in the Christian tradition is developed in company. There is no such thing as a private Christian: Christian spirituality has a communal dimension which is integral to the journey.

Christian spiritual formation infuses every aspect of living, with head, heart and hands – and it is about ultimate purpose. It is the growing into a personhood that reflects, in a way unique to the individual, a transforming engagement with the heart of God. It is about life to the full; it is about a particular vision of the world; and it is about living that out in the minutiae of each day.

This way of seeing the world and living in it constitutes a core belief system of reality that is shared and nurtured. In this sense alone, it poses a counter-cultural challenge to a post-modern time. While our post-modern culture tends to reject universal narratives, the reign of God is the transforming vision for those who choose to stand in the Catholic Christian tradition. And while the individual path to this reality is acknowledged and respected, the vision itself is a non-negotiable touchstone for all those choosing to be involved in the educational mission of the Church.

It is a mission founded on a sacramental view of the world, nurtured in the cradle of community, strengthened by pathways of prayer, challenged in the world to do what must be done for justice sake, and reflected in the compassionate hospitality that is the hallmark of all followers of Jesus.

While the vision remains constant, the journeys to the place where the heart catches fire are as different and sacred as each individual. Our challenge and responsibility is to facilitate formation that allows the spark to catch, to open the eyes of recognition, and to turn the feet to hasten home to Jerusalem, the heart of their being. It is the tending of this kind of fire that kindles the soul of Catholic educators.

There has been wonderful work in the formation of Catholic educators and leaders across Australia over the last ten years. This may be interpreted as confirmation that those who are involved in the work of spiritual formation in contemporary times are missionaries to a secularised people, doing the primary work of pre-evangelisation. However, the reality bears a far more nuanced missional dynamic. Those teachers and leaders who shouted 'We are!' in the anecdote shared at the beginning of this book, along with their many colleagues, indicate a depth and capacity for insight and connection that is not captured in the established language of evangelisation and ecclesial referencing: the theological horizon in their journey is wider; the transformative rupture personally and communally is deeper; and the anchor points are more cohesive. Thus, the work of formation today may be more appropriately described as the work of missional re-imagining. Unbinding the layers that can obscure the heart and light of the core narrative for contemporary travellers nurtures a personal and professional witness that follows very faithfully in Jesus' own footsteps.

The aim of formation is no more and no less than transformation, impacting every part of lives, personal and professional. A strategic approach must reflect in substance and process, both the core elements of the Catholic spiritual tradition and sound current theological and educational practice, demonstrating a capacity to meet the contemporary context of the adult Catholic educator. In so doing, it holds in creative balance the tension between respectfulness for the individual spiritual journey and systemic needs and expectations. It thus bridges the meaning-making of personal narrative and the mission shaping of the Christian meta-narrative in a way that maintains a deep integrity for both. Most of all, it proclaims the transformative reality we are called to in its deepest sense, drawing mission and meaning together in a divine fusion.

Then you will say the last word,
the only word
that abides and that one never forgets.
Then, when all is silent in death
and I have learned and suffered my last,
Then will begin the great silence, in which you alone resound,
You who are Word from eternity to eternity.
Then all human words will be dumb.
Being and knowing, knowing and experiencing,
will be all the same:
'I will know as I am known',
will understand what you have always said to me,
namely yourself.
No human word, no image and no concept
will ever stand between me and you;
you yourself will be
the one joyful word of love and life
that fills all the spheres of my soul.

(KARL RAHNER, MARCH 1984)

APPENDIX 1:

CATCHING FIRE PROGRAMS

Each program is briefly outlined below.

Keepers of the Flame Program

The Keepers of the Flame program is designed for experienced teachers in Brisbane Catholic Education schools. The program runs over three years in a sequential, developmental way.[1] In the first year of the school community involvement in *Catching Fire*, a group of three staff begin the Keepers of the Flame program. The following year, a second cohort of three staff is invited to begin the program. The participants in Keepers of the Flame are encouraged to support the community initiatives of the *SpiritFire* participants from their school.[2]

This program is informed by the work of Thomas Groome, Gloria Durka and Parker J Palmer, specifically Palmer's *The Courage to Teach* and his understanding of 'Circles of Trust.'[3] In keeping with Palmer's work, the program is underpinned by an understanding that we are engaged in 'inner work' or 'soul work' rather than in-service. Participants learn to read the narrative of their own lives.[4] Within that, they learn to read the presence of

---

1   The in-service mindset prevalent among educators has been discussed in an earlier section. Being so used to an in-service model of learning, there were a number of staff who took some time to understand the developmental approach of the CFP programs where there were no expected 'to-do's'. The use of the Boundary Markers in each program served to establish a performance- and outcomes-free zone.

2   This had enormous impact: 'The way we could just step up for each other – take the risk knowing we really did have the support of each other and knowing we were on about something real, made the difference for me when I got back and began to think who am I to be anything to these other people and who am I to get up and speak about anything at all! What have I got to give to the person next to me in the lunch room. But somehow I knew I did have something, and I was different and I couldn't help it. And when I looked over and saw ... well, all we had to do was look at each other and I felt an enormous sense of love and support' (Susannah, St Raphael's). And from another who was not part of the core group, but observed their dynamic (about the bond between participants): 'I truly felt it was much deeper than just that they had done the program together. I felt they shared the fire of the spirit with each other and within themselves. When I saw them around the school involved in different situations or different roles, I can only express what I saw or felt the following way – they all seemed to have an inner contentment – a glow that came from deep within – the Spirit! This is the key to Catholic leadership!' (Lydia – on staff, not a program participant.)

3   This concept is articulated in his book, *A Hidden Wholeness*.

4   Klein, 1993.

God and the deep places of their souls in ways they may not have imagined before.[5]

The wider ecclesial connection is introduced to this dynamic with the Jesus meta-narrative providing the connecting links. The local experience of Church and Catholic education is explored as the lived context for the participants. This personal and communal exploration is informed by theological and ecclesial perspectives.

Through this process, participants are invited to reflect on their vocation as a teacher in a Catholic school. Participants gain a richer appreciation for the place of prayer, silence and personal reflection in their personal and professional lives. Participants are introduced to a wide variety of prayer experiences (including the *Staff PrayerFire* resources) to support and enrich both their personal prayer life and the prayers they lead with the students in their classes.[6] In Year 2, participants are invited to prepare and lead prayer and ritual for the group and in the Year 3 retreat the prayer experiences focus on the capacities for Christian community.[7] A strong sense of community is nurtured as each participant develops a reflective capacity in company with other teachers,[8] and using narrative and the rich resources of the Christian tradition. In the course of three years very deep and rich bonds are formed between participants.

5　Many of the participants' summative reflections alluded to the different kind of space they accessed as being pivotal in *retaining* a sense of their deepest self and their connection to God: 'I know I need to keep going back to this place inside me to be with my God and know the me I am and want to be. When that's the place I come out of, I am better at home, at work and with my students and staff (KFCSFB).'

6　Even learning the simplicity of the basics in setting up a prayer space (a bible, a candle and a cross), and experiencing how to greet the space and each other in reverent welcome, echoed a lasting impression: 'Just seeing how to set the prayer space up and knowing what has to go there and what might go there and how to be with each other helped me learn so much. Every time we came back, it was so comfortable and quiet and safe. I think that's what a prayer circle should be' (KFPGFB).

7　As participants realised over time that the programs were designed in a staged approach, the realisation became a strong affirmation of their journey: 'As we talked about the program nearing the end of the year, I couldn't believe how much I'd moved, how much I'd learned. I knew that what I was doing at the end of the year I would have been incapable of doing at the beginning, and if you had told me what I'd be doing by the end of the year, I wouldn't have believed you' (APRE, PGFB).

8　Learning to be present and to listen was a challenging but powerful experience: 'I don't think I have ever in my life felt listened to in that way, without judging or without feeling I had to struggle to be heard or get air-play. It was the most amazing experience. I cried later because of the love in it, to be somehow that cared about that someone would just listen. Jesus must have been like that. I can be Jesus to someone else like that' (KFPGFB).

Guiding Lights

The *Guiding Lights Leadership Program* is designed for those in leadership positions in Brisbane Catholic Education schools. The program runs over three years in a sequential, developmental way. In the first year of the program, the principal attends. In the second year of the program, the rest of the school leadership team begins their program. Those in this program are expected to support and develop their own mission leadership within their school context.

This program is informed particularly by the work of Stephen Bevans, Daniel O'Leary, Elizabeth Johnson, Sandra Schneiders, Karl Rahner, Robert Kinast, Gerald Grace, and Gini Shimabukuro. It has been designed to deepen individual leadership vision and skill while developing capacity and confidence as a Catholic educational leader in the contemporary context. The Trinitarian model of Christian community and the heart of vocation are applied in the context of Catholic school leadership, focusing on the heart and soul of mission in Catholic leadership rather than content coverage or management skills.

During the three-year program, there is a focus on deepening participants' spiritual foundations for Catholic school leadership; understanding and developing an integrated leadership style; engaging with the school and Church contexts; and developing an understanding of mission that integrates faith, life and culture. The process includes encounters with homeless people 'on the streets' and the use of psycho-spiritual tools to explore a personal understanding of the role of spirituality in Catholic leadership.[9] The subsequent 'leader companioning' component offers a model of mentoring and continuing support that is characterised by flexibility in response to participant need.[10]

---

9   It became apparent that the inclusion of the justice/service dimension in the program deepened an authentic identification with the gospel challenge. From one principal: 'The street experience was difficult for me, on a personal level. But I see it as an absolute must for a leadership program. The impact on all of us was huge – I know that a couple of the principals met with past parents who have ended up on the streets. And I know others are going to organise for their staff and parent groups to be invited to experience something like we have here' (GLP5), (Gowdie, 2012).

10 The Guiding Lights program also afforded principals the opportunity to companion each other, and this was highly valued, confirming Flintham's research (2007) where the opportunity for sharing between principals in both honesty about the demands, and inspiration about the calling, was a recommendation of his findings. The literature highlights how important is the influence of significant people in the spiritual growth of leaders, with the capacity to inspire human connection with others a key element noted in a variety of studies (Moore, 1999; Newby & Hyde, 1992). *Catching Fire* confirms those general findings, and offers further insight into the importance of selection, the skill of the companions, and the mentoring dynamic.

   School leaders were afforded the option to be individually companioned themselves by a skilled person with a strong spiritual foundation. The concept was embraced well, with some having a significant experience of being mentored in this way: 'My sessions with the Leader Companion have been excellent. … I have found this an oasis in the hard work of

The program acknowledges that participants have the primary responsibility for their own spiritual formation. It recognises that each of us has a different and unique gateway to the spiritual journey. The program develops formation capacities through a head, heart and hands approach. The journey is not just one of cognition, it engages the very centre of our being[11] and then, with this head and heart learning, we are moved to witness and action in community. The Guiding Lights Leadership Breakfasts – held in conjunction with systemic Leadership Forums – bring participants together for opportunities to sustain and centre their leadership.

leadership. The flexibility of how we meet and my changing needs has been a great reason for success with this I think. It has been all about my needs and I haven't felt locked into another person to meet with' (Principal, GLPGFB).

It became apparent that the flexibility in the structure of companioning and the content focus of the companioning was critical to the success of the concept, confirming the literature around successful mentoring and coaching practice (Bennetts, 2001; Blackwell & McLean, 1996; Green, 2006; Law, 1987; Tausch, 1978). For those where this did not work as well, it was the calibre of the Leader Companion that seemed to be at issue: 'They just seemed to be pushing their own barrow – it wasn't about me' (Principal, PGFB). This disconfirming data underlined how important it was to be discerning in the choice of those invited to be involved as Leader Companions.

As program participants moved back to their school community, they became a supportive group to each other in the everyday unfolding of school life, a group who: 'understood a new language,' had a 'way of seeing, and maybe being, differently that we kind of saw in each other and it somehow made us stronger – more brave I think, not able to just do as we'd done before '(KFCSFB).

Schools were encouraged to organise semi-regular meetings for all participants involved in the separate programs (up to seven) to share their experiences and to plan initiatives in their schools. Where this happened, the general influence and change in the school community appeared to be most sustained. However, even where no meetings or get-togethers among participants occurred, the influence of this 'critical mass' was still evident and identified by the participants and critical friends in the research: 'There was an obvious special bond – a real connectedness – between all of them' (Lydia, CSFB). Others, particularly APREs, understood and appreciated the practical implications of this shift: 'I feel very supported. It's great that there's seven people here and everyone takes a role in supporting. It's not left to one person' (APRE, PGFB). The APRE of the case school, St Raphael's, had no doubt about the internal shift that had occurred: 'They now have not only the passion, but the ability. And they have a confidence and a belief in prayer and in God. I think that's the difference'. The shift was manifest most obviously in a broadening active participation in prayer, liturgies and professional learning days on spirituality and faith, and a more collaborative sense of ownership in staff meetings around the issues of identity and ethos and formation planning. This dynamic confirms research in critical mass theory (Dahlerup, 2005; Oliver & Marwell, 2002; Norris & Lovenduski, 2001; Stark, 1996), giving example to its application for spiritual formation in the Catholic school setting.

11   For leaders in particular, the trusted Kairos space to allow the shadows to emerge had significant impact. One participant described her experience this way: 'I did not want to look at this part of my life, and have avoided it diligently. And did so successfully during this retreat. But it kept bobbing up and finally I did [look at it]. I'm grateful there was no pressure or expectation to do so, otherwise my antenna for manipulation would have sent me to an angry place! I felt I had adult ways to look at this now. I was in a group I could trust – not that I shared with others – I just knew this was a safe place and they helped make it that way. And I had X and Y (facilitators) who just made a way for me. I found wisdom I didn't really think I ever had. What I was scared of was not really that big in the end once I stared it down. It really was a mouse with a megaphone in my heart. I'm incredibly grateful for this. It's changed me – I feel like I'm growing into an adult who is whole and loved and loving. God is real and close and in me. I can't tell you what that means (SFPGFB).

SpiritFire

This program is designed to develop a core group in each school community to animate the spiritual culture of the school community. Three people from each school in *SpiritFire* are drawn from the staff – one from the school leadership team, usually the APRE, and two other staff members. They are those who have an interest in, and recognised potential to animate, the staff community. The aims of the program are two-fold: to nurture the individual formation of participants and to develop skills for use in their own school staff communities. Participants have particular carriage in implementing school-based initiatives and systemic resources provided to schools, especially *Staff PrayerFire*.[12]

The *SpiritFire* program is informed by an understanding of theological reflection, scriptural exegesis, psychospirituality and group dynamics, through the work of Bernard Lonergan, Carolyn Osiek, Raymond Brown, Robert Wicks, Patricia O'Connell Killen and Robert Kinast.

The main activities within the *SpiritFire* program are the participants' 'reading' of their own lives through a deepened understanding of scripture and psycho-spirituality tools, as well as their learning of simple skills to facilitate small group prayer initiatives and reflection times with other staff. Over the course of four formation contact days through the year, participants learn how to engage with the layered meaning of scriptural passages, understand and lead personal and group reflection on the scriptures, facilitate a process of theological reflection, develop and lead ritual, and explore a range of approaches to prayer within the Catholic tradition.[13]

Throughout the *SpiritFire* program, participants explicitly explore the Capacities of Christian Community that are identified in the *Staff Formation Framework*. They examine the capacities in relation to their personal spiritual journey and the implications for the life of the school community.

Throughout the three years of the *SpiritFire* program a number of key elements are developed. Prayer experiences centre around the use of scripture as a way of making connections between inspired sacred writing and its relevance to everyday life. Theological reflection, Lectio Divina, and a four-level framework for understanding scripture, are key processes used

---

12 *Staff PrayerFire* is a systemic resource providing each school with an experiential and wide ranging program of prayer rituals derived from the Catholic tradition and adapted for staff prayer.

13 Other rituals, such as leaving a light on overnight in the sacred prayer space, re-introduces participants to the tradition of the sanctuary light. These practices had the effect of recovering or discovering what some called a deep pride in their Catholic inheritance: 'I had no idea how ... rich was the symbol and story of the Catholic tradition. It's like we seem to only have left the motions without the meaning. This is so different but I can see it's not too. It makes me feel we have as much depth and wisdom as the Buddhists who you always hear these days as being the most sacred or wise religious people. Why don't we know about this stuff?!' (KFCSFB)

throughout the program. Participants are invited into an experience of using scripture to reframe how they understand their lives, their vocation and the world.[14]

---

14 Participants appreciated what they perceived as 'solid process and content'. In particular, the use of psycho-spirituality (Leffel, 2007) and narrative reflection (Bons-Storm, 2002; Klein, 1993) in the interpretation of scripture provided them with a sense of personal engagement and challenge that most had not experienced: 'Sometimes, what is called holistic formation can be too fluffy – in trying to be something for all, there is nothing to grab onto. But *SpiritFire* has such gutsy stuff – very challenging but very caring of us too' (APRE, PGFB).

APPENDIX 2:

KEY PRINCIPLES OF PRACTICE FOR FACILITATORS OF *CATCHING FIRE* STAFF FORMATION PROGRAMS

Key principles include the following:

- Facilitators attend to their own continuing spiritual formation and psychological wellbeing aware of what they bring to each group encounter and in order to authentically lead and engage.
- Facilitators establish the use of the five Boundary Markers[1] as a way of holding the space and the group: Bring All of You; Listen with Soft Eyes; No Fixing; Extend and Presume Welcome; Double Confidentiality.
- Facilitators utilise an approach of co-facilitation in formation programs to powerfully model collaborative leadership, mutual respect for gift and skill, and genuine companioning.[2]
- Engaging in prayerful preparation prior to each formation program allows facilitators to bring to their work a sense of centred-ness, intentionality and awareness of the dynamic action of the Holy Spirit.
- Facilitators create an environment that is welcoming, prayerful and invitational.
- Facilitators are well-prepared in their organisation to ensure that they can be fully present to the formation process and the participants' contexts.

---

1   These principles are adapted from Parker Palmer's 'Circles of Trust' approach, and seek to establish an openness and honesty in the group that nurtures and challenges the identity and integrity of each member. They have been particularly powerful for participants in *Catching Fire* and widely adopted in school classrooms and staff rooms: 'The boundary markers I learnt on the first retreat was [sic] a skill I will never forget. Now that I am aware of them, I think I am more respectful of interactions I have with others. Likewise, I know I'm more tolerant of others who <u>don't</u> keep these markers, as they are still to learn them.'

2   All programs in *Catching Fire* were co-facilitated. This had an impact in itself: 'The way X and Y worked together was so ... honouring ... is the word ... of each other, but not all serious and precious. I haven't seen people REALLY work like this before' (SFPGFB); and 'They just slipped into each other's stream ... no competition or holding the floor – or any this bit that bit kind of stuff. It was fluid but you can see how much they like and respect each other' (SFPGFB).

- Facilitators apply best practice in group dynamics and spiritual direction to the work.[3]

---

3 Time, space, developed trust, and tools for reflection are all important elements in participant negotiation of the difficult parts of their lives. The invitational principle which operated throughout the *Catching Fire* programs was never more important than in reflecting on the difficult moments of life. Rather, if and when these moments did emerge for participants, they perceived that the reflective skilling they were building already helped them shift perspective, and the attentiveness of facilitators created a safe passage for deeper and honest reflection.

REFERENCES

ACBC Pastoral Projects Office (2007), *Catholics who have stopped attending mass*, Australian Catholic University, Melbourne, Vic.

ACBC & ACLRI (Australian Catholic Bishops Conference, and the Australian Conference of Leaders of Religious Institutes) (2000), *Towards healing: principles and procedures in responding to complaints of abuse against personnel of the Catholic Church in Australia*, National Committee for Professional Standards, Melbourne, Vic.

ACEL (2009), *Leadership Capability Framework*, Author, Penrith, NSW.

ACER (2010), *Who's coming to school today?* Catholic Education, Archdiocese of Brisbane, Brisbane, Qld.

ACR (1978), *Australasian Catholic Record*, RMIT, Sydney, NSW.

ACS (Australian Community Survey) (1998), *A survey of wider community values, religiosity and image of the church in the 1990's*, National Church Life Survey Research, Melbourne, Vic.

Adair, J (2001), *The leadership of Jesus and its legacy today*, Canterbury Press, Norwich, UK.

AITSL (2014), *Global trends in professional learning and performance & development: Some implications and ideas for the Australian education system*, prepared in partnership with the Innovation Unit, Australian Institute for Teaching and School Leadership (AITSL), Melbourne, Vic, retrieved from http://www.aitsl.edu.au/docs/default-source/default-document-library/horizon_scan_report.pdf?sfvrsn=2

AITSL (2014a), *The Essential Guide to Professional Learning: Innovation*, Australian Institute for Teaching and School Leadership (AITSL), Melbourne, Vic, retrieved from http://www.aitsl.edu.au/docs/default-source/professional-growth- resources/professional-learning-resources/essential_guide_innovation.pdf

AITSL (2014b), *The Essential Guide to Professional Learning: Leading Culture*, Australian Institute for Teaching and School Leadership (AITSL), Melbourne, Vic, retrieved from http://www.aitsl.edu.au/docs/default-source/professional-growth- resources/professional-learning-resources/essential_guide_leading_culture.pdf

Alford, H & Naughton, M (2001), *Managing as if faith mattered; Christian social principles in the modern organization*, University of Notre Dame Press, Notre Dame, Indiana.

Annenburg Institute for School Reform (2004), *Instructional Coaching: Professional Development Strategies that Improve Instruction*, Brown University Press, Providence, Mass.

Andrews, D & Crowther, F (2002), Parallel leadership: A clue to the contents of the 'black box' of school reform, *The International Journal of Educational Management, 16*(4), pp. 152-159.

Arbuckle, G (1996), *From Chaos to Mission: Refounding Religious Life Formation*, Geoffrey Chapman, London, UK.

Arthur, J (2002), Review of *Catholic Schools: Mission Markets and Morality* in *British Journal of Educational Studies, 50*(4), Blackwell, Oxford, UK.

Astley, J (2009), Emotion and transformation in the relational spirituality paradigm, Part 2: Implicit morality and 'minimal prosociality', *Proceedings of the Receptive Ecumenism and Ecclesial Learning Conference*, Ushaw College, 13 January, 2009.

APAPDC (2003), *Leaders Lead Project*, Author, Canberra, ACT.

Bacik, JJ (1993), *Tensions in the Church: facing the challenges, seizing the opportunities*, Sheed & Ward, Kansas, MS.

Bacik, JJ (2002), *Catholic spirituality – its history and challenge*, Paulist Press, New Jersey, NY.

Bailey, PA; Carpenter, DR & Harrington, P (2002), Theoretical foundations of service-learning in nursing education, *Journal of Nursing Education, 41*(10), 433-436.

Balia, DM & Kim, K (2010), *Witnessing to Christ today* (Vol. 2), OCMS.

Barcan, A (1980), *A history of Australian education*, Oxford University Press, Melbourne, Vic.

Barth, R (2004), *Learning by heart*, John Wiley and Sons, New York, NY.

Barty, K; Blackmore, J; Sachs, J & Thompson, P (2005), Unpacking the issues: Researching the shortage of school principals in two states in Australia, *The Australian Educational Researcher, 32*(3), pp. 1-18.

Bass, BM (1985), *Leadership and performance beyond expectations*, Free Press, New York, NY.

Bateson, G & Bateson, MC (1987), *Angels fear: Toward an epistemology of the sacred*, Macmillan, New York, NY.

Beal, R (2009), *In pursuit of a 'total ecclesiology': Yves Congar's 'De Ecclesia', 1931-1954* (doctoral dissertation), Catholic University of America, Washington, DC, AAT 3361304.

Beare, H; Caldwell, B & Millikan, R (1993), Leadership, in Preedy, M (ed.), *Managing the effective school*, Paul Chapman Publishing, London, UK, pp. 141-163.

Beare, H (1995), *What is the next quantum leap for school systems in Australia? The 1994 Currie Lecture*, Australian Council for Educational Administration, Hawthorn, Vic.

Beare, H (1998), O' for leaders who have great souls, *Proceedings of the national ACEA conference in Melbourne, Australia, 1998*, Australian Council for Educational Administration (renamed Australian Council for Educational Leaders in 2002, Penrith, NSW.

Beare, H (2001), *Creating the future school*, Routledge Falmer, London, UK.

Beare, H (2003), Creating future schools for future kids, *Proceedings of the 2003 Conference of the Australian Secondary Principals Association held in Sydney, 28 September to 1 October, 2003, ASPA*, Sydney, NSW.

Beattie, H (2001), *The theory practice interface: a case study of experienced nurses' perception of their role as clinical teachers* (doctoral dissertation), Australian Catholic University, Brisbane, Qld.

Beck, JR (2003), Self and soul: exploring the boundary between psychotherapy and spiritual formation, *Journal of Psychology and Theology, 31*(1), pp. 24-36.

Bellamy, J; Black, A; Castle, K; Hughes, P & Kaldor, P (2002), *Why people don't go to church*, Openbook Publishers, Adelaide, SA.

Bellanca, J (1996), *Designing professional development for change*, Hawker-Brownlow Education, Moorabbin, Vic.

Bellanca, J (2002), Professional development for a new age, in Thomas, N (ed.), *Perspectives on the Community College*, League for Innovation, Phoenix, AZ.

Belmonte, A (2006), *Voices of lay principals in an era of change* (doctoral dissertation), University of Queensland, St Lucia, Qld.

Belmonte, A; Cranston, N & Limerick, B (2006), Voices of catholic school lay principals: promoting a catholic character and culture in schools in an era of change, *Proceedings of the International Conference of the Australian Association for Research in Education held in Adelaide, 27-30 November 2006*, retrieved 4 October, 2009, from http://www.aare.edu.au/confpap.htm

Benedict XVI (2005), *Deus caritas est. God is love*, Vatican City, Rome, IT.

Benedict XVI (2008), A proper hermeneutic for the Second Vatican Council, in Lamb, M & Levering, M (eds.), *Vatican II: Renewal within tradition*, Oxford University Press, Oxford, UK.

Benet McKinney, M (1987), *Sharing wisdom: A process for group decision making*, Ave Maria Press, Notre Dame, Ind.

Bennett, N; Crawford, M & Cartwright, M (eds.) (2003), *Effective educational leadership*, Sage Publications, London, UK.

Bennetts, C (2001), Lifelong learners: In their own words, *International Journal of Lifelong Education, 20*(4), pp. 272-288.

Benson, PL (2004), Emerging themes in research: Spiritual and religious development, in *Applied Developmental Science, 8*(1), pp. 47-53.

Benson, PL; Roehlkepartain, EC & Rude, SP (2003), Spiritual development in childhood and adolescence: Towards a field of enquiry, in *Applied Developmental Science, 7*(3), pp. 205-215.

Berk, L (2001), *Development through the lifespan*, Allyn and Bacon, Needham Heights, MA.

Beuchner, F (1973), *Wishful thinking: A theological ABC*, Harper and Row, New York, NY.

Bevans, SB; Chai, T; Jennings, JN; Jorgensen, K & Werner, D (eds.) (2015), *Reflecting on and Equipping for Christian Mission* (Vol. 27), Wipf and Stock Publishers.

Bevans, S (2002), *Models of contextual theology*, Orbis, New York, NY.

Bevans, S (2005), Wisdom from the margins: Systematic theology and the missiological imagination, *Australian E-Journal of Theology*, 5(1), retrieved 3 March, 2008, from http://aejt.com.au/2005/vol_5,_no_1,_2005/?article=395502

Bevans, S (2009), *The mission has a church: An invitation to the dance*, Yarra Theological Union Melbourne, Vic.

Bevans, SB & Schroeder, RP (2004), *Constants in context: A theology of mission for today*, Orbis, Maryknoll, NY.

Bezzina, M (2008), More than just rhetoric: Putting moral purpose to work in complex times, *Proceedings of the ACEL Annual Conference, New Metaphors for Leadership in Schools held in Melbourne, 30 September – 2 October, 2008.*

Bezzina, M; Burford, C & Duignan, P (2007), Leaders transforming learning and learners: Messages for Catholic leaders, *Proceedings of the 4th International Conference on Catholic Education Leadership held in Sydney, 29 July – 1 August, 2007.*

Billig, S (2004), *Heads, hearts and hands: The research on K-12 service learning*, RMC Research Corporation, Denver, CO.

Bishops of NSW & ACT (2007), *Catholic schools at a crossroads: Pastoral letter of the Bishops of NSW and ACT*, Author, retrieved 7 May, 2009, from http://www.cecnsw.catholic.edu.au/Catholic_schools_at_the_crossroads

Blackburn, S (2005), *Truth. A guide for the perplexed*, Allen Lane, London, UK.

Blackwell, R & McLean, M (1996), Formal pupil or informal peer? in H. Fullerton (ed.), *Facets of Mentoring in Higher Education, Paper 94*, Staff and Educational Development Association, pp. 23-31.

Bloom, B (1956), *Taxonomy of Educational Objectives, the classification of educational goals – Handbook I: Cognitive Domain* (Vol. 1), McKay, New York, NY.

Bloom, B; Masia, B and Krathwohl, D (1964), *Taxonomy of educational objectives: The classification of educational goals. Handbook II: The affective domain*, David McKay & Co, New York, NY.

Blout, DL (2004), *Reflections on teaching in a Catholic high school: A qualitative case study* (doctoral dissertation), retrieved 25 March, 2010, from Dissertations and Theses Duquesne University, Pittsburgh, Penn: Publication No. AAT 3136704.

Boeve, L (2005), Religion after de-traditionalization: Christian faith in a post-secular Europe, *Irish Theological Quarterly, 70*(2), pp. 99-122.

Boeve, L (2007), *God interrupts history: Theology in a time of upheaval,* Continuum, New York, NY.

Boeve, L (2011), Communicating faith in contemporary Europe: Dealing with language problems in and outside the church, In J. Sullivan (ed.), *Communicating faith,* Catholic University of America Press, Washington, pp. 293-312.

Boff, L (1986), *Ecclesiogenesis: the base communities reinvent the Church,* Orbis Books, Maryknoll, NY.

Boff, L (1993), 'Trinity' in *Mysterium Liberationis: An encyclopedia of liberation theology,* Orbis Books, Maryknoll, NY.

Boiler Room Communications (BRC) (2003), *Australian Boiler Room Study,* Boiler Room Communications, Melbourne, Victoria.

Bolman, L & Deal, T (2001), *Leading with soul: An uncommon journey of spirit,* Jossey-Bass, San Francisco, CA.

Bons-Storm, R (2002), The importance of life and faith histories in the methodology of practical theology, *HTS Teologiese Studies/Theological Studies, 58*(1), pp. 26-42.

Borg, M (1994), *Meeting Jesus again for the first time: The historical Jesus and the heart of contemporary faith,* Harper Collins, New York, NY.

Bosch, D (1991), *Transforming mission: Paradigm shifts in the theology of mission,* Orbis Books, Maryknoll, NY.

Bouma, GD, (2006), *Australian soul: Religion and spirituality in the 21st century,* Cambridge University Press, Port Melbourne, Vic.

Boud, D; Keogh, R & Walker, D (eds.) (1985), *Reflection: Turning experience into learning,* Kogan Page, London, UK.

Boud, D & Miller, N (eds.) (1997), *Working with experience: Animating learning,* Routledge, London, UK.

Bourdieu, P (1977), *Outline of a theory of practice,* Cambridge University Press, Cambridge, UK.

Bourdieu, P (2000), *Pascalian meditations,* Polity Press, Cambridge, UK.

Bowgen, L & Sever, K (2014), *Differentiated Professional Development in a Professional Learning Community,* Solution Tree Press, Bloomington, IN.

Boyd, V (1992), *School context. Bridge or barrier to change?* Southwest Educational Development Laboratory, Austin, TX.

Boyd, V & Hord, SM (1994), Principals and the new paradigm: Schools as learning communities, *Proceedings of the annual meeting of the American Educational Research Association held in New Orleans, 1994.*

Bracken, JA (2008), *God: Three who are one*, Liturgical Press, Collegeville, MN.

Branson, C (2004), *An exploration of the concept of values-led principalship* (doctoral dissertation), Australian Catholic University, Brisbane, Qld.

Branson, C (2009), *Leadership for an Age of Wisdom*, Springer, Dordrecht, Netherlands.

Bredehoft, D (2003), The Catholic school leader: shaping mud into the reflection of our creator, *Momentum, 24*(2), pp. 70-72.

Brockett, RG & Hiemstra, R (1991), *Self direction in adult learning: perspectives on theory, research and practice*, Routledge, New York, NY.

Broken Bay CEO, (2008), *Our values, our mission*, Diocese of Broken Bay, Pennant Hills, NSW.

Brookfield, SD (2015), *The skilful teacher: on trust, technique and responsiveness in the classroom* (3rd ed.), Jossey Bass, San Francisco, CA.

Brookfield, SD & Hess, ME (eds.) (2008), *Teaching reflectively in theological contexts: promises and contradictions*, Jossey Bass, San Francisco, CA.

Brookfield, SD & Preskill, S (eds.) (2005), *Discussion as a way of teaching*, Jossey Bass, San Francisco, CA.

Brookfield, SD (1983), *Adult learning, adult education and the community*, Open University Press, Milton Keynes, UK.

Brookfield, SD (1995), *Becoming a critically reflective teacher*, Jossey Bass, San Francisco, CA.

Brookfield, SD (2005), *The power of critical theory: liberating adult learning and teaching*, Jossey Bass, San Francisco, CA.

Brueggemann, W (2001), *The prophetic imagination* (second edition), Augsburg Fortress Press, Minneapolis, MN.

Bruner, J (2004), Life as narrative, in *New School for Social Research, 71*(3), pp. 691-710.

Bryk, A; Lee, V & Holland, P (1993), *Catholic schools and the common good*, Harvard University Press, Cambridge, MA.

Buchanan, MT (2013a), Leadership dimensions associated with leadership roles in faith-based schools, in Buchanan, MT (ed.), *Leadership and religious schools: International perspectives and challenges*, Bloomsbury Academic, New York, USA, pp. 127-144.

Buetow, HA (1988), *The Catholic school: Its roots, identity and future*, Crossroad Publishing, New York, NY.

Burghardt, WJ (1989), Contemplation: A long, loving look at the real, *Church,* Winter 1989, pp. 14-18.

Burkitt, I (1990), *Social Selves: Theories of the social formation of personality*, Sage, London, UK.

Burley, S (1997), Lost leaders from the convent and the classroom, in McMahon, J; Neidhart, H & Chapman, J (eds.), *Leading the Catholic school*, Spectrum, Melbourne, Victoria, pp. 49-61.

Burley, S (2001), Resurrecting the religious experiences of Catholic girls' schooling in South Australia in the 1920s, *Education Research and Perspectives*, *28*(1), pp. 25-44.

Byrne, L (2001), *The journey is my home*, Hodder and Stoughton, London, UK.

Camille, AL & Schorn, J (2004), *A faith interrupted: An honest conversation with alienated Catholics*, Loyola Press, Chicago, Illinois.

Campbell, J (1972), *The hero with a thousand faces*, Princeton University Press, Princeton, NJ.

Campbell, J (ed.) (1971), *The Portable Jung*.

Canavan, K (1990), The Catholic Education Office: Birth of a complex organisation, *Unicorn, 16*(1), pp. 35-39.

Canavan, K (1999), The transformation of Catholic schools in Australia, *Journal of Religious Education*, *47*(1), pp. 19-24.

Cappel, C (1989), A Reflection on the Spirituality of the Principal, in Kealey, RJ (ed.), *Reflections on the role of the Catholic school principal*, National Catholic Educational Association, Washington, DC, pp. 29-33.

Cardonna, P (2000), Transcendental leadership, *Leadership and Organisational Development Journal*, *21*(4), pp. 201-207.

Carlin, P; d'Arbon, T; Dorman, J; Duignan, P & Neidhart, H (2003), *Leadership succession for catholic schools in Victoria, South Australia and Tasmania: Final Report*, Australian Catholic University, Strathfield, NSW.

Carlson, N (2003), *Community of practice: A path to strategic learning*, Idaho National Engineering and Environmental Laboratory, Idaho Falls, ID.

Carmichael, L (1982), Leaders as learners: A possible dream, *Educational Leadership*, *40*(1), pp. 58-59.

Carter, M & Francis, R (2001), Mentoring and beginning teachers' workplace learning, *Asia-Pacific Journal of Teacher Education, 29*(3), pp. 249-262.

Carotta, CC (2003), *The work of your life*, Harcourt Religion Publishers, Orlando, Florida.

Carotta, CC & Carotta, M (2005), *Sustaining the spirit: callings, commitments, and vocational challenges*, Harcourt Religion Publishers, Orlando, Florida.

Castelli, M (2000), The role of the headteacher in developing children holistically: Perspectives from Anglicans and Catholics, *Educational Management Administration and Leadership*, *28*(4), pp. 389-403.

Catholic Archdiocese of Brisbane (1996), *Shaping and Staffing Our Parishes*, Author, Brisbane, Qld.

Catholic Archdiocese of Brisbane (2000), *Understanding Evangelisation*, Author, Brisbane, Qld.

Catholic Archdiocese of Brisbane (2004), *Let your Light Shine*, Author, Brisbane, Qld.

Catholic Church Life Survey (CCLS) (1996), Australian Catholic Bishops Conference, Canberra, ACT.

Catholic Education, Archdiocese of Brisbane (2001), *Archdiocesan report: Catholic schools for the 21st century (defining features of Catholic schools)*, Author Brisbane, Qld.

Catholic Education, Archdiocese of Brisbane (2002), *Learning framework*, Author, Brisbane, Qld.

Catholic Education, Archdiocese of Brisbane (2004), *Vision statement for Catholic education in the Archdiocese of Brisbane*, Author, Brisbane, Qld.

Catholic Education, Archdiocese of Brisbane (2005), *Strategic renewal framework 2002-2006* (2nd ed.), Author, Brisbane, Qld.

Catholic Education, Archdiocese of Brisbane (2005), *Renewal process*, Author, Brisbane, Qld.

Catholic Education, Archdiocese of Brisbane (2005), *Celebration and challenge*, Author, Brisbane, Qld.

Catholic Education, Archdiocese of Brisbane (2007), *Guidelines for professional development and planning days*, Author, Brisbane, Qld.

Catholic Education, Archdiocese of Brisbane (2008), *Archdiocesan overview*, Author, Brisbane, Qld.

Catholic Education, Archdiocese of Brisbane (2009), *Employment of Staff Policy*, Author, Brisbane, Qld.

Catholic Education, Archdiocese of Brisbane (2009), *Report on the 2008 Primary Graduate Process Review*, Author, Brisbane, Qld.

Catholic Education, Archdiocese of Brisbane (2010), Who's coming to school today? *Summary of research findings*, Author, Brisbane, Qld.

Catholic Education Commission of Victoria Ltd (CECV) (2010), *Enhancing Catholic schools identity project*, Author, Melbourne, Vic, retrieved 16 December, 2010, from http://*www.schoolidentity.net*

Catholic Education South Australia (2013), *Like a mustard seed: A CESA Stimulus and Foundation Paper for Staff Spiritual and Religious Formation*, *https://online.cesa.catholic.edu.au/docushare/dsweb/Get/Document-27651/Staff+Spirituality+and+Religious+Formation+Framework+v1.0.pdf*

Catholic Education South Australi (2014), *Continuous improvement framework for catholic schools*, 23200/CESA_School+improvement_web+Final.pdf

Catholic Health Australia (2011), *Crafting Catholic identity in post modern Australia: A preferential option for the poor*, Catholic Health Australia Publications, Deakin West, ACT.

Code of Canon Law (CCL) (1983), *The Code of Canon Law: Latin-English Edition*, Canon Law Society of America, Washington, DC.

Catholic Education Commission of Victoria (CECV) (2010), *Enhancing Catholic schools identity project*, Catholic Education Commission of Victoria Ltd, Melbourne, Vic, retrieved 16 December, 2010, from http://*www.schoolidentity.net*

Chambers, P (2003), Narrative and reflective practice: Recording and understanding experience, *Educational Action Research, 11*(3), pp. 403-414.

Chambers, P (ed.) (2016), *Schools for human flourishing*, National Society (Church of England and Church in Wales) for the Promotion of Education, SSAT Ltd and the Woodard Corporation, London, UK.

Chapdelaine, A; Ruiz, A; Warchal, J & Wells, C (2005), *Service-learning code of ethics*, Anker Publishing Co Bolton, MA.

Cheung, T (2002), *A strategy to develop spiritual leaders* (doctoral dissertation), Fuller theological Seminary, Hong Kong.

Chopp, RS (1995), Saving work, in *Feminist practices of theological education*, Westminster John Knox, Louisville, KY.

Chittester, J (2000), *Illuminated life*, Orbis Books, New York, NY.

Chittester, J (2001), *Listen with the heart*, Sheed and Ward, London, UK.

Chittester, J (2003), Re-imaging the Catholic school in this new century, in Prendergast, N & Monahan, L (eds.), *Reimagining the Catholic school*, Veritas, Dublin, Ire.

Cioppi, MT (2000), *Evangelisation in Catholic secondary schools* (doctoral dissertation), UMI Dissertations Publishing, Immaculata College, East Whiteland, PN.

Ciriello, MJ (ed.) (1994), *The Principal as spiritual leader: Expectations in the areas of faith development, building Christian community, moral and ethical development, history and philosophy*, United States Conference of Catholic Bishops, Washington, DC.

Clark, M (1995), *A short history of Australia* (4th ed.), Penguin Books, Ringwood, NSW.

Clarke, S (2002), The teaching principal: from the shadowlands to a place in the sun, *Queensland Journal of Educational Research, 18*(1), pp. 23-37.

Clarke, S (2003), Mastering the art of extreme juggling: an examination of the contemporary role of the Queensland teaching principal, *Unpublished report of the Queensland Association of State School Principals (QASSP)*.

Codd, A (2003), The school and the parish: changing patterns of involvement, in Prendergast, N & Monahan, L (eds.), *Re-imagining the Catholic school*, Veritas Publications, Dublin, Ire.

Code of Canon Law http://www.vatican.va/archive/ENG1104/_INDEX.HTM

Cohen, L & Mannion, L (1994), *Research methods in education* (2nd ed), Croom Helm, London, UK.

Coleman, J & Hopper, T (1987), *Public and private schools: The impact of communities*, Basic Books, New York, NY.

Coles, R (1990), *The spiritual life of children*, Houghton Mifflin, Boston, MA.

Collins, P (2004), *Between the rock and a hard place: being Catholic today*, ABC Books, Sydney, NSW.

Collins, J & Porras, J (2004), *Built to last: successful habits of visionary companies*, Random House, London, UK.

Coloe, M (2010), A matter of justice and necessity –Women's Participation: A prophetic challenge to the contemporary church, ACU, Melbourne, Vic.

Compagnone, N (1999), Lay Catholic elementary principals in the State of Kansas and the perceptions of their spiritual leadership and ministerial role (doctoral dissertation), University of Dayton, Dayton, OH.

Congar, Y (1965), Lay People in the Church, translated by Donald Attwater, Chapman, London, UK.

Conger, JA (1994), *Spirit at work: Discovering the spirituality in leadership*, Jossey-Bass, San Francisco, CA.

Congregation for Catholic Education (1977), *The Catholic school*, St Paul Publications, Homebush, NSW.

Congregation for Catholic Education (1982), *Lay Catholics in schools: Witnesses to faith*, St Paul Publications, Homebush, NSW.

Congregation for Catholic Education (1988), *The religious dimension of education in a Catholic school: Guidelines for reflection and renewal*, St Paul Publications, Homebush, NSW.

Congregation for Catholic Education (1998), *The Catholic school on the threshold of the third millennium*, St Paul Publications, Homebush, NSW.

Congregation for Catholic Education (2007), *Educating together in Catholic schools: a shared mission between consecrated persons and the lay faithful*, St Paul Publications, Homebush, NSW.

Congregation for Catholic Education (2014), *Educating Today and Tomorrow: A Renewing Passion (Instrumentum laboris)*, n. 10.

Congregation for the Clergy (1997), *General directory for catechesis*, Canadian Conference of Catholic Bishops, Ottawa, Ontario.

Constitution on the sacred liturgy (sacrosanctum concilium), in Flannery, A (ed.) 1981, *Vatican Council II: The conciliar and post-conciliar documents*, Dominican Publications, Dublin, Ire.

Conn, W (1998), *The desiring self: Rooting pastoral counselling and spiritual direction in self-transcendence*, Paulist Press, Mahwah, NJ.

Connors, B (1991), Teacher development and the teacher, in Hughes, P (ed.), *Teachers professional development*, ACER, Hawthorn, Vic, pp. 53-81.

Cook, TJ (2001), *Architects of Catholic culture: Designing and building Catholic culture in Catholic schools*, National Catholic Educational Association, Washington, DC.

Cook, T (2008), *Responding to Leadership Challenges in U.S. Catholic Schools: The Lived Reality* Online Submission, updated keynote address delivered at the Annual International Conference on Catholic Leadership, Creighton University.

Cook, T J & Simonds, TA (2011), The charism of 21st-century Catholic schools: Building a culture of relationships, *Journal of Catholic Education, 14*(3).

Cooper, C (ed.) (1975), Theories of group process, in Kolb DA & Fry R, *Toward an applied theory of experiential learning*, John Wiley, London, UK.

Corban, J (2002), *Succession planning*, Inspired Business Solutions.

Coughlan, P (2010), *The mission of the Catholic school and role of the principal in a changing Catholic landscape* (doctoral dissertation), Australian Catholic University, Brisbane, Qld.

Cozzens, D (2002), *Sacred silence: denial and the crisis in the church*, John Garratt Publishing Mulgrave, Vic.

Craig, M (2010), A post-modern theological model for understanding the religious concept of ultimate reality and religious diversity, *Australian E-Journal of Theology, 15*(1), retrieved 13 June, 2010, from http://aejt.com.au/2010/issue_15/?article=225394

Cranton, P (2005), *Understanding and promoting transformative learning*, Jossey-Bass, San Francisco, CA.

Cranton, P (ed.) (2006), *Authenticity in teaching. New directions for adult and continuing education*, Jossey-Bass, San Francisco, CA, p. 111.

Crawford, M & Rossiter, G (2006), *Reasons for living: Education and young people's search for meaning, identity and spirituality*, Australian Council for Educational Research, Melbourne.

Creasy, J & Paterson, F (2005), *Leading Coaching in Schools*, Leading Practice Seminar Series, National College for School Leadership, www.ncsl.org.uk

Croke, B (2007), Australian Catholic schools in a changing political and religious landscape, in Grace GR & O'Keefe JM (eds.), *International handbook of Catholic education: Challenges for school systems in the 21st century, Parts one and two*, Springer, Dordrecht, The Netherlands, pp. 11-834.

Crotty, L (2003), *Religious leadership in the Catholic school: the position of the religious education co-ordinator* (doctoral dissertation), University of Sydney, Sydney, NSW.

Crotty, L (2005), The REC and religious leadership, *Journal of Religious Education, 53*(1), pp. 48-59.

Crotty, L (2006), Leadership in religious education: A critique from the Australian perspective, *Handbook of the religious, moral and spiritual dimensions in education, Part 3*, Springer, Dordrecht, The Netherlands, pp. 779-798.

Crowther, F; Kaagan, S; Furguson, M & Hann, L (2002), *Developing teacher leaders: how teacher leadership enhances school success*, Corwin Press, Thousand Oaks, CA.

Csikszentmihalyi, M (1998), *Finding flow: the psychology of engagement with everyday life*, Basic Books, New York, NY.

Curran, J (2015), Teaching and leading through dialogue: Pope Francis and Catholic Higher Education, *Journal of Catholic Higher Education*, 34:2, pp. 135-149.

Czerniawski, G (ed.) (2011), *Emerging teachers and globalisation*, Routledge, New York, NY.

Dahlerup, D (2005), *The theory of a 'critical mass' revisited*, prepared by Dept. of Political Science, Stockholm University for proceedings of the Annual Meeting of the American Political Science Association held in Washington DC, 1-4 September, 2005.

Daley, BJ (2001), Learning and professional practice: A study of four professions, *Adult Education Quarterly*, 52(1), pp. 39-54.

Daloz, L (1986), *Effective teaching and mentoring*, Jossey-Bass, San Francisco, CA.

Daloz, L (1999), *Mentor: Guiding the journey of adult learners* (2nd ed.), Jossey-Bass, San Francisco, CA.

Daloz, L (2000), Transformative learning for the common good, in Mezirow, J and Associates (eds.), *Learning as transformation*, Wiley and Sons, San Francisco, CA, pp. 103-123.

Daloz, LA; Keen, CH; Keen, JP & Daloz-Parks, S (2000), Lives of commitment, in DeZure, D (ed.), *Learning from change*, Stylus Publishing, Sterling, Virginia.

D'Arbon, T (2000), School principals for the new millennium, *Proceedings of a national AARE conference of the Australian Association for Research in Education held in Sydney, Australia, 2000*, retrieved 10 July, 2009, from http://www.aare.edu.au/confpap.htm

D'Arbon, T (2003), Future principals for schools of the future, *Proceedings of 'Thinking about tomorrow', a national ACEL conference held in Sydney, 29 September – 1 October, 2003*, Australian Council for Educational Leaders, Penrith, NSW.

D'Arbon, T; Duignan, P & Duncan, D (2001), *Leadership succession: A research project on behalf of Catholic Education Commission*, Australian Catholic University, Sydney, NSW.

D'Arbon, T; Duignan, P; & Duncan, J (2002), Planning for future leadership of schools: an Australian study, *Journal of Educational Administration*, 40(5), pp. 468-485.

D'Arbon, T; Duignan, P; Dwyer, J & Goodwin, K (2001), *Leadership succession in Catholic schools in New South Wales: A Research Project on behalf of the Catholic Education Commission, New South Wales, phase two final report*, Australian Catholic University, Strathfield, NSW.

D'Arbon, T; Neidhart, H & Carlin P (2002), Principal succession in Catholic primary and secondary schools in Victoria, South Australia and Tasmania: Opportunities and challenges, *Proceedings of a national conference of the Australian Association for Research in Education held in Brisbane, Australia, 1-4 December, 2002*, retrieved 15 March, 2008, from http://www.aare.edu.au/02pap/car02106.htm

Date, J (2008), *Implications of Canon Law for Church Organisations Operating in Australia*, Masters Law Research thesis, the University of Melbourne, pp. 27-28.

Daughtry, P (2002), The Current Spiritual Climate, *Magazine of the Evangelical Alliance*, 2(4).

Day, C (1999), *Developing teachers: The challenge of lifelong learning*, Falmer Press, London, UK.

Day, C & Harris, A (2000), *Leading schools in times of change*, Open University Press, London, UK.

De Souza, M; Durka, G; Engebretsen, K; Jackson, R & McGrady, A, (2006), *International handbook of the religious, moral and spiritual dimensions in education*, Springer, Dordrecht, The Netherlands.

Deal, TE & Kennedy, AA (1982), *Corporate cultures: The rites and rituals of corporate life*, Addison-Wesley, Reading, MA.

Deal, T & Peterson, T (2003), *Shaping school culture: the heart of leadership*, Jossey-Bass, San Francisco, CA.

Declaration on Christian education *(Gravissimum educationis)*, in Flannery, A (ed.) 1981, *Vatican Council II: The conciliar and post-conciliar documents*, Dominican Publications, Dublin, Ire.

Declaration on the relation of the Church to non-Christian religions (Nostra aetate), in Flannery, A (ed.) 1981, *Vatican Council II: The Conciliar and Post-Conciliar Documents*, Dominican Publications, Dublin, Ire.

Decree on the apostolate of lay people (Apostolicam actuositatem), in Flannery, A (ed.) 1981, *Vatican Council II: The conciliar and post-conciliar documents*, Dominican Publications, Dublin, Ire.

Delio, I (2014) (ed), *From Teilhard to Omega: Co-creating an Unfinished Universe*, Orbis, Maryknoll, NY.

Delio, I (2015), *Making All Things New: Catholicity, Cosmology, Consciousness*, Orbis Books, Maryknoll, NY.

Department of Education and Training (2004), *The privilege and the price: A study of principal class workload and its impact on health and well-being - final report*, Author, Melbourne, Vic.

Derbyshire, MA (2005), *Supporting spiritual formation of teachers in Catholic schools*, University of Lethbridge, Lethbridge, Alberta.

Dewey, J (1925), *Experience and nature*, Open Court, Chicago, IL.

Dewey, J (1933), *How we think*, Heath, New York, NY.

Dewey, J (1934), *Art as experience*, Perigee Books, New York, NY.

Dillon, J & Maguire, M (eds.) (2011), *Becoming a teacher: issues in secondary teaching*, McGraw Hill, New York, NY.

Dimmock, C (2012), *Leadership, Capacity Building and School Improvement: Concepts, themes and impact*, Routledge, New York, NY.

Dinham, S (2008), *What forms of leadership, leadership structures and leadership learning are required for enabling teacher effectiveness?* Paper presented at National Leadership Learning Network, Adelaide, retrieved from http://slideplayer.com/slide/3743585/

Di Paola, L (1990), *A study of a staff development program for Catholic elementary school lay teachers* (doctoral dissertation), Fordham University, New York, NY, retrieved 25 March, 2010, from Dissertations and Theses: AandI. (Publication No. AAT 9109230).

Dirkx, JM & Prenger, S (1997), *Planning and implementing instruction for adults: A theme-based approach*, Jossey-Bass, San Francisco, CA.

Dixon, R (2002), *Who goes when? Mass attendees and their usual Mass time*, Pastoral Projects Office, Australian Catholic Bishops Conference, Melbourne, Vic.

Dixon, R (2005), *The Catholic community in Australia*, Openbook Publishers, Adelaide, SA.

Dixon R (2006), *Why Catholics have stopped going to Mass*, Pastoral Projects Office, Australian Catholic Bishops Conference, Melbourne, Vic.

Dogmatic Constitution on the Church (Lumen gentium), in Flannery, A (ed.) 1981, *Vatican Council II: The conciliar and post-conciliar documents*, Dominican Publications, Dublin, Ire.

Doherty, B (1981), *I am what I do*, St. Mary of the Woods Books, St. Mary of the Woods, Ind.

Doherty, T (2008), The many ways of telling the story of Jesus. *Compass, 42*(2), pp. 6-8.

Donnelly, C (2000), In pursuit of school ethos. *British Journal of Educational Studies, 48*(2), pp. 134-154.

Donovan, K (2000), *From separation to synergy – Receiving the richness of gen X*, Zadoc Papers, Hawthorn, Vic.

D'Orsa, J & D'Orsa T (1997), Reimagining Catholic school leadership for the third millennium, in Keane, R & Riley, D (eds.), *Quality Catholic schools: Challenges for leadership as Catholic education approaches the third millennium*, Brisbane Catholic Education, Brisbane, Qld, pp. 72-82.

D'Orsa, J & D'Orsa, T (2013), *Leading for Mission*, Integrating Life, Culture and Faith in Catholic Education, Vaughan Publishing, Mulgrave, Vic.

D'Orsa, T (2008), in the second modernity it takes the whole curriculum to teach the whole gospel, *Proceedings of the QCEC Curriculum Conference held in Brisbane*, 2008.

D'Orsa, J & D'Orsa, T eds. (2015), New Ways of Living the Gospel, Spiritual Traditions in Catholic Education, Vaughan Publishing, Mulgrave, Vic.

Doyle, D (2000), *Communion ecclesiology*, Orbis Books, Maryknoll, NY.

Dorney, JA (1997), Maria Harris: An aesthetic and erotic justice, in Keeley, BA (ed.), *Faith of our foremothers: Women changing religious education*, John Knox Press, Louisville, KY.

Dorr, D (2006), *Spirituality of leadership*, The Columba Press, Blackrock, Dublin, Ire.

Downey, M (1991), Current trends understanding Christian spirituality *Spirituality Today*, *43*(3), pp. 271-280.

Downey, M (1994), Christian spirituality: Changing currents, perspectives, challenges. *America*, *172*, pp. 8-12.

Downey, M (2006), *Experiences of Teachers' Daily Work Which Nourish and Sustain the Spirituality of Lay Teachers in Catholic High Schools* (unpublished doctoral dissertation), ACU, Banyo, Qld.

Dowson, M & McInerney, D M (2005), For what should theological colleges educate? A systematic investigation of ministry education perceptions and priorities. *Review of Religious Research*, *46*(4), pp. 403-421.

Doyle, T (1989), Context of Catholic education beyond 1988, in *NCEC Celebration and challenge: Catholic education in the future*, St Paul Publications, Homebush, NSW, pp. 35-54.

Drahmann, T & Stenger, A (1989), *The Catholic school principal: An outline for action*, National Catholic Educational Association, Washington, DC.

Drane, JW (2000), *The mcdonaldization of the church: spirituality, creativity, and the future of the church*, Darton, Longman and Todd, London, UK.

Draper, J & McMichael, P (2003), The rocky road to headship, *Australian Journal of Education*, *47*(2), pp. 185-196.

Drazenovich, G (2004), Towards a phenomenologically grounded understanding of Christian spirituality and theology, *Quodlibet Journal* *6*(1).

Dreyer, EA & Burrows, MS (eds.) (2005), *Minding the spirit: The study of Christian spirituality*, Johns Hopkins, Baltimore, MD.

Driedger, P (1999), *Finding our way home: The Church, our story: Catholic tradition, mission and practice*, Ave Maria Press, Notre Dame, Ind.

DuFour, R & Eaker, R (1998), *Professional learning communities at work: Best practices for enhancing student achievement*, National Educational Service, Bloomington, Ind.

DuFour, R & Eaker, R (eds.) (2005), *On common ground: The power of professional learning communities*, Solution Tree Press, Bloomington, Ind.

Duignan, P (2002), Formation of authentic educational leaders for Catholic schools, in Duncan, DJ & Riley, D (eds.), *Leadership in Catholic Education*, Harper Collins, Sydney, NSW.

Duignan, P (2004), Forming capable leaders: From competencies to capabilities. *New Zealand Journal of Educational Leadership, 19*(2), pp. 5-13.

Duignan, P (2007), *Educational leadership: Key challenges and ethical tensions*, Cambridge University Press, Melbourne, Vic.

Duignan P & Bhindi, N (1997), Leadership for a new century, *Educational Management and Administration, 25*(1), pp. 117-132.

Duignan, P; Burford, C; d'Arbon, T; Ikin, R & Walsh, M (2003), *Leadership challenges and ethical dilemmas for leaders of frontline service organisations*, A three-year ARC funded research SOLR Project, Australian Catholic University, Sydney, NSW.

Duignan, P & Cannon, H (2011), The power of many: building sustainable collective leadership in schools, Acer Press, Camberwell, Vic.

Dulles, A (1978), *Models of the Church*, Doubleday Image Books, New York, NY.

Dulles, A (1986), *Vatican II and the Extraordinary Synod*, The Liturgical Press, Collegeville, MN.

Duncan, B (2003), 'A schizophrenic process in the church: the conservative retreat from the social dimension of the gospel', *Compass, 37*(4), pp. 32-38.

Dunne, T (1985), *Lonergan and spirituality*, Loyola University Press, Chicago, IL.

Durka, G (2002), *The Teacher's Calling: A Spirituality for those who Teach*, Paulist Press, Mahwah, NJ.

Earl, PH (2003), *Formation of lay teachers in Catholic schools: The influence of virtues/spirituality seminars on lay teachers, character education, and perceptions of Catholic education* (doctoral dissertation), George Mason University, Fairfax, VA.

Earl, PH (2005), Spiritual formation for Catholic educators: Understanding the need, *Journal of Catholic Education, 8*(4), pp. 513-530.

Earl, PH (2007), Challenges to faith formation in contemporary Catholic schooling in the USA: Problem and response, in Grace, GR, & O'Keefe JM (eds.), *International handbook of Catholic education: Challenges for school systems in the 21st century, Parts one and two*, Springer, Dordrecht, The Netherlands, pp. 40, 43.

Edwards, D (1999), *The God of evolution: A trinitarian theology*, Paulist Press, Mahwah, NJ.

Egan, H (2010), *Soundings in the Christian mystical tradition*, Liturgical Press, Collegeville, MN.

Ellison, C (1983), Spiritual well-being: conceptualization and measurement, *Journal of Psychology and Theology*, *11*(4), pp. 330-340.

English, L; Fenwick, T & Parsons, J (2005), Interrogating our practices of integrating spirituality into workplace education, *Australian Journal of Adult Learning*, *45*(1), Adult Learning Australia, Canberra, ACT, pp. 7-28.

Erikson, E (1950), *Childhood and society*, Norton, New York, NY.

Erikson, E (1994), *Identity, youth and crisis*, Norton, New York, NY.

Evers, C & Lakomski, G (1996), *Exploring educational administration: Coherent applications and critical debates*, Pergamon, Oxford, UK.

Fabella, V (1989), A common methodology for diverse Christologies? In Fabella, V & Oduyoye, MA (eds.), *With passion and compassion: Third world women doing theology*, Orbis Books, Maryknoll, NY.

Fairholm, GW (2000), *Capturing the heart of leadership: Spirituality and community in the new American workplace*, Praeger Publishers, Westport, CT.

Faller-Mitchell, S (2010), The impact of core reflection on the practices of teacher educators, *Proceedings of the 13th Annual Conference of the Oregon Association of Teacher Educators, held at Western Oregon University, 5 March, 2010*.

Fawcett, G (1996), Moving another big desk, *Journal of Staff development*, *17*(1), pp. 34-36.

Feldman, DH (2000), Forward. In V. John-Steiner, *Creative collaboration*, Oxford University Press, New York, NY, pp. ix–xiii.

Fenwick, T (2001), Teacher supervision through professional growth plans: Balancing contradictions and opening possibilities, *Educational Administration Quarterly*, *37*(3), pp. 401-424.

Fischer, K (1989), The imagination in spirituality, *The Way Supplement, 66*, Autumn.

Finlay, R (2015), *Mission Integrity: Holding on by our fingertips*, https://webclasscommunity.wordpress.com/category/mission-integrity/ 19/5/2015

Finke, R (1997), An orderly return to tradition: explaining the recruitment of members into Catholic religious orders, *Journal for the Scientific Study of Religion, 36* (2).

Fisher, JW (1999), Helps to fostering students' spiritual health, *International Journal of Children's Spirituality*, *4*(1), pp. 29-49.

Fisher, JW (2001), Comparing levels of spiritual well-being in state, Catholic and independent schools in Victoria: Australia Research Report, *Journal of Beliefs and Values, 22*(1).

Flannery, A (ed.) (1981), *Vatican Council II: The conciliar and post-conciliar documents*, Dominican Publications, Dublin, Ire.

Fletcher, S & Mullen, CA (eds.) (2012), *Sage handbook of mentoring and coaching in education*, Sage, London, GB.

Flintham, A (2007), *Grounded in faith: the spiritual formation, development and sustainability of Catholic school principals across 12 dioceses in England and Australia*, National College for School Leadership, Liverpool, UK.

Flowers, BS (ed.) (1988), *The power of myth with Bill Moyers*, Doubleday, New York, NY.

Flynn, M (1993), *The culture of Catholic schools*, Society of St Paul, Homebush, NSW.

Flynn, M & Mok, M (2002), *Catholic Schools 2000*, Sydney, Catholic Education Commission, NSW.

Forbes, S (2003), *Holistic education: An analysis of its ideas and nature*, Solomon Press, Portland, OR.

Foster, W (1986), *The reconstruction of leadership*, Deakin University, Waurn Ponds, Vic.

Fowler, DL (2009), *Effectiveness of experiential learning strategies* (doctoral dissertation), retrieved from Dissertations and Theses: AandI. (Publication No. AAT 3399047), Texas Woman's University, Dallas, TX.

Fowler, JW (1981), *Stages of faith: The psychology of development and the quest for meaning*, Harper and Row, San Francisco, CA.

Fowler, JW (2000), *Becoming adult, becoming Christian: Adult development and Christian faith*, Jossey-Bass, San Francisco, CA.

Fowler, JW (2004), *Faithful change: The personal and public challenges of postmodern life*, Abingdon Press, New York, NY.

Frank, P (1995), *The wounded storyteller*, University of Chicago Press Chicago, IL

Fraser, W (1995), *Learning from experience: empowerment or incorporation*, National Institute of Adult Continuing Education, Leicester, UK.

Frost, P & Egri, C (1994), The shamanic perspective on organisational change and development, *Journal of Organisational Change, 7*, pp. 1-23.

Fullan, M (2001), *Leading in a culture of change*, Jossey-Bass, San Francisco, CA.

Fullan, M (2002), Principals as leaders in a culture of change, *Educational Leadership*, Special Issue, May 2002.

Fullan, M (2005), Professional learning communities writ large, in DuFour, R; Eaker, R & DuFour, R (eds.), *On common ground: The power of professional learning communities*, Solution Tree Press, Bloomington, IN, pp. 209-223.

Fullan, M (2010), *All systems go: the change imperative for whole system reform*, Corwin Sage, Thousand Oaks, CA.

Fullan, M & Fink, D (2003), Sustaining leadership, *Phi Delta Kappan, 84*(9), pp. 693-700.

Gallagher, MP (2004), *Clashing Symbols: An introduction to faith and culture*, Paulist Press, Dublin, Ire.

Gardner, H (1993), *Frames of mind: The theory of multiple intelligences*, Basic Books, New York, NY.

Gardner, H (2000), *Intelligence reframed: Multiple intelligences for the 21st century*, Basic Books, New York, NY.

Gardner, H (2006), *Five minds for the future*, Harvard Business School Press, Boston, MA.

Garvin, D (1993), *Building a learning organization*, Harvard Business Review (July –August), Harvard Business Review Press, Boston, MA.

Gittins, AJ (1993), *Bread for the journey: The mission of transformation and the transformation of Mission*, Orbis Books, Maryknoll, NY.

Gleeson, C (2003), *A canopy of stars*, Ringwood, David Lovell Publishing, Vic.

Gorman, M (1989), The spirituality of the Catholic school principal, in Kealey, R (ed.), *Reflections on the role of the Catholic school principal)*, National Catholic Educational Association, Washington, DC, pp. 29-33.

Gowdie, JD (2006; 2009), *Catching Fire – Staff with spirit: staff formation framework for the mission of Catholic education* (second edition), Catholic Education, Archdiocese of Brisbane, Brisbane, Qld.

Grabinger, RS & Dunlap, JC (1995), Rich environments for active learning: a definition, *ALT-J, 3*(2), pp. 5-34.

Grace, G (1995), *School leadership: Beyond education management*, Falmer, Lewes, UK.

Grace, G (1996), Leadership in Catholic Schools, in McLaughlin T; O'Keefe, J & O'Keefe, V, *The Contemporary Catholic School: Context, Identity and Diversity*, The Falmer Press, London, UK.

Grace, G (1997), *School leadership: Beyond education management. An essay in policy scholarship*, The Falmer Press, London, UK.

Grace, G (2000), Wanted: spiritual school leaders, *The Times Educational Supplement,* March 10, 2000. Issue 4367.

Grace, G (2002), *Catholic schools: mission, markets and morality*, Routledge Falmer, London, UK.

Grace, G (2010), *Mission Integrity: Contemporary challenges for Catholic school leaders*, Paper presented at the Fifth International Conference on Catholic Educational Leadership, Sydney, Australia, August 2010.

Grace, G (2010), *Renewing spiritual capital: an urgent priority for the future of Catholic education internationally*, International Studies in Catholic Education, 2:2, pp. 117-128.

Grace, G (2012), *Digital Journal of Lasallian Research (4)*, 07-19, p. 11.

Grace, G (2015), *Faith, Mission and Challenge in Catholic Education: The Selected Works of Gerald Grace*, Taylor and Francis, London, UK.

Grace, GR & O'Keefe, JM (eds.) (2007), *International handbook of Catholic education: Challenges for school systems in the 21st century, Parts one and two*, Sprenger, Dordrecht, The Netherlands.

Graham, J (2006), *An exploration of primary school principals' perspectives on the concept of community as applied to Catholic schools* (doctoral dissertation), Australian Catholic University, Melbourne, Vic.

Granberg-Michaelson, W (2013), *From Times Square to Timbuktu: The Post-Christian West Meets the Non-Western Church*, Eerdmans, Grand Rapids, MI.

Granberg-Michaelson, W (2012), *Global Christianity: A Report on the Size and Distribution of the World's Christian Population*, Pew Research Center, New York NY.

Granovetter, M (1978), Threshold Models of Collective Behavior. *American Journal of Sociology 83(6)*, doi:10.1086/226707, pp. 1420–1443.

Grant, A (2016), What can Sydney tell us about coaching? Research with implications for practice from down under, *Consulting Psychology Journal: Practice and Research, 68(2)*, pp. 105-117.

Greeley, A (2004), *The Catholic revolution: New wine, old wineskins, and the Second Vatican Council*, University of California Press, Berkeley, CA.

Green, PM (2006), Service reflection learning: An action research study of the meaning making processes occurring through reflection in a service learning course (unpublished doctoral dissertation), Roosevelt University, Chicago, IL.

Greene, M (1999), Releasing the imagination, *NJ (Drama Australia Journal)*, 23(2), pp. 9-17.

Greenberg, A & Berktold, J (2004), *Evangelicals in America survey*, sponsored by Religion and Ethics Newsweekly, conducted by Greenberg, Quinlan, Rosner Research, 16 March – 4 April, 2004, Washington, DC.

Greenleaf, R (1977), *Servant Leadership: A Journey into the Nature of Legitimate Power and Greatness*, Paulist Press, Mahwah, NJ.

Gregson, V (ed.) (1988), *The desire of the human heart: An introduction to the theology of Bernard Lonergan*, Paulist Press, New York, NY.

Griffiths, W & McLaughlin, D (1999), Towards an understanding of the administration of Australian Catholic education, *International Studies in Education Administration, 28*(1), pp. 25-41.

Grimmett, PP & Crehan, EP (1992), The nature of collegiality in teacher development: the case of clinical supervision, in Fullan, M & Hargreaves, A (eds.), *Teacher development and educational change*, The Falmer Press, London, UK, pp. 56-85.

Groen, J (2001), How leaders cultivate spirituality in the workplace: What the research shows, *Adult Learning 12/13*, American Association for Adult and Continuing Education, Arlington, VA, pp. 20-23.

Groen, J (2004b), The experience and practice of adult educators in addressing the spiritual dimensions of the workplace, *Canadian Journal for the Study of Adult Education, 18* (1), pp. 72-92.

Groen, J; Coholic, D & Graham, JR (eds.) (2013), *Spirituality in social work and education: theory, practice and pedagogies.*

Groeschel, B (1984), *Spiritual passages: The psychology of spiritual development*, Crossroad, New York, NY.

Gronn, P (1999), *The making of educational leaders*, Cassell, London, UK.

Gronn, P (2002), Leader formation, in Leithwood, K; Hallinger, P; Seashore, L; Furman-Brown, G; Gronn, P; Mulford, W & Riley, K (eds.), *Second international handbook of educational leadership and administration*, Springer, Dordrecht, The Netherlands, pp. 1031-1070.

Gronn, P & Rawlings-Sanaei, F (2003), Principal recruitment in a climate of leadership disengagement, *Australian Journal of Education, 47*(2), pp. 172-184.

Groome, T (1996), What makes a school Catholic? In McLaughlin, T; O'Keefe, J & O'Keeffe, B (eds.), *The contemporary Catholic school: Context, identity and diversity*, The Falmer Press, London, UK, pp. 107-125.

Groome, T (1998), *Educating for life: A spiritual vision for every teacher and parent*, Thomas More Press, Allen, TX.

Groome, T (1999), Education for wisdom: Catholic education instills a wisdom for life, *Momentum, 30*(4).

Groome, T (2002) *What makes us Catholic: Eight gifts for life*, Harper Collins, San Francisco, CA.

Groome, TH (2003), *What makes us Catholic: Eight gifts for Life*, Harper, San Francisco, p. 37.

Groome, TH & Horrell, HD (eds.) (2003) *Horizons and hopes*, Paulist Press, New York, NY.

Good Samaritan Education (2011a), *GSE: A Handbook*, Good Samaritan Education, Sydney.

Good Samaritan Education (2011a), *GSE: A Handbook*, Good Samaritan Education, Sydney.

Good Samaritan Education (2011a), *GSE: A Handbook,* Good Samaritan Education, Sydney.

Good Samaritan Education (2011b), *Immersion Handbook,* Good Samaritan Education, Sydney.

Good Samaritan Education (2012), *GSE Staff Immersion Guidelines,* Good Samaritan Education, Sydney.

Guenther, M (1992), *Holy listening,* Darton, Longman and Todd, London, UK.

Guillory, W (1997), *The living organization: Spirituality in the workplace,* Innovations International, Salt Lake City, UT.

Guinan, MD (1998), Christian spirituality: Many styles, one Spirit, *Catholic Update, C0598.*

Gunter, H (2001), *Leaders and leadership in education,* Paul Chapman, London, UK.

Gurr, D (2001), Directions in educational leadership, in White, P (ed.), *Hot topics,* Australian Council for Educational Administration, No. 5, 2001.

Gutierrez, G (1971), *A theology of liberation: History, politics, and salvation,* Orbis Books, Maryknoll, NY.

Habermas, J (1972), *Knowledge and human interests,* Heinemann, London, UK.

Habermas, J (1974), *Theory and practice,* Heinemann, London, UK.

Habermas, J (1987), *Lifeworld and system: A critique of functionalist reason,* Beacon Press, Boston, MA.

Hall, G & Hord, S (2015), *Implementing change: Patterns, principles, and potholes* (4th ed.), Pearson Education, Boston, MA.

Hall, G & Hendricks, J (eds.) (2012), *Dreaming a New Earth: Raimon Pannikar and Indigenous Spiritualities,* Mosaic Press, Preston, VIC.

Hallinger, P & Heck, R (1997), Exploring the principal's contribution to school effectiveness, *School Effectiveness and School Improvement, 8*(4), pp. 1-35.

Hjalmarson, L & Hellend, R (2011), *Missional spirituality,* InterVarsity Press, Downer's Grove, IL.

Halpin, D (2003), *Hope and education: The role of the utopian imagination,* Routledge-Falmer, London, UK.

Hamilton, DM & Jackson, MH (1998), Spiritual development: paths and processes. *Journal of Instructional Psychology, 25*(4), pp. 262- 270.

Hammonds, B (2002), In *Leading and learning for the 21st century, 1*(3), online newsletter retrieved 22 April, 2008, from www.leading-learning.co.nz

Handy, C & Aitkin, R (1986), *Understanding schools as organisations,* Penguin Books, London, UK.

Hanifin, P (2000), *The role of reflection in leading the professional development of the advanced skills teacher* (doctoral dissertation), ACU, Ascot Vale, Vic.

Hansen, P (2000), The shape of Catholic primary school lay principalship: round pegs in square holes? *Journal of Religious Education, 48*(4), pp. 28-34.

Hansman, C; Kimble, C; Hildreth, P & Bourdon, I (eds.) (2008), *Communities of practice: Creating learning environments for educators*, Information Age Publishing, Charlotte, NC.

Hargreaves, A (2007), Sustainable leadership and development in education: creating the future, conserving the past, *European Journal of Education, 42*(2), pp. 223-233.

Hargreaves, P (1994), *Changing teachers changing times: teachers work and culture in the postmodern age*, Continuum, London, UK.

Harman, GS (1975), The political constraints on catholic education, in Tannock, PD (ed.), *The organization and administration of Catholic education in Australia*, University of Queensland Press, St Lucia, Qld, pp. 161-183.

Harris, M (1989), *Fashion me a people*, Westminster John Knox Press, Louisville, KY.

Harris, M (1991), *Dance of the spirit*, Westminster John Knox Press, Louisville, KY.

Harris, M (1996), *Proclaim jubilee: A spirituality for the twenty-first century*, Westminster John Knox Press, Louisville, KY.

Harris, M & Moran, G (1998), *The curriculum of education: Reshaping religious education: Conversations on contemporary practice*, Westminster John Knox Press, Louisville, KY.

Harrison, W (2007), *Youth leadership: Discovering the educational background attainment and sense of adequacy of active youth leaders in NSW AOG Churches* (Masters thesis), Sydney College of Divinity, Sydney, NSW.

Hartwell, A (1996), *Scientific ideas and education in the 21st century*, retrieved 20 October, 2008, from http://www.21learn.org/arch/articles/ash_complexity.html

Harvey, A (2003), *Towards a 5th gospel via schillebeeckx and solle* (doctoral dissertation), Australian Catholic University, Melbourne, Victoria.

Hay, D (1987), *Exploring inner space – Is God still possible in the twentieth century?* AR Mowbray, Oxford, UK.

Hay, D, 2006, *Something There*, Darton, Longman and Todd Ltd, London.

Hay, D (2002), *Why is implicit religion implicit?* Dept of Divinity and Religious Studies, University of Aberdeen, Aberdeen, Scotland.

Hay, D & Nye, R (1998a), *Understanding the spirituality of people who don't go to Church*, Church of Scotland, Nottingham, UK.

Hay, D & Nye, R (1998b), *The spirit of the child*, HarperCollins, London, UK.

Hay Group (2013), *Coaching Environmental Scan: Summary of selected literature, models and current practices*, AITSL, Melbourne, Australia.

Healy, H (2005), Nurturing the spirituality of religious educators in Catholic schools within a professional development framework, *Journal of Religious Education*, 53(1), pp. 29-35.

Hecht, D (2003), The missing link: Exploring the context of learning in service-learning, in Billig, S & Eyler, J (eds.), *Deconstructing service-learning: research exploring context, participation and impacts*, Information Age Publishing, Nashville, TN, pp. 25-49.

Heft, J (1991), *The Catholic identity of Catholic schools and the future of Catholic schools*, National Catholic Educational Association, Washington, DC.

Heibert, DW (1992), The sociology of fowler's faith development theory, *Studies in Religion*, 21, pp. 321-335.

Heifetz, R (1995), *Leadership without easy answers*, Harvard University Press, Cambridge, MA.

Heifetz, R & Laurie, D (2001), *The work of leadership*, Harvard Business Review -Breakthrough Leadership, Harvard Business School Publishing, Cambridge, MA.

Heifetz, R & Linsky, M (2002), *Leadership on the line: Staying alive through the dangers of leading*, Harvard Business School Press, Cambridge, MA.

Hellwig, MK (1990), A history of the concept of faith, in Lee, JM (ed.), *Handbook of faith*, Religious Education Press, Birmingham, UK, pp. 3-23.

Hellwig, MK (1993), *What are the theologians saying now?* Collins Dove, Melbourne, Vic.

Hellwig, M (1998), The hallmarks of Christian apprenticeship, *Momentum*, 29, pp. 7-8.

Hendriks, J & Hall, G (2009), The natural mysticism of indigenous Australian traditions, *Australian E-Journal of Theology, March 2009*, ACU, Brisbane, Qld, retrieved 19 January, 2010, from http://aejt.com.au/2009/issue_13/?article=158315

Hendriks, J & Heffernan, G (1993), *A spirituality of catholic aborigines and the struggle for justice, No 68 Living Religion*, Aboriginal and Torres Strait Islander Apostolate, Catholic Archdiocese of Brisbane.

Hetherington, M & Leavey, C (eds.) (1988), *Catholic beliefs and practices*, Collins Dove, Melbourne, Vic.

Hicks, C (2004), Don't just survive! *The Encompass Connection* (June).

Hide, K (2004), Insights from the revelations of divine love and the contemplation to attain love. *Australian E-Journal of Theology*, 3(1), retrieved 7 November, 2007, from http://aejt.com.au/2004/vol_3,_no_1,_2004/?article=395661

Hill, B (2004), *Exploring religion in school: A national priority*, Openbook, Adelaide, SA.

Hirst, E; Renshaw, P & Brown, R (2009), A teacher's repertoire of practice in a multi-ethnic classroom: The physicality and politics of difference, in Cesar, M & Kumpulainen, K (eds.), *Social interactions in multicultural settings*, Sense Publishers, Rotterdam, The Netherlands, pp. 329-348.

Hodgkinson, C (1991), *Educational leadership. The moral art,* University of New York Press, Albany, NY State.

Hoge, D; Dinges, W; Johnson, M & Gonzales, J (2001), *Young adult Catholics: Religion in the culture of choice*, Notre Dame Press, Notre Dame, IN.

Holmes, E (2005), *Teacher well being: Looking after yourself and your career in the classroom*, Routledge Falmer, New York, NY.

Holohan, G (2009), Revisioning Catholic schools in an education revolution, *Proceedings of a conference of Diocesan Directors of Catholic Education, Melbourne, Australia, April, 2009.*

Hord, SM (1992), *Facilitative leadership: The imperative for change*, Southwest Educational Development Laboratory, Austin, TX.

Hord, SM (1997), Professional learning communities: What are they and why are they important? *Issues about Change, 6*(1), Southwest Educational Development Laboratory, Austin, TX.

Horner, R (2008), The presence of leadership, *Topics, 18*(2), Australian Catholic Primary Principals Association, Glenelg, SA, retrieved 12 January, 2009, from http://www.acppa.catholic.edu.au/news/pdfs/2008/RossHorner_PresenceofLeadership.pdf

Hough, M (2004), Why a learning organisation? *Independent Education: Exploring Partnerships – Exploring the Potential, 34*(1), pp. 23-26.

Houle, C (1980), *Continuing learning in the professions*, Jossey-Bass, San Francisco, CA.

Hughes, P (2000), Comparison of church attendance trends in the UK and Australia, in *Pointers, 10*(1), Christian Research Association, Melbourne, Vic, pp. 4-5.

Hughes, P (2003), Profiling Australians, in *Pointers, 13*(2), Christian Research Association, Melbourne, Vic, p. 16.

Hughes, P (2007), *Putting life together: Findings from Australian youth spirituality research*, Fairfield Press, Melbourne, Vic.

Hughes, P (2009), *The spirituality of teachers in Catholic schools: Project report*, prepared for the Principals' Association of Victorian Catholic Secondary Schools, John Garratt Publishing, Mulgrave, Vic.

Hughes, P (2010), Are Australians 'losing their religion'? in *Pointers, 20*(2), Christian Research Association, Melbourne, Vic, pp. 1-3.

Huitt, W & Robbins, J (2003), An introduction to spiritual development, *Proceedings of 11th Annual Conference: Applied Psychology in Education, Mental Health, and Business*, 4 October 2003, held at University of Valdosta, Georgia, retrieved January 2010, from http://www.edpsycinteractive.org/brilstar/chapters/spirituality.pdf

Hull, G (ed) (1997), *Changing work, changing workers: Critical perspectives on language, literacy and skills*, State University of New York Press, Albany, NY.

Hutton, D (2002), Many faces, one reality: the Catholic school in Australia, in Duncan, D & Riley, D (eds.), *Leadership in Catholic education: Hope for the future*, Harper Collins, Sydney, NSW, pp. 48-59.

Huxley, A (1945), *The perennial philosophy*, Harper and Row, San Francisco, CA.

Illeris, K (2002), The Three Dimensions of Learning, *Contemporary Learning Theory in the Tension Field between the Cognitive, the Emotional and the Social* (trans. Reader, D & Malone, M), Roskilde University Press.

Illeris, K (2003), Towards a contemporary and comprehensive theory of learning, *Journal of Lifelong Education, 22*, pp. 396-406.

Illeris, K (2004), Transformative learning in the perspective of a comprehensive learning theory, *Journal of Transformative Education, 2*(2), pp. 79-89.

Intrator, S (2002), *Stories of the courage to teach: Honoring the teacher's heart*, Jossey-Bass, San Francisco, CA.

Intrator, S (ed.) (2005), *Living the questions: Essays inspired by the life and work of Parker J. Palmer*, Jossey-Bass, San Francisco, CA.

Intrator, S & Kunzman, R (2006), Starting with the soul, *Educational Leadership, 63*(6), pp. 38-42.

Intrator, S & Scribner, M (2000), *Courage to teach longitudinal program evaluation*, Centre for Teacher Formation, Bainbridge Is, WA.

Iversen, GY; Mitchel, G & Pollard, G (eds.) (2009), *Hovering over the face of the Deep: Philosophy, theology and children*, Waxman Verlag, Munster.

Jackson, KA (2006), 'You can never have enough tiaras': Reflective practice and the annual school concert in a small, rural primary school (Masters thesis), University of Melbourne, Parkville, Vic.

Jaen, N (1991), *Towards a liberation spirituality*, Loyola University Press, Chicago, IL.

Jarvis, P (1987), *Adult learning in the social context*, Croom Helm, London, UK.

Jarvis, P (2004), *Adult and continuing education: Theory and practice*, Routledge, London, UK.

Jarvis, P (2007), *Globalization, Lifelong Learning and the Learning Society: Sociological Perspectives*, Routledge, London, UK.

Jewison, N; Stein, N; Topol, J; Crane, N; Frey, L; Picon, M & Mann, P (2006), *Fiddler on the Roof*, National Film Board of Canada, distributed by Twentieth Century Fox Home Entertainment, Beverly Hills, CA.

John XXIII (1963), Statement 24 May, retrieved from http://vatican2voice. org/2need/deroo.htm

John Paul II (1984), Homily, *Canadian Catholic Review*, University of Laval Stadium, Quebec City, October, pp. 323-325.

John Paul II (1984), *Address to the European Bishops, October 1984*, Vatican City, Rome, IT.

John Paul II (1989), Christifideles Laici, *The vocation and the mission of the lay faithful in the church and in the modern world*, Vatican City, Rome, IT.

John Paul II (1994), Tertio Millennio Adveniente, *The coming of the third millennium*, Vatican City, Rome, IT.

John Paul II (2001), *Novo millenio inuente*, retrieved 24 February, 2008, from http://www.vatican.va/holy_father/john_paul_ii/apost_letters/ documents/hf_jp-ii_apl_20010106_novo-millennio-ineunte_en.html

John Paul II (2001), *Ecclesia in Oceania*, St Paul's Publications, Homebush, NSW.

John Paul II (1997), *Catechism of the Catholic Church*, Double Day, New York, NY.

Johnson, DW & Johnson, FP (1996), *Joining together: Group theory and group skills*, Allyn and Bacon, Boston, MA.

Johnson E (2002), *She who is: The mystery of God in feminist theological discourse*, Crossroad, New York, NY.

Johnson, EA (1994), Jesus and salvation, in Crowley, P (ed.), *Proceedings of the Forty-Ninth Annual Convention, Catholic Theological Society of America, held in Baltimore, 1994*.

Johnson, H & Castelli, M (2000), Catholic head teachers: the importance of culture building in approaches to spiritual and moral development and the transmission of faith tradition, *International Journal of Children's Spirituality*, 5(1), pp. 75-90.

Johnson, JR (1998), Embracing change: A leadership model for the learning organisation, *International Journal of Training and Development*, 2(2), pp. 141-150.

Johnson-Miller, B (2000), *The complexity of religious transformation* (doctoral dissertation), School of Theology, UMI Dissertation Publishing, Lincoln University, Claremont, CA.

Johnson-Miller, B (2005), Visiting the labyrinth of religious transformation, *Journal of Beliefs and Values*, 26(1), retrieved 28 September, 2007, from http://www.tandfonline.com/doi/abs/10.1080/13617670500046576?jour nalCode=cjbv20

Jones, J (2002), Recapturing the courage to teach, An interview with Parker J. Palmer, in *TeacherView.Com*, retrieved 18 September, 2007, from http://www.teacherview.com/joyjones/dec2002.htm

Joseph, E (2002), Faith leadership, in Hunt, T; Joseph, E & Nuzzi, R (eds.), *Catholic schools still make a difference: Ten years of research 1991-2000*, National Catholic Education Association, Washington, DC.

Jung, C (1981), *The archetypes and the collective unconscious*, Princeton University Press, Princeton, NJ.

Jung, C (1976), *The Portable Jung*, edited by Joseph Campbell and translated by RFC Hull, Penguin, New York, NY.

Kalantzis, M & Cope, B (2008), *New learning: Elements of a science of education*, Cambridge University Press, Melbourne, Vic.

Kauanui, S & Bradley, J (2003), Comparing spirituality on three southern California college campuses, *Journal of Organizational Change, 16*, pp. 448-462.

Keating, JR (1990), *A pastoral letter on Catholic schools*, Diocese of Arlington, Arlington, VA.

Keating, T (1987), *The mystery of Christ: The liturgy as spiritual exercise*, Element Inc, Rockport, MA.

Keating, T (2009), *Intimacy with God – an introduction to centring prayer*, Crossroads, New York, NY.

Keely, BA (2002), Spiritual formation: Personal formation and educational practices, *The Clergy Journal, 78*(5), pp. 17-18.

Keeton, MT (ed.) (1976), *Experiential learning*, Jossey-Bass, San Francisco, CA.

Kelleher, P (2000), *The faith formation of Catholic high school administrators: The unique role of the laity* (doctoral dissertation), UMI Dissertations Publishing, University of Dayton, OH.

Kelly, A (1995), *Consuming passions: Christian faith and the consumer society*, ACSJC Publications, Sydney, NSW.

Kelly, A (2004), Reflections on spirituality and the Church, *Australian E-Journal of Theology, 3*(1), retrieved 4 March, 2008, from http://aejt.com.au/2004/vol_3,_no_1,_2004/?article=395648

Kelly, A (2009), Catholic identity: Lost, and found, *Aquinas Lecture delivered 23 November, 2009 at Australian Catholic University, Brisbane, Queensland*, retrieved 4 March, 2008, from http://library.acu.edu.au/other_collections_and_catalogues/aquinas_memorial_lectures/?a=22031

Kelly, B; Woolfson, L & Boyle, J (2008), *Frameworks for practice in educational psychology: a textbook for trainees*, Jessica Kingsley Pub, London, UK.

Kelly, T (2002), Grace, meaning and Catholic education, in Duncan, DJ & Riley, D (eds.), *Leadership in Catholic education: Hope for the future*, Harper Collins, Pymble, NSW:

Kenary, J (2009), *Service learning experience and undergraduate leadership behaviours: an action research case study*, (doctoral dissertation), University of Hartford, West Hartford, CT.

Kennedy, E (2004), Featured in Spurling, F (Producer), & Rutledge, D (Presenter), *Poor Church* [Radio Broadcast, Encounter Program 25 July, 2004], Radio National, Australian Broadcasting Commission, Sydney, NSW, retrieved 8 May, 2008, from http://www.abc.net.au/rn/relig/enc/stories/s1152547.htm

Kessler, R (2000), *The soul of education: Helping students find connection, compassion, and character in school*, Association for Supervision and Curriculum Development, Alexandria, VA.

Killeen, A (1997), *The impact of positions of leadership in Catholic primary schools*, University of Melbourne, Melbourne, Vic.

Killeen, P & De Beer, J (1994), *The art of theological reflection*, The Crossroads Publishing Company, New York, NY.

Kilpatrick, S; Barrett, M & Jones, T (2003), *Defining learning communities*, Faculty of Education, University of Tasmania, Hobart, Tas, retrieved 23 November 2007, from www.aare.edu.au/03pap/jon03441.pdf

Kinast, R (1996), *Let ministry teach*, Liturgical Press, Collegeville, MN.

Kinast, R (1999), *Making faith-sense: Theological reflection in everyday life*, Liturgical Press, Collegeville, MN.

Kinast, R (2000), *What are they saying about theological reflection?* Paulist Press, Mahwah, NJ.

King, PE & Boyatzis, CJ (2004), Exploring adolescent spiritual and religious development: Current and future theoretical and empirical perspectives, *Applied Developmental Science, 8*(1), pp. 2-6.

King, R; Hill, D & Retallick, J (eds.) (1997), *Exploring professional development in education*, Social Science Press, Katoomba, NSW.

King, U, 2008, *The Search for Spirituality*, Blue Bridge, New York.

Kirk, JA (2000), *What is mission? Theological explorations*, Fortress Press, Minneapolis, MN.

Klein, S (1993), *Theologie und empirische biographie-forschung*, Verlag W Kohlhammer, Stuttgart.

Knights, P (2005), *Catholic evangelisation: an overview*, Case, April 2005, retrieved 14 September, 2007, from http://www.margaretbeaufort.cam.ac.uk/research/knights.pdf

Knowles, M (1980), *The modern practice of adult education: From pedagogy to androgogy*, The Adult Education Company, Cambridge, NY.

Kohlberg, L (1984), *Essays on moral development: The psychology of moral development*, Harper and Row, New York, NY.

Kohlberg, L (1987), *Child psychology and childhood education: A cognitive-developmental view,* Longman, New York, NY.

Kolb, A & Kolb DA (2001), *Experiential learning theory bibliography 1971-2001,* McBer and Co, Boston, MA, retrieved 28 September, 2007, from http://www.infed.org/biblio/b-explrn.htm

Kolb, DA (1976), *The learning style inventory: Technical manual,* McBer and Co, Boston, MA.

Kolb, DA (1981), Learning styles and disciplinary differences, in Chickering, AW (ed.), *The modern American college,* Jossey-Bass, San Francisco, CA.

Kolb, DA (1984), *Experiential learning,* Prentice Hall, Englewood Cliffs, NJ.

Kolb, DA (with Osland, J & Rubin, I) (1995a), *Organizational behavior: An experiential approach to human behavior in organizations,* 6e, Prentice Hall, Englewood Cliffs, NJ.

Kolb, DA (with Osland, J and Rubin, I) (1995b), *The organizational behavior reader,* 6e, Prentice Hall, Englewood Cliffs, NJ.

Kolb, DA & Fry, R (1975), Toward an applied theory of experiential learning, in Cooper, C (ed.), *Theories of group process,* John Wiley, London, UK, pp. 35-36.

Korthagen, F (2004), In search of the essence of a good teacher: towards a more holistic approach in teacher education, *Teaching and Teacher Education, 20,* pp. 77-97.

Korthagen, F & Vasalos, A (2005), Levels in reflection: core reflection as a means to enhance professional growth, *Teachers and Teaching: Theory and Practice, 11*(1), pp. 47-71.

Koyama, K (1979), *Three-miles-an-hour God,* Orbis Books, Maryknoll, NY.

Krietemeyer, R (2000), *Leaven for the Modern World: Catholic Social Teaching and Catholic Education,* National Catholic Educational Association, p. 65.

Kwakman, K (2003), Factors affecting teachers' participation in professional learning activities, *Teaching and Teacher Education, 19*(2), pp. 149-170.

Kyle, N (1986), *Her natural destiny,* New South Wales University Press, Sydney, NSW.

Lacey, BM (2003), Catholic school leadership topics, *Journal of Australian Catholic Primary Principals Association, 13*(3).

Lacey, K (2002a) Avoiding the principalship, *Principal Matters, November 2002,* pp. 25-29.

Lacey, K (2002b), *Understanding principal class leadership aspirations: Policy and planning implications,* Leadership Development Unit, Department of Education and Training Victoria, Melbourne, Vic, retrieved 9 February, 2008, from http://www.sofweb.vic.edu.au/pd/schlead/pdf/understanding_prin_class_leadership aspirations_report.pdf

Lacey, K (2003), Executive summary: Principal class aspirations research project, in *Succession planning in education*, Department of Education and Training Melbourne, Vic, retrieved 10 February, 2008, from http://www.apapdc.edu.au

LaCugna, CM (ed.) (1993), Freeing theology: The essentials of theology in feminist perspective, Harper, San Francisco, CA.

LaCugna, CM (1992), *God for Us: The Trinity and Christian Life*, Harper, San Francisco, CA.

Lakeland, P (1997), *Postmodernity: Christian identity in a fragmented age*, Fortress Press, Minneapolis, MN.

Lakeland, P (2003), *The liberation of the laity: in search of an accountable church*, Continuum Publishing, New York, NY.

Lakeland, P (2008), *Church: Living communion*, Liturgical Press, Collegeville, MN.

Lakeland, P (2008), Ecclesiology and post modernity: Questions for the Church in our time, *Theol Studies, 69*(3), p. 729.

Land, KC; Deane, G & Blau JR (1991), Religious pluralism and church membership: A spatial diffusion model, *American Sociological Review, 56*, pp. 237- 249.

Langford, J (2008), Seeds of faith: practices to grow a healthy spiritual life, Paraclete Press, Brewster, Mass.

Largent, E (2009), Contributing factors to meaningful service-learning and intentions for future volunteerism: A case study at a community college, (unpublished doctoral dissertation), University of Oklahoma, Norman, OK.

Laser, R et al. (2010), *Beyond the God gap: A new roadmap for reaching religious Americans on public policy issues*, Third Way and Public Religion Research, Washington, DC.

Lawrence, B (1998), Transformation, in Taylor MC (ed.), *Critical terms for religious studies*, University of Chicago Press, Chicago, IL.

Leavey, C & Hetherton, M (eds.) (1988), *Catholic beliefs and practices: research report*, Collins Dove, Melbourne, Vic.

Leffel, GM (2007), Emotion and transformation in the relational spirituality paradigm part 2: Implicit morality and 'minimal prosociality,' *Journal of Psychology and Theology, 35*(4), pp. 281-297.

Leithwood, K & Duke, D (1999), A century's quest to understand school leadership, in Murphy, J & Louis, KS (eds.), *Handbook of research in educational administration* (2nd ed.), Jossey-Bass, San Francisco, CA, pp. 45-72.

Leithwood, K; Jantzl, D & Steinbech, R (1999), *Changing leadership for changing times*, Open University Press, Buckingham, UK.

Leithwood, K & Jantzi, D (2005), A review of transformational school leadership research 1996-2005, *Leadership and Policy in Schools*, *4*(3), pp. 177-199.

Lennan, R (ed.) (1995), *Redefining the church: Vision and* practice, Dwyer, EJ, Sydney, NSW.

Lennan, R (2013), 'The Church as Mission: Locating Vocation in Its Ecclesial Context', in *The Disciples' Call: Theologies of Vocation from Scripture to the Present Day*, Jamison, C (ed.), Bloomsbury, London, UK, pp. 43-63.

Lessing, J; Morrison, D & Nicolae, M (2010), '*Educational Institutions, Corporate Governance and Not-For-Profits*', Corporate Governance e-Journal 1, (5).

Lincoln, YS & Guba, EG (1985), *Naturalistic inquiry*, Sage, Newbury Park, CA.

Lindholm, JA & Astin, HS (2008), Spirituality and pedagogy: Faculty's spirituality and use of student-centered approaches to undergraduate teaching, *The Review of Higher Education*, *31*(2), pp. 185-207.

Lingard, B; Hayes, D; Mills, M; Christie, P & Wilson, M (2003), *Leading learning: making hope practical in schools*, Open University Press, Berkshire, UK.

Lisrel, A (2003), Relationship between school and classroom environment and teacher burnout: An analysis, *Social Psychology of Education*, *6*(2), Springer, Dordrecht, The Netherlands, pp. 107-127.

Loder, J (1998), *The logic of the spirit: Human development in theological perspective*, Jossey-Bass, San Francisco, CA.

Lonergan, B (1972), *Method in theology*, Darton, Longman and Todd, London, UK.

Lount, M & Hargie, O (1998), Preparation for the priesthood: A training needs analysis, *Journal of Vocational Education and Training*, *50*(1), pp. 61-77.

Lovat, T & Clement, N (2008), Quality teaching and values education, *Journal of Moral Education*, *3*(1), pp. 1-16.

Lyons, W & Scroggins, D (1990), The mentor in graduate education, *Studies in Higher Education*, *15*(3), pp. 277-285.

Ma, W & Ross, K R (eds.) (2015), *Mission spirituality and authentic discipleship* (Vol. 14), Wipf and Stock Publishers.

Macdonald, M; Carpenter, P; Cornish, S; Costigan, M; Dixon, R; Malone, M; Manning, K & Wagner, S (1999), *Woman and man: One in Christ Jesus: Report on the participation of women in the Catholic Church in Australia*, Harper Collins Religious, Sydney, NSW.

Mackay, H (1997), *Generations*, Pan McMillan, Sydney, NSW.

Mackay, H (2000), *Turning point: Australians choosing their future*, Pan McMillan, Sydney, NSW.

Mackay, H (2008), *Advance Australia ... where?* Hachette, Sydney, NSW.

Mackay, H (2016), *Beyond belief: how we find meaning with or without religion*, Pan McMillan, Sydney, NSW.

MacLaren, D (2000), *Principles of Engagement on International Development through the Lens of Catholic Social Teaching.*

Mahan, B (2002), *Forgetting ourselves on purpose – vocation and the ethics of ambition*, Jossey Bass, San Francisco, CA.

Manternach, D (2002), Fostering reflective teachers in a globalized age, *Religious Education, 97*(3), pp. 271-287.

Maréchal, C (1999), *Toward an effective partnership between religious and laity in fulfilment of charism and responsibility for mission, Charism and spirituality*, Proceedings of the 56th Conference of the Unione Superiore Generali, Rome.

Marsick, V (ed.) (1987) *Learning in the workplace*, Croom Helm, London, UK.

Marsick, V & Watkins, K (1990) *Informal and incidental learning in the workplace*, Routledge and Kegan Paul, London, UK.

Marsick, V & Watkins, K (2015), *Informal and incidental learning in the workplace*, Abingdon Press, Routledge Revivals, London, UK.

Marsick, V & Watkins, K (1993), *Sculpting the learning organisation: Lessons in the art and science of systemic change*, Jossey-Bass, San Francisco, CA.

Martoo, GV (2006), *Reculturing a school as a learning organisation: Investigative narratives in two Queensland schools* (doctoral dissertation), University of Technology, Brisbane, Qld, retrieved 25 March, 2008, from http://eprints.qut.edu.au/16294/1/Gladys_Martoo_Thesis.pdf

Maslow, A (1983), *Motivation and personality* (3rd ed.), Harper and Row, New York, NY.

Mason, M; Webber, R; Singleton, A & Hughes, P (2006), Summary of the final report of a 3 year study, Christian Research Association, ACU National, Monash University, Melbourne.

Mason, M; Singleton, A & Webber, R (2007), *The spirit of generation Y: Young people's spirituality in a changing Australia*, John Garratt Publishing, Mulgrave, VIC.

Masson, R (1984), Spirituality for the head, heart, hands, and feet: Rahner's legacy, *Spirituality Today, 36*(4), pp. 340-354.

May, G (1982), *Will and spirit: A contemplative psychology*, Harper and Row, San Francisco, CA.

Maynes, C (2002), The teacher as archetype of spirit, *Journal of Curriculum Studies, 34*(6), pp. 699-718.

McAdams, DP (1993), *The stories we live by: Personal myths and the making of the self*, Morrow, New York, NY.

McAdams, DP (1996), Personality, modernity, and the storied self: A contemporary framework for studying persons, *Psychological Inquiry*, 7, pp. 295-321.

McCann, J (2003), Improving Our Aim: Catholic School Ethos Today, in Prendergast, N & Monahan, L, *Reimagining the Catholic School*, Veritas Publications Dublin, Ire, pp. 157-167.

McCormack, B (2002), Removing the chaos from the narrative: Preparing clinical leaders for practice development, *Educational Action Research*, 10(3), pp. 335-351.

McCormack, C (2004), Storying stories: a narrative approach to in-depth interview conversations, *International Journal of Social Research Methodology*, 7(3), pp. 219-236.

McCrindle (2015), last retrieved August 25, 2016, from http://mccrindle.com.au/research-resources#media

McGilp, E (2000), Leadership: some messages worth hearing, *Catholic School Studies*, 73(1), pp. 22-24.

Massam, K (1996), *Sacred threads: Catholic spirituality in Australia: 1922-1962*, University of NSW Press, Sydney, NSW.

Macdonald, M et al. (1999), *Woman and man: One in Christ Jesus: Report on the participation of women in the Catholic Church in Australia*, Harper Collins Religious, Sydney, NSW.

McDonald, WM & Palmer, PJ (eds.) (2002), *Creating campus community: In search of Ernest Boyer's legacy*, Jossey-Bass, San Francisco, CA.

McGinn, B (1991), *The foundations of mysticism*, Crossroad, New York, NY.

McFadden, S & Gerl, R (1990), Approaches to understanding spirituality in the second half of life, *Generations*, 14(4), p. 35.

McLaughlin, TH; O'Keefe, J & O'Keefe, BO (eds.) (1996), *The contemporary Catholic school: Context, identity, and diversity*, (Included papers from the conference at St Edmund's College in Cambridge on 'The contemporary Catholic school and the common good', 1993.), Routledge, London, UK.

McLaughlin, MW (1991b), Learning from experience: lessons from policy implementation, in Odden, AR (ed.), *Education policy implementation*, State University of New York Press, Albany, NY, pp. 185-195.

McLaughlin, D (1997), *Beliefs, values and practices of Catholic students: a research project*, Australian Catholic University, Brisbane, Qld.

McLaughlin, D (1998), Catholic schools for the twenty-first century: challenges for educational leadership, in Duignan, P & D'Arbon, T (eds.), *Leadership in Catholic Education: 2000 and Beyond*, Australian Catholic University, Strathfield, NSW, pp. 9-30.

McLaughlin, D (2000), Quo Vadis the Catholic education? A post conciliar perspective, in McLaughlin, D (ed.), *The Catholic School: Paradoxes and Challenges*, St Pauls Publications, Strathfield, NSW, pp. 24-41.

McLaughlin, D (ed.) (2000a), *The Catholic school: Paradoxes and challenges*, St Pauls Publications, Sydney.

McLaughlin, D (2000b), The Catholic school: Avenue to authenticity, *Catholic Education: a Journal of inquiry and practice, 3*(3), pp. 274-292.

McLaughlin, D (2000c), The Catholic school on the threshold of the third millennium: a challenge to parochial myopia, *Journal of Religious Education, 48*(1), pp. 14-26.

McLaughlin, D (2002), Aspiring towards authenticity, The dialectic of Australian Catholic education, *Proceedings of a conference of the Association of Principals of Catholic Secondary Schools of Australia entitled 'A Journey to the Heart, A Journey to the Spirit: Catholic schools into the future'*, held at Coolangatta, Qld, 2-5 October, 2002.

McLaughlin, D (2005), The dialectic of Australian Catholic education, *International Journal of Children's Spirituality, 10*(2), pp. 215-233.

McLaughlin, D (2008), Educating together in Catholic schools: A shared mission between consecrated persons and the lay faithful, *Journal of Catholic School Studies, 80*(2), pp. 37-53.

McMahon, LG (2003), Rekindling the spirit to teach: A qualitative study of the personal and professional renewal of teachers (unpublished doctoral dissertation), Gonzaga University, Spokane, Washington.

McMillan, DW (1996), 'Sense of Community', in *Journal of Community Psychology, 24*(4), pp. 315-325.

McPherson, CW (2002), *Keeping silence: Christian practices for entering stillness*, Morehouse Publishing, Harrisburg, PA.

McQuillan, P (2002), *Encounters beyond the pond: The limit experience of senior high school students*, Occasional Paper 34, 2nd series, Religious Experience Research Centre, Lampeter, Wales.

McQuillan, P (2004), Youth spirituality, a reality in search of expression, *Journal of Youth and Theology, 3*(2).

Mead, GH (1934), *Mind, self, and society*, University of Chicago Press, Chicago, IL.

Merkel, J (1998), Sacred circles. *Momentum, 29*, pp. 36-38.

Merriam, SB & Brockett, RG (2007), *The profession and practice of adult education*, Jossey Bass, San Francisco, CA.

Merriam, SB & Caffarella, RS (1999), *Learning in adulthood*, Jossey-Bass, San Francisco, CA.

Merton, T (1961), *New seeds of contemplation*, New Directions, New York, NY.

Meyer, M & McMillan, R (2001), The principal's role in transition, *International Electronic Journal for Leadership in Learning, 5*(13).

Mezirow, J (1990), *Fostering critical reflection in adulthood: A guide to transformative and emancipatory learning*, Jossey-Bass, San Francisco, CA.

Mezirow, J (1991), *Transformative dimensions of adult learning*, Jossey-Bass, San Francisco, CA.

Mezirow, J (1997), Transformation theory out of context. *Adult Education Quarterly, 48*(1), pp. 60-63.

Mezirow, J (2000), *Learning as transformation: Critical perspectives on a theory in progress*, Jossey-Bass, San Francisco, CA.

Miedema, S (1995), The beyond in the midst: The relevance of Dewey's philosophy of religion for education, in Garrison, J (ed.), *The New Scholarship on Dewey* Dordrecht/Boston/London: Kluwer Academic Publishers, pp. 61-73.

Miller, J (2000), *Education and the soul: Toward a spiritual curriculum*, State University of New York Press, Albany, NY.

Miller, J (2006), *Educating for wisdom and compassion: Creating conditions for timeless learning*, Corwin, Thousand Oaks, CA.

Miller, J (2007), *The holistic curriculum* (2nd ed.), University of Toronto Press, Toronto, ON.

Miller, J (2007), Whole teaching, whole schools, whole teachers, *Educational Leadership, 64*, Summer 2007, retrieved 1 May, 2008, from http://www.ascd.org/publications/educational-leadership/summer07/vol64/num09/Whole-Teaching,-Whole-Schools,-Whole-Teachers.aspx

Miller, JM (2007), *The Holy See's teaching on Catholic schools*, St. Paul's Publications, Strathfield, NSW.

Mills, CW (1959), *The sociological imagination*, Oxford University Press, New York, NY.

Mitroff, IA & Denton, EA (1999), *A spiritual audit of corporate America: A hard look at spirituality, religion, and values in the workplace*, Jossey-Bass, San Francisco, CA.

Moore, L (1999), *Personal characteristics and selected educational attainment of Catholic principals in relation to spiritual formation activities* (doctoral dissertation), University of Dayton, Dayton, OH.

Moran, G (1983), *Religious education development*, Winston Press Inc, Minneapolis, MN.

Moran, G (2000), Building on the past, in Lee JM (ed.), *Forging a better religious education in the third millennium*, Religious Education Press, Birmingham, AL, pp. 134-154.

Morson, GC & Emerson, C (1990), *Mikhail Bakhtin: Creation of a Prosaics*, Stanford University, Stanford, CA.

Morneau, R (1996), *Spiritual direction: Principles and practices*, Crossroad, New York, NY.

Morwood, M (2007), *Tomorrow's Catholic: Understanding God and Jesus in a new millennium*, Twenty-Third Publications, Mystick, CT.

Moxley, R (2000), *Leadership and spirit: Breathing new vitality and energy into individuals and organisations*, Jossey-Bass, San Francisco, CA.

Mullen, CA (ed.) (2009), *The Handbook of Leadership and Professional Learning Communities*, Palgrave Macmillan, New York, NY.

Mulligan JT (1994), *Formation for evangelization*, Novalis, Ottawa, ON.

Mulligan JT (2005), *Catholic education ensuring a future*, Novalis, Ottawa, ON.

Murdoch, D (2002),Teaching principals in smaller primary schools: Their issues, challenges and concerns, *Proceedings of a Conference of the Australian Association of Research in Education held in Brisbane in 2002*, retrieved 27 February, 2008, from http://www.aare.edu.au/02pap/abs02.htm

Myers, S (1999), Service learning in alternative education settings, *The Clearing House: A Journal of Educational Strategies, Issues and Ideas, 73*(2), pp. 114-117.

National Catholic Education Commission (1996), *Top ten challenges in Catholic education*, Author, Canberra, ACT, retrieved 27 February, 2008, from http://www.ncec.catholic.edu.au/

National Catholic Education Commission (1997), *The National Catholic Education Commission 1997 Annual Report*, Author, Canberra, ACT,retrieved 1 March, 2008, from http://www.ncec.catholic.edu.au/

National Catholic Education Commission (1998), *Australian Catholic schools: Why we have them? What they aim to achieve? What Catholic schools do?* Author, Canberra, ACT, retrieved 3 March, 2008, from http://www.ncec.catholic.edu.au/

National Catholic Education Commission (1998), *NCEC response to MCEETYA national goals taskforce discussion paper*, Author, Canberra, ACT, retrieved 3 March, 2008, from http://www.ncec.catholic.edu.au/goals.htm

National Catholic Education Commission (2005), *Leadership in the religious domain. Leading in Catholic schools*, Author, Melbourne, Vic, retrieved 5 March, 2008, from http://www.ncec.catholic.edu.au/

National Catholic Education Commission (2009), *Australian Catholic Schools 2008*, Author, Canberra, ACT, retrieved 2 August, 2009, from http://www.ncec.catholic.edu.au/

National Church Life Survey, *NCLS survey reports 2001, 2006*, Author, Sydney, NSW, retrieved 2 August, 2009, from http://www.ncls.org

National Church Life Survey (2008), *NCLS occasional paper 10: Moving beyond forty years of missing generations*, Author, Melbourne, Vic.

National Church Life Survey (2009), *NCLS occasional paper 13: Faith-sharing activities by Australian Churches*, Author, Melbourne, Vic.

Neidhart, H & Carlin, P (2004), Developing school leaders with the commitment and capacity to pursue the common good, *Proceedings of a Conference of the Australian Association for Research in Education held in Melbourne, Nov/Dec. 2004*, retrieved 4 October, 2008, from http://www. aare.edu.au/confpap.htm

Neal, JA(1997), Spirituality in management education: A guide to resources, *Journal of Management Education, 21*(1), pp. 121-139.

Neal, JA (2000), *Spiritual evolution*, retrieved 17 March, 2006, from www. spiritatwork.com

Neal, JA (ed.) (2013), *Handbook of Faith and Spirituality in the Workplace: Emerging Research and Practice*, Springer, New York, NY.

Neidhart, H & Carlin, P (2004), Research implications for preparation of Catholic school principals, *Catholic School Studies, 10,* pp. 5-10.

Neidhart, H & Lamb, J (2013), Forming faith leaders in Catholic schools, *Leading and Managing* Spring/Summer *19*(2).

Newby, TJ & Hyde, A (1992), The value of mentoring, *Performance Improvement Quarterly, 5*, pp. 2-15.

Newport M (1997), *Australian Catholic Bishops' Statements*, Ligare Pty Ltd, Sydney, NSW.

New Zealand Catholic Education Office (NZCEO) (2007), New Zealand Catholic integrated schools, in *Catholic Special Character Review and Development* (2nd ed.), Author, Wellington, NZ, retrieved 12 December, 2007, from http://www.nzceo.catholic.org.nz/media/resources/special-character-rev-dev07.pdf

Niebuhr, H (1993), *Radical monotheism and western culture: with supplementary essays*, John Knox Press, Westminster, UK.

Nolan, A (2008), *Jesus today*, Orbis Books, Maryknoll, NY.

Norris, P & Lovenduski, J (2001), *Critical mass theory, gender, and legislative life*, Bloomsbury, London, UK.

Nouwen, H (1976), *Reaching out*, Collins, Glasgow, UK.

Nouwen, H (1991), *Way of the heart – Desert spirituality and contemporary ministry*, Harper Collins, San Francisco, CA.

Nuzzi, R (2000), To lead as Jesus did, in Hunt, T; Oldenski, T & Wallace T (eds.), *Catholic school leadership: An invitation to lead*, Falmer Press, London, UK.

Nuzzi, R (2002), Catholic identity, in Hunt, T; Ellis, J & Nuzzi R (eds.), *Catholic schools still make a difference: Ten years of research 1991-2000*, National Catholic Educational Association, Washington, DC.

Oblate Communications (2004), *International Symposia on Missionaries to Secularity*, retrieved 8 May, 2008, from http://www.omiworld.org/default.asp

O'Brien, RP (2004), *Assessing the characteristics of effective professional learning and training programs: Perceptions of teachers, principals and training personnel within Catholic education in Melbourne* (unpublished doctoral dissertation), ACU, Fitzroy, Vic.

Ochs, C (1983), *Women and spirituality*, Rowman & Allanheld, Totowa, NJ.

O'Donnell, S (2001), *The character and culture of the Catholic school*, New Council for Educational Research, Wellington, NZ.

O'Donoghue, J (1997), *Anam Cara: A book of Celtic wisdom*, Harper Collins, New York, NY.

O'Donoghue, T (2004), Come follow me and forsake temptation: The recruitment and retention of members of Catholic teaching orders, 1922-1965, Peter Lang, Bern, Switzerland.

O'Donoghue, T (2007), *Planning your qualitative research project: An introduction to interpretivist research in education*, Routledge, London, UK.

O'Donoghue, T & Burley, S (2008), God's antipodean teaching force: An historical exposition on Catholic teaching religious in Australia, *Teaching and Teacher Education, 24,* pp. 180-189.

O'Donoghue, T & Dimmock, C (1998), *School restructuring: International perspectives*, Kogan Page, London, UK.

O'Donoghue, T & Potts, A (2004), Researching the lives of Catholic teachers who were members of religious orders: Historiographical considerations, *History of Education, 33*(4), pp. 469-481.

O'Farrell, PJ (1992), *The Catholic church and community: An Australian history* (3rd ed.), New South Wales University Press, Kensington, NSW.

O'Hara, KA (2000), *Perceptions of Catholic school principals' spiritual leadership role: Toward an operational definition* (doctoral dissertation), University of Missouri, Kansas City, MO, retrieved from Dissertations and Theses: A and I, (Publication No. AAT 9970752).

O'Keefe, J (2003), Catholic Schools as Communities of Service: the US Experience, in Prendergast, N & Monahan, L, *Reimagining the Catholic School*, Veritas Publications, Dublin, Ire, pp. 93-106.

O'Keefe, J (1996), No margin, no mission, in McLaughlin T; O'Keefe, J & O'Keeffe, B (eds.), *The contemporary Catholic school*, Falmer Press, London, UK.

O'Kelly & Bishop, G (2015), *Address to Faith Formation & Religious Education Standing Committee*, National Catholic Education Commission at the Australian Catholic University, North Sydney on Tuesday, 17 March, 2015, p. 7.

Oliver, M (2004), *Why I wake early*, Beacon Press, Boston, MA.

Oliver, O (2006), *Dorothy*, Solle, Orbis, New York, NY.

Oliver, PE & Marwell, G (1988), The paradox of group size in collective action: A theory of the critical mass, II, *American Sociological Review, 53,* pp. 1-8.

Oliver, PE & Marwell, G (2002), recent developments in critical mass theory, in Berger J & Zelditch, M (eds.), *New directions in contemporary sociological theory,* Rowman and Littlefield, Lanham, UK.

Oliver, PE; Marwell, G & Teixeira, R (1985), A theory of the critical mass, I: Interdependence, group heterogeneity, and the production of collective action, *The American Journal of Sociology, 91*(3), pp. 522-556.

O'Leary JD (2001), *Travelling light: Your journey to wholeness,* Columba Press, Dublin, Ire.

O'Leary, JD (2011), *Unmasking God: Revealing God in the ordinary,* Columba Press, Dublin, Ire.

O'Leary, D (2004), *Seeds of Desire,* retrieved October 8, 2016, from http://archive.thetablet.co.uk/article/20th-november-2004/13/travelling-light-d-aniel-ol-eary, p. 13.

O'Leary, D (2008), *Begin with the Heart,* The Columbia Press, Dublin.

O'Loughlin, F (2007), The new evangelization of the twenty first century, *Australian Catholic Record, 84*(4), pp. 401-413.

O'Murchu, D (1997, 2007), *Reclaiming spirituality,* Claretian Publications, Manila, Philippines.

O'Murchu, D (2004), *Quantum theology,* Crossroad, New York, NY.

Ortberg, J (2014), *Soul Keeping: caring for the most important part of you,* Zondervan, Grand Rapids, MI.

Osmer, R (2008), *Practical theology: An introduction,* Eerdmans, Grand Rapids, MI.

Palmer, PJ (1983), *The company of strangers: Christians and the renewal of American public life,* Crossroad, New York, NY.

Palmer, PJ (1990), *Leading from within: Reflections on spirituality and leadership,* The Servant Leadership School, Washington, DC.

Palmer, PJ (1993a), *To know as we are known: Education as a spiritual journey,* Harper, San Francisco, CA.

Palmer, PJ (1993b), Good talk about good teaching: Improving teaching through conversation and community, *Change, 25*(6), Heldref Publications, Washington, DC, pp. 8-13.

Palmer, PJ (1997), The grace of great things: Recovering the sacred in knowing, teaching and learning, *Spirituality in Education Online,* retrieved 18 November, 2007, from http://csf.colorado.edu/sine/transcripts/palmer.html

Palmer, PJ (1999), Evoking the Spirit, *Educational Leadership, 56*(4), pp. 6-11.

Palmer, PJ (2000), *Let your life speak: Listening for the voice of vocation,* Jossey-Bass, San Francisco, CA.

Palmer, PJ (2004), *A hidden wholeness: The journey toward an undivided life*, Jossey-Bass, San Francisco, CA.

Palmer, PJ (2007), *The courage to teach: Exploring the inner landscape of a teacher's life* (10th Anniversary Ed.), Jossey-Bass, San Francisco, CA.

Parks, SD (2000, 2011), *Big questions, worthy dreams: Mentoring emerging adults in their search for meaning purpose and faith*, Jossey Bass, San Francisco, CA.

Parks, SD (2005), *Leadership can be taught: A bold approach for a complex world*, Harvard Business Review Press, Boston, MA.

Parramatta Catholic Education Office (2007), *Values that matter*, Author, Parramatta, NSW.

Pastoral Constitution on the Church in the Modern World (Gaudium et Spes) in Flannery, A (ed.) 1981, *Vatican Council II: The conciliar and post-conciliar documents*, Dominican Publications, Dublin, Ire.

Paul VI (1965), *Gravissimum Educationis: Declaration on Christian education*, Daughters of St. Paul, Boston, MA.

Paul VI (1975), *Evangelii nuntiandi: On evangelisation in the modern world*, St. Paul Publications, Homebush, NSW.

Paulson, S (Presenter) (2008), *You are the river:* An interview with Ken Wilber, Radio Broadcast 28 Apr, 2008, in *Atoms and Eden – Conversations about faith and science*, retrieved 19 May, 2010, from www.salon.com/life/feature/2008/04/28/ken_wilber

Peck, MS (1993), *Further along the road less travelled: The unending journey toward spiritual growth*, Simon and Shuster, New York, NY.

Peers, EA (2002), *The complete works of Teresa of Avila, Volume 1*, Burns and Oats, London, UK.

Pargament, KI & Park, CL (1995), Merely a defense? The variety of religious means and ends, *Journal of Social Issues, 51*, pp. 13-32.

Piaget, J (1955), *The child's construction of reality*, Routledge and Kegan, London, UK.

Pius X (1905), *On the teaching of Christian doctrine*, Daughters of St. Paul, Boston, MA.

Phan, PC (2000), The gift of the Church: A textbook on ecclesiology, The Liturgical Press, Collegeville, MN.

Phan, PS (2006), 'Reception' or 'subversion' of Vatican II by the Asian Churches? A new way of being Church in Asia, *Australian E-Journal of Theology, 6*(1), retrieved 3 March, 2008, from http://aejt.com.au/2006/vol_6,_no_1,_2006/?article=395185

Pink, D (2010), Drive, *The surprising truth about what motivates us*, Canongate Books, Edinburgh, Scotland.

Polkinghorne, D (1988), *Narrative knowing and the human sciences*, State University of New York Press, Albany, NY.

Poll, JB & Smith, TB (2003), The spiritual self: toward a conceptualization of spiritual identity development, *Journal of Psychology and Theology, 31*(2), p. 129.

Pollefeyt, D (2008), Difference matters: A hermeneutic-communicative concept of didactics of religion in a European multi-cultural context, *Journal of Religious Education, 56*(1), pp. 9-17.

Pollefeyt, D (2009), *How do Catholic schools respond to today's secular, pluralist context?* (Discussion paper), ECSIP Enhancing Catholic School Identity Project, Melbourne.

Pollefeyt, D (2011), Assessing and enhancing Catholic school identity (ECSIP): Empirical and practical-theological instruments that help Catholic schools in (re)shaping their identity in a pluralizing cultural context, *Presentation at the National Catholic Education Convention, Adelaide, September.*

Pollefeyt, D & Bouwens, J (2010), Framing the identity of Catholic schools: Empirical methodology for quantitative research on the Catholic identity of an education institute, *International Studies in Catholic Education, 2*(2), pp. 193-211.

Pope Francis (May 18, 2013), Q&A *Session with members of movements, communities and ecclesial associations,* http://www.vatican.va/holyfather/francesco/speeches/2013/may/documents /papa-francesco_20130518_v glia-pentecosteenhtml

Pope Francis (July 28, 2013), *Meeting with the bishops of brazil address of Pope Francis,* Archbishop's House, Rio de Janeiro, http://w2.vatican.va/content/francesco/en/speeches/2013/july/documents/papa-francesco_20130727_gmg-episcopato-brasile.html

Pope Francis (Oct 1, 2013), Interview with Eugenio Scalfari, 'How the Church Will Change,' *La Repubblica,* http://www.repubblica.it/cultura/2013/10/01/news/popes_conversation_with_scalfari_ english-67643118/ (accessed March 10, 2015).

Pope Francis (Feb 13, 2014), Pope Francis offers three proposals for improving Catholic education, *Address to the Congregation for Catholic Education,* http://www.catholicworldreport.com/Blog/2929/pope_francis_offers_three_proposals_for_improving_catholic_education.aspx

Pope Francis (May 13, 2014), Address to Catholic Students, Teachers: It Takes A Village To Raise A Child, *Catholic Communications, Sydney Archdiocese,* http://www.sydneycatholic.org/news/latest_news/2014/2014513_1189.shtml

Pope Francis (Sept 27, 2015), Address to Families, https://zenit.org/articles/pope-s-off-the-cuff-address-to-families/2015ZENIT STAFFFRANCIS

Pope Francis (Nov 23, 2015), by Junno Arocho Esteves, Catholic News Service http://www.romereports.com/2015/11/23/pope-francis-you-cannot-speak-of-catholic-education-without-speaking-about-humanity

Pope Francis (Nov 25, 2015), by Daniel Guernsey, http://www.crisismagazine.com/2015/challenges-and-ambiguities-at-the-world-congress-on-education

Power, T (2002), Dancing on a moving floor: lay women and the principalship in Catholic primary education, in Duncan, D & Riley D (eds.), *Leadership in Catholic Education*, Harper Collins, Sydney, NSW.

Porteous, J (ed.) (2008), *The new evangelization: developing evangelical preaching*, Connor Court Publishing, Ballan, Vic.

Prahl, R; Marwell, G & Oliver, P (1991), Reach and selectivity as strategies of recruitment for collective action: A theory of the critical mass, V, *Journal of Mathematical Sociology, 16*(2), pp. 137-164.

Preedy, M; Glatter, R & Wise, C (eds.) (2003), *Strategic leadership and educational improvement*, Paul Chapman Publishing, London, UK.

Prendergast, N & Monahan, L (eds.) (2003), *Reimagining the Catholic School*, Veritas, Dublin, Ire.

Prest, J, *The spirituality of the lay Catholic educator in Australian catholic secondary schools* (unpublished doctoral dissertation), Monash University, Melbourne, Vic.

Price, D (2008), *An exploration of participant experience of the service learning program at an Australian Catholic boys school* (doctoral dissertation), Australian Catholic University, Brisbane, Qld.

Queensland Catholic Education Commission (1995), *What strategies and models best support the faith development of teachers?* QCEC Research and Review Committee Research Report, Author, Brisbane, Qld, retrieved 6 July, 2007, from http://www.qcec.qld.catholic.edu.au/

Queensland Catholic Education Commission (2000), *Religious dimension of senior educational leadership*, Author, Brisbane, Qld, retrieved 7 July, 2007, from http://www.qcec.qld.catholic.edu.au/

Queensland Catholic Education Commission (2001), *The Queensland Bishops Project - Catholic Schools for the 21st Century*, A report to the Queensland Bishops, Author, Brisbane, Qld, retrieved 14 July, 2007, from http://www.qcec.qld.catholic.edu.au/

Queensland Catholic Education Commission (2005), *Accreditation to teach in a Catholic school*, Author, Brisbane, Qld, retrieved 14 July, 2007, from http://www.qcec.qld.catholic.edu.au/

Queensland Catholic Education Commission (2005), *Spiritual and Faith Formation for Leadership*, Author, Brisbane, Qld, retrieved 15 July, 2007, from http://www.qcec.qld.catholic.edu.au/

Queensland Catholic Education Commission (2008), *Queensland Catholic Schools Curriculum Paper*, Author.

Queensland Catholic Education Commission (2010), *Formation for Staff in Catholic Schools in Queensland*, Author, Brisbane, Qld, retrieved 8 December, 2010, from http://www.qcec.qld.catholic.edu.au

Quillinan, J (2002), The call for courageous renewal for Catholic schools of the third millennium, *Australasian Catholic Record* 79(1), p. 48ff.

Quillinan, J (2012), *Shaping an Australian spirituality*, Compass, No. 4.

Radford Reuther, R (1993), *Sexism and Godtalk: Toward a feminist theology*, Beacon Press, Richmond, VA.

Rahner, K (1970), *The Trinity*, Herder & Herder, New York, NY.

Rahner, K (1963), *The Christian commitment*, Sheed & Ward, London, UK.

Rahner, K (1973), The spirituality of the Church of the future, *Theological Investigations*, XX, Herder and Herder, New York, NY, pp. 149-150.

Rahner, K (1990), *Faith in a wintry season: conversations and interviews with Karl Rahner in the last years of his life*, Crossroad, New York, NY.

Ramsay, W & Clark, EE (1990), *New ideas for effective school improvement*, Falmer Press, Hampshire, UK.

Ranson, D (2002), *Across the Great Divide*, St Paul's Publications, Society of St Paul, Sydney, Australia.

Ranson, D (2006), Forming a New Generation of Catholic School Leaders, *Australasian Catholic Record,* 83(4), pp. 415-421.

Reck, C (1991), *Catholic identity*, National Catholic Educational Association, Washington, DC.

Rieckho, BS (2014), The Development of Faith Leadership in Novice Principals, *Catholic Education: A Journal of Inquiry and Practice,* 17(2), retrieved from http://digitalcommons.lmu.edu/ce/vol17/iss2/3

Riessman, CK (1993), *Narrative analysis*, Sage, London, UK.

Ribbins, P (1997), Heads on deputy headship: Impossible roles for invisible role holders? *Educational Management and Administration,* 23(3), pp. 295-308.

Richards, L (2005), *Handling qualitative data,* Sage, London, UK.

Ricour, P (1984), *Time and narrative,* 3 volumes, translated by McLaughlin, K & Pellauer, D, University of Chicago Press, Chicago, IL.

Robertson, B (1990), Storytelling in pastoral counselling: A narrative pastoral theology, *Pastoral Psychology, 39*, pp. 33-45.

Robinson, SP (2007), *Starting mission shaped churches*, St Pauls, Chatswood, NSW.

Rogers, EM (1995), *Diffusion of Innovations* (4th ed.), The Free Press, New York, NY.

Rogus, JF & Wildenhaus, CA (2000), Ongoing staff development in Catholic schools, in Hunt, TC; Oldenski, TE & Wallace, TJ (eds.), *Catholic School Leadership – an invitation to lead* London, Falmer Press, UK, pp. 157-173.

Rohr, R (2003), *Everything belongs: The gift of contemplative prayer*, Crossroads, New York, NY.

Rohr, R (2008), *Things hidden: Scripture as spirituality*, St Anthony Messenger Press, Cincinnati, OH.

Rohr, R (2009), *The naked now: Learning to see as the mystics see*, Crossroads, New York, NY.

Rohr, R (2010), Emerging Christianity, *Proceedings of a conference held at Albuquerque 8-10 April, 2010*, Mustard Seed Resources, Albuquerque, NM.

Rolheiser, R (1998), *Seeking spirituality*, Hodder and Stoughton, London, UK.

Rolheiser, R (2006), *Secularity and the Gospel*, The Crossroad Publishing Company, New York, NY.

Rolheiser, R (2008), *Old and new struggles with the Church*, Weekly reflection published online on 9 November, 2008, retrieved 15 April, 2008, from www.ronrolheiser.com

Rolph, J (1991), Can there be quality in teacher education without spirituality? *Assessment and Evaluation in Higher Education, 16*(1), pp. 49-55.

Romney, M (2000), *Stages of faith in Christian perspectives on faith development*, Eerdmans, Mosley, MI.

Rossiter, G (1999), Historical perspective on the development of Catholic religious education in Australia: Some implications for the future, *Journal of Religious Education, 47*(1), pp. 5-18.

Rossiter, G (2001), Reasons for living: Religious education and young people's search for spirituality and identity, in Roebben, B & Warren, M (eds.), *Religious education as practical theology: Essays in honour of Professor Herman Lombaerts*, Annua Nuntia Lovaniensia Series, Peeters Publishing, Leuven, BE, pp. 53-105.

Rossiter, G (2003), Catholic education and values: A review of the role of Catholic schools in promoting the spiritual and moral development of pupils, *Journal of Religion in Education, 4*, pp. 105-136.

Rossiter, G (2004), The nature, psychological function and construction of meaning, *An Introductory Study*, ACU, Strathfield, NSW.

Rossiter, G (2005), From St Ignatius to Obi Wan Kenobi: An evaluative perspective on spirituality for school education, *Journal of Religious Education, 53*(1).

Rossiter, G (2013), Perspective on the use of construct 'Catholic Identity' for Australian Catholic schooling: Sociological background and literature – part 1, *Journal of Religious Education, 61*(2), pp. 4-16.

Rossiter, G (2013), Perspective on the use of the construct 'Catholic Identity' for Australian Catholic schooling: Areas in the discourse in need of more emphasis and further attention – part 2, *Journal of Religious Education, 61*(2), pp. 17-29.

Rossiter, G (2013), Perspective on the use of the construct 'catholic identity' for Australian Catholic Schooling – part 1, the sociological background and the literature, *Journal of religious education, 61*(2), pp. 1-12.

Rosov, W (2001), *Practising the presence of God: Spiritual formation in an American rabbinical school* (doctoral dissertation), Stanford University, Palo alto, CA, Publication Number AAT 3028162.

Rowan, B & Miskel, CG (1999), Institutional theory and the study of educational organizations, in Murphy, J & Louis, KS (eds.), *Handbook of research in educational administration* (2nd ed.), Jossey-Bass, San Francisco, CA, pp. 359-384.

Rshaid, G (2009), The spirit of leadership, *Educational Leadership, 67*(2), pp. 74-77.

Rubin, H and Rubin, I (1995, 2005), *Qualitative interviewing: The art of hearing data*, Sage, Thousand Oaks, CA.

Ryan, M & Malone, P (2003), *Exploring the religion classroom: a guidebook for Catholic schools*, Social Science, Sydney, NSW.

Ryan, J (2006, 15 Sept), Mystics in action: Albert Schweitzer and Dorothy Soelle are figures who speak to the modern world, *National Catholic Reporter*, retrieved 16 July, 2007, from http://findarticles.com/p/articles/mi_m1141/is_40_42/ai_n16753276/?tag=content;col1

Ryan, E (1997), *Rosemary Haughton witness to hope*, Sheed and Ward, Kansas City, MO.

Ryan, T (2014), Our pathway to God: Drawn by Desire, *Compass: A Review of Topical Theology, 48*(3), pp. 3-9.

Rymarz, R (2002), Postconciliar Catholics: Gen X and religious education, *Journal of Religious Education, 50*(4), pp. 52-56.

Rymarz, R (2004), Lost generation: the cultures of generation X Catholics, *Australian Catholic Review, 82*(2), pp. 144-154.

Rymarz, R & Graham, J (2005), Going to church: attitudes to church attendance amongst Australian core Catholic youth, *Journal of Beliefs and Values, 26*(1), pp. 55-64.

Sampson, EE (1993), *Celebrating the other. A dialogic account of human nature*, Harvester Wheatsheaf, Hemel Hempstead, UK.

Sarros, J (2002), The heart and soul of leadership: The personal journey, McGraw Hill, Melbourne, Vic.

Schaps, E (2003), Creating a school community, *Educational Leadership, 60*(6), pp. 31-33.

Schein, E (1997), *Organisational culture and leadership* (2nd ed.), Jossey-Bass, San Francisco, CA.

Schelling, TC (1978), *Micromotives and Macrobehavior*, Norton, New York, NY.

Schillebeekx, E (1990), *Church: The human story of God*, Crossroad, New York, NY.

Scharmer, C (2007), Addressing the blind spot of our time: An executive summary of the new book by Otto Scharmer, *Theory U: Leading from the Future as It Emerges,* The Society for Organisational Learning, Cambridge, USA.

Schneiders, S (2000), *Finding the treasure: locating Catholic religious life in a new ecclesial and cultural context*, Paulist Press, New York, NY.

Schneiders, S (2003), Religion vs. spirituality: A contemporary conundrum. *Spiritus: A Journal of Christian Spirituality, 3*(2), pp. 163-185.

Schneiders, SM (2006), *Exploring Christian spirituality*, Paulist Press, New York, NY.

Schön, D (1983), *The reflective practitioner*, Basic Books, New York, NY.

Schreiter, RJ (1984), The new catholicity: Theology between the global and the local, Orbis Books, Maryknoll, NY.

Schreite, RJ (1996), Cutting-edge issues in theology and their bearing on mission studies, *Missiology: An International Review, XXIV*(1).

Schroer (2016), last retrieved August 25, 2016, from http://socialmarketing. org/archives/generations-xy-z-and-the-others/

Schussler Fiorenza, E (1984), *In memory of her*, Crossroads, New York, NY.

Schuttloffel, MJ (2003), *Report on the future of Catholic school leadership*, National Catholic Educational Association, Washington, DC.

Scott, D (1996), Education policy: the secondary phase, *Journal of Education Policy, 11*(1), pp. 133-140.

Scott, G (2003), *Learning principals. Leadership capabilities and learning research in the New South Wales Department of Education and Training*, University of Technology, Quality Development Unit, Sydney, NSW.

Scott, WR (1995), *Institutions and organizations*, Sage, Thousand Oaks, CA.

Scottish Catholic Education Commission, (2007), *Values for Life*, Author, Glasgow, UK.

Schuttloffel, M (2007), Contemporary challenges to the recruitment, formation and retention of Catholic school leadership in the USA, in Grace, G & O'Keefe, J (eds.), *International Handbook of Catholic Education*, Springer, London, UK, pp 85-102.

Selby Smith, R (1971), Independent schools, in Maclaine, AG & Selby Smith, R, *Fundamental issues in Australian education*, Ian Novak, Sydney, NSW, pp. 249-278.

Seligman, MEP & Csikszentmihalyi, M (2000), Positive psychology: An introduction, *American Psychologist, 55*(1), pp. 5-14.

Senge, PM (1990), *The fifth discipline: The art and practice of the learning organisation*, Double Day, New York, NY.

Senge, PM (2000), *Schools that learn: A fifth discipline fieldbook for educators, parents and everyone who cares about education*, Double Day, New York, NY.

Senge, PM (2008), *The necessary revolution: How individuals and organizations are working together to create a sustainable world*, Double Day, New York, NY.

Senge, PM; Scharmer, C; Jaworski, J & Flowers, B (2005), *Presence: An exploration of profound change in people, organisations and society*, Doubleday, New York, NY/Society for Organisational Learning, Cambridge, MA.

Sergiovanni, T (1984), Leadership and excellence in schooling, *Educative Leadership, 41*, pp. 4-13.

Sergiovanni, T (1987), *The principalship: A reflective practice perspective*, Allyn and Bacon, Boston, MA.

Sergiovanni, T (1992), *Moral leadership*, Jossey-Bass, San Francisco, CA.

Sergiovanni, TJ (1994a), *Building community in schools*, Jossey-Bass, San Francisco, CA.

Sergiovanni, TJ (1994b), Organizations or communities? Changing the metaphor changes the theory, *Educational Administration Quarterly, 30*(2), pp. 214-226.

Sergiovanni, TJ (1996), *Leadership for the schoolhouse*, Jossey-Bass, San Francisco, CA.

Sergiovanni, TJ (2000), The lifeworld of leadership: Creating culture, community, and personal meaning in our schools, Jossey-Bass, San Francisco, CA.

Sergiovanni, TJ (2001), *Leadership (what's in it for schools?)*, Routledge Falmer, London, UK.

Sergiovanni, T (2003), The lifeworld at the centre: values and action in educational leadership, in Bennett, N; Crawford, M & Cartwright, M (eds.), *Effective educational leadership*, Sage, London, UK.

Shackle, E (1978), *Christian mysticism*, Clergy Book Service, Butler, Wisconsin.

Sharkey, P (2002), Building our capacity and commitment, in Duncan, D & Riley, D (eds.), *Leadership in Catholic education*, Harper Collins, Sydney, NSW.

Shaw, P (2014), *Transforming theological education: A practical handbook for integrative learning*, Sheldrake, P (2007), *A brief history of spirituality*, Blackwell Publishing, Malden, MA.

Sheehan, O & Kirkland, R (2007), *6 steps in curriculum development*, Office of Faculty Development, Ohio University College of Osteopathic Medicine, Athens, OH.

Sheldrake, P (1998), *Spirituality and Theology*, Darton, Longman and Todd, London, p. 35.

Shimabukaro, G (1998), The authentic teacher: Gestures of behavior, *Momentum, 29*, pp. 28-31.

Shimabukaro, VH (2001), A role analysis based on Church documents, dissertations and recent research, in Hunt, T & Nuzzi, RJ, (eds.), *Handbook of research on Catholic education*, Greenwood Press, Westport, CT.

Shimabukaro, VH (2008), Supporting the Catholic Identity of Catholic Elementary Schools in Virginia: A Study of Teachers' Perceptions of Professional Formation Experiences in Catholic Schools, Michigan University Press, MI.

Shimabukaro, G (1998), A call to reflection. 'A teachers' guide to Catholic identity for the 21st century, National Catholic Educational Commission, Washington, DC.

Shinohara, A (2002), Spiritual formation and mentoring: An approach from the Christian tradition of spiritual direction, *Christian Education Journal, 6*(2), pp. 105-17.

Showers, B & Joyce, B (1996), The Evolution of Peer Coaching, *Educational leadership, 53*(6), pp. 12-16.

Shults, FL & Sandage, SJ (2006), *Transforming spirituality: Integrating theology and psychology*, Baker Academic, Grand Rapids, MI.

Silf, M (2007), *Roots and wings: the human journey from a speck of stardust to a spark of God*, Eerdmans, London, UK.

Simone, G (2004), *Professional development as a process of renewal: Case studies of the courage to teach program* (unpublished doctoral dissertation), University of Colorado, Boulder, CO.

Slattery, MJ (1999), *The role of the Catholic school principal in the face of modern day changes and demands* (doctoral dissertation), Australian Catholic University, Melbourne, Vic, retrieved 12 may, 2008, from http://dlibrary.acu.edu.au/digitaltheses/public/adt-acuvp216.04092009/index.html

Smith, A (1996), *The God shift: Our changing perception of the ultimate mystery*, New Millennium London, UK.

Smith, C (2006), The use of census and other data in Australian Catholic education, *Proceedings of the ABS Census Analysis Conference conducted in Sydney by the Catholic Education Commission of NSW,19 July 2006*, Catholic Education Commission NSW, Sydney, NSW.

Smith, C (2007), *Enrolment trends in Catholic schools: Challenges for our systems and schools*, Catholic Education Commission NSW, Sydney, NSW.

Smith, MK (2001), 'David A. Kolb on experiential learning', *the encyclopedia of informal education*, retrieved 28 May, 2008, from http://www.infed.org/biblio/b-explrn.htm

Snyder, MH (2001), *Spiritual questions for the twenty-first century*, Orbis Books, Maryknoll, NY.

Söelle, D (1981), *Choosing life*, Philadelphia, Fortress Press, PA.

Söelle, D (1990), *Thinking about God: An introduction to theology*, SCM Press, London, UK.

Söelle, D (2001), *The silent cry: Mysticism and resistance*, Fortress Press, Minneapolis, MN.

Sparks, D (2003), Interview with Michael Fullan, *Journal of Staff Development, 24*(1), pp. 55-58, retrieved 9 January, 2008, from http://www.learningforward.org/news/jsd/fullan241.cfm

Sparshott, F (1963), *The structure of aesthetics*, University of Toronto Press, Toronto, Can.

Spry, G & Duignan, P (2004), *Framing leadership in Queensland Catholic schools: A report*, Catholic Educational Leadership, Flagship of Australian Catholic University, Brisbane, Qld.

Spry, G (2007), The history of leadership frameworks, *Proceedings of the Queensland Primary Principals' Conference held in Cairns, May 2007*, Personal notes.

Stark, R (1996), *The rise of Christianity: A sociologist reconsiders history*, Princeton University Press, Princeton, NJ.

Starratt, RJ (2004), *Ethical leadership*, Jossey Bass, San Francisco, CA.

Stenlund, K (1995), Teacher perceptions across cultures, *The Alberta Journal of Educational Research 4*, pp. 1-2.

Stott, J (2002), *Basic Christian leadership: Biblical models of Church, Gospel and Ministry*, InterVarsity Press, Downers Grove, IL.

Sullivan, J (2001), *Catholic Education: Distinctive and Inclusive*, Kluwer Academic Publishers, Dordrecht, The Netherlands.

Sullivan, J (2011), Promoting the mission: Principles and practice, *International Studies in Catholic Education, 3*(1), pp. 91-102.

Tacey, D (1995), *Edge of the sacred: Transformation in Australia*, Harper Collins, Sydney, NSW.

Tacey, D (2000), *ReEnchantment: The new Australian spirituality*, Harper Collins, Sydney, NSW.

Tacey, D (2003), *The spirituality revolution – the emergence of contemporary spirituality*, Harper Collins, Sydney, NSW.

Tacey, D (2006), Mysticism, cornerstone of the future Church. The Benedictine spirituality lectures, *Online Catholics (Issue 94, 8 March, 2006)*, retrieved 23 August, 2007, from onlinecatholics.acu.edu.au/issue94/news1.html

Tacey, D (2015), *Beyond literal belief: religion as metaphor*, Garratt Publishing, Mulgrave, Vic.

Tannock, PD (ed.) (1975), *The organization and administration of Catholic education in Australia*, University of Queensland Press, St Lucia, Qld.

Tausch, R (1978), Facilitating dimensions in interpersonal relations: Verifying the theoretical assumptions of Carl Rogers in school, family education, client-centred therapy, and encounter groups, *College Student Journal, 12*, pp. 2-11.

Taylor, C (1996), Spirituality of life – and it's shadow, *Compass, 14*(2), pp. 10-13.

Taylor, C (2014), *Dilemmas and Connections*, The Belknap Press of Harvard University Press, Cambridge and London.

Taylor, C & Dreyfus, H (2015), *Retrieving Realism*, Harvard University Press.

Taylor, E (1997), Building upon the theoretical debate: A critical review of the empirical studies of Mezirow's transformative learning theory, *Adult Education Quarterly, 48*(1), pp. 34-60.

Taylor, E (2007), An update of transformative learning theory: A critical review of the empirical research (1999-2005), *International Journal of Lifelong Education, 26*(2), pp. 173-191.

Tennant, M (1997), *Psychology and adult learning* 2e, Routledge, London, UK.

The Age (24 March, 2004), *Of priests and principals: power struggles in Catholic schools between lay and religious leaders must be resolved.*

The Bulletin (19 April, 2005) *Contraception, celibacy, right to life: Challenges facing the Catholic Church*, pp. 23-29.

Theissen, VW (2005), The great work to be born: Spiritual formation for leaders, *Direction, 34*(1), pp. 54-63.

Thomson, P (2004), *Severed heads and compliant bodies? A speculation about principal identities*, University of Nottingham, Nottingham, UK.

Thompson, M (1995), *Soul feast: An invitation to the Christian spiritual life.* John Knox Westminster, UK.

Thompson, M (2005), *Soul feast*, Westminster/John Knox, Louisville, KT.

Thompson, S. (2004). Leading from the eye of the storm, *Educational Leadership, 61*(7), 60–63.

Tillich, P (1957), *Systematic theology, Volume 2: Existence and the Christi*, University of Chicago Press, Chicago, IL.

Tinsey, W (1998), *Teachers, clergy and Catholic schools: A study of perceptions of the religious dimension of the mission of Catholic schools and relationships between teachers and clergy in the Lismore Diocese* (doctoral dissertation), Australian Catholic University Digital Theses, 2000-2011, Sydney, NSW.

Tinsey, W (2002), The gospel, Church and culture historical and contemporary perspectives on mission, evangelisation and the dialogue with culture, *Australian E-Journal of Theology*, Issue 2, August 2002, Australian Catholic University, Brisbane, Banyo Campus, Qld.

Tisdell, EJ & Tolliver, TD (2001), The role of spirituality in culturally relevant and transformative adult education, *Adult Learning, 12*(3), pp. 13-14.

Tolle, E (2005), *A new earth*, Penguin Group, New York, NY.

Tomal, DR; Schilling, CA & Trubus, M (2013), *Leading School Change: Maximizing Resources for School Improvement*, Rowman & Littlefield Education, Plymouth, UK.

Treston, K (1992), *Transforming Catholic schools: Visions and practices for renewal*, Creation Enterprises, Brisbane, Qld.

Treston, K (1994), *Following the heart*, Creation Enterprises, Brisbane, Qld.

Treston, K (1997), Ethos and identity: Foundational concerns for Catholic schools, in Keane, R & Riley, D (eds.), *Quality Catholic schools: Challenges for leadership as Catholic education approaches the third millennium*, Archdiocese of Brisbane, Brisbane, Qld, pp. 9-18.

Treston, K (1998), The school as an agent in evangelisation, in Feheney, J (ed.), *From ideal to action: The inner nature of a Catholic school today*, Veritas, Dublin, Ire.

Treston, K (2000), *Visioning a future church*, Creation Enterprises, Brisbane, Qld.

Treston, K (2001), *Wisdom schools: seven pillars of wisdom for Catholic schools*, Creation Enterprises, Brisbane, Qld.

Treston, K (2007), *Five key challenges for leadership in Catholic schools for 21st century*, last accessed 15th August 2011, http://www.acu.edu.au/__data/assets/pdf_ le/0010/89893/Five_Key_Challenges_For_Leadership.pdf

Treston, K (2008), *Queensland Catholic schools and curriculum*, QCEC, Brisbane, Qld.

Trimingham-Jack, C (2003), *Growing good Catholic girls: Education and convent life in Australia*, Melbourne University Press, Melbourne, Vic.

Tuite, K (2007), *Making the Edmund Rice ethos a reality: A case study in the perceptions of principals in Christian Brothers' schools in Queensland* (unpublished doctoral dissertation), ACU, Banyo, Qld.

Turkington, M (2004), *The Catholic Education Office (CEO) Sydney as a learning organization and its perceived impact on standards* (doctoral dissertation), Australian Catholic University, Sydney, NSW.

USCCB (United States Conference of Catholic Bishops) (1972), *To teach as Jesus did*, Daughters of St. Paul, Boston, MA.

USCCB (United States Conference of Catholic Bishops) (2005), *Co-workers in the vineyard of the Lord: A resource for guiding the development of lay ecclesial ministry*, Author, Washington, DC.

Underhill, E (2002), *Mysticism*, Dover, New York, NY.

Vaill, PB (1998), *Spirited leading and learning: Process wisdom for a new age*, Jossey-Bass, San Francisco, CA.

Van Eyk, B (2002), The new ethos: Catholic schooling in a post-modern world, *Catholic School Studies, 75*(May), pp. 33-36.

Van Kaam, A & Muto, S (1978), *Am I living a spiritual life? Questions and answers on formative spirituality*, Dimension Books, Denville, NJ.

Voas, D & Crockett, A (2005), Religion in Britain: Neither believing nor belonging, *Sociology, 39*(1), pp. 11-28.

Vorgrimler, H (1986), *Understanding Karl Rahner: an introduction to his life and thought*, Crossroad, New York, NY.

Vygotsky, L (1978), *Mind in society*, Harvard University Press, Cambridge, MA.

Wainwright, G (1987), *Christian spirituality*, Macmillan, New York, NY.

Wallace, TJ (1998), The faith leadership issue, *Momentum, 29*, pp. 46-49.

Wallace, TJ (2000), We are called: The principal as faith leader in the Catholic school, in Hunt, TC; Oldenski, T & Wallace, T, *Catholic School Leadership: An Invitation to Lead*, Falmer Press, London, UK, pp. 193-206.

Walker, D (1989), Holiness: Pattern or journey? *Australian Catholic Record, 66*(1).

Walker, D (1998), Notes on the Cloud of Unknowing, in the Master of Arts Program *Formative Spirituality*, CCS Broken Bay, Hard copy.

Walsh, M (2001), *The Good Sams: Sisters of the Good Samaritan 1857-1969*, John Garratt, Mulgrave.

Warhurst, J (2012), 50 years since Australia's 'most poisonous debate', *Eureka Street, 22*(13), p. 33.

Weil, SW & McGill, I (eds.) (1989), *Making sense of experiential learning. Diversity in theory and practice*, Open University Press, Milton Keynes, UK.

Westerhoff, JH (1976), *Will our children have faith?* Dove Communications, Melbourne, Vic.

Westerhoff, JH (1980), *Bringing up children in the Christian faith*, Winston Press, Minneapolis, MN.

Wheatley, M (2002), Leadership In Turbulent Times Is Spiritual, *Frontiers of Health Services Management, Summer 2002*.

Whelan, M (1994), When anomalies consistently appear at the interface between learning and experience we must act: Reflections on the emergence of a new science, *Journal of Spiritual Formation, 14*(2), pp. 271-285.

Whitehead, E & Whitehead, JD (1997), *Method in ministry: Theological reflection in Christian ministry*, Sheed & Ward, Franklin, WI.

Wicks, R (2003), *Riding the dragon*, Sorin Books, Notre Dame, IN.

Wicks, (2006), *Crossing the desert*, Sorin Books, Notre Dame, IN.

Wicks, R (2009), *Prayerfulness: Awakening to the fullness of life*, Sorin Books, Notre Dame, IN.

Wicks, R & Parsons D (eds.) (1993), *Clinical handbook of pastoral counseling, Volume II – Selected topics*, Paulist Press, Mahwah, NJ.

Wicks, R; Parsons, D & Capps, D (eds.) (1993), *Clinical handbook of pastoral counseling, Volume I – Expanded edition*, Paulist Press, Mahwah, NJ.

Wicks, R; Parsons, D & Capps, D (eds.) (2003), *Clinical handbook of pastoral counseling, 3*, Paulist Press, Mahwah, NJ.

Wilber, K (2000), *A Theory of Everything*, Shambhala, Boston, MA.

Wilber, K (2006), *Integral Spirituality: A Startling New Role for Religion in the Modern and Postmodern World*, Shambhala, Boston, MA.

Wilkinson, PJ (2011), *Catholic parish ministry in Australia: Facing disaster?* Catholics for Ministry, Manuka, ACT.

Williams T (2000), *Keynote address at the Biennial Conference the Association of Catholic School Principals (NSW/ACT) held in Tamworth, NSW.*

Williams, K (2010), The common school and the Catholic school: A response to the work of T.H. McLaughlin, *International Studies in Catholic Education, 2*(1), pp. 19-36.

Wolski, CJ (1994), *Spirituality and personal maturity*, University Press of America Lanham, MD.

Wolski, CJ (1999), Spiritual formation, *Theology Today, 56*, pp. 86-97.

Woods, R (2002), *Enchanted headteachers: sustainability in primary school headship*, National College for School Leadership Practitioner Enquiry Report, NCSL, Nottingham, UK.

Wright, CJH (2006), *The Mission of God: Unlocking the Bible's Grand Narrative*, IVP, Downers Grove, IL.

Wright, W (2002), *Sacred heart, gateway to God*, Darton, Longman and Todd, London, UK.

Wubbolding, R (2002), *Reality Therapy for 21st Century*, Footprint Books, Warriewood, Australia.

Wuthnow, R (1998), *After heaven: Spirituality in America since the 1950s*, University of California, Berkerley, CA.

Zanzig, T (2004), Fostering discipleship in the Catholic community, *Hot Topics*, Pearson Education Inc.

Zappone, K (1991), *The hope of wholeness*, Twenty Third Publications, Connecticut, USA.

Zinn, LF (1997), Supports and Barriers to Teacher Leadership: Reports on Teacher Leaders, *Paper Presented at the Annual Meeting of the American Educational Research As References.*

Zinnbauer, B; Pargament, K & Scott, A (1999), The emerging meanings of religiousness and spirituality: Problems and prospects *Journal of Personality*, 67(6), pp. 889-919.

Zohar, D & Marshall, I (2000), *Spiritual intelligence*, Bloomsbury Press, London, UK.

INDEX

OTHER BOOKS IN THE MISSION
AND EDUCATION SERIES

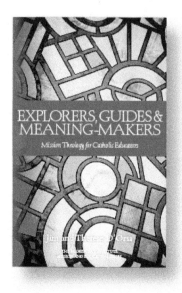

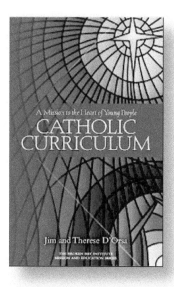

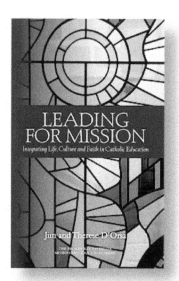

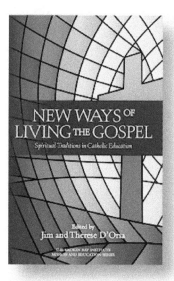

For more information see **www.vaughanpublishing.com.au**

CPSIA information can be obtained
at www.ICGtesting.com
Printed in the USA
BVHW040934170821
614608BV00018B/563